Collective Memory, National Identity, and Ethnic Conflict

Collective Memory, National Identity, and Ethnic Conflict

Greece, Bulgaria, and the Macedonian Question

VICTOR ROUDOMETOF

Westport, Connecticut
London

Library of Congress Cataloging-in-Publication Data

Roudometof, Victor, 1964–
   Collective memory, national identity, and ethnic conflict : Greece, Bulgaria, and the
Macedonian question / Victor Roudometof.
     p. cm.
   Includes bibliographical references and index.
   ISBN 0–275–97648–3 (alk. paper)
   1. Macedonian question. 2. Nationalism—Macedonia. 3. Albania—Relations—Balkan
Peninsula. 4. Balkan Peninsula—Relations—Albania. 5. Balkan Peninsula—Politics and
government. I. Title.
DR2195.R68 2002
949.5′6—dc21   2002067937

British Library Cataloguing in Publication Data is available.

Library of Congress Catalog Card Number: 2002067937
ISBN: 0–275–97648–3

First published in 2002

Praeger Publishers, 88 Post Road West, Westport, CT 06881
An imprint of Greenwood Publishing Group, Inc.
www.praeger.com

Printed in the United States of America

∞™

The paper used in this book complies with the
Permanent Paper Standard issued by the National
Information Standards Organization (Z39.48–1984).

10 9 8 7 6 5 4 3 2 1

Copyright Acknowledgments

The author and publisher gratefully acknowledge permission for use of the following material:

Excerpts from Victor Roudometof. 1996. "Nationalism and Identity Politics in the Balkans:
Greece and the Macedonian Question." *Journal of Modern Greek Studies* 14 (2). Published
by The Johns Hopkins University Press.

Excerpts from Victor Roudometof. 2000. "Culture, Identity, and the Macedonian Question:
An Introduction." Pp. 1–24 in Victor Roudometof (ed.), *The Macedonian Question: Culture,
Historiography, Politics*. Boulder, CO: East European Monographs.

Excerpts from Victor Roudometof, Bonka Stoyanova-Boneva, and Stephan E. Nikolov. 2000.
"In Search of 'Bigfoot': Competing Identities in Pirin Macedonia, Bulgaria." Pp. 237–58 in
Victor Roudometof (ed.), *The Macedonian Question: Culture, Historiography, Politics*. Boulder,
CO: East European Monographs.

Excerpts from Victor Roudometof. 2002. "National Minorities, Nation-States, and External
National Homelands in Southeastern Europe." In George Kourvetaris, Victor Roudometof,
Kleomenis Koutsoukis, and Andrew Kourvetaris (eds.), *The New Balkans*. Boulder, CO: East
European Monographs, distributed by Columbia University Press.

Contents

Illustrations

Acknowledgments

My original interest in this topic dates back to the early 1990s, when the Greek mobilization against the international recognition of the Republic of Macedonia brought this issue to the attention of the international community. While I was writing my doctoral dissertation on the origins of ethnic conflict in the region, I pursued this topic because of its contemporary relevance and because it allowed me to use my comparative-historical approach to shed light on an ongoing political affair. Over the years, I followed up this topic with a variety of chapters, edited volumes, and paper presentations. This monograph is the cumulative outcome of all this work.

In preparing and revising the various articles and chapters that eventually became this manuscript, I have sought the assistance and feedback of numerous individuals. I would like to thank professors Loring Danforth (Anthropology, Bates College), Dennison Rusinow (Center for International Studies, University of Pittsburgh), Anastasia Karakasidou (Anthropology, Wellesley College), William Dunn (Graduate School of Public and International Affairs, University of Pittsburgh), Adamantia Pollis (Political Science, New School for Social Research), John Markoff (Sociology, University of Pittsburgh), and an anonymous reviewer of the *Journal of Modern Greek Studies* (JMGS) for their useful comments. Special thanks go to Melissa McGary and Rachelle Schaaf for their help in editing earlier versions of my 1996 JMGS article.

For further assistance, encouragement, and feedback, I would like to thank Peter Bien (English, Dartmouth College), George Kourvetaris (Sociology, Northern Illinois University), Anna Karpathakis (Sociology, CUNY-Kingsborough), Keith Brown (Anthropology, Brown University), and

Constantinos Danopoulos (Political Science, San Jose State University). For his help with bibliographical sources, I should thank Vassilis Gounaris, Director of the Research Department of the Museum for Macedonian Struggle, Thessaloniki. For their help with Bulgarian sources and for their permission to reproduce portions of a jointly authored chapter, I should express my deep appreciation to my co-authors Stephen E. Nikolov (Institute of Sociology, Bulgarian Academy of Science, Sofia, Bulgaria) and Bonka Stoyanova-Boneva (Anthropology, University of Pittsburgh). Moreover, I express my gratitude to Carol Baily (Center for Media Studies, Washington and Lee University) and Buffy Hanna (Scripps Gerontology Center, Miami University) for their assistance with historical and contemporary maps of the region.

For their assistance in the final preparation of the manuscript, I would like to express my thanks to the following Miami University students: Tim Helin, Kera Wilson, Elizabeth Tulipana, and Chelsey Wagner. My work was made easier with their help and support, thereby allowing me to conclude work on the final manuscript in a timely fashion. Finally, I should express my thanks to Mrs. Betty Marak, for her assistance with proofreading and cross-checking the manuscript; as well as to the editorial staff at Greenwood/Praeger for their copyediting of the manuscript's final draft.

Abbreviations

ASNOM	Anti-Fascist Assembly of National Liberation of Macedonia
AVNOJ	Anti-Fascist Council for the National Liberation of Yugoslavia
BCP/BSP	Bulgarian Communist Party (after 1989, Bulgarian Socialist Party)
CSCE	Conference on Security and Cooperation in Europe
CUP	Committee of Union and Progress (the Young Turk Party)
DAG	Democratic Army of Greece (controlled by the Greek Communists)
DLK	Democratic League of Kosovo (the main Albanian party in Kosovo)
EAM	National Liberation Front of Greece (Ethniko Apeleutherotiko Metopo)
EU	European Union
FYROM	Former Yugoslav Republic of Macedonia
KLA (or UCK)	Kosovo Liberation Army (or Ushtria Clirimtare e Kosoves [UCK])
KKE	Greek Communist Party (Elliniko Kommounistiko Komma)
MAKIVE	Macedonian Movement for Balkan Prosperity (Makedoniko Kinima Valkanikis Evimereias)
NATO	North Atlantic Treaty Organization
NLA	National Liberation Army
NOF	Narodnoosloboditelniot Front, or National Liberation Front (of Slavo-Macedonians in Greece)
OAED	Organization for the Employment of Human Resources (of Greece) [Organismos Apascholiseos Ergatikou Dynamikou]
OMO-Ilinden	United Macedonian Organization-Ilinden

PASOK   Panhellenic Socialist Movement (Panellinio Socialistiko
                         Kinima)
PDP   Party for Democratic Prosperity (of Albanians in FYROM)
SNOF   Slovenomakedonski Narodno Osloboditelen Front, or Slav
                         National Liberation Front (of Slavo-Macedonians in Greece)
UN   United Nations
VMRO (or IMRO)   Internal Macedonian Revolutionary Organization
VMRO-DPMNU   Internal Macedonian Revolutionary Organization–Democratic
                         Party for Macedonian National Unity (of FYROM)
VMRO-UMCS   Internal Macedonian Revolutionary Organization–Union of
                         Macedonian Cultural Societies (of post-1989 Bulgaria)
VMRO-United   The Internal Macedonian Revolutionary Organization–United,
                         instituted by the Comintern during the interwar period

Chapter 1

Collective Memory, National Identity, and the Macedonian Question

On 24 March 1999 U.S. President Bill Clinton addressed the U.S. public to inform them that the United States and NATO has just begun their military campaign to remove the Serb forces from Kosovo. It was the beginning of what the U.S. media labeled the "Kosovo Crisis"—or what can be more accurately described as the NATO-led war against Serbia. In Clinton's statement, there are clear and unequivocal references that the necessity of military involvement was due to fear that the war would engulf Kosovo's neighboring state of the Republic of Macedonia, eventually leading to a wider Balkan war. In Clinton's own words,

We have acted . . . to prevent a wider war; to diffuse a powder keg at the heart of Europe that has exploded twice before in this century with catastrophic results. . . . Ending this tragedy is . . . [also] important to America's national interest. . . . Kosovo is a small place, but it sits on a major fault line between Europe, Asia and the Middle East, at the meeting place of Islam and both the Western and Orthodox branches of Christianity. To the south are our allies, Greece and Turkey; to the north, our new democratic allies in Central Europe. And all around Kosovo there are other small countries, struggling with their own economic and political challenges—countries that could be overwhelmed by a large, new wave of refugees from Kosovo. All the ingredients for a major war are there: ancient grievances, struggling democracies, and in the center of it all a dictator in Serbia who has done nothing since the Cold War ended but start new wars and pour gasoline on the flames of ethnic and religious division.

In large part, then, the goal of military intervention in Kosovo was to prevent the "spill over" of war toward Macedonia and to contain the crisis in the region (Tiryakian, 2002).[1] The widespread, common-sense belief that

war would soon extend into the southern Balkans (including a confrontation between Greece, Turkey, and possibly Bulgaria) has been an object of
speculation for the better part of the 1990s (for example, see Larrabee,
1994).[2] Clinton implicitly alluded to the Macedonian Question in his speech
as one of the reasons that led to the U.S. involvement in Kosovo. Specifically, Clinton suggested that the Kosovo Crisis could lead to a wider war
because of the presence of "ancient grievances" and newly born struggling
democracies in the region.[3]

Certainly, making a more explicit reference to the Macedonian Question
was not possible at the time of Clinton's speech. This was not only because
of the U.S. public's lack of general familiarity with such issues but also because the Macedonian Question consists of mutually opposing interpretations that render any attempt at neutrality highly problematic. Indeed, for a
long time, the issue has been discussed among international relations specialists, political scientists, journalists, and historians. All these groups have
displayed a tendency to reproduce the viewpoints present in the Balkan nation-states, and, consequently, they have reproduced the academic equivalent of a Babel of opinions and perspectives.[4] It is tempting, then, to adopt
the view that such conflicts are too complicated and difficult to grasp because of their inherent "Balkan" nature. Such viewpoints have helped the
articulation of a neo-Orientalist perspective on the Balkans and the ethnic
or national rivalries in the region. Clinton's own reference to "ancient grievances" is an apt illustration of this viewpoint.

What is lacking in current scholarship—and what I hope that this book is
going to contribute—is a *sociological perspective* on the issues involved in the
various controversies over Macedonia.[5] I would argue that our understanding of the Macedonian Question (and the public policy that was based on
such an understanding) is quite partial and incomplete. This is not due to
lack of interest or data. The recent (and still unresolved) political controversy over the "naming" of the former Yugoslav Republic of Macedonia
(FYROM or FYR Macedonia) is a topic of great importance to anthropologists, historians, sociologists, and political scientists.[6] Certainly, the
Macedonian Question is by no means new to the politics of the Balkan peninsula. On the contrary, there is plenty of literature on this issue, both in
the Balkans as well as on the shelves of libraries in Western Europe and North
America. Therefore, it is important to realize that the sheer production of
more books on this topic is not necessarily going to improve our state of
knowledge. By and large, the Macedonian Question has not been approached
sociologically, that is, as an issue involving the construction of mutually an-
tagonistic worldviews over the definition and cultural legacy of "Macedonia."
On the contrary, the Macedonian Question has been (and to large degree
still remains) a domain for journalists, amateur historians, and activists of all
persuasions.

All these cultural workers have reproduced the rival viewpoints espoused by the different nation-states, groups, and individuals involved in this symbolic battle. Indeed, heated arguments flare up whenever the issue of Macedonian minorities is raised, and the "affirmation" of the Macedonian nation by its neighbors Greece and Bulgaria (and, to a lesser extent, Serbia and Albania) remains an elusive goal. History and its interpretation lie at the heart of the Macedonian saga. In the simplest terms, the Macedonian Question concerns competing claims to Macedonia's soil. Who holds the legitimate "rights" over Macedonia? Is the former Yugoslav Republic of Macedonia (FYROM) the legitimate carrier of the name of Macedonia? Or does the name belong to the Greek historical tradition and culture, as the Greek nation-state insists? Are the modern-day Macedonians the legitimate inheritors of the historical legacy of Macedonian kings like Philip II and Alexander the Great? Or are they Bulgarians who have been indoctrinated into Macedonian nationhood by Tito's partisans, as Bulgarians and Greeks insist?

These are questions that raise the issue of national identity construction, especially in connection to the production of different socio-historical interpretations. It is for this reason that an inquiry into the Macedonian Question necessitates a discussion of the intertwining between collective memory and national identity. Hence, my goal in this book is to inquire into the construction of the Greek, Bulgarian, and Macedonian narratives that shape collective memory and produce specific political identities that are mutually exclusive. The presence of these mutually exclusive political identities is the source of conflict in Macedonia. Indeed, the Macedonian Question provides one of the best research sites worldwide for studying the relationship between collective memory and national identity.

Because the adjective "Macedonian" has both an ethnic or national and a geographical connotation, it is important to clarify my own usage of the word. The term "Macedonian" is used throughout this book to refer to people who use this label for their own national self-identification. Currently, this is the standard international use of the word. However, people throughout geographical Macedonia (see Map 1.1) use the adjective "Macedonian" for the purposes of regional identification. Greeks and Bulgarians can identify themselves as Macedonians without attributing a sense of national identity to the term. When referring to such individuals and groups, I have added the words Greek or Bulgarian as modifiers. While this description is helpful for an international audience, it is not consistent with local practice. Within Greece, a Macedonian is a Greek from Macedonia (in the same sense that a Cretan is a Greek from Crete); and within Bulgaria, a Macedonian is a Bulgarian from Macedonia. The reader should keep in mind this interplay between regional and ethnic or national labels. In many respects, slipping in and out of the different connotations of the same word is a strategy that serves the purposes of nationalists from all sides.

Map 1.1
Geographical Macedonia in Relation to Contemporary States in the Region

=== Nation-State boundaries
——— Coastlines
●●● Approximate extent of 'Geographical Macedonia'

   To help the reader grasp the transition from a regional to a national label, I have employed a number of terms to designate Macedonia's Slavic-speaking inhabitants over the last centuries. These terms were used at the time and their employment might serve as a way to mark the articulation of Macedonian national identity over the last two centuries. Terms such as "Slavo-Macedonians" were popular in interwar Greece—while the term "Macedonian Slavs" was used by Serbs to designate the Slavic-speaking inhabitants of their respective part of Macedonia. In contemporary discussions, Macedonians frequently consider these terms to be offensive. Indeed, they are correct in insisting that others address them by the national name of their choice. But the situation was different in the first half of the twentieth century, and there is little to be gained by applying a recent national label in a different historical and social context. On the contrary, awareness of this context can be tremendously useful in tracing the articulation of Macedonian identity, as well as the reasons for the Greek and Bulgarian negation of such an identity.
   This book provides a general guide to these contemporary controversies and illuminates the relationship between national identity and collective memory. In constructing the book's main arguments, I have drawn upon literature from a variety of fields—including anthropology, history, political science, and sociology. In this introductory chapter, I outline the connec-

tion between the contemporary controversies among the Balkan nation-states and the social-scientific field of social memory or collective memory. Next, I outline the manner in which this book's individual chapters are going to address different facets of the Macedonian Question.[7]

I should point out that, in its current form, the Macedonian Question is not restricted to the symbolic battle over the "ownership" of the cultural and historical tradition of the region. More specifically, in contemporary politics, this symbolic struggle has been further modified by the presence of a sizeable Albanian minority within FYROM, a minority that feels treated as second-class citizens by the Macedonian Slav majority and government. Therefore, because of Macedonia's sensitive geographical location, an analysis of the Macedonian issue has to address aspects of the Albanian "national question" in the post-1989 former Yugoslavia, Albania, and Greece.

NATIONAL NARRATIVES, MEMORY, AND IDENTITY

The Macedonian issue has divided Balkan nation-states since the middle of the nineteenth century. In the second half of the nineteenth century, the region was fiercely claimed by all the neighboring nation-states (Serbia, Greece, and Bulgaria). The Balkan nation-states used the educational system and the local Orthodox churches as instruments to acculturate the population to their respective imagined community. Such nationalist antagonisms were part of the export to the Ottoman Balkan society of the Western idea of the nation-state and its concomitant secular identity. The redeployment of the Eastern Orthodox religion as a people's expression of national identity helped the construction of their passages into modern-day nationhood (Roudometof, 2001; Karakasidou, 1997). Unfortunately, in the case of Macedonia (and in the better-publicized cases of Bosnia, Kosovo, and Cyprus), this redeployment produced division and animosity.

In contemporary politics, the conflicting ethnocentric national narratives of the different sides have generated the Greek-Bulgarian-Macedonian dispute of the 1990s. Such narratives illustrate the manner in which "culture" becomes an important site for political conflict in the twenty-first century (Wallerstein, 1990). In 1991, the People's Republic of Macedonia declared its independence from the Yugoslav federation and set off a political, cultural, and diplomatic struggle with Greece. Greece's government opposed the recognition of the new state with the name "Macedonia" and the acknowledgment of the Macedonians as a nation. Between 1991 and 1995 Greece challenged the attempt by the new state to gain official recognition by the international community. Although a 1995 interim accord restored normal relations between Greece and the FYROM/Republic of Macedonia, the issue did not disappear from public discourse. Greek and Macedonian diasporic communities in Canada, Australia, and the United States became involved in the political and symbolic struggle over the name Macedonia

(Danforth, 1995). The European Union (EU) and the United Nations (UN) were (and continue to be) involved in the efforts to provide a resolution to the international dispute. Greek, Bulgarian, and Macedonian internal politics were also influenced by the developments that occurred on the issue.

According to the FYROM's official viewpoint, geographical Macedonia is the national homeland of the Macedonian nation. Its 1913 partition among Bulgaria, Greece, and Serbia was a national disaster that divided Macedonians into different states, all set on acculturating them into the Greek, Bulgarian, and Serb nations. In sharp contrast to this viewpoint, Greeks and Bulgarians consider their struggles over Macedonia as part of their process of national liberation. They reject the Macedonians' claim to be a distinct nation. In their view, post-1945 communist-led nation building "fabricated" the existence of the Macedonian nation.

The modern nature of all these national identities and their subsequent conflicts clashes directly with the tendency of misinformed journalists and extreme nationalists to transform them into transhistorical titanic struggles against mythical enemies. As the different nationalist agendas became enshrined in regional national history, schoolbooks, songs, and folk tradition, they gradually provided "invented traditions," (Hobsbawm and Ranger, 1983) to be enacted in public lectures, national holidays, official histories, and other forms of "banal nationalism" (Billig, 1995). The collective memory constructed and maintained by the daily reproduction of such national "commemorations" (Gills, 1994) is perhaps the main obstacle in finding mutually acceptable solutions to the various political problems associated with the Macedonian issue.

In fact, collective memory stands in the way of developing evenhanded treatments of the issue and of revising some of the most nationalistic viewpoints that still persist in regional literature. Academic writing on this subject has long been characterized by political and nationalistic prejudices that have forestalled the development of social scientific viewpoints on the ethnic and national controversies concerning "Macedonia." Even today one would be hard-pressed to find regional specialists competent and willing to undertake critical evaluations of the local historiographies. Hence, in order to analyze the Macedonian issue in an evenhanded manner it is necessary to view the narratives of the various sides as forms of collective memory—and not as objective accounts of historical processes.

Collective or social memory is an area of study that has only recently attracted the attention of historians and sociologists (for two very useful overviews of the literature, see Olick and Robbins, 1998, and Zelizer, 1995). Indeed, it might be predicted that the field is going to grow in significance and importance in the coming years. The reasons behind the relative lack of attention vary widely in different disciplines. In history, the long-standing tradition of "scientific objectivity" until recently did not allow the examination of historical writing in relationship to the articulation of collective memory (Novick, 1989; Lukacs, 1985). In sociology and anthropology, the legacy of pioneers such as Emile Durkheim, Maurice Halbwachs (1992), and Karl Mannheim was eclipsed in mid-twentieth century by the more empirically oriented and positivist tradition of U.S. mainstream sociology.[8]

The fundamental argument put forward by these pioneers was that social (or collective) memory is sustained only within specific social contexts. Hence, memory of events is closely connected to the collective representations produced and reproduced by social groups.[9] In *The Past is a Foreign Country,* David Lowenthal (1985) puts forward an important interpretation concerning the relationship between memory and history. He argues that it is us, the contemporaries, who construct our past selectively and for a variety of different reasons. Out of many possible pasts, some are lost, while others are the subjects of careful strategies of maintenance and reproduction. Lowenthal's work highlights the importance of visual representations as instruments that help the organization of a people's appropriation of the past. It also highlights the critical role of commemorations for the social reproduction of collective memory. This particular insight has been exploited in recent studies of nationalism, especially with regard to the manner in which modern nation-states construct their own sense of past through a variety of public rituals, monuments, and exhibits (see, for example, Spillman, 1997; Horne, 1984; MacDonald and Fyfe, 1996).

Over the last two decades, scholars of nationalism have strongly suggested that modern nations are intimately involved in rituals, the construction of national myths, and other symbolic elements that help construct and maintain the peoples' sense of belonging to an "imagined community" (Hobsbawm and Ranger, 1983; Smith, 1986, 1999; Anderson, 1991). From this point of view, the collective memory of a nation is part of its cultural heritage and tradition, the set of symbols invoked in order to produce elements of social solidarity and cultural cohesion. Within different societies, historical events serve as focal points for the reproduction of collective representations that shape the contemporaries' own understanding of their identity and their relationship to the past and a nation's soil.[10] Key controversies over the interpretation of historical events become highly publicized issues—such as the Masada myth in Israel (Ben-Yehuda, 1995; Schwartz, Zerubavel, and Barnett, 1986) or the role and significance of the Confederate flag in the American South. The Macedonian Question, then, is one such example. It is not a unique case, but rather an exemplary case study of processes present in varying degrees in societies around the globe.

In theoretical terms, there is a multitude of ways through which collective memory is standardized and reproduced. These include: national holidays, public lectures, articles in the popular press, documentaries, pictures, statues, and other media of a bewildering variety (for specific examples, see Lowenthal, 1985; also Le Goff, 1992: 86–88). While these media allow for the exposition and description of a rich tapestry of details, they have to follow a particular logic inherent in nation building. This cultural logic is crystal-lized in what I refer to throughout this book as *national narrative*.[11] By that I mean the historical tale of the evolution of a particular people through the ages.[12] Although nationalists often like to present modern-day nations as possessing a long and glorious history, it is important to take into account the fact that most national narratives have come into existence during the nineteenth century, the golden age of nation building, as well as the epoch that witnessed the birth of history as an academic discipline. The fundamental logic of these narratives entails the following steps:

1. A "quest for origins" according to which the researcher's task is to trace the be-ginnings of a people as far back in history as possible;
2. The construction of continuity among the different historical periods, thereby showing the preservation of a "people's" culture, tradition, and mentality;
3. The identification of periods of glory and decline, including moral judgments regarding the actions of other collectivities vis-à-vis the nation; and
4. The quest for meaning and purpose, the identification of a destiny revealed in the progression of history, or what might be called a semi-Hegelian interpretation of history.

All these elements can readily be recognized as indispensable components of "national history," a genre popular in nineteenth-century Europe, where newly born nations from the Italians to the Greeks to the Poles or the Serbs sought to use history as a method of legitimizing their nationalist move-ments.[13]

According to the logic outlined in the preceding paragraphs, identifying a nation's destiny also provides a moral imperative for completion of the nation-building process or the process of national integration. When two or more nations identify the same territory as their own "unredeemed land" (i.e., their *irredenta*), bitter disputes follow, as each side cannot truly accept compromises without in a sense betraying the national mission. For example, Alsace-Lorraine became the bitter object of territorial disputes between France and Germany from the nineteenth century up until 1945—not un-like Bosnia-Herzegovina in the 1990s. In another instance of a similar dis-pute, Italy became engulfed in a dispute with Austria and Yugoslavia over the city of Trieste. To this day the Irish Republic does not recognize Britain's official name—i.e., the United Kingdom of Great Britain and Northern Ireland.

The Macedonian issue is part of this same pattern of regional disputes that is present throughout Europe (as well as in other regions around the globe). It is worth pointing out the significance and power of the moral imperatives codified into a national narrative. In Europe's interwar period, these moral imperatives provided the rising Fascist and Nazi movements with a glow of morality and righteousness. It might be argued that these tendencies belong squarely in Europe's past; yet, their ghost was invoked as late as the 1989–90 German unification. Following Poland's strong objections, Germany had to explicitly accept the post-1945 eastern border between the two countries, thereby putting to rest all possible future territorial claims into Polish territory.

All these examples aptly illustrate the power of national narratives over public imagination. It is with these broader examples in mind that one should approach the Macedonian Question. The theoretical issue underlying the Macedonian Question concerns the usage and construction of national narratives as a way of developing the "imagined community" (Anderson, 1991) of the nation. In turn, these national narratives must be interpreted in the context of the competing Greek, Bulgarian, and Macedonian nationalisms. While most scholars of nationalism consider this phenomenon to be a product of the last few centuries,[14] many national narratives trace the history of a nation back many hundreds of years.[15] The national narratives of Serbia, Bulgaria, Greece, Poland, and even France can easily trace their people's origins back to the Middle Ages, or even to antiquity. To inquire into such narratives in a critical fashion, it is necessary to move beyond the narrative structure of the genre of national history.

Michel Foucault has articulated perhaps the most explicit principles for the examination of ruptures and discontinuities, and his approach can be used as a useful strategy to counter the implicit assumption of continuity present in national narratives. Foucault (1984) argues in favor of a genealogy, not a history. Genealogy does not seek to establish the continuities sought and cherished by "national history" or the national narratives of the modern nation-states. On the contrary, its goal is to subvert the "quest for origins" in historical discourse, by inserting the dynamics of power and domination and their relationship to knowledge into the circuits of knowledge production. After all, the modern nation-state (and its multitude of agents) is largely responsible for shaping the territory of the globe according to its own image (Lewis and Wigen, 1997). It is easy to forget the relative novelty of this process. Even in France, the paradigmatic case of nation-state building, this process was completed only during the second half of the nineteenth century (Weber, 1976). Both cultural representation and state institutions subsequently helped the territorialization of identity in connection to a nation's soil (Malkii, 1992). It is through these processes that people have developed a sense of belonging associated with a specific homeland. Indeed, identity has only recently been conceptualized as entailing collective forms of social solidarity within a particular group (Handler, 1994; Gupta and Ferguson, 1992). In this recent reconceptualization of identity, historical memory (in the form of historical writing or folklorist and ethnographic studies) has provided for the production and reproduction of the newly formed identities

(Lowenthal, 1994). The use of the historical record is therefore political, because national histories provide a population with heroes, monuments, and other evidence for the existence of national identity through the ages.[16]

THE SENSE OF PAST IN THE COLLECTIVE MEMORY OF THE BALKAN NATION-STATES

The production of collective memory in the Balkan nation-states follows closely the cultural logic of their national narratives.[17] National holidays provide an occasion for an explicit manifestation of this cultural logic:

By defining a nation's beginning, such holidays temporally insulate the entity. When U.S. citizens observe the Fourth of July, the French celebrate Bastille Day (July 14) or Argentinians commemorate National Day (May 25), they acknowledge a figurative "starting line" that separates each nation's history from that of all others. Such symbols enforce a sense of inclusion and exclusion, a boundedness that is vital to every nation's identity. (Cerulo, 1995: 57)

This process is readily observable in the national holidays of Greece, Serbia, Bulgaria, and the Republic of Macedonia. Table 1.1 provides a list of these countries' national holidays. For our purposes, it is necessary to exclude purely religious holidays such as Easter and Christmas Day, alongside holidays that have no clearly defined "national" significance. For example, May 1st (International Labor Day) and January 1st (New Year's Day) are in reality "international" holidays—as opposed to purely national ones. Additionally, holidays commemorating World War II and related phenomena (such as the *Ohi* Day in Greece or the Yugoslav holidays in Serbia) are too diffuse to provide good cases for the study of the relationship between national holidays and national identity. Holidays commemorating World War II events are common to a number of European countries, while the holidays established by communist regimes to celebrate their coming into power are explicitly connected to the political regime and, hence, tend to be short-lived.

Once these considerations are taken into account, it is easier to grasp those holidays that are directly connected to a specific nation—either Serbia or Bulgaria or Greece or Macedonia. In all instances, the major national holiday is a commemoration of an uprising, revolution, battle, or other military victory (or defeat) that signaled a world-historical event that shaped the nation's collective memory and national narrative. National commemorations are occasions that help with the construction, reproduction, and maintenance of national identity. As Table 1.1 shows, the national commemorations of the Balkan nation-states are closely connected with their national narratives, the tales of the peoples' struggles for independence, self-assertion, and national liberation.

Moreover, mass public education is closely connected to the teaching of specific tales aimed to instill a sense of belonging into the general public,

Table 1.1
National Holidays in Greece, Bulgaria, Serbia, and Macedonia[1]

Country	Date	Holiday	Occasion
Greece	March 25th	Independence Day	The official proclamation of the Greek revolution in 1821.
	October 28th	Ohi (No) Day	The date Italy invaded Greece, initiating Greece's involvement into World War II. The date is also used as an occasion to commemorate the resistance during the Occupation.
Bulgaria	September 22nd	Independence Day	The official proclamation of Bulgaria as a sovereign state (1908)
	March 3rd	Liberation Day	The liberation of Bulgaria by the Russian military in their war against the Ottoman Empire (1877–78)
Republic of Macedonia	August 2nd	Ilinden Uprising	The day of the initial uprising of the Macedonians against Ottoman rule (1903)
	October 11th		The anti-Fascist Resistance against German Occupation
	September 8th	Independence Day	Declaration of Macedonian independence (1991)
Serbia[2]	June 28th	St. Vitus Day [3]	The anniversary of the Kosovo Battle (1389)
	November 29th	Republic Day	The foundation of the "second Yugoslavia" (1943)
	March 28th	Constitution Day	Established by the Milosevic regime to celebrate the 1989 abolition of autonomy for the provinces of Vojvodina and Kosovo

[1]This table lists only national holidays. Holidays that are affiliated with religions or the labor movement—such as January 1st or Christmas Day (January 7th in Serbia and December 25th in Bulgaria and Greece) or May 1st—are excluded. I would like to thank Stephan E. Nikolov (Institute of Sociology, Bulgaria) and Zlatko Isakovic (lecturer, visiting scholar, and research fellow, Carleton University, Canada) for their assistance in collecting the information.

[2]As a member of the Yugoslav federation, Serbia observed also Yugoslav federal holidays, such May 9th (Victory Day) and April 27th (Yugoslav National Day).

[3]St. Vitus Day was the major holiday for pre-1917 Serbia. It was a national holiday during the interwar period—but did was not a national holiday during the communist regime (1945–1989). Slobodan Milosevic's regime restored this holiday in the late 1980s.

Source: Roudometof (2002a)

thereby transforming peasants into members of a specific nation (Weber, 1976; Mosse, 1975). Research, writing, and discussion in the fields of human and social sciences—ranging from archaeology to politics or sociology—have to confront the national narrative. This can be done in two ways: either the researcher situates his or her argument within the general structure of the national narrative; or, alternatively, the researcher challenges the national narrative directly or indirectly. Needless to say, it is extremely difficult to have an academic career in case one's work is set in opposition to perceived orthodoxy.

Perhaps the most prominent example that illustrates these processes is the case of archaeological work on ancient Macedonia. In 1978, the excavation of the ancient Macedonian royal tombs at Vergina in Greek Macedonia gave a more physical aspect to the historical legacy of the ancient Macedonians. In the aftermath of the discovery, the issue of whether the ancient Macedonians were culturally and genealogically tied to the ancient Greek world of city-states has become an issue of paramount importance for contemporary cultural politics. It should be noted that the ancient Macedonians do not bear any genealogical connection to modern-day Macedonians. But both Greeks and modern-day Macedonians claim to be the legitimate inheritors of the legacy of ancient Macedonians. The use of archaeology in the service of the national narrative compels the researchers in the field to take a stance on this issue—for, quite simply, they cannot escape the controversy (for a review, see Danforth, 1995: 45–46).

Extreme Macedonian nationalists have developed the viewpoint that modern Macedonians are not Slavs, but rather the descendants of ancient Macedonians. Moderates, like the Republic's former President Kiro Gligorov (1999: 102) suggest that Macedonians should not be "slaves to recent hypotheses that we are direct descendants of Alexander the Great." Yet, at the level of popular discourse, both Greeks and Macedonians make extensive use of Alexander the Great as a powerful symbol of historical and cultural continuity.

The use of archaeology in nationalist legitimization has provided the background for a major confrontation over symbols. At stake was the appropriation of the sun or star of Vergina, an archaeological artifact discovered in an ancient Macedonian tomb in the late 1970s in the Greek part of Macedonia. Although the specifics of the meaning of the artifacts (and the identity of the persons buried in the tomb) have remained a topic of discussion among specialists, the sun or star of Vergina was soon appropriated by Macedonian and Greek nationalists as their own symbol. When in 1992 the Macedonian Assembly selected it as the state symbol and placed it on the new state's flag, Greeks viewed this action as nothing less than straightforward theft of their own cultural heritage (Brown, 1994).

Of course, the issue is meaningful only in the context of the local national narratives. Today's Macedonians are Slavs and have little to do with an ancient people who lived approximately one thousand years before the coming of Slavs into the Balkans. More importantly, the thorny issue of whether the ancient Macedonians were part of the ancient Greek world or whether they were "barbarians" who were acculturated into the ancient Greek civilization has been a topic of discussion for close to 2,500 years. Ancient Greek authors offered different opinions on this issue, and their judgment was colored by partisanship. Given the fact that the issue could not be settled even in the fourth century BC, it is very unlikely that archaeological research could ever prove one or the other argument conclusively. But even were this possible, no legitimate conclusions about contemporary Macedonia can be drawn from such an analysis.

The maintenance of national narrative and its grip on popular imagination rests on its successful transmission to future generations. This transmission is accomplished through public oratories in national commemorations, school textbooks, and the media reproducing popular orthodox views in everyday life. These institutions have the ability to shape public perception even in cases where their proclaimed past lacks any connection to real historical events. Consider for example the public outcry caused in Greece by the publication of Alkis Angelou's book, *The Underground School: Chronicle of a Myth* (Angelou, 1999). This short monograph set out to delegitimize the widely held belief that during the period of the Ottoman rule, Greek educational institutions and schools were closed down and students had to attend school at night in secret. In the popular song that exemplifies this oral tradition, education and religious belief are linked, the function of education being to instill the Orthodox faith into the pupils' souls. The four verses, known practically to all Greek pupils, read: "Oh bright moon / shine on me so I would walk / and go to school / to learn of things, God's own things" (translation mine). The conventional, "mythological" interpretation of the song is that this was the folk song sung by Greek pupils who were going to school at night, fearful of Ottoman persecution. Angelou's careful study pointed out the lack of any proof with regard to such prosecution during the Ottoman period, and traced the development of this myth in the second half of the nineteenth century. Suffice to say, the book's main thesis goes against the entrenched belief of generations of Greeks who have been told again and again in various public commemorations that their forefathers' desire for education was forcibly forestalled by the Ottoman Turks, and that the Orthodox Church was the only institution that allowed them access to education. Indeed, this version of history is at odds with the historical record. During the second half of the eighteenth century the Orthodox Church fought against the import of Enlightenment ideas in the Balkans and persecuted many of the native intellectuals who advocated them (see Roudometof, 1998a).

In his monograph, Angelou points out that this particular national myth has its origins not in the scholarly work of historians, but rather in nineteenth-century public commemorations of the Greek war of independence. It was in the context of such occasions that poetic license gradually gave rise to a national myth both powerful and devoid of any real substance. His analysis illustrates the manner in which mass media, journalists, politicians, and the clergy are frequently in a position to shape collective memory against the reality of the historical record.

While this particular example aptly illustrates the ability of public oratory to shape popular collective memory against the reality of the historical record, it is important to point out the extent to which the educational systems of the Balkan nation-states, and more specifically, the school textbooks, have been a major component in the construction and reproduction of these nations' national narratives. As early as 1926, Dimitris Glinos, one of the modernizing intellectuals of the interwar period, conducted a survey of ninety Greek books—seventy-nine of which were school textbooks covering the 1914–26 period. Glinos lamented the texts' ethnocentrism and pointed out the tendency to transform recent conflicts into transhistorical struggles. In doing so, the textbooks contributed to the construction of stereotypes alienating the Balkan peoples from each other (Iliou, 1993). In sharp contrast to post–World War II Western Europe, the educational institutions and textbooks of the Balkan states were not cleansed of nationalistic propaganda and ethnocentric stereotypes. In most of the Yugoslav republics, the failure to address the "national question" in a fair and open manner helped the proliferation of historical revisionism in the 1980s and 1990s. In the post-1990 period, history education was renationalized, providing the ideological infrastructure for the armed conflicts of the period. While Serbian textbooks provide the paradigmatic case for this tendency, post-1989 Macedonian and Bulgarian textbooks provide additional evidence for a regional ethnocentric cultural turn.

The 1991–92 Bulgarian history textbooks also provide a distorted image of neighboring countries and peoples. In the textbooks, Greeks are presented as having political, religious, and military power, which they use to exploit and subordinate the Bulgarian people. Of the themes specifically mentioned in the history textbooks, the "national unification of the Bulgarian areas" remains a dominant theme. In the 1992 textbooks it was mentioned seventy times versus only thirty for the 1991 textbooks. Other themes include "Greece's denationalization policy," mentioned twenty-four times in 1991 and twenty times in 1992, and "Greece's territorial expansion pursuits," mentioned forty-two times in 1991 and thirty-four times in 1992 (Vouri, 1996: 70).

Moreover, history textbooks provide selective interpretation of their histories. Greek textbooks attribute the success of the 1821 Greek revolution to the heroic deeds of the revolutionaries—while the Turkish textbooks attribute the revolution's success to Great Power interference. Macedonian and Albanian textbooks trace their people's national liberation efforts back to the

1821 revolution, thereby legitimizing these two latecomer nations (Katsoulakos and Tsantinis, 1994). Key events of recent Balkan history are presented in a highly ethnocentric manner. For example, the 1912–13 Balkan wars receive a highly selective treatment in the Greek, Macedonian, Serb, and Bulgarian textbooks (Belia, 1993; Vouri, 1993). Generally speaking, the wars are presented from within nationalistic lenses. The nation's suffering is exalted and "injustices" are pointed out. The rest of the Balkan states are blamed, and the nation is assumed to bear no responsibility for the turn of events. Good deeds are generally reserved for one's nation and bad deeds are the work of others.[18]

In the 1990s, extensive qualitative and quantitative research has provided ample evidence of ethnocentrism in the Greek educational system.[19] Mirroring their Balkan counterparts, the basic themes of Greek schoolbooks revolve around the concepts of continuity, preservation, homogeneity, resistance, and superiority. National identity is viewed as transcendental and continuous from antiquity to the present. The "West" is viewed as a threatening presence, while neighboring countries become targets for exalting Greek superiority. Such stereotypes are also reflected in the public's attitudes. For example, a survey conducted in 1995–96 in Greek Macedonia found that 64.6% of the respondents "disliked" the Macedonians (Mihalopoulou et al., 1998: 201). Just like the Bulgarians or the Serbs, Greeks appear to have been unfairly treated in key historical moments (Dragona, 1997: 84–85; Hopken, 1996). The growing socioeconomic gap between the Balkans and the "West" is contextualized as a threat to national identity (Dragona, 1997: 87–89). Technological progress is viewed as an element alienating people from their own identity and ultimately threatening national authenticity.

Practically in all Balkan countries, the Ottoman legacy is viewed as purely negative. Students are led to believe that the Ottomans conquered the Balkans by force, violently converted Orthodox Christians into Muslims, and lacked any claim to civilization itself.[20] These images account for the negative attitudes of Serbs, Bulgarians, and Greeks vis-à-vis Turkey. Being entrenched in public discourse and everyday life, these attitudes inevitably become major obstacles in conflict resolution and contribute to the negative image of Muslim minorities in the Balkan states. For example, in a 1992 survey a reported 83.8% of the Bulgarian public considered the Turks to be "religious fanatics," and, subsequently, refused to marry them (80.8%) or even to be friends with them (38.7%) (Hopken, 1997: 77).

It is important to stress that the link between memory and a sense of belonging is not restricted to those inhabiting a particular territory. On the contrary, the transnational movement of peoples facilitates the migration of human communities across boundaries. In these instances, belonging is closely associated with feelings of longing for the original homeland. Diasporas and transnational communities often display a long-distance nationalism vis-à-vis their original place of origin (Schiller et al., 1992;

Anderson, 1993). In the globalized world of the twenty-first century, the traditional notion of a community based on a territorial sense of place is gradually replaced by a de-territorialized sense of locality (Appadurai, 1995). In the case of Macedonia, such communities of immigrants can be found in Australia, Canada, and a few other countries around the globe. For these communities, the issue of identity is a direct expression of their experiences in a setting where national origin and citizenship are clearly distinguished from each other. Multiculturalism and the acceptance of ethnic diversity in advanced industrialized societies have paradoxically strengthened the ethnic or ethno-national identity of immigrants from Macedonia. In the immigrant communities of Australia and Canada, the Macedonian issue is a domain of strife among Greek, Bulgarian, and Macedonian immigrants (Danforth, 1995, 2000). Hence, far from a topic confined to the boundaries of the Balkan peninsula, the Macedonian Question has become a transnational site of conflict—as evidenced by the numerous Web sites competing for rival interpretations (for example, www.macedon.org, or www.makedonika.org).

NATIONHOOD AND CITIZENSHIP IN THE BALKANS

While the discussion thus far has provided some solid examples of the significance of national narrative for the Balkan nation-states, it is further necessary to specify the particular direction of nationalism in the Balkans. National narratives are not a feature unique to Eastern European countries—on the contrary, they are present in all nations around the globe. However, there are marked regional differences between the foundational principles for the development of local national identities.

National identity is the outcome of conflicting claims that are generated by more or less selective references to, and interpretations of, written and oral historical narratives, a process that establishes collective beliefs in the legitimacy of claims to a territorial "fatherland."[21] Prevalent among the southeastern European societies, this form of national identity stands in sharp contrast to the Western European and U.S. model of national identity, which emphasizes the importance of citizenship rights and the territorial nature of the state. Although it is tempting to juxtapose Eastern and Western European nationalisms, it should be emphasized that Western societies are by no means immune to particularistic trends. In the post-1945 period, the rise of peripheral nationalisms in Ireland, Spain, France, Italy, and Great Britain has seriously undermined the proposition that ethnic nationalism is absent from Western European societies (Guibernau, 1999). This trend illustrates the rather simplistic nature of analyses—for example, Plamenatz's (1976)—that conflate the methodological differentiation between civic and ethnic nationalisms with the concrete historical and geographical differentiation between Western and Eastern European societies.

It is therefore important to place the broader theoretical themes discussed here within the specifics of the Balkan case. The Macedonian Question has to be placed within the context of the broader Balkan route toward modernity. It is well known that southeastern European nationalisms generally tend to emphasize a population's cultural heritage and its ethnic continuity (Stavrianos, 1958; Jelavich and Jelavich, 1977; Jelavich, 1983). While this outcome is not in doubt, the social processes that have led to this particular route are less well known. The older (nineteenth and early twentieth century) Orientalism in European writings about the Balkans has indeed been coupled with a more recent neo-Orientalism that attributes the presence of ethnic conflict in the region to the people's cultural attributes (Kaplan, 1993; Kennan, 1993; Huntington, 1996).

To move beyond these simplistic viewpoints, it is necessary to look upon the contemporary realities as the outcome of the historical process of nation building in the region over the last 150 years. Although the consequences of nationalism are multifaceted, what is particularly important for the issues addressed here is the fact that nationalism is an ideology that facilitates not only the growth of a political movement—it also colors the contemporaries' worldview and identity. The shape of subjective national identity is determined by the manner in which nationalism shapes the individual's sense of belonging. In turn, this process is influenced by a variety of social processes—economic, political, and cultural. From this point of view, the solidity of the concepts of "nation" and "national identity" is rendered problematic, and the conceptual ground shifts from issues regarding a population's "nationality" to issues concerning the creation of a "nation" as a category that provides emotional and political identification for a given population.[22]

As I have argued in my *Nationalism, Globalization, and Orthodoxy* (2001), the development of national identities in the region was the product of a competition between the two rival discourses of *citizenship* and *nationhood*. An important feature of the Balkan pattern of nation building (as it emerged in the post-1850 period) has been the systematic subordination of citizenship rights to the principle of nationhood. Citizenship and nationhood represent two discourses that provide for the foundation of an "imagined community" (Anderson, 1991). Citizenship does not simply imply formal membership in a state's political body; it also assumes that all citizens are members of the nation owing to their adherence to universal principles (the United States provides the "ideal type" of such a nation). Nationhood, as the basic foundation for the construction of a distinct national identity, implies the employment of particularistic criteria most often derived from a local culture. In most (but not all) cases, this process involves the politicization of earlier *ethnies* or ethnic communities (Smith, 1986) as a means through which cultural characteristics (language and religion) become politically relevant (Roudometof, 1999). Although elements of citizenship and nationhood are to be found in almost every national culture, the two discourses are typically structured in a hierarchical manner. One of the two is selected as the normative standard that provides the foundational principle of social organization. For example, French membership in the nation is derived from membership in the state (signifying the subordination of ethnic particularism to civic universalism), while in Germany membership in the state (and the civic rights and obligations associated with it) is derived from a person's membership in the ethnic community of the German nation (for an analysis, see Brubaker, 1992).

Eighteenth-century early Balkan nationalists such as Rigas Velestinlis and the Balkan federalists of the 1850–1950 period offered an alternative to the model of the nation-state. Their goal was to divorce state organization from national groups in order to provide for a federation or a state where different nations or ethnic communities could coexist peacefully.[23] However, these Balkan attempts did not materialize. By the mid-nineteenth century, the Ottoman bureaucracy as well as prominent members of the Ottoman Greek-Orthodox community championed a reform program, aiming at providing equality among all Ottoman subjects. This attempt to establish interethnic citizenship among the Ottoman population was a deliberate effort to provide a meaningful alternative to the rising Greek, Serb, and Bulgarian nationalisms. To accomplish such a goal the reformers championed parliamentary democracy as the effective mechanism that would help transform the Ottoman subjects into citizens (for details, see Roudometof, 2001: 75–95). These efforts led to the 1876 revolution and the establishment of the first Ottoman parliament. The experiment proved short-lived. Caught in the midst of the international crisis of 1875–78, the parliament was not given sufficient time (and adequate authority) to transform Ottoman political culture. In 1878, Sultan Abdul Hamid II prorogued the parliament and established his own semi-theocratic authoritarian regime. For the next thirty years, the issue of political reform was stalled, and it did not surface until the Young Turk revolution of 1908. Indeed, the Young Turks attempted to find a solution to the thorny problem of ethnic coexistence. However, their proposed solution entailed the acculturation of non-Muslim Ottoman minorities into the Ottoman Muslim society of the time. The ethnic and national communities of the Balkan Christians opposed this solution. By that time, the Greek, Serb, and Bulgarian national propaganda machines had been rather successful in gaining loyalty among a considerable number of Ottoman subjects— most of them in the European part of the Ottoman Empire.

During the nineteenth and twentieth centuries, Balkan nation building has emphasized nationhood at the expense of citizenship (Roudometof, 2001: 101–56). The origin of this trend lies in the Ottoman practice of granting collective rights to members of a confessional association (*Rum millet*) rather than to individuals (Karpat, 1973, 1982; Ramet, 1989). In the *millet* system, collective rights were tied to particularistic rather than universalistic criteria (the latter being the case in Western democracies). As a result, Balkan nation-states claimed the loyalty of prospective nationals living within the Ottoman Empire on a similar basis, since this was the only way that prospective nationals could be legally identified. Membership in a state came to be viewed as the natural consequence of membership in a nation (defined in terms of an ethnic or religious group), yet state membership implied participation in the dominant ethnic or religious "imagined community." Thus little room was left for a genuine interplay between state and national membership, as the two had become closely intertwined.

In fact, during the 1923 Greco-Turkish exchange of populations, the definition of "Greek" and "Turk" followed religious criteria, a feature that testifies to the extent that particularistic criteria have been employed in defining membership in modern Balkan nations. In nineteenth- and early twentieth-century Macedonia, ethnicity was also employed as a major characteristic with which to decide a person's nationality. The foundation of the Bulgarian Exarchate (1870) aimed specifically at differentiating the Bulgarian from the Greek population on an ethnic and linguistic basis, hence providing the conditions for the open assertion of Bulgarian national identity (Kofos, 1964: 13–16). In fact, the rationale for creating a separate religious institution, like the Exarchate, was predicated on the assumption that it was possible to readily identify the two groups (Bulgarians and Greeks)—and that people who belonged to the two groups would invariably identify with the one or the other national church. It is worth adding that the Bulgarian Exarchate maintained all the rituals and other features of the Eastern church; its sole difference from the Greek-Orthodox church was its employment of Bulgarian as liturgical language. In this case, however, the employment of language as a means to differentiate between Bulgarians and Greeks further complicated matters; a portion of the population that remained faithful to the Orthodox Patriarchate of Constantinople was Slav-speaking. The identity of this (often bilingual) population constituted the centerpiece of the nineteenth-century Macedonian Question (Lunt, 1984: 108).

By 1912 the Balkan nation-states (Serbia, Bulgaria, and Greece) finally formed a political and military coalition and, in the 1912–13 Balkan wars, were able to defeat the Ottoman forces and to partition Ottoman Macedonia among them. The partition of Macedonia signified the triumph of nationhood over projects of transnational or interethnic citizenship. Consequently, the Balkan nation-states pursued homogenization policies, attempting to transform their citizens into members of their respective nations. Yet, these nations were conceived of as communities constructed around the dominant ethnicity, religion, or language. In accordance to the European standards of the interwar period, minorities were "anomalies within a nation-state" and were subsequently treated accordingly. For the last two centuries, then, nation building in Greece, Bulgaria, and Serbia has emphasized nationhood rather than citizenship as the major criterion for establishing a person's membership in the national "imagined community." The creation of the first

Yugoslavia (1918) might appear as a deviation from this trend. However, both the interwar as well as the post-1945 Yugoslavia had to deal with precisely these issues, attempting to develop stable solutions to the problems associated with the coexistence of multiple ethnicities (Serbs, Croats, Slovenes, and other smaller groups) within the boundaries of a single unit (Djilas, 1991; Banac, 1984; Ramet, 1992; Lampe, 1996).

The employment of particularistic criteria for deciding the Balkan peoples' national status has had serious consequences. Minority rights are articulated within a discourse of citizenship. Since in the Balkans it is nationhood and not citizenship that provides for membership in the nation, concern for minorities is understood as implying irredentist activity. It should thus be noted that the issues of minority rights and irredentism are closely intertwined, and that the confusion between the two is not accidental. For inclusion into their respective nations, Greek, Bulgarian, Serb, and Macedonian identities stress the importance of particularistic criteria at the expense of civic-oriented universalism. For example, Greek national identity has been historically determined by Greek Orthodoxy (that is, membership in the Greek Orthodox Church) and, secondarily, by competency in the Greek language. Modern Greek identity is conceived as an integral, transcendent entity, a conceptualization that operates in an exclusive manner vis-à-vis non-ethnic Greeks:

[N]on-Greeks are not—and cannot be—members of the *éthnos* [nation]; hence . . . they are not entitled to those rights that are available to members of the Greek *éthnos*. . . . Beginning with the founding of modern Greece, the conceptualization of the Greek *éthnos* as coterminous with the Greek state rejects, except for historic religious minorities, the existence of other ethnicities within its boundaries. (Pollis, 1992: 189)

Similarly, the definition of the Macedonian "imagined community" is also based on a religious criterion (membership in the Macedonian Orthodox Church) and a linguistic one (competency in the Macedonian language). But, contrary to Greek identity, both criteria are contested; the Macedonian Church is considered schismatic by the other Eastern churches and the autonomous status of the Macedonian language has been similarly questioned.[24]

In order to foster subjective identification with the principles of nationhood, the Balkan nation-states have developed national narratives to help justify their irredentism and their historical rights in different parts of the Ottoman Empire.[25] The visions of a Greater Bulgaria, a Greater Serbia, and the Greek "Great Idea" each employed a historical narrative to justify irredentist claims. Such narratives aim at establishing a connection between the particular nation and the territory it occupies—or the territory it should occupy—thus legitimizing the possession of a territory by a particular collectivity. To a considerable extent, the international dispute among Greece,

Bulgaria, and FYROM concerns a similar issue. What is at stake in this debate is a collectivity's "power to nominate," which in this case is the power to obtain, via a particular national narrative, a past and thus an identity that legitimizes a group as an entity that has a "right" to a territory as its "natural" habitat (Bourdieu, 1989). The conflict that has been played out in international conferences as well as in street demonstrations concerns, to a considerable degree, the official recognition of legitimate rights to Macedonia—the name, the territory that bears it, and the loyalty of the subjects living in it.

OUTLINE OF THE BOOK

The book's individual chapters explore different aspects of the broad issues outlined above. Elsewhere, I have discussed the evolution of the various national identities in the Balkan peninsula over the last two centuries (Roudometof, 2001). In this book I am concerned with the contemporary issues surrounding the Macedonian Question. Therefore, although my discussion takes into account the significant consequences of past historical events into the contemporary situation, it is not my intention to provide "a history of Macedonia."

In Chapter 2, I provide an overview of the political and cultural mobilization of the 1990s. The Macedonian Question officially became an issue for the international community after the 1991 declaration of independence by the People's Republic of Macedonia. Between 1991 and 1995 the Greek state opposed the official recognition of the new state by the international community. After 1995, the issue assumed a less visible profile in international relations, yet it remained an important domestic issue. Of course, although Greece was the most visible state opposing the use of the word "Macedonia" by the People's Republic, it was not the only one. Bulgaria has considered the (Slavic) Macedonians of the People's Republic to be Bulgarians. Bulgaria recognized the new state as "Macedonia," but this should not conceal the fact that the Bulgarian state did not really recognize the fact that the Macedonian nation is distinct from the Bulgarian nation. In addition to the formal or official exchanges involved in these controversies, the Macedonian Question became a transnational conflict, as various immigrant associations of Greeks, Bulgarians, and Macedonians were involved in lobbying for their particular side. In Australia, Canada, and the United States, states with considerable numbers of southern European immigrants, these issues became important rallying points for the mobilization of the local communities. Both among the immigrant communities and within the Balkan nation-states, the local intelligentsia played a key role in promoting the local national narratives, hence adding "oil to the fire" of nationalist passions. Dissenters, whose beliefs and writings did not follow the collectively held beliefs, were castigated and persecuted.

What is the story of Macedonia and its people? What are the narratives that have led to such passions? This is the issue explored in Chapter 3, where I review the Macedonian narrative and spell out the reasons that have led both Greeks and Bulgarians to fiercely oppose it. I should point out that it is fairly easy for third-party observers to reconstruct Macedonia's history on the sole basis of one of these narratives, and, then, to criticize the other narratives from that point of view (for a comparative review of the competing perspectives, see Danforth, 1995). In fact, fairly well-researched and well-intentioned monographs have fallen prey to this tendency (for example, see Poulton, 1995; Shea, 1997). My own approach aims at looking at these narratives comparatively, setting off one against the other, and thereby explaining why people who believe in one of these narratives find the other narrative so insulting to their sense of national identity. In order to accomplish this task, I depend heavily upon Michel Foucault's approach toward the history of ideas and call for an archaeology of the Macedonian Question. Only by examining the presuppositions of the different national narratives and their relationship to political projects (such as nation building) within the context of the local states is it possible to provide an interpretation for their emergence and nature. I hope that this enterprise makes a contribution toward opening up the field and allowing for the production of less ethnocentric perspectives. My discussion in Chapter 3 does not include an extensive overview of the Bulgarian-Macedonian dispute. This is a reflection of the fact that in the post-1989 period it has been the Greek-Macedonian dispute over the name of the new state that occupied the attention of the international community.

Following the description of the contrasting perspectives, in Chapter 4, I provide an account or an interpretation of the historical evolution and pattern of cultural history that led to the construction and reproduction of Macedonian national identity. My interpretation relies heavily on the role of conflicting national claims upon the European territories of the Ottoman Empire, as well as on the role of the state-sponsored policies of cultural homogenization pursued during the interwar period by the Balkan nation-states. Additional factors, ranging from geopolitical rivalry to the resettlement of Ottoman Greek refugees in the Greek Macedonia to the role of communist parties during the interwar period and post–World War II immigration waves, also shaped the historical trajectory of the peoples of Macedonia, contributing to the construction of rival identities. My discussion in Chapter 4 stresses the transnational character of Macedonian and Greek nation-building in the twentieth century (for a general discussion, see Roudometof, 2002a). Of course, such transnational nation-building was also present in earlier periods; however, the recent advent of electronic media has contributed significantly to the new immigrants developing close bonds with their homeland—albeit without actually setting foot on its soil.

Having discussed the symbolic or theoretical issues underlying the Macedonian Question, I proceed with a more policy-oriented discussion of the controversies surrounding the issues of minorities in the southern Balkans. In Chapters 5 and 6 I inquire first into the issue of Macedonian national minorities in Bulgaria and Greece, and, then, into the better-publicized "Albanian Question." Over the last two decades, Macedonian human rights activists in Bulgaria and Greece have raised the issue of Macedonian minorities within these two states and have sought to use international forums in order to force the two states to grant them "cultural rights" as minority people. These efforts have met great resistance in both states and have been depicted as thinly veiled efforts to question these states' territorial integrity by Macedonian nationalists. It is worth pointing out that both Greece and Bulgaria were initially not well prepared for dealing with these issues; and the fact that these issues were raised in international meetings and by nongovernmental organizations is but an apt illustration of the shifting norms in international relations and the reconfiguration of state sovereignty (Jacobson, 1996; Sassen, 1996). Despite the rhetorical claims and the large informal estimates produced by the Macedonian side, my overview of the literature and research in this area suggests that reality does not in fact support the claim that sizeable Macedonian *national minorities* exist within Greece and Bulgaria today. Of course, Macedonian minority groups exist in both states—but they lack the numerical strength attributed to them in the early 1990s.

The situation is quite different with the Albanians, who are currently dispersed in the northern and western part of FYROM (see Map 1.2), the "international protectorate" of Kosovo (whose status is practically in limbo after the NATO-led war of 1999), and the Albanian state. Moreover, several hundreds of thousands of Albanians have immigrated (legally or illegally) to Greece, thereby adding a further twist to the story. As a result, the Albanian Question has to be examined comparatively, and, more specifically, it is necessary to take into account the regional dynamics present within each region. Only in such a fashion is it possible to gain a better understanding of regional geopolitics as well as the local states' attitudes. In sharp contrast to the symbolic conflict over Macedonia reviewed in the book's earlier chapters, the Albanians' claims to statehood both in Kosovo and Macedonia are rooted in straightforward demography and the peoples' right to self-determination. In Chapter 6, I review the Greek-Albanian dispute over the status of the Greek minority in Southern Albania. Furthermore, I examine the manner in which the regional developments in Kosovo during the 1990s have impacted ethnic relationships between Albanians and (Slavic) Macedonians in FYROM. In the book's final chapter, I synthesize the arguments developed in the various chapters of the book and provide a final summary of the interpretation advanced throughout the monograph. In addition

Map 1.2
The Albanian Population in the Southern Balkans

Source: U.S. Institute for Peace, http://www.usip.org/oc/sr/kosovomap.html.

to clarifying, debunking, and challenging the various arguments put forward by the different sides involved in this controversy, I also provide a short overview of the recent developments in the region in the book's postscript.

NOTES

1. The mythology of humanitarian intervention was used to convey the impression that the Kosovo intervention was a "just war" fought on behalf of the refugees and for the protection of their human rights. Such considerations were just a small part of the rationale. For a critique, see Chomsky (1999).

2. Still, the very next day following Clinton's statement, Constantinos Stephanopoulos, the President of the Republic of Greece, publicly questioned this scenario. For Stephanopoulos, Clinton's line of argument was beyond his understanding. The President's statement fueled the belief that the reasons behind the U.S.-led campaign were not the ones officially stated. Over the next few months, the overwhelming majority of the Greek public became radically opposed to the NATO campaign, forcing the government to adopt a policy of careful maneuvering in order to avoid an open confrontation with NATO while at the same time taking public opinion into consideration.

3. Clinton's references to "ancient grievances" and "newly born struggling democracies" were indirect but clear statements referring to the problem of international recognition of FYROM. Ironically, less than two years after the U.S.-led war against Yugoslavia, civil war broke out in the Republic of Macedonia between the Macedonian majority and the Albanian minority—indeed, the very outcome that the U.S.-led NATO intervention ought to have prevented.

4. There are numerous books, articles, and monographs published on the topic, in both Western and Balkan languages. Among the most notable of the 1990s Anglophone publications are Poulton (1995), Danforth (1995), Mackridge and Yannakakis (1997), Shea (1997), Karakasidou (1997), Gounaris et al., (1997), Pettifer (1999a), Cowan (2000), and Roudometof (2000a).

5. To my knowledge, there is not a single sociologist among the international specialists who have produced works on the Macedonian Question. The 1990s anthropological scholarship (and in particular the books by Karakasidou and Danforth) have come fairly close to a sociological analysis of the social construction of the Macedonian Question. However, both books focus on ethnographic material and thick description—and in this manner they provide solid examples of excellent anthropological work. My analysis in this book is aimed to supplement these analyses by providing a more theoretical discussion of the Macedonian Question.

6. The very name of the state has become part of this controversy. I am using the acronym FYROM because this is the name under which the United Nations has recognized the state. I am acutely aware that a large number of states have recognized the state under the name it has chosen for itself, that is, the Republic of Macedonia. For further comments and discussion on the "naming" of Macedonia and the different connotations of the word "Macedonian," see Danforth (1995: 6–7) and Karakasidou (1997: 22–24).

7. In this book, I am discussing the Macedonian Question from its very emergence in the nineteenth century. As Pettifer (1999b) has argued, there are two distinct phases of this dispute—the "old" pre-1945 Macedonian Question, and the "new" post-1945 Macedonian Question. This distinction is useful, although I think that for the purposes of this book it is necessary to examine the evolution of this saga in its totality. For further discussion on the differences between the "old" and the "new" questions, see Chapters 4 and 7.

8. Moreover, the study of collective memory has become entangled in the controversies surrounding relativism and its use in social-scientific inquiry. See Burke (1997), Lukacs (1985), Lowenthal (1985; 1996), Hutton (1993), and Le Goff (1992) for discussions about the role, impact, and influence of memory in history writing.

9. Pierre Norra's *Les Lieux de memoire* (1984–92), a history of the collective memory of France as revealed through its representations, is perhaps the most influential contemporary project that bears the mark of Halbwachs's approach.

10. Halbwachs (1992: 193–235) himself showed how the people used the spatial location of the Holy Land to generate schemes that were superimposed on Palestine. Historians have explored this dimension of memory studies by focusing on the role of the various commemorations of the two World Wars. For examples, see Mosse (1975; 1990) and Winter (1995). The U.S.-based research has focused on the construction of the mythology surrounding key figures of U.S. history, such as George Washington and Abraham Lincoln (see Schwartz, 1987; 2000). Another,

potentially more fruitful line of research focuses on the competing interpretations of U.S. national identity and the different groups that espoused different ideological projects (O'Leary, 1999).

11. The notion of narrative as a central dimension in the politics of nation building and memory has received some attention in the literature. See for example Bhabha's (1990) original discussion on the use of narrative as a nation-building mechanism. My own perspective, however, is closer to the approach of Stuart Hall (1992); (see also Hall and De Gray, 1996, and Smith, 1999). More recently, Lukic and Brint (2001) also refer to "national cultural narratives."

12. The Old Testament might be considered as the first such written source of a particular national narrative. For a discussion of the Jewish experience as it relates to issues of collective memory and history, see the classic work by Yerushalmi (1996).

13. For some informative discussions on the decline of nationalist historiography in Western countries, see Oestergaard (1991) and Kennedy (1970). See Smith (1999: 29–56) for a discussion of the intertwining between historical knowledge and nationalism. The role of historians in nation building is also the focus of Deletant and Hanak (1988).

14. The field of nationalism has experienced a revolution over the last twenty years, leading to a completely new body of literature written predominantly by social scientists (instead of historians, who used to be the scholars originally interested in nations). The list of some of the most influential works includes Gellner (1983), Smith (1986, 1991, 1995), Anderson (1991), Greenfeld (1991), Alter (1989), Kedourie (1985), Hobsbawm (1990), Hobsbawm and Ranger (1983), Brieully (1993), Hechter (1975), and Connor (1994). In addition to the scholarly works, there is also a multitude of journalistic accounts addressing issues of nationalism— such as the best sellers by Ignatieff (1994) and Kaplan (1993).

15. Seton-Watson's (1977) distinction between "old" continuous nations and "new" discontinuous nations bears the mark of the influence of various national narratives. Ironically, for Seton-Watson the "old" nations are those of Western Europe, while Eastern European nations are mostly considered among the "new" nations. In the geopolitical nationalist game of legitimization, tradition (and claims to antiquity) is a valuable resource. In sharp contrast to Seton-Watson's description, many of the so-called "new" nations of Eastern Europe and the Third World have been eager in constructing genealogies that explicitly connect the present-day inhabitants of these nations to antiquity. There is an abundance of such examples, ranging from Greece to Egypt or Turkey and Iraq.

16. Smith (1986) refers to these processes as the essential *mythomoteur* that guides nation building in the modern era. Contemporary nations frequently depend upon narratives of historical reconstruction. Such narratives provide revisionist accounts of the past as a means of justifying the actions taken in the present. Yet, it is easy to perceive such narratives as "objective accounts" and to forget their biases and presuppositions. The long-standing proposition of modernization theory—that the ethnic conflict will subside with modernization—has blinded many researchers to the fact that such conflicts are in many respects part of the modernization project (see Roudometof, 1999; Bhabha, 1996: 59).

17. Spatial boundaries and temporal continuities are a necessary ingredient for nation-formation. Therefore, the politics of collective memory necessarily involve confrontations about the significance of particular spatial markers as well as the tem-

poral markers that signify events that shaped the nation's image of itself. For a discussion, see Boyarin (1994).

18. It is important to point out that none of these features are unique to the Balkan countries. On the contrary, these features are shared among the majority of Eastern European nation-states. For example, Verdery (1993: 195) writes that "across the region, local historiographies represented nations as innocent victims, victimized nearly always by *other* nations, rather than by their own members" (emphasis in the original). Poland and Romania display characteristics similar to those of the Balkan nation-states discussed here.

19. Frangoudakis and Dragona (1997). The project is based on an analysis of textbooks as well as interviews with teachers. The massive nature of the project does not allow a detailed description of the specifics, and, consequently, my discussion simply highlights some key aspects of the overall tendencies. Suffice to say the evidence suggests a twist in Todorova's (1997: 43–45) account of the Greeks' view of the Balkans. Increasingly, Greeks distance themselves from the Balkans in an effort to avoid precisely the stereotypes Todorova analyzes in her brilliant book.

20. While teaching a class of Serbs, Macedonians, Greeks, and Albanians at the American College of Thessaloniki in 1998, I asked them whether they attributed the spread of Islam to violence and forced conversion. Despite the information provided in their textbook, nearly all students responded that this was indeed the case. The students doubted the reliability and accuracy of their "American textbook" and preferred to rely upon the knowledge they accumulated in their elementary and high school years.

21. On national identity as a process, see Schlesinger (1987) and Connor (1990). The assumption that this form of identification is distinctly modern does not entail the conclusion that "identity" in general is a particularly modern phenomenon. National identity is seen as a modern manifestation of people's awareness of their membership in a group. Regarding the existence of collective identity in pre-modern times, see Armstrong (1982) and Smith (1986, 1991).

22. This does not mean that nation-formation is a phenomenon without deep roots in the collective consciousness of a society—as some social theorists have suggested (for a critical review, see James, 1996). Nor does the fact that nation is a socially constructed entity mean that nation is a fabricated concept that serves the ideological processes of legitimization by specific social classes and dominant groups. Such interpretations are clearly shortsighted and tend to view cultural categories in an instrumentalist fashion—as categories that have no content on their own.

23. On Rigas Velestinlis, see Vranousis (1957), Kitromilides (1978), and Todorov (1991). On federalist plans within nineteenth-century Greek society, see Todorov (1991). For federalist plans between Serbs and Bulgarians, see Shashko (1974). Two excellent general overviews of these projects are offered by Djordjevic (1970) and Stavrianos (1944). For a more detailed discussion of the evolution of Balkan nationalisms in the eighteenth and early nineteenth centuries, see Roudometof (1998b).

24. However, an important difference between Greece and FYROM does exist regarding the relationship between state and nation. In Greece, the state operates as a depository of the nation; its policies aim at serving the good of the nation, and no distinction is made between national and state interests. In contrast to Greece, FYROM's engagement with these issues has been quite complex. The constitutional debates that took place in FYROM in the 1990s were attempts to clarify the

relationship between state and nation. These debates are reviewed in Chapter 6. According to Hayden (1992b), FYROM's constitution is an example of the peripheral nationalism that caused the breakup of Yugoslavia; it clearly states that the Republic of Macedonia is the "national state of the Macedonian people." Albanians, Turks, Serbs, Vlachs, and other non-ethnic Macedonian citizens belong to a separate "nationality" (Perry, 1994a: 83). Such an orientation was bound to cause severe disagreement from within the ranks of the large Albanian minority—an issue explored in Chapter 6.

   25. See Kitromilides (1983). "Official" historical narratives postulate the existence of a nation back in time and then proceed to interpret the historical record as the continuous evolution of this "imagined community" from that particular point. As a comparison of Albanian, Turkish, Bulgarian, and Macedonian history textbooks demonstrates, the Balkan national narratives diverge from each other as they interpret historical events such as the 1821 revolution and the Balkan wars of 1912–13 in quite a different light (cf. Katsoulakos and Tsantinis, 1994; Skoulatou et al., 1983). Historical facts are either deleted from the narrative or presented in a selective manner.

Chapter 2

The Symbolic Struggle
for Macedonia

In the early 1990s, the latest twist in the Macedonian Question occurred as a direct consequence of the disintegration of the second Yugoslavia.[1] On 17 November 1991 the People's Republic of Macedonia declared its independence and asked for international recognition. Unlike Slovenia and Croatia (see Hayden, 1992a, 1992b), the declaration was not the result of long-held grievances. It simply followed the regional pattern of Yugoslav disintegration. Indeed, the People's Republic of Macedonia was, by all measures, an economic backwater—and its economic security was closely tied to the existence of the Yugoslav federation. In 1990, the People's Republic of Macedonia accounted for 6.7% of Yugoslavia's industrial product, 6.6% of its agricultural product, 9.2% of its agricultural population, 4.9% of investment, and 5.6% of imports. By all accounts, the public was strongly Titoist in orientation, and, unlike Slovenia and Croatia, they did not harbor dreams of succession (Ramet, 1996: 212–14).

The declaration set off a diplomatic, cultural, and international struggle over the recognition of the new state. Greece opposed recognition of the new state because of its use of the name "Macedonia" and engaged in intensive diplomatic efforts to prevent its recognition by the international community. At the heart of the dispute lies the thesis that the Republic is the official homeland of the Macedonian nation. Although the diplomatic dispute has subsided in magnitude after 1995, it has remained an important factor influencing both Greek and Bulgarian politics. In this chapter, I describe the evolution of this symbolic conflict over the name of the new state. Because Greece has been the most visible adversary of Macedonian recognition, I devote considerable space to the way in which this conflict has shaped Greek politics in the 1990s. The other major adversary of Macedonian nationalism is Bulgaria. However, Bulgaria avoided the costly route of turning the name into a subject of diplomatic confrontation. Therefore, throughout the 1990s, Bulgaria was less visible in the international scene in its opposition to the Macedonian state. But this does not imply that Bulgarians recognized the Macedonians as a separate nation—at least in the first half of the 1990s.

GREECE AGAINST THE MACEDONIAN REPUBLIC

On 4 December 1991, Greece declared that recognition of the Republic of Macedonia depended on its constitutional guarantees against claims to Greek territory, cessation of hostile propaganda against Greece, and exclusion of the term "Macedonia" or its derivatives from the new state's name. The first of the three conditions was a response to Article 49 of FYROM's new constitution, which states that "the Republic cares for the status and rights of those persons belonging to the Macedonian people in neighboring countries as well as Macedonian expatriates, assists in their cultural development, and promotes links with them" (Constitution of the Federal Republic of Macedonia, cited in Perry, 1992: 40). It should be noted that Article 49 is indeed similar to Article 108 of the Greek constitution; nevertheless, the reference to Macedonian peoples in "neighboring countries" was interpreted by Greece as an indirect reference to a Macedonian minority within Greece—an issue discussed in greater length in Chapters 4 and 5.

In December 1991, the European Union (EU), at the insistence of Greece, stated that it would not recognize the new state until it guaranteed that it had no territorial claims against any neighboring state and would not engage in acts against any such state, including the use of a name that implied territorial claims. In January 1992, the Macedonian parliament adopted two amendments stating that the republic had no territorial claims against any neighboring state, that the republic's borders could not be changed except in a manner consistent with international norms, and that it would not interfere with the affairs of other states. Following these amendments, a European Union arbitration commission issued the Batinder Report, which found that the republic had fulfilled all conditions for recognition (Danforth, 1994: 327–28). However, Article 49 remained in FYROM's constitution, causing considerable dissatisfaction in Greece. Of the two other conditions set by the Greek state, the question of the republic's name has stirred the fiercest debates in the international press, with numerous journal and/or newspaper articles having addressed some aspect of this conflict. Some commentaries argued for the right of the Macedonian people to self-determination, whereas dissenting voices considered the employment of the term Macedonia by the new state to be a usurpation of Greek heritage by a small group of Slav nationalists.[2]

Within Greece, but also among the Greek diaspora, the issue provoked a strong emotional response. Many of the reactions to this issue included an element of righteous indignation regarding FYROM's claim to be the homeland of the Macedonian nation. The Greek popular press reflected the general Greek attitude; it referred to FYROM as a *morfoma* ("formation") and a *kratidio* ("little state"), both expressions serving to belittle FYROM's status as a sovereign state. Moreover, in the Greek discourse, the new entity was always called "the Republic of Skopje" and never Macedonia (unless the word were placed between quotation marks). Macedonians were referred to as "Skopjians" (the equivalent of calling Greeks "Athenians"). Archbishop Serafim, head of the Greek Church at the time, is on record as declaring "The propagandists of Skopje should shut up and not provoke us" (interview in the newspaper *Eleytherotypia*, 3 January 1993). This colorful statement is characteristic of the prevailing attitude among Greeks.

Throughout 1992, various rumors suggested the formation of a coalition between Turkey (Greece's traditional political adversary) and FYROM that could lead to war and the potential annexation of parts of Greece by both countries. This scenario was quite improbable at the time—especially since Skopje lacked military capacities of any significance (Ramet, 1996: 217). However, the reaction to these potential (and to some extent, imaginary) threats was revealed in the Greek press by virtue of headlines such as "Turkey sends army for intervention in the Balkans" (*To Vima*, 22 November 1992) or "The ungrateful West strikes Greece" (*Oikonomikos Tachidromos*, 19 November 1992). Such headlines reflected a general tendency to see "enemies" wherever disagreement was expressed. Consider these headlines: "We & the barbarians of Europe" (*Eleftheros Typos*, 14 June 1992), "The Europe of the Idiots" (*Eleftheros Typos*, 13 December 1992), or "Athens is a Victim of a German Plot" (*Kathimerini*, 26 July 1992). A growing nationalist fervor led to actions that violated the right of free speech. For example, members of a leftist organization were persecuted because of their dissenting views on the Greece-FYROM dispute. When 169 intellectuals aligned themselves with this persecuted leftist group in the name of freedom of speech, nationalist fervor led to the solicitation of more than 2,000 signatures of prominent figures and intellectuals advocating the righteousness of the official viewpoint (for details, see Helsinki Watch 1993).[3]

Additionally, other rumors suggested that the new state would not constitute a viable political entity and would most likely be partitioned among the neighboring states. In 1992, the Serb president Slobodan Milosevic proposed to the Greek government the partitioning of FYROM between Serbia and Greece. Greece, however, rejected the offer and reported the Serbian proposal to the European Union (Zahariadis, 1994: 663).[4] This proposal coincided with protests from the Serb minority throughout the 1991–92 period—as well as exaggerated Serb reports that some 300,000 Serbs were living in the new state (Ramet, 1996: 222–23). Consequently, at least for a while, the new state had to face the spectrum of Serb military involvement (just like Slovenia and Croatia did in the early 1990s).

Beyond the reaction registered in the popular press, the reemergence of the Macedonian Question stimulated a strong popular response as well.[5] Huge demonstrations were organized both in Greece and abroad. On 14 February 1992 and again on 31 March 1994, approximately one million people turned out in the streets of Thessaloniki to declare "Macedonia is Greek." In Munich, 10,000 Greeks took to the streets on 5 April 1992 to make the same claim. In the United States, a rally sponsored by the Hellenic-American Council reportedly drew 20,000 people to Washington, D.C. Additionally, in Greece, private companies initiated advertising campaigns that aimed at "proving" the "Greekness" of (Greek) Macedonia. In the United States, Greek-Americans issued a plea to President George Bush through advertisements in the *New York Times* on 26 April and 10 May 1992. EU governments considered hostile to the Greek viewpoint—in particular, Italy and the Netherlands—were threatened with a Greek boycott of their exports. Following the recognition of FYROM by Bulgaria, Greece suspended a $50 million line of credit to that country, but Greek-Bulgarian relations were improved some time later (Zahariadis, 1994: 662). Within Greece, songs, pamphlets, and stickers declaring "Macedonia is Greek" proliferated in less than a year. In sum, there has been a plethora of material published or reprinted within a few years arguing in favor of the Greek viewpoint.[6]

The Greek and the Macedonian diasporas have both been an audience as well as an international agent in this international struggle over "Macedonia." In Canada and Australia, where large Greek and Macedonian diasporas live— many originating from Greek Macedonia—the issue became an explosive one, with family members and community organizations coming into sharp conflict with each other. An especially acute conflict broke out between the two diasporas in Melbourne, where 113,000 Greek-speaking and 21,000 Macedonian-speaking immigrants reside (Danforth, 1995). For these two immigrant groups, the competing claims are much more than symbolic; at stake is each group's right to call its local immigrant clubs and associations "Macedonian" and its denial of the other group's right to do the same.[7] The involvement of diasporas in this dispute is a prime example of "long distance" nationalism (Anderson, 1993).[8] This was facilitated by the migration of Macedonian peasantry (Greek and Slavic) overseas during the late nineteenth century and also after World War II (Petrovski, 1981; Gounaris, 1989). This entire process is part of the transnational articulation of Greek and Macedonian nationhood worldwide. The emergence of these diasporas and the manner in which they came to be drawn into this dispute is discussed in Chapter 4.

All the activities reviewed in the preceding paragraphs demonstrate that the Greek reaction vis-à-vis the new state was a genuine response that bears the mark of late twentieth-century nationalism. Talk of a Macedonian state was (and still is) perceived as an insult by most Greeks. During the 1992–93 period, this issue became a dominant theme in Greek politics. The attitude of Antonis Samaras, Greek minister of foreign affairs at the time, was a major factor contributing to Macedonia's elevation as an issue of great political concern. The minister adopted a rigid position that denied the existence of a Macedonian nation and the recognition of the new state. Fears concerning Macedonian irredentism were instrumental in legitimizing this standpoint. In an attempt to pressure the new state into compliance, a trade embargo was put in place, causing serious economic dislocation within the republic (Petkovski et al., 1992).

On 4 April 1992, Constantinos Mitsotakis, the Greek premier, forced Samaras out of the Ministry of Foreign Affairs, but the ex-minister's strong political views remained influential in Greek policy. Samaras continued to voice his independent views on the matter until he was compelled to retire from both his seat in Parliament and his membership in the conservative party (New Democracy) because of his opposition to the party's official policy regarding this issue. The presence of a right-wing critic within the party's ranks as well as the employment of the Macedonian issue as a political weapon by the socialist opposition (PASOK) were important obstacles in preventing the adoption of a more flexible attitude toward the Macedonian Question.

During 1993, Samaras finally broke ranks with the conservatives and started his own party, called "Political Spring." When conservative deputies who had been allied with him withdrew their support of the government, new elections became necessary. The conservative government was forced out of office in the 10 October 1993 elections, and the socialist party (PASOK) was returned to power. The new government claimed that no negotiations could take place between FYROM and Greece.[9] This led to the termination of any dialogue between the two sides—and a Greek embargo against Skopje.

In the diplomatic field, Greece initially appeared to be successful since the EU, in its 27 June 1992 meeting in Lisbon, aligned itself with the Greek viewpoint, denying official recognition of the republic if it used the term "Macedonia" in its official title. The EU decision prompted popular reaction in Skopje, where, in mid-July, some 50,000–100,000 people protested against EU refusal to recognize their nation (Ramet, 1996: 219). Although by September 1992, Skopje had been recognized only by eight states (Ramet, 1996: 221), the situation improved in the following years. Already in early 1993 the new state was successful in gaining membership in the International Monetary Fund (IMF) under the title "Former Yugoslav Republic of Macedonia" (FYROM). It applied for membership in the United Nations

(UN). Following strong Greek mobilization against FYROM's acceptance into the UN and a French recommendation for UN-sponsored mediation, the controversy surrounding the usage of the term "Macedonia" became the subject of international mediation until the post-1993 Greek socialist government withdrew from the negotiating table. In January 1993, the three EU members of the UN Security Council (Britain, France, and Spain) tabled a plan of confidence-building measures between Athens and Skopje and proposed the acronym FYROM. The UN assumed the mediation between the two parties, eventually leading to accession of FYROM into the UN—with Greece's approval (Veremis, 1995a: 83).

On 16 December 1993, six EU states decided to recognize the new state as FYROM, a decision that was interpreted by the Greek press as a major defeat for the official Greek position. In early 1994, the United States and Australia were added to the list of states that had recognized the new state as FYROM. The recognition was interpreted as a major defeat for the Greek "hard line" on the issue of FYROM's international recognition—and was quite important because the two states were able to overcome the quite vocal objections of their Greek diaspora communities.

Faced with these changes in the diplomatic field, the Greek government imposed on 16 February 1994 a strict new trade embargo banning the movement of goods from the port of Thessaloniki to the new state (Veremis, 1995a: 90). The new embargo reduced FYROM's export earnings by 85%, while food supplies were dropped by 40% (Dunn, 1994: 19).[10] The Greek embargo against FYROM elicited criticism from the Western press and the international community at large; in fact, the EU Commission unsuccessfully challenged the embargo's legitimacy in the European Court. However, when the new embargo was announced, a reported 66.2% of Athenian Greeks supported the "hard line" adopted by the socialists (poll results published in *Eleytherotypia*, 18 February 1994). Over time, the Greek position became increasingly untenable because the international community was quite aware that lack of international recognition contributed to long-term instability in the region. The wars in Croatia and Bosnia-Herzegovina reinforced the necessity to adopt a more pragmatic attitude toward a state that had succeeded in leaving the Yugoslav federation peacefully. By 1995, close to sixty states—including Bulgaria, Turkey, and the Russian Federation—had recognized the new state either as "Macedonia" (the majority of them) or as FYROM. Reports of the damage caused to FYROM's economy by the embargo prompted U.S. intervention and eventually led to the 1995 Interim Accord between Athens and Skopje.

In the interim accord the two parties bypassed the issue of the name and provided for lifting Greece's embargo. In return, FYROM removed from its flag the sixteen-ray star of Vergina, an archeological artifact of the Ancient Macedonian kingdom that was discovered in Greek Macedonia—and whose significance for the parties has been discussed in Chapter 1. Figures 2.1 and

2.2 allow for a comparison between the old and new flags of FYROM. Signed on 13 September 1995 the agreement consisted of twenty-three articles (United Nations, 1995). Its principal points are summarized below:

The First Party [i.e., Greece] recognizes the Party of the Second Part [i.e., FYROM] as an independent sovereign state and the two Parties shall establish diplomatic relations at an agreed level with the ultimate goal of relations at ambassadorial level (Article 1)

The Parties hereby confirm their common existing frontier as an enduring and inviolable international border (Article 2)

Each Party undertakes to respect the sovereignty, the territorial integrity and the political independence of the other Party (Article 3)

Figure 2.1
The Star of Vergina in the Pre-1995 Macedonian Flag

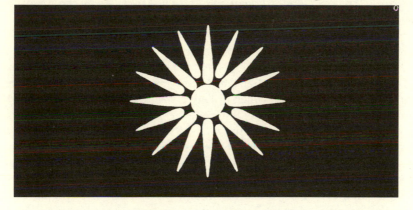

Figure 2.2
The Current Flag of the Former Yugoslav Republic of Macedonia

The Parties shall cooperate with a view to facilitating their mutual relations notwith-
standing their respective positions as to the name of the Party of the Second Part
[i.e., FYROM] (Article 5.2)

The Party of the Second Part [i.e., FYROM] hereby solemnly declares that nothing
in the Constitution can or should be interpreted as constituting any claim by the
Party of the Second Part to any territory not within each existing border (Article
6.1)

Each Party shall promptly take effective measures to prohibit hostile activities or
propaganda by State-controlled agencies and to discourage acts by private entities likely to incite violence, hatred or hostility against each other (Article 7.1)

While the interim accord normalized relations between Athens and Skopje,
it did not completely remove the issue from public debate.[11] As a matter
of fact, coverage of the accord by the Greek media was rather limited
and invited neutral or even hostile comments by the press (Demertzis,
Papathanassopoulos, and Armenakis, 1999). This attitude stood in sharp
contrast to the open endorsement of nationalist passions by the majority of
the press during the pre-1995 period. An analysis of the Sunday press between December 1991 and April 1993 reveals that the overwhelming majority of commentaries reflected ethnocentric viewpoints (Armenakis et al.,
1996).

The post-1995 Greek foreign policy has been influenced by the general
postulate of modernization, which provided the slogan for the "new PASOK"
under the leadership of Costas Simitis. The pursuit of modernization and
Westernization has meant that the post-1995 Greek government has been
more willing to engage with international organizations and the international
community at large. Substantively, however, the post-1996 Greek foreign
policy combined both a nationalist orientation (inherited from the pre-1995
PASOK cabinets) with a more pro-Western orientation. The goal of this
fusion has been to satisfy both wings of the party and the electorate—on the
one hand the social democrat modernizers, and, on the other hand, the
populists (Kazamias, 1997).

In fact, for the more populist (or nationalist) oriented of PASOK's deputies, the recognition of FYROM became directly connected to the outcome
of the cultural and political struggle between FYROM and Greece. For them,
the Macedonian Question has been a mechanism through which they can
register their discontent with the policy of the post-1995 Simitis government.[12] This attitude is consistent with the socialists' use of the Macedonian
Question as a political weapon between 1991–93, when they were in opposition. Suffice it to say that within Greek politics, the issue is a crown of
thorns—skillfully employed by those criticizing the party in power to un-
dermine its popular following.

Hence, after 1995, the Greek government continued the negotiations with
FYROM and normalized trade relations between Athens and Skopje. How-

ever, the Simitis government has publicly maintained that no compromise solution can be made on the "name issue" under any circumstances. Specifically, the government has opposed the so-called "compound name solution"—that is, a concession by the Greeks of the term "Macedonia" preceded by a qualifying epithet to indicate its geographic as opposed to its ethnic content.[13] The government has maintained its hard line despite the fact that this solution is favored by the modernizing wing of the party and is said to be favored even by Prime Minister Simitis himself (Kazamias, 1997: 84). The reason for this impasse is the government's fear that any move on the "name issue" is bound to meet the strong opposition of the populists within the party.

During the post-1995 period the associations of the Greek diaspora have been equally vocal when the issue of a compromise solution with FYROM has been raised. The associations do not hesitate to oppose declarations of Greek officials that do not meet the standard "hard line" on the Macedonian Question. For example, the associations responded swiftly when on 21 July 1997 the Greek Foreign Minister Theodoros Pangalos reportedly expressed in a *New York Times* interview the desire of the Greek government to resolve the infamous issue of FYROM's official name. The PanMacedonian Associations of the United States and Canada, then holding their meetings in Thessaloniki, held a special session to issue a statement calling the minister's views "irresponsible and unacceptable for our national interest" (*Nea Makedonia,* 23 July 1997, p. 6) and demanding his resignation.

In May 1998 the publication of the *Dictionary of Modern Greek Language* by the Greek linguist Giorgos Babiniotes added new flame to the passions involved. The dictionary indicated as a possible employment of the word "Bulgarian" its use by hooligans from southern Greece as a derogatory term for the followers of sports teams from northern Greece. On 29 May 1998, at least forty-five faculty members from the Aristotelian University of Thessaloniki publicly expressed their disagreement with the inclusion of this connotation in the dictionary. The wave of protest was led by Pontic Greek activists from Greek Macedonia and practically dominated the Greek media for almost a week. Theodoros Aspasides, a member of the Municipal Council of Thessaloniki, sued Babiniotes and on 14 July 1998, the Lower Court of Thessaloniki declared that the suit had merit and ordered the professor to remove this interpretation from the dictionary. According to the court, this interpretation is used by only a handful of hooligans and "it creates confusion about the national origins of the players and followers of PAOK [local football team] and the Macedonians in general." Dissenting voices pointed out that the decision amounted to nothing less than censorship—and that it violated the constitutional guarantees of free speech.[14] During the first half of the 1990s, Professor Babiniotes had been an advocate of Greek "hard core" views on the Macedonian Question, and, therefore, this turn of events was quite ironic. Although he publicly defended his scientific duty to record this usage of the word "Bulgarian" and to pursue "scientific truth" independently of nationalistic "political correctness," Babiniotes (1998) later suggested that all slang terms be moved to a different section of the dictionary, and the latest edition of his dictionary bows to the overwhelming majority of these criticisms.[15]

The ease with which a Greek "cultural warrior" found himself on the defensive aptly illustrates the difficulties of conducting social scientific research on these issues and of expressing one's opinion freely (Karakasidou, 1994). More ominous, however, is the harassment of organizations and individuals conducting research on the topic of minorities within Greece.[16] Right-wing groups have taken the lead in such actions but their activities do not encounter universal rejection, as right-wing newspapers frequently thrive on the publication of imaginary conspiracy scenarios involving individuals associated with research on minority issues. Such individuals are portrayed as agents of foreign powers or as people whose motives are suspect and potentially harmful to the nation.

During the early 1990s, the promotion of ethnocentric stereotypes in the Greek press helped such political views gain legitimacy in the eyes of the public, especially in northern Greece (see Panagiotopoulou, 1996; Triandafyllidou and Mikrakis, 1998). Research conducted in 1995–96 in all the counties of Greek Macedonia by a team from the Greek Center for Social Research led to interesting conclusions regarding ethnocentrism and xenophobia—especially toward the Macedonians. While 60% of the 1,200 respondents expressed their conviction that Greek Macedonia should be a center of regional economic development and interstate relations with the rest of the Balkans, they also expressed negative attitudes against people from neighboring states. For example, despite strong evidence to the contrary, "foreigners" were blamed for an increase in crime (70.2%) and a decline in wages (77.3%), while a reported 44% desired some kind of border control to prevent immigration from the neighboring countries (Mihalopoulou et al., 1998: 204–5, 540).

While these concerns are by no means unique to Greece (California, for example, has experienced a similar situation in the 1990s), the association between ethnicity and prejudice greatly promotes a nationalistic outlook. The Macedonians hold the dubious distinction of being the first among the groups despised (64.6% of respondents disliked them), followed by the Jews (55.6%), and the Muslims (or Turks) of western Thrace (54.2%) (Mihalopoulou et al., 1998: 201). These attitudes are, at least in part, a reflection of the post-1989 wave of legal and illegal immigration into Greece from the post-communist countries (Voulgaris et al., 1995; Panagiotopoulou, 1997). During the 1990s, unofficial estimates put the total number of (mostly illegal) immigrants close to one million.[17] Still, the rise of ethnocentrism converges with the cultural struggle against FYROM to provide distorted images of the Other, images that certainly do not promote the goal of peaceful coexistence.

THE MACEDONIAN QUESTION IN BULGARIAN POLITICS

Important as Greece became in this whole affair during the 1990s, it is only one of the parties involved. Of the others, Bulgaria is the country most closely engaged with the issue. Bulgaria has recognized FYROM as the Republic of Macedonia, but at the same time explicitly denied the recognition of Macedonia as a separate nation. In fact, Bulgaria has insisted that all those who declare themselves "Macedonians" are in reality Bulgarians, an official viewpoint advocated consistently for almost four decades (and for more than a century before that with minor variations and occasional respites). The first Bulgarian national state, created by the 1878 San Stefano Treaty, included most of geographical Macedonia, but the subsequent revision of the treaty only a few months later, at the Congress of Berlin, excluded Macedonia from the territory of the Bulgarian state (see Maps 2.1 and 2.2). Ever since, both the Bulgarian state and its intelligentsia have repeatedly asserted their claims to Macedonian territory, claims that are viewed as part of Bulgaria's process of national unification (for a brief overview, see Mahon, 1998). The

Map 2.1
The Bulgarian State According to the San Stefano Treaty (1878)

Source: Roudometof (2001: 141)

Map 2.2
Macedonia and Bulgaria According to the Treaty of Berlin
(1878)

Source: Roudometof (2001: 142)

Bulgarian-Macedonian relations in the nineteenth and early twentieth centuries are discussed in greater detail in Chapters 3 and 4. In the post-1989 period, Bulgaria had to confront Macedonian statehood and international recognition. In 1992 President Zhelev expressed Bulgaria's official viewpoint as follows:

We have a common history, a common language, a common religion. . . . For the vast majority of Bulgarians, and for our historians, the idea has therefore arisen that Macedonia is not a nation in its own right. But politically, we cannot allow ourselves to impose a national identity on the Macedonians. They have the right to choose for themselves—that is the most essential democratic right of the individual. (Quoted in Lefebvre, 1995: 458).

In line with this viewpoint, Bulgaria has consistently opposed the designation of medieval and contemporary historical figures as Macedonian (for an overview, see Rusinow, 1968). Minor issues, in this regard, serve as exemplars of the larger underlying political difference: for example, Bulgarians refuse to employ interpreters in their official dealings with Macedonian representatives on the grounds that there is no need for them. The implication here is that the Macedonian language is really Bulgarian, an implication acutely understood—but fiercely protested—by the Macedonians. In sharp contrast to the Bulgarian-Macedonian debate over the need for interpreters, Scandinavian diplomats (Danes, Swedes, and Norwegians) take pride in the fact that they do not use interpreters in Scandinavian-only negotiations.[18] Scandinavians respect the distinctiveness and autonomy of each other's respective languages, while at the same time recognizing that they are mutually intelligible. On the other hand, Bulgarian refusal of and Macedonian demands for interpreters has much more to do with legitimizing differences than with questions of intelligibility.

The above examples represent only a small proportion of the many issues that have become targets of the political and cultural struggle. They do indicate, however, that the central contemporary controversy concerns the manner in which Bulgarians, Greeks, and Macedonians view and interpret Macedonian identity. In fact, human rights advocates in Bulgaria and Greece have suggested the existence of Macedonian minorities in both these states. This issue is discussed in detail in Chapter 5. Where both Athens and Sofia agree is in their categorical denial that Macedonian minorities exist within the boundaries of Greece and Bulgaria. For Greek and Bulgarian nationalists, as well as for a majority of the public in the two countries, the Macedonian nation itself is nothing more than an ideological construct of the Cold War and Tito's efforts to expand his reach into the southern Balkans. Indeed, Greeks and Bulgarians have suggested that ethnic heterogeneity and state-sponsored ethnogenesis cast doubt even on the Macedonians' claim to be a distinct nation or ethnic group. The long-standing position of Bulgarians has been that all Slavic-speaking Macedonians are Bulgarians. In a 1999 nationwide survey, an estimated 51% of the Bulgarian population considered the citizens of the Republic of Macedonia to be ethnic Bulgarians (ACG, 1999).

While the Bulgarian state has been persistent in its persecution of organizations and individuals that advocate Macedonian separatism, Bulgarians react quite differently when it comes to Macedonian organizations that adopt a nationalistic posture. In 1990, probably the most controversial year on the troubled way to Bulgarian democracy, it was not difficult to register the Union of the Macedonian Cultural Societies, an organization already operating during the communist regime, as a political party.[19] The Union of the Macedonian Cultural Societies was a nationwide organization that emerged during the communist regime in the 1950s. It provided a mechanism through which the Bulgarian Communist Party (BCP) was able to infiltrate the numerous Macedonian Bulgarian organizations throughout the country. Despite communist control and infiltration, these organizations remained preoccupied with their traditional social functions—such as the commemorations connecting the Macedonian Bulgarians to their original places of origin.[20]

Throughout the 1980s, as the Bulgarian communists assumed a more nationalist stance toward the Turkish and Muslim minorities in Bulgaria, a group of Bulgarian communist reformers began demanding a more nationalist position on the Macedonian issue. They enjoyed some support within the party elite and were able to assume leadership positions in the Macedonian clubs in Sofia, where they proceeded to revive the nationalist agenda of the pre–World War II nationalist (or "fascist" in communist jargon) VMRO (to be discussed in detail in Chapter 4). By 1986–87 these communist reformers were able to establish a new organizational structure and to attract students from the Sofia and Veliko Turnovo universities. The new nationalists took advantage of the post-1989 democratization wave to publish the newspaper *Makedonia* in 1989 and to establish Macedonian societies in Pirin Macedonia—in the towns of Blagoevgrad and Petrich (Nedeva and Kaytchev, 1999: 178–79). On 5–6 January 1990 they held a congress restoring the Union of Macedonian Cultural Societies. On 15–16 December 1990, another congress formally adopted the name VMRO-UMCS (International Macedonian Revolutionary Organization–Union of Macedonian Cultural Societies).

The name and the legacy of the Internal Macedonian Revolutionary Organization (VMRO) lie at the very heart of the Bulgarian-Macedonian dispute. The original VMRO was formed in 1893 in Thessaloniki. Actively involved in terrorist activities, the organization staged the 1903 Ilinden Uprising (for further discussion, see Chapter 4). The uprising failed, and the popularity of VMRO receded in the following years. However, reconstituted and regenerated, VMRO re-entered Bulgarian politics in the interwar period as a powerful political force, uniting a diverse group of refugees, activists, former guerrilla fighters, and some criminal elements. This is perhaps as far as an unbiased description may go since, in the post-1945 period, Skopje and Sofia have been fighting over VMRO's orientation: Was it a Bulgarian national organization or did it represent a Macedonian national liberation movement?

In post-1990 Macedonian politics, the emergence of a nationalist party bearing the same name (VMRO-DPMNU) was accompanied by an openly irredentist agenda, aiming at a "reunification" of the pre-1913 Macedonia (see Chapters 3 and 6 for further discussion). Despite the initial popularity of the party, the harsh economic realities of the 1990s illustrated the unrealistic nature of its demands and gradually led to a shift toward the politics of accommodation and coexistence. By 1998, after a long period of exclusion from the post-1991 cabinets, VMRO-DPMNU became one of the partners in the Skopje coalition government.

Like its counterpart (VMRO-DPMNU) in the post-1991 Republic of Macedonia (FYROM), the reconstructed VMRO-UMCS of Bulgaria assumed a nationalistic posture. Although not a political party originally, it became one later—by dropping the useless appendage of the "Union of

Macedonian Cultural Societies." By 2000 VRMO had become part of the rightist ruling coalition of the Reunited Democratic Forces. While attempts by the former secret services to prompt nationalistic parties, particularly on the basis of their alleged strong anti-Turkish sentiment, were in vain, the VMRO alone comes close to satisfying the "demand" for such a party.

In the 1990s young VMRO members, carrying traditional red and black banners and burning torches, became the most typical component of patriotic rallies, and they were the most militant participants in the anti-communist unrest during the winter of 1996–97. VMRO representatives, elected in the municipal authorities and as mayors, became known for establishing curfews for young people. VMRO leaders took an extremely militant position against the so-called "sects" (which in Bulgaria means every religious group outside the ranks of the Bulgarian Orthodox Church) and undertook violent measures (beating, torture) against Mormon and Jehovah's Witness preachers. VMRO's leader and MP, Krassimir Karakachanov, also tried to prevent the abolition of the death penalty. Such tactics set the VMRO against the clearly pro-European orientation of its coalition partners.

VMRO leaders also revealed an astonishing lack of understanding of the realities in FYROM. On the occasion of a friendly soccer match between the Bulgarian and Macedonian national teams, VMRO organized a massive invasion of fans, including MPs and students, who marched through Skopje carrying Bulgarian flags and singing patriotic songs. None of the local population revealed any intention to meet them as liberators (as was the case with Bulgarian troops in 1941), nor did the local police attempt to prevent such a demonstration. More seriously, the VMRO imposed a sort of "embargo" on Bulgaria's contacts with the Br. Cervenkovski government, openly expressing its expectations that after Macedonian elections, its namesake in Skopje, VMRO-DPMNU, would overnight reject every kind of hesitation and prejudice toward Bulgaria, including possible moves toward reunification. Of course, these unrealistic expectations were not met, but such immature tactics created many problems for VMRO-DPMNU.

VMRO's heavy influence upon Bulgaria's foreign policy has been one of the principal factors that led to the stagnation in Bulgarian-Macedonian relations during most of the 1990s. Yet, for all the sound and the fury it has created, VMRO has failed to win widespread following among the Bulgarian public. Even after a relatively strong and visible presence in the public protests of the 1996–97 winter, VMRO remained an unintelligible, perplexing organization in the eyes of the Bulgarian public. This is reflected in the results obtained by a nationwide survey listed in Table 2.1.

Table 2.1 confirms the public's skeptical attitude and indicates the importance of the Macedonian issue for VMRO's visibility. This, of course, is perhaps inevitable since the name alone contains a strong connection to its historical predecessor of the early twentieth century. Yet, the public does not necessarily identify this legacy with the modern-day VMRO. According to

Table 2.1
VMRO Activities

Question: What do you connect the activities of the contemporary VMRO with?

	Yes	No	No Answer
—With the historical tradition	47.2	8.6	44.2
—With the events of January 1997	14.3	29.9	55.8
—With the Macedonian Issue	44.9	8.9	46.1
—With their civil position for defense of Bulgarianism	36.1	11.8	52.0
—With their stance against the sects	20.1	22.2	57.6
—With their stance for preserving the death penalty	11.5	24.1	64.4
—With draft legislation introduced by them	9.3	25.3	65.4
—With their leader	14.6	23.0	62.4
—With their partnership with SDS	19.8	21.5	58.6
—With the MPs from VMRO	8.2	28.4	63.3
—With their representatives in your municipal council	7.0	29.5	63.5
—None of the above	10.3	20.9	68.8
—Something different from the list above	2.2	13.7	84.1

Source: Analytical Creative Group ACG Ltd. 1999. Unpublished Survey Results, courtesy of Stephan E. Nikolov.

a nationwide representative survey by the National Center for Public Opinion Research (NCPOR), 64.9% of respondents have "No opinion" about VMRO and 13.8% "Have never heard" of it. Thus, only 21.3% of the population has an opinion about VMRO, and these opinions are very diverse, as can be seen from Table 2.2.

Thus, if we put aside the vague "organization which contributes to the democracy," positive attitudes toward VMRO are bound up with the perception of it as a patriotic and nationalistic organization, while negative views are concentrated around the image of a coercive, extremist, fascist, or simply "suspicious" organization (an image imposed by communist propaganda), coupled with demands, albeit without evidence to justify them, that the party be banned. Most opponents of the VMRO are in the sixty years old and above age range, i.e., those who have direct memory of VMRO's terrorist activities in the 1920s and early 1930s.

There is also a small number of respondents who consider VMRO as a "Macedonian" organization—while it is not clear what this means. These ambiguities of the label "Macedonian" in Bulgaria are discussed in greater

Table 2.2
Opinions about VMRO

Question: What do you think about VMRO?
(only these who express opinion)

Item	Percentage
1. An organization, which contributes to the democracy	33
2. It has to be closed, I do not approve it	22
3. A patriotic organization	9
4. Coercive, extremist, fascist organization	9
5. Feckless, without any influence	6
6. Suspicious	4
7. Macedonian organization	3
8. Nationalists, who care about Bulgaria	3
9. Other	11

Source: NCIOM (1997: 108–9).

length in Chapter 5. Finally, others consider it an organization of Bulgarians from Macedonia or one of the Macedonians. Interestingly enough, attitudes toward VMRO are clearly distributed according to the various regions of Bulgaria. In the city of Sofia; southwestern Bulgaria (i.e., Pirin Macedonia); most of central Bulgaria; and the Varna, Vidin, and Silistra regions (a total of twelve regions) the prevailing attitudes are positive. In southern Bulgaria (Rhodopes and Burgas); northeastern Bulgaria with the exceptions of Varna, Dobrich, and Silistra; and Montana, a negative attitude prevails. The remaining group of five regions appears to be "neutral." Regions with positive attitudes are more urbanized with a more highly educated population, while negative attitudes dominate where the population is chiefly Turk and, in general, Moslem. The sole exception is Montana, where none of these features are present, but which leans heavily to the left, or post-communist parties.

Results from this survey indicate that VMRO is far from being what the organization itself claims, that is, "all-Bulgarian and nation wide," and could not receive significant electoral support outside a large coalition. Of great relevance to our current discussion, however, is that VMRO's main base is in Pirin Macedonia (see Map 1.1). If nationally the image of the VMRO is ambiguous and contentious, it is mainly in Pirin that people are unable to forget the kind of legacy this organization tries to revive, and its rigid nationalistic attitude concerning the Bulgarian character of the local population could hardly go unmentioned.[21] It is also in Pirin Macedonia that we observe the strongest electoral support for VMRO. Even if we accept rumors of corruption, nepotism, and bribes (for example, giving students stipends in exchange for affiliation and support), the significance of such a level of support should not be underestimated.

The latest twist in the ambiguous relationship between Bulgaria and FYROM came with the signing of a joint declaration between the prime ministers of the two states. The 22 February 1999 joint declaration was aimed at ending the long-standing language dispute between the two sides— that is, the degree to which the Macedonian language was to be recognized officially as a separate language by the Bulgarian state. However, in practical terms, the Republic of Macedonia (FYROM) had to withdraw any claims regarding a Macedonian minority in Bulgaria; more precisely, citizens of both countries are now permitted to identify themselves as they wish, without any pressure from outside.

Reaction in Bulgaria to this development in Bulgarian-Macedonian relations was unusually muted. Surprisingly, the VMRO has kept a low profile, stating that nothing in the bilateral declaration implies recognition of the Macedonian language as such, while Skopje is prevented from making any claims regarding the Macedonian minority in Bulgaria. Ognyan Minchev and Ivan Krustev, who had been in close contact with the government experts, interpreted the agreement in this light. They said that the formulation regarding language is so precise that it would be valid even if Skopje suddenly chose to accept German as its official language. The only strong protest has come from the (former Communist) Bulgarian Socialist party (BSP), which maintains that the joint agreement represents the surrender by Bulgaria of its "language, historic legacy, and its future."[22]

A BATTLE FOR THE INTELLIGENTSIA

As the review of the political developments in Greece and Bulgaria illustrates, the Macedonian Question is predominantly a concern of middle-class, educated people.[23] Not surprisingly, the issue has become a lucrative domain where the pursuit of professional advancement meets nationalist fervor. Numerous web pages are devoted to the presentation of the Greek, Macedonian, or Bulgarian viewpoints, reciting well-known facts, presenting personal testimonials, reproducing archival material and maps, and using the social-scientific literature to promote their own viewpoints. This mostly middle-class intelligentsia, eager to assume the role of "legislators" (Bauman, 1987), reacts strongly to any suggestion that their passions might be misplaced, that their strongly held opinions might be beliefs—a *doxa* in Bourdieu's (1977) words—that tell us more about the power of cultural reproduction and less about the topics under discussion.

For example, my own work on the Macedonian Question has been the subject of selective interpretation. Quotes from one of my articles were used in a website devoted to "provide the reader with documented evidence about the differences between the ancient Macedonians and the ancient Greeks"; to "illustrate the uniqueness and the grandeur of the ancient Macedonians from whom the legacy has been stolen"; and "[to] some degree, counterbalance the overwhelming Greek propaganda."[24] I was much surprised to find my work selectively quoted on one particular page on this website,[25] where the author enlisted my "aid" in his effort to "prove" that ancient Greeks and ancient Macedonians were different peoples. The author's conclusion was as follows:

These passages alone provide the reader with granite-solid proof that ancient Macedonians were just that—Macedonians—and Greece's racist propaganda against today's Macedonians is laced with venom and hate and represents a classic case of modern fabrication of history. Their highly vocal assertions that "ancient Macedonians were Greeks," and "Macedonia is Greece" are exposed for what they really are—lies and fabrications—and are being obliterated to smithereens once and forever.

Of course, my own research on this issue cannot be used in support of such polemics—even more so in the case of *ancient* Macedonia, which has never been the subject of my studies. In recent years, anthropologists have found themselves in the eye of the storm—as their accounts have become the subject of much controversy and heated debate. Perhaps the most famous example is that of the Greek-American anthropologist Anastasia Karakasidou, who in the early 1990s wrote a dissertation on the nation-building process in Greek Macedonia. Incomplete and inaccurate information about the dissertation was disseminated, and the publication of an article that seemingly advocated the viewpoints of Macedonian human rights activists (Karakasidou, 1993a) turned the Greek-American anthropologist (and native of Greek Macedonia) into a target for nationalist hysteria. The first such attack was published in the pages of the widely circulated weekly *Oikonomikos Tachidromos* (Kargakos, 1993).[26]

Soon it was followed by more scholarly critiques (see Gounaris, 1993; Hatzidimitriou, 1993; and Zahariadis, 1993). The result was a protracted debate concerning academic freedom, a debate that exemplified in many respects the differences in political and scientific agendas between academics writing on Macedonia within the U.S. context and those working within the Greek context. In the meantime, Karakasidou became a target for Greek nationalists: her post-1992 ordeal included an e-mail hate campaign, death threats, and the ultra–right-wing newspaper *Stochos* publishing her car number plates and phone number—hence, turning her into a target for right-wing extremists.[27] When fear of Greek retaliation led to the refusal of Cambridge University Press to publish her dissertation, the flames of controversy went up once again (see Mazower, 1996). Coming after so much controversy, the final publication of the book was quite anti-climactic (Karakasidou, 1997). Indeed, the book did not, as a matter of fact, contain any truly controversial statement. Contrary to the impression generated by shallow readings of her early work, Karakasidou (1997: 136) clearly stated that simplistic theories suggesting the existence of coherent ethnic communities in early twentieth-century Macedonia are theoretically and empirically unsound. In this regard, the amount of ink that was spilled over a study of a *single* village simply shows the heat and the passion that the Macedonian Question arouses among Greeks even to this day.

Indeed, perception of and reaction to scholarly work on Macedonia is routinely influenced by the extent to which an author is perceived to agree or disagree with the arguments set forward by nationalists and politicians. For example, within Greece, authors such as Poulton (1995), Danforth (1995), and Karakasidou (1997) would be among the "villains" of the Greek national cause. This classification is an extension of the authors' viewpoint: Poulton (1995) studies the Slavic Macedonians and adopts mostly their point of view; while Danforth (1995) and Karakasidou (1997) offer a more nuanced perspective, albeit one that recognizes the existence of Macedonians or Macedonian Slavs. Critiques and reaction by Greek specialists are directly linked to considerations of these political issues, as opposed to academic merit alone.[28] More important, scholarship by Greek academics is frequently written with the local audience in mind—and with the constant worry that one's reputation might be adversely affected if academic scholarship does not conform to nationalist rhetoric.[29]

However, it is important to realize that such nationalist biases are not the exclusive domain of Greek historians and social scientists. On the contrary, the Macedonian narrative is equally biased. Writing about the institution of Macedonian National History, Keith Brown (2000a) observes that the central institution associated with the writing and interpretation of national history in FYROM, the Institute of National History, has a virtual monopoly over the production and dissemination of knowledge about the Macedonians. Moreover, the intellectuals working in the institution (originally built under Tito's communist regime) work with a sense of moral mission to uncover the history of an overlooked and victimized people.

Brown's observations about the Institute's structure, organization, and professional culture are worth quoting at length:

In 1992–93 I was struck by the rigid hierarchy of the Institute's personnel structure and the shape of individual careers. Apart from trained individuals at museums elsewhere in the Republic, virtually all national historians in Macedonia worked in the same building and knew each other at least by sight. At that time there were a total of between eighty and one hundred staff. Historians rose through the ranks of the Institute by incremental stages, publishing as they went, completing their master's in their late twenties or early thirties and then their doctorate, usually at around the age of forty. The individual career within the discipline was conceived of as a progression in and of itself, in which the historian (almost always male) acquired more and more knowledge as he matured. The career of the national historian was considered as a job for life. In the Institute, there were no one-year visiting positions or three-year fixed-term grants—everyone was on "tenure track." Additionally, the scholars at the Institute for National History had no teaching obligations—they were pure researchers, judged by their peers on that basis.

However, the term "peer" is one that would be difficult to translate into Macedonian. . . . The contours of national history as *struka* (science) buttress the discipline's status as *nauka* (profession), creating a certain homology between the notion of national history itself and the careers of its successful practitioners. Senior historians are deeply involved in the progress of juniors, as they serve as mentors and play a large part in shaping the projects that younger historians undertake. After all, if knowledge is progressive, then more senior historians are, of course, better equipped to deal with it than younger ones. . . . The kind of disputes that might occur between an "older statesman" and a "young Turk" within a department or in the pages of a learned journal is not likely to occur in Macedonia.

Indeed, the idea of dissent, especially when it emerges from younger members, is repugnant. . . . In some sense, such a view comes out of the firmly held belief that there is a single correct version of the past, which all senior historians share. (Brown, 2000a: 152–53)

In other words, the overlapping of strategies for professional self-legitimation with the construction of a (largely) orthodox Marxist interpretation of history creates a conceptual universe that does not allow for critical thinking or rigorous critical peer review of arguments.

To this situation it is necessary to add an important geographical and autobiographical component, namely the fact that many of the senior researchers at the Institute are refugees from northwestern Greek Macedonia. They fled to Vardar Macedonia (see Map 1.1) following the defeat of the Communist forces in the Greek Civil War (1944–49). The historical events and the post–World War II situation are discussed in Chapter 4. For our purposes, it is important to stress the consequence of these events on individual biographies. The lives of many among the Macedonian intelligentsia have been shaped by the events of defeat, exile, and resettlement (Mihailidis, 2000). In many respects, their intellectual contours (and the "single correct version of the past" invoked by Brown) are an extension of the need to accomplish in their intellectual field the very feat they were denied in the battlefield: the official recognition and "affirmation" of the Macedonians as a nation. All of the above, of course, suggest that it is at best naive to look upon the Institute's historiography as "objective history" told by detached and careful researchers determined to discover the Truth.[30]

For example, one of the Institute's senior researchers, Krste Bitoski, had seventy-two publications from 1958 to 1986 (Brown, 2000a: 148). Bitovski was born in the village of Gavros, in the prefecture of Kastoria (in Greek

Macedonia) in 1926 and fled to the People's Republic of Macedonia during the Greek Civil War. Other such examples among the Institute's prominent historians include Risto Kiriajovski (born in Ayia Anna in the prefecture of Kastoria in 1927), Hristo Antonovski (born in the village of Hryssa in the prefecture of Pella) and Todor Simovski (born in the village of Piyi in the Kilkis prefecture) (Mihailidis, 2000: 76–77). The fact that these (and other) senior researchers set the tone for the Institute's research agenda reveals the extent to which professional development and resurgent irredentism (alongside the nostalgia of the refugees for their original homelands) are intertwined in the Institute's scholarship. The systematic attempt to "construct" and "prove" the existence of Macedonians through the centuries has been a life-goal that fused both professional goals and revisionist nostalgia.

CONCLUSIONS

In this chapter I have provided a review of the post-1989 symbolic struggle for "Macedonia"—the name; the cultural legacy associated with its historical legacy; and the legitimate "ownership" of this legacy by Greeks, Bulgarians, and Macedonians. As this overview clearly illustrates, throughout the 1990s, the Macedonian Question has been an important factor in international relations as well as in domestic politics. It has influenced the fate of Greek governments, as well as the recognition of the Macedonian state (FYROM) by the international community. It also played an important role in the evolution of U.S. and EU policy in the region. It would be a grave mistake to assume that the agencies, states, and organizations involved in this controversy have had a sound understanding of the history, the internal disputes, and other nuances associated with the Macedonian Question. On the contrary, each side proceeded to pursue its own agenda, often with unanticipated results.

The international political conjuncture of the post-1989 period has significantly aided the international recognition of Macedonian national identity. With the collapse of the Soviet bloc during the 1989–90 period and the concomitant "springtime of nations" in eastern Europe and the former USSR, FYROM's declaration of independence occurred in an extremely favorable international environment. Therefore, it is fair to say that the open confrontation between FYROM and Greece was quite detrimental to Greece's international image and quite positive for FYROM's image. Greece stood accused of opposing the international recognition of the only state that was successful in making a peaceful exit from the collapsing Yugoslavia. FYROM's small size and meager population stood in sharp contrast to Greece, the most prosperous country in the region. Consequently, Greece was cast in the role of a "bully" attempting to intimidate its neighbors—with little attention to the specifics and even less attention to the internal political and cultural dynamics of this issue. In this respect, the 1995 interim accord was a helpful step in the right direction. It allowed both parties to save face and move toward better bilateral relations. It would be, nevertheless, a serious mistake to assume that this meant that the issue was resolved. As I have shown in this chapter, the Macedonian Question remains a useful tool to be employed by politicians, journalists, and other cultural warriors.

The involvement of Bulgaria in the post-1989 dispute in many respects mirrors the Greek experience. VMRO's almost comical efforts to represent itself as an agent of Bulgarian nationalism reveal the extent to which the issue remains alive in Bulgarian politics. The particular context of the Greek (and Bulgarian) reaction to FYROM's declaration of independence has rarely been articulated in a manner that made it comprehensible to agents unfamiliar with the history of the region. Instead, most (mainly Greek) authors and politicians operated from within the Greek national narrative, hence making it difficult to communicate the gist of this issue to an international audience. To approach this issue requires a critical reading of the national narratives of the different sides involved in this controversy. To move beyond the perspectives of the national narratives of each side it is necessary to suspend the structure that gives them coherence and step outside the cultural logic of "national history." To accomplish such a goal requires attention to the multifaceted nature of social and cultural processes and the ways in which continuity is artificially constructed by disregarding ruptures, discontinuities, and other inconvenient material. This task is undertaken in the next two chapters. In the following chapter, I provide a critical overview of the Macedonian national narrative and spell out the conceptual consequences that have led to the Greek and Bulgarian negation of Macedonian identity. In Chapter 4, I go a step beyond the critique and comparison of the different narratives—and toward a critical account of the evolution of national identity in Macedonia.

NOTES

1. The Macedonian assembly introduced thirty-two amendments to the constitution in 1989, thereby paving the way for multi-party elections. Macedonian politicians hoped for the preservation of the Yugoslav federation. In August 1990, the Movement for All Macedonian Action endorsed succession and six months later, the newly created political party VMRPO-DPMU seconded the call. This party's activities are discussed later on in this chapter. On 25 January 1991 the Macedonian assembly adopted a declaration of sovereignty, modeled after the declarations of Slovenia and Croatia. The question of possible independence entered public debate on 26 June 1991. Eventually, the republic carried out a referendum on 8 September 1991, producing a 74% support for independence (Ramet, 1996: 214–15). In January 1992, the new state formally declined Serbian invitation to associate itself with the new "federal republic of Yugoslavia" (e.g., the "rump Yugoslavia" consisting of Serbia and Montenegro).

2. There have been hundreds of articles published in the international press on

the Greece-FYROM controversy. A good example of this controversy is the exchange between Malcolm (1992a) and Leigh Fermor (1992). Also see the *New York Times* editorial of 23 November 1992 in favor of Skopje and the response by J.S. Regas and L.Z. Acevska (letters to the Editor, the *New York Times,* 7 December 1992). Kaplan (1991), Moore (1992a), and Perry (1992) offer more comprehensive and careful accounts.

3. This issue had serious repercussions for Greece, which stood accused of denying the right of dissenting voices to air their opinions. Characteristically, a letter voicing these concerns was published in the *New York Review of Books* (17 December 1992, pp. 77–78) citing a number of prominent intellectuals as supporters and asking for more people to join a write-in campaign. The five members of the so-called Revolutionary Socialist Organization accused of the dissemination of "heretical" views were acquitted of all charges but the whole issue represented a major public relations disaster (for reviews, see Shea, 1997; Koutrovik, 1997). The role of the intellectuals in nationalist mobilization is strongly criticized by Karakasidou (1994). See also the discussion in the last section of this chapter.

4. See Giannakos (1992) for a policy analysis that raises the issue of the new state's viability. In August 1992, Slobodan Milosevic told Greek reporters of his offer to the Greek government to partition the territory of FYROM, and the Greek Foreign Ministry confirmed this information.

5. For brief overviews of the nationalist reaction, see Perry (1992: 37–40) and Karakasidou (1993a). See Danforth (1995) and Tamis (1994) for discussions of the conflict between the Macedonian and Greek diasporas.

6. A good summary of the "official" Greek position in Greek, English, and French can be found in Mazarakis-Aenian (1992). See also Papakonstantinou (1992). Probably, the most notable and comprehensive publication is by Koliopoulos and Hasiotis (1992). This two-volume work attempts to document the Greek presence in Macedonia. Also, Holevas (1991) offers a typical Greek response to the issue of Slavic minorities in northern Greece. A dissenting and critical approach to the popular nationalist viewpoints of the Greek press can be found in Liakos et al. (1993) and Kirkos (1993).

7. When in 1994, the Australian government decided to recognize FYROM, it also instructed all Commonwealth departments to use the prefix "Slavic-" before the adjective "Macedonian." It was a clumsy solution to the contradictory claims put forward by Macedonian and Greek diaspora communities. The Macedonians interpreted the action as a Greek victory (see Balalovski, 1995).

8. The involvement of the Greek and Macedonian diaspora communities in lobbying for each side had an effect upon the foreign policy of countries such as the United States or Australia. In Australia, the numerical supremacy of the Greeks has translated into a favorable stand by the government (see Bivell, 1995). Most important, the Clinton administration recognized the new state as FYROM and not as Macedonia, causing the dissatisfaction of some U.S. diplomats (see Harris, 1999).

9. This turn of events stood in sharp contrast to the suggestion made by conservative Prime Minister Costantinos Mitsotakis in February 1993 that a compound-name solution should be accepted by the Greek side (Ramet, 1996: 226–27). The compound-name issue is discussed later on in this chapter.

10. For FYROM, the embargo came on top of an already deteriorating economic situation. During the 1991–94 period, GNP dropped by 37% and unemployment

reached 28% (or 173,000) by 1994. Additionally, FYROM absorbed approximately 60,000 refugees from Bosnia, an element adding to the financial constraints (Zografos, 1994: 94). As a result of its economic collapse, FYROM was forced to freeze payments to international organizations. By the end of 1992, the public debt was $846 million. By the end of 1993 inflation was estimated at 350%.

11. In fact, Macedonian legal experts have argued that the international recognition of Skopje as the Republic of Macedonia by the UN cannot be modified by the 1995 Interim Accord because the rules governing the UN do not link the conditions for recognition of a state by another state to the conditions for admission to the UN (Janev, 1999).

12. For example, in March of 1998, the Socialist deputies L. Verivakis, G. Kapsis, P. Oikonomou, and S. Papathemelis voted against the nomination of professor N. Oikonomides for the Presidency of the Hellenic Foundation of Civilization on the grounds that the nominee had written a newspaper article expressing the viewpoint that Greece is not entitled to demand that the FYROM's population change their country's name. The defection of the deputies to the opposition temporarily postponed Oikonomides' nomination (reported in the daily *Exousia*, 6 March 1998, p. 7). After a few weeks of negotiations, two of the deputies were persuaded to remove their objections and the nomination was approved.

13. During the initial 1992–93 period, Greek authors suggested a bewildering array of alternative names for the new state. The list includes the following: Central Balkan Republic, South Slavia, Dardania, Paeonia, and Illyria (Danforth, 1995: 155–56). On 14 May 1993 Cyrus Vance proposed a draft of a treaty between the two parties. According to the draft, FYROM was to be called "Nova Makedonija" (Veremis, 1995a: 83). In practical terms, it became clear from early on in the negotiations between Athens and Skopje that the only possible compromise was the compound solution, whereby Skopje would keep the label "Macedonia" with the addition of a geographical epithet (such as Vardar or Northern). In this manner, it would be clear that the state did not include all of geographical Macedonia—and would allow for the successful separation of the diplomatic issues from the cultural war between the two sides.

14. Parts of the court decision and commentaries by the parties were reported in the dailies *Exousia*, 14 July 1998, p. 20, and *Eleytherotypia*, 14 July 1998, pp. 24–25. The "political correctness" syndrome in this affair was not limited to Macedonia. Petros Prokopidis, president of the Euxeinos Club, protested the interpretations of other terms (Turkish-speaking, Turkish-seed, and Cyprus) on similar grounds. Perhaps the most amusing case is his protest of the derogatory use of the term "Pontios" [Pontic] because Babiniotes recorded its connotation of "exceedingly naive" (Pontic jokes are the Greek equivalent of "Polish jokes"). To conclude this rather comical issue (referred to as the "trial of the words" in the popular press), the Greek Supreme Court (Areios Pagos) intervened into the issue. The court deemed the lower court's prohibition of the dictionary unconstitutional (*To Vima*, 13 December 1998, p. A63, and 20 December 1998, p. A56).

15. For a comparison between the first and second version of the dictionary, see Ios, *Eleytherotypia*, 17 October 1998, pp. 24–25. It is perhaps indicative of the uneven treatment of the various cases that Pontic Greeks are no longer "exceedingly naive" in the second edition, while ethnic stereotypes vis-à-vis other ethnic groups (Gypsies, Vlachs, and Jews) are still recorded as such.

16. For example, in late May 1998, a conference organized in Larissa, Thessaly, by the Greek Center for Research of Minority Groups was portrayed in the local press as an effort to stir up the issue of the Vlach minority in Greece. As a result, not only did local representatives of Vlach associations and of the local government publicly criticize the participants, but also approximately fifteen members of the recently formed "Patriotic Association of Thessaly" showed up at the conference and began to verbally abuse them—leading the conference to a premature end. Ironically, the Center's activities are sponsored by the European Union and among its members are some of the best-known Greek academics (see Ios, *Eleytherotypia*, 21 June 1998).

17. Unofficial estimates are obviously more reliable than official counts when it comes to illegal immigration. Following the Greek government's initial amnesty to illegal immigrants and the creation of a green card program, illegal immigrants were invited to submit their petitions to the Greek unemployment agency (OAED) in order for them to become eligible for a green card. In 1998, after the end of the period allowed for such petitions, OAED had received a total of 372,672 petitions. Still, at the same time, unofficial estimates of immigrants were closer to one million. The breakdown was as follows: 82,000 immigrants from various African countries (78,000 of which were from Egypt alone); 74,000 from various Asian countries (of whom 35,000 were from the Philippines, 10,000 from Syria, and 10,000 from Pakistan); and more than 400,000 from Europe. Of this last group, the largest contingencies were the Albanians (approximately 250,000), the Bulgarians (70,000), the Poles (50,000), and the Serbs (20,000). To these figures one should add a total of 140,000 Pontic Greeks who had been "repatriated" from the former USSR—and are full citizens of the Greek state. Another 100,000 of them were waiting on naturalization at the time (reported in the daily *Exousia,* 24 December 1998, pp. 22–23).

18. I owe the information on Scandinavia to Victor Friedman (personal communication). In February 1999 an interstate agreement was signed between the two states aiming at the resolution of the language question. See the discussion in the second part of this chapter.

19. For an overview of the Bulgarian transition to democracy, see Bell (1997). It was a real shock for many in Bulgaria when in 1990 the popular TV anchor K. Kevorkyan contacted the notorious VMRO leader Ivan ("Vanche") Mihailov, who had for a long time been thought dead, and took a long interview from him. This interview paved the way for representing to the seemingly unprepared Bulgarian public such personalities as Tsar Simeon II and members of the royal family, as well as other émigrés, whom official propaganda considered "enemies of the people."

20. In the post-1945 period, these organizations had originally resisted the official BCP policy with regard to the Macedonian Question (Matzureff, 1978) and were subsequently brought under direct communist control. The two traditional holidays of Bulgarian Macedonians are the Ilinden Uprising and the commemoration of Gotse Delchev. The original Union of Macedonian Societies was formally disbanded in 1977, and the societies came under the direct control of the communist-led Fatherland Front (Nedeva and Kaytchev, 1999: 174–77).

21. Moreover, VMRO fiercely opposes any attempt for a more flexible position on the matter of the Republic of Macedonia's majority population and its language, stating resolutely that both Bulgaria and Macedonia are "mononational states" and in Macedonia the "Bulgaromacedonians" prevail.

22. BSP daily *Duma* commented on all this under a huge title on the first page in Macedonian: "Go priznavme makedonskiot jazik," *Duma Daily,* 11 February 1999, No. 34, pp. 1–2. See also in the same issue the commentary "Unforgivable Manipulation" by Goran Gotev. Chief Prosecutor Ivan Tatarchev has been another fierce critic, but his retirement (20 February 1999) has lessened the significance of his opinion.

23. Such intellectual conflicts were played out in international conferences throughout the post–World War II period. Each side involved presented its own experts who put forward radically opposed viewpoints concerning the interpretation of history, language, literature, and folklore. For some excellent examples of such disputes, see Matzureff (1978: 234–59).

24. The website is: *http://www.gate.net/~joegrez/intent.htm* maintained and periodically updated by J. S. G. Gandeto, who "represents and works for himself only"—according to the declaration in the website. There are many websites devoted to the Macedonian Question; however, the problem rests not on the absence of information, but, rather, on their radically opposite viewpoints.

25. The exact web page address is *http://www.gate.net/~joegrez/greeks_on_ancient_macedonians.htm* and the document is called "A Search for a Nation-Building Material." The article that was the victim of selective (and out of context) quotation was my "Nationalism and Identity Politics in the Balkans," *Journal of Modern Greek Studies* 1996 (14) 2: 253–301.

26. The initial publication of the commentary spurred a protracted debate that followed the rulebook of a reality TV show. Moral crusaders proceeded to castigate "renegade" academics. The debate was conducted mainly in the form of letters to the publisher and lasted several months. Among the people who intervened were Dimitris Gondikas, director of the Hellenic Studies Program at Princeton University (where Karakasidou was a post-doctoral fellow at the time) and the inhabitants of Assiros (the village studied by Karakasidou), who felt they had to publicly defend their Greekness. For a brief recapitulation of these exchanges, see Karakasidou (1997: 229–33).

27. The ultra–right-wing newspaper *Stochos* reached a weekly circulation of 10,000 issues in 1992—of which 6,000 issues were distributed outside the capital Athens. Kostopoulos (2000: 321) claims that the newspaper is funded by the Greek Foreign Ministry. According to the newspaper's editor G. Kapsalis, *Stochos* received information by agents of the Greek Intelligent Service (Ethniki Ypireseia Plyroforion or EYP). Such information aimed to stigmatize those who did not fall in line with the Greek nationalist rhetoric of the period.

28. For example, Greek anthropologist Giorgos Agelopulos writes (1997: 105–6) that "a series of recently published analyses and descriptions of Macedonia, take as a given the division of at least a portion of Macedonia in concrete groups. . . . [In these analyses] there is an impression . . . that there are regions in Macedonia, where, under certain conditions, various populations coexist, rigorously preserving their boundaries." Agelopulos is careful to distinguish between the appropriation of such perspectives by Macedonian nationalists and the actual work undertaken by fellow anthropologists. See Agelopulos (1995) for further discussion. For a more bitter (and far less nuanced) critique, see Koliopoulos (1997).

29. For example, Gounaris (1997a) argues that the arguments put forward by Macedonian human rights advocates and Macedonian historians in FYROM are

nothing else than a recycling of past Bulgarian propaganda against Greek Macedonia. This line of argument fails to acknowledge the shifts in the international political environment of the post–World War II period and does not allow the Greek historiography to deal effectively with the new approaches to the study of the history of Macedonia. It is, however, an argument that is bound to appear quite appealing to the Greek public—for it is largely in line with the popular rhetoric of journalists and amateur historians.

30. For an analysis of the intertwining between communist internationalism and Macedonian nationalism as manifested in the pages of the journal *Macedonian Review,* see Krapfl (1996) and my discussion in Chapter 3.

Chapter 3

Toward an Archaeology of the Macedonian Question

The social trajectory of memory . . . extends the act of remembering for recall's sake into a consideration of the use of memory to shape belonging, exclusivity, social order, and community. . . . Remembering becomes a marker that signals social existence and all that such existence invokes. . . . Collective memory provides narratives about the past, artifacts that signal central events of the past, and ways of meaningfully signifying the past.

Barbie Zelizer (1995: 227)

In this chapter, I am pursuing an "archaeology" of the Macedonian Question (Foucault, 1972). By that I mean the critical examination of the national narratives put forward by the parties involved in the current phase of the Macedonian Question. My goal is to expose the gaps, discontinuities, and, more generally, the ruptures within these narratives. This critical examination of the national narratives aims to illustrate the partial character of the national narratives and their role in providing the local nation-states with an ideological apparatus that conceals the claims of others in Macedonia's soil. The national narratives aim at negating rival identities and, consequently, their function is to provide for the monopolization of Macedonia by one of the parties involved in the controversy.

I begin with the Macedonian national narrative. This narrative was formally articulated in the post-1945 period by the institutions of the People's Republic of Macedonia. It is this narrative that has become the contested terrain of the post-1945 "new" Macedonian Question (Petiffer, 1999b). The origins of the official Macedonian national narrative are to be sought in the establishment in 1944 of the Yugoslav Republic of Macedonia. This open acknowledgment of the Macedonian national identity led to the creation of a revisionist historiography whose goal has been to affirm the Macedonian nation (Kofos, 1986). Of course, since the Greek and Bulgarian narratives emerged during the course of the nineteenth century, the post-1945 Macedonian narrative has been "revising" narratives that were themselves "revisionist" when they first appeared. But to argue along these lines is to accept the logic of a "quest for origins" whereby locating the "authentic" origins of a modern-day people into the distant past provides these people with a special claim to the soil they inhabit today.[1] Therefore, in the following analysis, claims of historical precedence are not taken into account as factors determining the legitimacy of the one or the other national narrative.

In the following discussion, I present the Macedonian national narrative as well as the arguments made against it by Greeks and Bulgarians. Because of the importance and publicity surrounding the Greek opposition to FYROM's recognition as "Macedonia," I spend considerable space elaborating the rationale, arguments, and presuppositions behind the Greek national narrative. I should point out that in the first half of the twentieth century, the Macedonian issue was mainly discussed in terms of the extent and degree to which the population of the region was identified mostly with Greece, Bulgaria, or Serbia (see Gounaris, 1996). This is not to refute the reality of Macedonian separatism and nationalism in that period—indeed, this issue is discussed further in Chapter 4. Nevertheless, the conceptual elaboration and intellectual production of the post-1945 period make it clear that the post–World War II period warrants special attention. The institutions of the post-1945 People's Republic of Macedonia contributed extensively to the consolidation of the Macedonian national narrative. In many respects, this support is quite typical of the situation in numerous other countries around the globe. Therefore, discussing the Macedonian national narrative in those terms does not imply—nor should it be interpreted as—a statement about the status of Macedonians as a nation or ethnic group in the earlier periods of Macedonian history.

THE MACEDONIAN NARRATIVE AND ITS IMPLICATIONS

Given the nation-building efforts undertaken during the last fifty years within the Yugoslav federation, FYROM can make a strong case regarding its people's right to self-determination. There is a substantial amount of factual evidence that can be used to support this goal: a language, a literature, universities and other institutions, as well as an entire generation that grew up during the postwar period. By 1983, only 10% of FYROM's population had been born before 1923. This means that a considerable portion of FYROM's current population has been socialized into the Macedonian national culture (as it evolved through the course of the post-1944 period) and has no personal experience of the Macedonian Question as it was expressed during the interwar period (1918–41) or earlier (Lunt, 1984: 14).[2]

Just like many of the neighboring nations, the Macedonian narrative suggests that, over the post-1850 period, the Macedonian nation was victimized by the irredentist policies of Serbia, Greece, and Bulgaria. The operating assumption of the literature is that most of the people of pre-1913 Ottoman Macedonia were ethnic Macedonians, not Serbs, Greeks, or Bulgarians. This viewpoint has been presented in numerous publications, including Apostolski and Polenakovich (1974), the official history of the Macedonian people edited by Apostolski et al., (1979), the influential book, *Macedonia: Its People and History* (1982) by Stoyan Pribichevich, and various articles in the journal *Macedonian Review*. The *Macedonian Review* and its related publications have provided considerable elaboration of the Macedonian viewpoint in English and have made them available on a global scale. Publication of the journal began in 1971. Up until 1989, the journal was a main vehicle for the simultaneous pursuits of nation building and socialism within the People's Republic of Macedonia. Approximately 20% of its essays between 1971 and 1989 mention the Ilinden Uprising, which serves as the unifying theme of the literature. Authors published in the journal ranked highly in the socialist hierarchy (e.g., university professors, bureaucrats, and high-level party functionaries). Most articles are translations or revisions of articles that were originally published in Macedonian.

For the purposes of the analysis pursued in this chapter, I focus on two issues that provide the building blocks of the Macedonian narrative: first, the geographical definition of Macedonia as an object of inquiry; and second, the national narrative, the historical tale of the origins and evolution of the Macedonians as a people. The Macedonian Question is linked to the definition of "Macedonia" as a geographical region as well as a national homeland for the Macedonian people—and consequently, it is necessary to pay close attention to issues of geography. In many respects, the narratives of collective memory espoused by the different sides involved in the Macedonian saga rely upon very different (and competing) definitions of space—that is, of geographical Macedonia (for general overview, see Zelizer, 1995: 223–25).

According to Macedonian authors, the term Macedonia refers to a territory in the Central Balkans that in the early twentieth century (1912–20) was partitioned among Bulgaria ("Pirin Macedonia"), Greece ("Aegean Macedonia"), and Serbia (the current territory of the Yugoslav Republic of Macedonia, sometimes called "Southern Serbia" or "Vardar Macedonia"). See Map 1.1 for a visual presentation of this point of view. More specifically,

Macedonia extends over a part of the Balkan peninsula, bordered to the north by the mountains of Shar, Skopska Tsrna Gora, Kozyak, Osogovo, and Rila, to the east by the western parts of the Rhodopes and the River Mesta, to the south by the

Aegean Sea and the River Bistritsa, and to the west by the mountains of Korab, Yablanitsa, Mokra, and Pindus. Its total area is one of 67,741.2 sq. kms., of which 25,411 sq. kms., that is to say 37.51%, constitute the Socialist Republic of Macedonia, while the rest lies within the frontiers of Greece and the People's Republic of Bulgaria (Apostolski et al., 1979: 7).

From a historical standpoint and despite the presumed clarity of the above statement, it should be noted that the geographical boundaries and ethnological composition of this territory are not clear. To begin with, Macedonia was not an administrative unit of the Ottoman Empire; the Porte referred to the region as the three provinces (vilayets) of Selanik (Thessaloniki), Manastir (Monastir or Bitola), and Kosovo, including Uskup or Skopje (Adanir, 1984–85: 43). Throughout the course of the nineteenth century, the various sides involved in the Macedonian Question manipulated boundaries and ethnological data to such an extent that it is impossible to achieve consensus. Wilkinson's characteristic statement that "hardly two authorities can be found to agree on [Macedonia's] exact delineation" is revealing (1951: 1). According to this same authority, the major causes of this diversity of opinion are the misrepresentation of the facts by nationalist scientists, the ignorance of the ethnographic situation, the changes brought by the passage of time, and the different methods of depiction and criteria employed by various scholars.[3]

Keeping in mind the contested character of any definition of Macedonia and the recent establishment of the Macedonian nation, let us proceed with the description of the "official" Macedonian national narrative. According to this viewpoint, the Macedonians are a nation inhabiting, since AD 600–700 when Slavs first appeared in the Balkans, the geographical territory bearing the same name. That is, these people are called Macedonians because they have inhabited the geographical Macedonian territory since medieval times (Mojsov, 1979; Tashkovski, 1976; Apostolski et al., 1979). In other words, it is argued that Slavs occupied the Macedonian countryside during the Middle Ages. A significant part of what Bulgarians (and Greeks) consider Bulgarian medieval history, including the reign of Tsar Samuil, is considered by the Macedonians to be part of Macedonian history. Additionally, it is also claimed that the Macedonian nation was instrumental in developing, first among the Slavic people, a written language and alphabet—namely, the Cyrillic alphabet. Macedonian authors consider the local autocephalous archbishopric of Ohrid to represent a depository of local Macedonian identity and describe the evolution of religious institutions in the area in national terms (Ilievski, 1973). Seen from this perspective, historical events such as the abolition of Ohrid's autocephaly in the late eighteenth century are viewed as hostile actions aiming at the acculturation of local Macedonians into Hellenism (see Roudometof, 1998a, for further discussion).

In terms of the modern manifestation of this consciousness, the Ilinden Uprising (2 August 1903) was a major turning point in the struggle for national independence. However, Macedonian historians trace nationalist activity at least as far back as the Eastern Crisis of 1875–78—and sometimes back even further to the 1821 Greek Revolution (Pandevski, 1979; Katardzhiev, 1980; Apostolski et al., 1979: 110–11). The establishment of the short-lived Krusevo republic is seen as a premonition of the independent status of the Macedonian state. The activities of the VMRO, founded in Thessaloniki in 1893, represented the most decisive step toward national liberation.

The post-1944 People's Republic of Macedonia was founded on a carefully constructed symbiosis of socialism and nationalism. The legitimization of this fusion was expressed in the transformation of the establishment of the Socialist Republic of Macedonia into a "second Ilinden"—analogous in this respect to the legendary uprising of 1903 (Krapfl, 1996: 302). Lazar Kolisevski, the president of the People's Assembly, delivered a commemorative speech published in 1959 where he argued that the republic was in need of a "scientific, Marxist explanation of history" (Kolisevski, 1959: 10). According to Kolisevski,

Some of our historians and writers have attempted to adopt, with regard to some events and questions of our history, not a scientific approach, but, so to say, a current political approach. I consider this to be profoundly erroneous not only with regard to history but also in relation to our policy. . . . It is probable that many of our ancestors considered themselves Bulgarians, Greeks, or Serbians. There is no need to pass over this in silence or to be ashamed because of it. . . . What is essential in this case were their aspirations, the substantial process expressed by their movement, the objective purpose of this process and the results this process has eventually produced. We can not like bourgeois historiography, determine history in accordance with this or that fact taken separately, and in contradiction with its whole objective development and its results.

All such and similar phenomena show that the Macedonian nation has not been born suddenly but came into being as a result of a process; they describe the conditions under which this process has developed; they point out that Macedonian nation has been formed under its own specific conditions and it has followed the same road of development as all other nations in the past. . . . In order to be convinced of the correctness of such an interpretation of the process of national development, it is sufficient to throw a cursory glance at the history of our people and see that the Macedonian nation has not emerged as a result of any political combination, beginning in the twentieth century, but that it has emerged from the general struggle, resistance, and awareness of the people, which began early in the nineteenth century. (Kolisevski, 1959: 10–12)

For the post-1945 Macedonian socialist historiography, the first Ilinden Uprising (1903) was essentially a bourgeois-democratic revolution that failed because of the inadequate integration of the "masses" into revolutionary struggle (Krapfl, 1996: 303). In sharp contrast to this "first" Ilinden, the socialist-sponsored "second" Ilinden of 1944 was successful because—

according to solid Marxist logic—the communists were able to integrate the "masses" into their struggle.

Consequently, it is not surprising that, for the Macedonian historiography, the partition of Macedonia among Bulgaria, Greece, and Serbia during the Balkan Wars of 1912–13 was a national disaster that divided Macedonians among three different states. Greeks, Bulgarians, and Serbs are accused of trying to assimilate the indigenous population, with heavy emphasis placed upon Bulgarian irredentism and the desire to create a Greater Bulgaria (Hristov, 1971; Katardzhiev, 1973; Lape, 1973). The Yugoslav communists were ultimately the champions of the Macedonian cause since they were responsible for making possible the creation of a Macedonian state within the Yugoslav federation.[4]

Soon after the 1944 proclamation of the People's Republic of Macedonia, an attempt at unification was undertaken by Tito and Dimitrov, who suggested that a Macedonian state, encompassing all three parts of Macedonia, was to be created. The new state would be part of a broad Yugoslav federation that would include Bulgaria as well (for details, see Palmer and King, 1971; King, 1973). The plan failed when Bulgarian and Yugoslav policies collided and Tito was forced out of the pro-Soviet camp, while Bulgaria also pulled out of the deal. The inhabitants of Pirin Macedonia were officially classified as Macedonians, and for a time the plan seemed to work (Korobar 1987).[5]

The Bulgarian communists held on this policy even after the Tito-Stalin split of 1948. The Bulgarian communists considered the Macedonian nationality an offshoot of the Bulgarian nation, a version that differed from the line followed by the Skopje-based communist regime—as Kolisevski's commemorative speech, quoted earlier in this chapter, aptly illustrates. Hence, the December 1956 census showed the presence of 187,789 Macedonians in Pirin, or Bulgarian Macedonia. It was only in 1958 that the Bulgarian Communist Party reversed its policy and decided to withdraw its recognition of a separate Macedonian nationality (Matzureff, 1978: 222). By 1960 the official statistical record had ceased to have a separate entry for Macedonians (Cviic, 1991: 39–40).

Greek policy toward the Macedonians in Aegean Macedonia aimed to assimilate them to Hellenism.[6] This policy was followed more consistently than Bulgaria's own policy. The Greeks maintained that those Slavs who identified themselves as "Bulgarians" were part of the interwar Greek-Bulgarian population exchange, when approximately 30,000 Greeks left Bulgaria and 53,000 Bulgarians left Greece (Pentzopoulos, 1962: 60). The VMRO, however, opposed the implementation of the population exchange because it would weaken claims to Greek Macedonia (Barker, 1950: 30). For the Greek state, the remaining population was "Slavophone Greek"—that is, Slav-speaking but Greek in terms of subjective national identification. Yet the Greek state also took specific measures to force the Slav-speaking population to speak Greek and to assimilate into Greek society. The Greek government changed Slavic place names and personal names to Greek ones and ordered religious services to be performed in Greek. These measures entailed considerable force, especially during the Metaxas regime (1936–41), when the use of the Slavic language was forbidden and education in Greek was enforced (Hristov, 1994: 6–7). Milder versions of these tactics remained in place during the 1950s and early 1960s.

The goal of unifying geographical Macedonia into a single state was put forward by the partisan movement that led to the foundation of the People's Republic of Macedonia. The 1943 Report of the Organizing Committee of the Anti-Fascist Assembly of National Liberation of Macedonia (ASNOM) declares that "the fighting Piedmont of Macedonia has fiercely proclaimed that it will not stint on support or sacrifice for the liberation of the other two segments of our nation and for the general unification of the entire Macedonian people." The manifesto issued at the first session of the Slavo-Macedonian Liberation Front (*Slovenomakedonski Narodno Osloboditelen Front,* or SNOF) also explicitly stated its aspiration "for the unification of the whole Macedonian people" (Kondis et al., 1993: 36; for details on SNOF see Chapter 4). The preamble of the 1991 FYROM constitution makes a direct reference to these proclamations, hence establishing an emotional (albeit not legally binding) connection with statements that directly challenged the sovereignty and territorial integrity of the Greek state.

The implication, then, is that up to this day a large part of geographical Macedonia remains "unredeemed." In the official history of the Macedonian nation (Apostolski et al., 1979), the authors' assumption is that the geographical Macedonia is the national homeland of Macedonians. Since other ethnic groups (Albanians, Greeks, Bulgarians, Serbs) are not included in the Macedonian nation, they are excluded—in an indirect but forceful manner—from any legitimate "historical" claim to the geographical Macedonia. In the 1993 book *Macedonia and Its Relations with Greece,* a publication by the Council for Research into Southeastern Europe of the Macedonian Academy of Sciences and Arts, the authors argue that the Macedonian people are the product of an ethnic mixture between the Ancient Macedonians and the Slavs. The authors claim that the Macedonian people occupied the whole of geographical Macedonia beginning in the Middle Ages. Throughout the course of the nineteenth century, national consciousness also developed, and by 1900 the Macedonian people were already a nation. The occupation of Macedonian territory by Greece (1913) led to its colonization by Greek settlers. In 1926 the Greek government proceeded to change the place names of the Aegean part of Macedonia. The authors write that these changes were achieved through a policy of state terror. In fact, as early as the Balkan War of 1913, " . . . Greece had begun the ethnic genocide of the Macedonian people. The cruelty displayed by the Greek soldiers in their dealings towards the Macedonian people was merciless" (Council for Research, 1993: 72). It is clear, therefore, that, in the eyes of the Macedonians, the occupation of Aegean Macedonia by Greece was an infringement upon their national right to self-determination and that the sole justification for the Greek occupation was the force of arms.

For these Macedonian authors, consequently, Greek rule over Aegean Macedonia lacks both a "historical" and a moral foundation. Greek Macedonia, for them, constitutes a segment of the Macedonian homeland. School textbooks reflect this mentality and encourage this perception. In the school texts issued by FYROM during 1992–93, a crucial distinction is made between geographical-ethnic borders (*geograftsko-etnitska granitsa*) and state boundaries. The former includes the totality of geographical Macedonia, while the latter include only FYROM's territory (Kofos, 1994: 14). Consequently, the homeland of the Macedonian nation extends beyond FYROM's state boundaries.[7] The political reasons for the contested character of the Macedonian narrative become clearer at this point. According to this narrative, Greeks and Bulgarians attempted to satisfy their irredentist dreams by ignoring the rights of the Macedonian nation to self-determination.

This turn toward an irredentist stand is related to FYROM's domestic politics. During the elections of November–December 1990, the Democratic Party for Macedonian National Unity (VMRO-DPMNU), which claimed a membership of 150,000, adopted an irredentist program asserting its desire to "unite" geographical Macedonia under the auspices of a single state (Andrejevich 1990a, 1990b; Perry, 1994a: 85). The electoral success of the Albanian party pushed the electorate toward the nationalists, who were successful in capturing the plurality of seats in the new parliament (38 out of 120). The VMRO-DPMNU was excluded from government, however, and a coalition of the former communists and the Albanian parties emerged as the new government. Ante Popovski, leader of the VMRO-DPMNU, publicly made statements arguing that "two thirds of Macedonia is under foreign occupation and still to be liberated" whereas slogans like "Solon [the Greek city of Thessaloniki] is ours" proliferated among Macedonian nationalists (Kaplan, 1991). It should be pointed out that Macedonian domestic politics in the 1990s have evolved in response both to Greek hostility toward FYROM and to the rising Albanian autonomist (and later on separatist) movement within FYROM. In the long run, the Albanian issue turned out to be far more important. Therefore, the political evolution of VMRO-DPMNU and the post-1993 Macedonian domestic politics are discussed in Chapter 6.

Nevertheless, the printing of maps including Greek Macedonia as part of the Macedonian state and the suggestion—unsuccessfully made by the parliamentary opposition VMRO-DPMNU—to print bills with the White Tower of Thessaloniki on them have been interpreted by the Greeks as clear indications of irredentism. Interpreted similarly has been the inclusion of the sixteen-ray star of King Philip II, a historical artifact of the ancient

Macedonian kingdom discovered in Greek Macedonia, on FYROM's flag. The specifics of the controversy over the sun or star of Vergina have been already reviewed in Chapters 1 and 2. It is important to note that in the early 1990s, the issue assumed paramount symbolic significance for both parties. On 16 February 1993, a law was submitted to the Greek parliament making the sixteen-ray star a national symbol for Greece as well.[8]

Following Skopje's entrance into the UN, FYROM's secretary of foreign affairs, Risto Nikovski, reportedly asserted that, owing to the recognition of a new state in the Balkans, the Treaty of Bucharest (1913) had ceased to have any validity (Holevas, 1993: 14–15). Since this treaty guaranteed the boundaries of the neighboring states, Nikovski's statement was perceived as the first step toward the pursuit of an expansionist policy. Still, the military threat from the new state was (and still is) practically nonexistent. In practical terms, Greek foreign policy aspires to prevent a future coalition between FYROM and Turkey (Greece's long-standing adversary) since Greece is afraid that such a coalition would present a formidable challenge to Greek strategic interests. Just as Turkey has a traditional concern for Muslim minorities in the Balkans, so FYROM has an interest in the plight of minorities throughout the region. Additionally, given its internal political and economic weakness and its disputes with its neighbors, FYROM is expected to welcome Turkey as a regional benefactor and protector (Zahariadis, 1994: 664). Moreover, Turkey's Macedonian policy includes its traditional concern for the welfare of the approximately 100,000 ethnic Turks in FYROM, the use of FYROM as a counterforce against Greece, and the desire to insure itself against a possible influx of Turkish refugees from FYROM into Turkey (Perry, 1994b: 54; for a general overview, see Poulton, 1997).

BULGARIAN AND GREEK ARGUMENTS AGAINST MACEDONIAN IDENTITY

As a rule, national narratives should not be accepted uncritically since they entail a considerable element of "myth-making." The Macedonian national narrative is no exception. With respect to the Macedonian narrative, both Greek and Bulgarian historiography have questioned its factual basis. Two points are especially controversial: first, that the word "Macedonian" was employed as a national (and not simply regional) identification during the second half of the nineteenth century; second, that the majority of the Slav population in the region identified with the separatist movement.[9]

For our purposes, it is worth pointing out that the legitimization of Macedonian national identity by the Yugoslav Republic of Macedonia and the "affirmation" (as Macedonian authors call it) of Macedonians as a nation does not necessarily imply a "fabrication" or an "invention" by the communist regime. To argue for such a thesis it is necessary to assume that state agencies have the power to impose their will upon the people and to act

without regard for the cultural and institutional context in which they operate. No one doubts the existence of a considerable number of Slavs in
Macedonia during the course of the nineteenth century. Their national identity, however, was the object of fierce competition among Greeks, Bulgarians, Serbs, and Macedonian "separatists" (that is, nationalists). This was
because the majority of Slavs in Macedonia in the middle of the nineteenth
century probably had no strong ethnic consciousness and was content with
the label Christian, essentially meaning non-Muslim. The remaining minority
included some, particularly in the south, who accepted the label Greek;
others, particularly in the north, who allowed themselves to be called Serbian;
then another—surely larger—group who as non-Greek and non-Serb used
the ethnonym Bulgar; and finally those who insisted they were non-Bulgarian
as well and who, for lack of any better name, declared themselves to be
Macedonians (Lunt, 1984: 108).

Moreover, no clear distinctions can be made between Bulgarian and
Macedonian intelligentsias during the first half of the nineteenth century,
since the writers of that period were united in their opposition to Grecophone
religious and cultural supremacy. For this period, "the distinction between
Macedonian and Bulgarian is essentially immaterial" (Friedman, 1985: 33).
Following the 1840s, there was a growing differentiation between northeastern Bulgarian and southwestern Macedonian elites regarding the standardization of their linguistic medium. Each side supported its own dialect.
Eventually this growing gap led to the Macedonians publishing textbooks
in their own medium. Between 1857 and 1880 a total of sixteen textbooks
were published in the southeastern Bulgarian-Macedonian linguistic medium
(Friedman, 1975: 90). Their publication serves as an indicator of the growing differentiation between the two Slavic intelligentsias.

Given the strong and ambivalent relationship between Bulgarians and
Macedonian Slavs, Macedonian national identity should probably be understood in negative terms—that is, as a denial of Bulgarian identity. Such a
relationship between national identities is not unique to this particular case:
one finds a similar relationship between the Southern Cone countries of
Argentina and Uruguay. Uruguay's identity rests on a negation of
Argentinean national identity.[10] But no new nation can accept being a
derivative of another nation (such a premise would negate the very purpose
of nation building). On the contrary, each nation needs a unique and hon-
orable "myth" of ancestry (Smith, 1986). Hence, history becomes an instrument employed to foster national consciousness and create a sense of unity
and loyalty.[11]

It is owing to these considerations that the relationship between Yugoslav
Macedonia and Bulgaria has been clouded by the problem of the interpretation of the historical record. During the 1960s, the relationship between
the two states was especially problematic because the proclamation of historical figures, events, and monuments as being Macedonian became a point

of friction between Yugoslavia and Bulgaria (Rusinow, 1968). The result has been a political and cultural conflict among Greeks, Bulgarians, and Macedonians in which the appropriation of the historical record as part of a particular nation's past is bitterly contested by the other sides. In this context, historical record is of special importance since it provides a genealogy that demonstrates a particular population's cultural distinctiveness and identity. The employment of the historical record is political—an effort to embed particular conceptions of nationhood in a people's foundations in order to create cultural cohesion.

In the Bulgarian case, historical figures and medieval monuments constitute the points of friction between FYROM and Bulgaria. A good example is the case of Gotse Delchev, one of the central figures of the VMRO leadership who is claimed (rather unsuccessfully) by the Macedonians as their own national hero.[12] Kaplan (1991: 99) offers the following contrasting views on this issue:

"Do not tell me about Macedonia," the Bulgarian diplomat I met in Greece told me. "There is no Macedonia. It is Western Bulgaria. The language is eighty percent Bulgarian. . . . Gotse Delchev was a Bulgarian. He was educated in Sofia. Bulgaria funded his guerrilla activities. He spoke a Western-Bulgarian dialect. How could he be something that does not exist?"

"The Bulgarians are well-known falsifiers of documents . . . ," Odre Ivanovski, a state historian for the Yugoslav Republic of Macedonia, explained when I met him in his office at Skopje. "What can you expect of Tartars?" . . . Ivanovski went on: "The Bulgarians, you know, have specialized teams who invent books about Gotse Delchev. They bribe foreign scholars with cash and give them professorships in order to put their names on the covers of these books. . . . How could Gotse Delchev be Bulgarian? He was born in Macedonia. He spoke Macedonian, not Bulgarian. How could he be a Bulgarian?"

The tone of the debate and the contrasting lines of argumentation indicate the strong emotional appeal of this issue. The fact that local historians and diplomats are greatly involved in these affairs does not help the situation, since historians and administrators often have professional reasons for adopting the most nationalist viewpoints. In such a case, they are awarded prestige and power because they confirm the collectively held beliefs supporting the righteousness of the national narrative. Even more so, as I have already discussed in Chapter 2, the post-1989 revived Bulgarian VMRO-UMCS has been a political party that explicitly raises the issue of "reunification" between Bulgaria and FYROM.

In the Greek case, reactions center upon the name "Macedonia" and the relationship between Macedonia's modern inhabitants and the legacy of the ancient Macedonians.[13] Greece accuses FYROM of usurping the heritage of ancient Greece by constructing a national history that implicitly links its inhabitants with those of ancient Macedonia. Indeed, it is for this reason that the 1995 interim accord between Athens and Skopje (presented in Chapter 2) included a specific declaration by FYROM that it does not harbor territorial aspirations vis-à-vis Greek Macedonia. Greek intellectuals present historical and archaeological evidence in order to demonstrate that the ancient Macedonians were ethnically, culturally, and linguistically part of the ancient Greek world, and that non-Greek claims to Macedonia are therefore illegitimate.[14] Greece does not recognize the Macedonians as a separate nation, insisting that they are of Bulgarian origin, and that the usage of the term Macedonia with respect to the new state's territory was part of a communist plot to annex parts of Greece to Tito's Yugoslavia.

To understand the reasons why affirmation of Macedonian national identity caused such a strong reaction in Greece, one must examine the Greek discourse on Macedonia. In Greece, there is a long tradition of writing about the Macedonian Question. However, writing about the Republic of Skopje (as Greeks call the new state) has been less prolific. It should be emphasized that Greek historians are not ignorant of the activities of VMRO and the Macedonian separatist movement. But Greeks fail to differentiate sufficiently between Supremacists and Separatists (the two movements favoring an autonomous or independent Macedonia during the 1893–1913 period), tending to view both groups as Bulgarian nationalist organizations aiming at the annexation of Macedonia by Bulgaria. This issue is discussed in greater detail in Chapter 4. For our purposes in this chapter, however, it is important to note that the Greek historiography (and the Greek national narrative) does not acknowledge the Separatists' argument that the Macedonian Slavs are a nation of their own—the Macedonian nation.[15] Historically, Greeks have insisted that the Orthodox Slav population that remained faithful to the Orthodox Patriarchate during the 1870–1913 period was Greek in terms of subjective national identification. The same people were claimed by VMRO, however, as their own prospective nationals. Owing to these considerations, the national narratives of the two sides appear to diverge from one another. Yet, despite this apparent divergence, both sides agree on most of the factual events of the period.

For example, Greek historiography considers the Ilinden Uprising not a revolt by the Macedonian liberation movement but an attempt by Bulgarian agents to stir up revolt in order to force the Ottoman government to offer autonomy to Macedonia, autonomy being, in turn, the first step toward the annexation of the region to a Greater Bulgaria. The VMRO revolutionaries are considered responsible for starting the rebellion and then leaving the mainly Greek and Hellenized Vlach population of Krusevo to be slaughtered by the Ottomans.[16]

Regarding FYROM's claim to represent the Macedonian nation, Greek authors have questioned this claim's literary and historical foundations. As early as 1960, the Greek linguist Nikolaos Andriotis (1992, 1st edition 1960) published a book about the artificial character of the Macedonian language. After a short historical account of the ancient Macedonians and the presence of Slavs in Macedonia, the book examines the relationships between the Serbian, Macedonian, and Bulgarian languages, concluding that the standardization of the Macedonian language in the post–World War II Yugoslav Republic of Macedonia was an artificial construction fabricated "from above" for political purposes. Andriotis's work has been severely criticized by other linguists. The general consensus is to treat Macedonian as a language and not as a regional dialect (de Bray, 1980; Lunt, 1984; Friedman, 1975, 1985). The reason for the divergence of opinion is that Andriotis's critics believe that "language and dialect are in no way definite quantities" (Lunt, 1984: 91) and that "the decision as to whether a given transitional South Slav dialect belongs to one or another language is not a linguistic one but a sociopolitical one" (Friedman, 1985: 36). Given the fact that all South Slav languages are closely connected, it does seem that the task of differentiating a language from a dialect is a political, not a scientific one. In other words, the establishment of the People's Republic of Macedonia constituted a sufficient criterion for considering the local linguistic medium a language (and not, as Bulgarian scholars have suggested, a Bulgarian dialect). But Andriotis did not follow this criterion. Instead, he considered the creation of the Macedonian republic to be an artificial construction and proceeded to give an interpretation of its language that was highly tainted by his own particular value judgments.

DEFENDING THE GREEK NARRATIVE

The next important book espousing Greek nationalism was Nikolaos Martis's 1983 book *The Falsification of the History of Macedonia*.[17] Martis, a Greek Macedonian from the city of Kavala, a former member of Parliament, and a former minister of northern Greece, writes that he was inspired to start his project by the ignorance of foreign audiences concerning the "realities" of the Macedonian Question. Like Andriotis, but at considerable length this time, Martis sets out to describe the history of ancient Macedonia and to trace the cultural and linguistic origins of the ancient Macedonians back to ancient Greece. He also insists that in antiquity the name Macedonia was applied only to the western part of Greek Macedonia, where the ancient kingdom of Macedonia was located. Later on, during the reigns of Philip II (359–36 BC) and Alexander the Great (336–23 BC), the kingdom was expanded to include the eastern part of Greek Macedonia as well as the Vardar region, and, later, to incorporate huge territories in the eastern Mediterranean. From this, Martis concludes that the name Macedonia is falsely used by the Republic of Macedonia, since this part of the Balkans did not have any relationship with ancient Macedonia. Martis's book (which also includes a summary of interwar developments) won a distinguished award from the Greek Academy of Athens.[18] Greek officials and the Greek press have adopted its line of argument in various instances, thus it has become the foundation on which the Greek reaction to FYROM is based.

Martis's argument raises the question of whether the evidence that he puts forward does indeed support his conclusions. Although the Macedonian side has averred that the ancient Macedonians were not ancient Greeks, they have also emphasized the Slavic character of the modern Macedonian identity. Furthermore, Martis's argument does not pay sufficient attention to the modern character of subjective national identification. The fact of the matter is that the term Macedonia was applied during the nineteenth century to an ill-defined territory larger than the ancient kingdom (which existed 2,000 years ago). With respect to the Ottoman territory of the central Balkans, the term Macedonia surfaced in the nineteenth-century maps of the region concomitantly with the rise of Balkan nationalisms (Wilkinson, 1951). In fact, Bulgarians, Greeks, and Serbs directly link the very definition of Macedonia to the national claims to this part of the Ottoman Empire.

But these objections are beside the point. Martis's argument is not about the historical record or the origins of national identity. Rather, it is based upon an ingenious manipulation of the repercussions implied in the narrative of the Greek ethnogenesis. Therefore, its importance and its special weight for modern Greeks can be understood only in the context of the official version of Greek history. Modern Greeks consider themselves to be the heirs of ancient Greece. Putting aside for the moment the actual validity of the claim itself, the origins of this notion can be located in the period following the 1750s. The claim itself plays a central role in the development of the Greek national narrative and is closely related to the influence of the Enlightenment in Southeastern Europe (Kitromilides, 1983, 1990; Dimaras, 1977). During the eighteenth century, the West's preoccupation with a "mythical" ancient Greece conceived as the birthplace of Western civilization and the neoclassicism that dominated the intellectual discourse of the period influenced Greek-Orthodox intellectuals to develop their own genealogy that linked modern Greece with Hellenic antiquity.

Elie Kedourie (1971) considers Greek nationalism the antecedent of third-world nationalisms in that the Western idea of the nation had a radical impact on transforming the Balkan theocratic social structure. The desire to "upgrade" the social and cultural conditions of the "backward" Ottoman state was seized upon by Balkan intellectuals to postulate the new idea of the nation as a concept that would enhance the modernization of their part of the world. In redeploying the Western idea of the nation in the Balkan context, these thinkers not only seized upon the heritage of the Enlightenment; they also connected the legacy of classical antiquity with the modern inhabitants of the region. Adamantios Koraes was the protagonist of this intellectual movement. He outlined a political program that mixed the ideas of Enlightenment with those of "national liberation," producing an explosive combination (Koraes, 1971). The decline of the nation during the modern era was seen as the outcome of foreign domination. By adopting the knowledge of the ancients that had been preserved by the West, the moderns could rise again and reclaim their proper position in the world. Of fundamental importance in such a program was the assumption of continuity between the ancients and the moderns. Following the Greek commercial breakthroughs of the late eighteenth century and the impact of the Enlightenment on Ottoman Balkan society,

... the Greeks raise their heads in proportion as their oppressors' arrogance abates and their despotism becomes somewhat mitigated. This is the veritable period of Greek awakening. Minds, emerging from lethargy, are amazed to observe this deplorable state; and that same national vanity which hitherto prevented them from seeing it, now increases their amazement and irritation. For the first time the nation surveys the hideous spectacle of its ignorance and trembles in measuring with the eye the distance separating it from its ancestors' glory. This painful discovery, however, does not precipitate the Greeks into despair: We are the descendants of Greeks, they implicitly [tell] themselves; we must either try to become again worthy of this name, or we must not bear it. (Koraes, 1971: 183–84)

For Koraes, the claim to the historical continuity from ancients to moderns was a reason for modernizing the Hellenic world. As he says, the Greeks must become "worthy" of their name or cease to bear it. Koraes's modernist program was a mixture of nationalist aspirations and Enlightenment rationalism. However, its impact on the local society was to strengthen the moderns' claim to be heirs of the ancients through a process of revitalizing Greek cultural identity. This genealogical tie between the ancients and the moderns was soon to become divorced from the political context in which Koraes formulated it—that is, the Enlightenment's liberal doctrines and its ideology of progress and modernization:

By means of this neoclassicism, the modern Greeks came gradually to conceive of themselves as the descendants and heirs of the ancients whose land they inhabited and whose language they spoke. This conception of ethnic continuity between the classical and modern Hellenes, which was the direct product of the reception of Enlightenment neoclassicism into Greek thought, provided the basic ingredient of the self-definition of the modern Greeks. (Kitromilides, 1983: 59)

Although modern Greek identity has been based on this assumption of continuity, the "proper" geographical boundaries of Greece and the ethnic characteristics of the Greeks remained vague for some time. Only during the second half of the nineteenth century did the consolidation of the national narrative take place. As late as 1824, the Phanariot Theodore Negris identified Serbs and Bulgarians as Greeks, a definition that was closer to that of the Orthodox religious community of the *Rum millet* than to the definition of a modern secular Greek identity (quoted in Skopetea, 1988: 25). But between 1839 and 1852 an important ideological change occurred. The challenge to the historical continuity thesis by the German historian Jacob Fallmerayer (1830), the gradual rise of the Bulgarian national movement, and the religious revival within the Greek kingdom all collided, suggesting the need for a different evaluation of Greece's historical past (Politis, 1993: 36–39; Dimaras, 1985). In the modern Greek Enlightenment, the ancients and the moderns were connected through a genealogical tie, while the Orthodox and Byzantine past had been undermined.

Suppressing Orthodoxy and Byzantinism was a political necessity for people such as Koraes who aimed at transforming the religiously based identity of the Greek-Orthodox ethnoconfessional community (known as the *Rum millet)* into a modern, secular national identity. But this project did not put down strong roots in the local "Romaic" popular consciousness. In a speech to the Greek Parliament in 1844, Ioannis Koletis declared that the Greek nation's boundaries were not identical with those of the Kingdom of Greece. This is generally considered to be the first articulation of Greek irredentism, more widely known as the "Great Idea." Koletis's aim was to safeguard the public sector positions of the "non-indigenous" Greeks—that is, those not born in the kingdom (Dimakis, 1991). Although he was not completely successful, his speech became a turning point for the development of Greek nationalism. Koletis supported Konstantinos Paparrigopoulos, the future author of the *History of the Greek Nation* (1865–74), who was born in Constantinople and who, therefore, was not an "indigenous" Greek (Dimaras, 1986: 119–24).

Rectifying the Orthodox and Byzantine past was the task undertaken by the Greek Romantic historiography of the second half of the nineteenth century. This Romantic historiography provided an ideological legitimization for the inclusion of the *Rum millet* in the Greek nation by constructing a history that aided the articulation of the "Great Idea." The official version of Greek history, published during the late 1860s by Paparrigopoulos, was grounded in the notion of an unbroken historical continuity between ancient and modern Greece. His historical narrative bridged the "gap" between the ancient world and the modern era by reinterpreting medieval Byzantium as a manifestation of Hellenism during the Middle Ages. Thus, the narrative of Greek ethnogenesis now spanned a period of 3,000 years, assuming a fundamental continuity that transcended the different historical periods. The Romantic historiography's reinterpretation of Greek history has provided the official narrative for the modern Greek state.[19] Intellectually, it has remained largely unchallenged since its consolidation in the late 1870s.[20]

An indispensable component of the thesis concerning unbroken historical continuity was the Hellenic character of the ancient Macedonian kingdom. In the early years of the Kingdom of Greece (1832–44), the boundaries of modern Greece were conceived as identical to those of ancient Greece; the ancient Macedonians were viewed as conquerors of ancient Greece and not as part of it.[21] In sharp contrast to this vision, for Paparigopoulos, Alexander the Great was a national heroic ancestor who bridged the gap of Classical Greece with Byzantium. Alexander emerged as a symbol of national unity, while his achievement provided an example for the project of national unification.[22]

Locating Romantic historiography's narrative in the context of nineteenth-century Balkan politics makes it possible to clarify the relationship between nationalism and historical narrative. Historical claims and nationalist claims were intertwined during the nineteenth century. Greek irredentism is a prime example of the close relationship between historical narrative and nationalist aspirations. Constantinos Paparrigopoulos was an ardent nationalist. Heavily involved in the political debates of his day, he was co-founder of the Society for the Propagation of Greek Letters (1869), one of the major nationalist organizations of the late nineteenth century (Dimaras, 1986: 241; Vergopoulos, 1994: 180–83). Paparrigopoulos considered his duty to be twofold—"national as well as scientific" (quoted in Politis 1993: 147)—which was indeed the case. The gradual publication of his *History of the Greek Nation* during the late 1860s and early 1870s was a project partially financed by state agencies and national societies. Provisions were also made for copies to be distributed to municipalities and to Athens University (Dimaras, 1986: 227–34). In 1877, the Greek parliament appropriated 6,000 drachmas so that the work could be translated into French (Paparrigopoulo, 1878). In 1879 a conference was held in Athens with participation by all Greek associations active outside the kingdom of Greece; Paparrigopoulos oversaw the coordination of the associations' efforts to turn his *History of the Greek Nation* into a foundational text. In 1882, the Historical and Ethnological Society of Greece was founded with the goal of "proving" the unbroken unity and continuity of Hellenism from antiquity to the present (Vergopoulos, 1994: 180–81).

During the nineteenth-century contest among Greeks, Serbs, and Bulgarians over Ottoman Macedonia, the Greeks employed this national narrative as an effective weapon to counteract Bulgarian claims to the region (Kofos, 1989a: 238). The Greeks utilized the continuity between ancients and moderns to strengthen their "historical" claims to Macedonian territory. In this interpretation, "Macedonia" means the territory of the ancient kingdom in the era of Philip II. Operating under these assumptions, Greek historiography does not allow for the development of divergent views. In this respect, it is not accidental that works nearly one hundred years old have preserved their centrality in the Greek national narrative.[23] The Balkan Wars of 1912–13 led to the occupation of most of this territory by Greece, satisfying national aspirations concerning the liberation of Macedonia. The complex Macedonian Question appeared to have been resolved, at least from the Greek standpoint.

While the pre-1913 Greek national narrative stressed Greece's cultural continuity from antiquity to modern times, the post-1913 narrative was modified in important ways, ways that significantly contributed to the conceptual gap between the versions of national history put forward by Athens and Skopje in the 1990s. The contemporary observers of pre-1913 Macedonia were quite aware of the fact that, while Greeks predominated in influence in the urban sector, they lacked any widespread influence in the countryside. But the Greek nationalists generally employed religion and the vague notion of "national predisposition" to bridge the gap between rhetoric and reality.

Between 1913 and 1941 the Greek historiography was preoccupied with "proving" the Greek character of Greek-held Macedonia, an effort aiming directly at combating revisionist Bulgarian publications at the time (Todorova, 1995). The Greek discourse assumed a marked new direction in the period of the Greek Civil War (1944–49), when the national preoccupation became that of defending Greek sovereignty in Macedonia. It was during the Civil War and in the post-1945 decades that Greek discourse sought to eliminate the very fact of the presence of Slavic-speakers in Greek Macedonia, a fact readily admitted in official documents, public speeches, and newspapers during the interwar period. The key instruments of this new effort included the *Society for Macedonian Studies* (founded in 1939) and, later on, the *Institute for Balkan Studies* (originally founded by the Society). The two institutions provided the material support and ideological nexus for the articulation of the new post-1945 Greek literature on Macedonia. Far from providing a simple "recycling" of past claims (cf. Gounaris and Mihailidis, 2000: 116–17), this new literature was—in large part—an expression of post–World War II and post–Civil War Greek right-wing nationalism. Its goal was to depict the Greek communists as collaborators with Tito's partisans, while it also aimed to "prove" that there were not (and there had never been) any Slavs in Greek Macedonia.[24]

In the post-1944 period, following the establishment of the Yugoslav Republic of Macedonia, this issue became the source of political strain in the Athens-Belgrade relationship; however, the difficulty remained in a subdued form insofar as the Yugoslav federation was preserved (for overviews, see Zahariadis, 1994, and Kostopoulos, 2000). During the 1950s the Greek state did not recognize the legitimacy of the People's Republic of Macedonia. However, the necessity for Greece to develop a Balkan strategy of engagement and cooperation as well as the Yugoslav communists' need for regional alliances after their break with the pro-Soviet camp (1948) gradually led to a policy of limited cooperation, whereby the two sides agreed to disagree over the Macedonian issue. Within Greece, the Macedonian issue became a bitterly contested political issue during the 1959–65 period.[25] Following the collapse of Yugoslavia, the issue surfaced once again and, with it, a considerable part of the controversies of the nineteenth- and twentieth-century Macedonian Question (see Chapter 4 for further discussion).

COLLECTIVE MEMORY AND THE LOGIC OF NATIONAL NARRATIVES

In light of the overview provided in this chapter, the significance and emotional character of Martis's argument may be clarified. The stickers proclaiming "Macedonia is Greek" are not intended to state the obvious—that Greek Macedonia is Greek—but instead to proclaim a different and more abstract thesis: that the name Macedonia is an integral part of Greek identity and that no one can claim to be a Macedonian without being Greek. Needless to say, Martis's argument is meaningful only in this context. Since, according to that argument, the ancient Macedonians were Greeks, and since the modern Greeks are the descendants of the ancients, it follows that the name and the territory of ancient Macedonia are "legitimately" Greek. Any claim to the contrary impugns Greek identity (by claiming that the ancient or modern Macedonians were or are not Greek) and therefore impugns the integrity of the Greek nation. This, precisely, is the Greeks' accusation against FYROM.

The rallying of the Greek public to defend the "Greekness" of Macedonia serves not only the political goal of asserting that Greek Macedonia is populated overwhelmingly by Greeks but also the emotional goal of affirming the Greek people's sense of national identity. Of course, by doing so, Greeks claim exclusive rights over Macedonia, denying to Macedonians the right to employ this word for their own self-identification.

All sides involved in the symbolic conflict over Macedonia (Bulgaria, Greece, and FYROM) operate with the assumption that nationhood provides the essential component for nation building. All parties consider their cherished national narratives as an essential ingredient for their national identity. These national narratives, however, encroach upon one another, tending to claim Macedonia (the name and, for Macedonian and Bulgarian irredentists, the territory as well) exclusively for their particular side. For Greeks, Macedonia is a name and a territory that is an indispensable part of the modern Greek identity. For Macedonians, it provides the single most important component that has historically differentiated them from Bulgarians. For Bulgarians, Macedonia is the *irredenta* (the unredeemed land) claimed by modern Bulgaria for more than one hundred years.

In the 1990s, the Greek-Macedonian dispute achieved a high-profile status and, as shown in Chapter 2, it became the center of a diplomatic, symbolic, cultural, and transnational struggle between Macedonians and Greeks. As I have argued in this chapter, the reason for the Greek nationalist mobilization is the fact that the Macedonian national narrative clearly questions the validity of the Greek national narrative. Still, this threat to the long-cherished "unbroken historical continuity" of the Greek nation is felt in differing degrees by Greeks, depending upon their regional identity, political affiliation, extent of nationalist attitudes, and so on. It is not surprising that Greek Macedonians feel this implicit threat to modern Greek identity much more intensely than the southern Greeks. This is due to a number of factors. First of all, Greek Macedonia has a number of elements that reveal the strong regionalism of its inhabitants. It has its own capital city, Thessaloniki, often referred to as the "co-capital" of Greece; it also has its "own" national heroes, the Ancient Macedonians and the warriors of the Macedonian Struggle (1903–8), and its own post-1991 "national" symbol, the sixteen-ray sun or star of Vergina (Danforth, 1995: 83).[26]

Second, and far more important, is the fact that Greek Macedonians have their own heavier accent of spoken Greek. This distinction is similar with the distinctions between the English spoken in southern England versus the northern, heavier English.[27] Use of the heavier, Macedonian Greek accent readily identifies a person as coming from northern Greece. The presence of a different accent further fosters regionalism. Third, and perhaps the most important factor, is that Bulgaria has occupied portions of Greek Macedonia three times in the course of the twentieth century, and the local Greek population has particularly bad memories associated with these events. Moreover, the large refugee population that lives in Greek Macedonia today has carried the memory of forceful expatriation and resettlement. The memory of these events plays a pivotal role in making Greek Macedonians particularly sensitive to perceived national threats.

The strong Greek mobilization against FYROM's claim to represent the Macedonian nation constituted a response to an implicit threat to modern Greek identity. Greek reaction centered upon the name of the new state more than any other issue because the name in itself raised important questions concerning the validity of the Greek national narrative. The Macedonian saga cannot be explained without a reference to the significance of collective memory in the contemporaries' attitude. Each side involved in this conflict is socialized into a specific national narrative that directly clashes with the narratives of the other side. The national narratives of each nation are the major conceptual obstacles in the improvement of bilateral relations among Athens, Skopje, and Sofia. National narratives help define a population and therefore provide the basis for claiming a particular population's loyalty. These national narratives shape collective memory and influence political and diplomatic efforts and agreements.

Moreover, the thorny question of Macedonian minorities in Bulgaria and Greece further suggests that concern with national narratives is not an academic activity but one that carries with it significant political repercussions. This issue is discussed in detail in Chapter 5. Suffice it to say, the political rallies and other forms of diplomatic and cultural struggle for Macedonia that I described in Chapter 2 rest on the mutually exclusive national narratives that I have reviewed in this chapter. Certainly, the transformation of this clash of national narratives into diplomatic disputes was unfortunate and counterproductive. Still, issues of national legitimacy are central to modern nation-states. Therefore, such issues should be clarified in order for good bilateral relations to develop.

In pursuing this "archaeology" of the Macedonian Question, I am quite aware of the objection that such an enterprise can be charged with relativism (Mazower, 1996; Zelizer, 1995: 227–28). Indeed, it might be reasonable to conclude that no description, no narrative could describe the evolution of national identity in Macedonia. Such a postmodernist interpretation would suggest that all sides involved in this controversy (FYROM/Macedonia, Greece, and Bulgaria) possess narratives that are equally valid, and no distinction can be made with regard to their claims to the truth. Insofar as the basic presuppositions of the national narratives are uncritically accepted, such a suggestion might not be a bad idea. Yet, it is by questioning these presuppositions that it becomes possible to gain an insight into the evolution of national identity in the region.

NOTES

1. For a literature review concerning the manner in which various authors and sides have approached the Macedonian Question over the last two centuries, see Gounaris and Mihailides (2000). As these authors point out, the evolution of the Macedonian saga was seriously impacted by the declining role of French as a language of scientific and political communication. Following the end of World War II, English became the new international language. Post-1945 Macedonian literature was written in English or it was made available in English through translations. For many among the public in Western Europe and the United States, this was the only language in which they could read sources about Macedonia. Consequently, the debates and arguments of the pre-1945 literature escaped the attention of the Anglophone world.

2. Moreover, the spread of literacy was simultaneous with post-1945 Macedonian nation-state building. In 1944, close to 67.5% of the population was illiterate (Troebst, 1994: 128). Hence, Macedonian nation-state building coincided with the transformation of a peasant society into a modern society. Already by the late 1940s, the emerging school system encompassed 200,000 adult students and, by 1949–50, close to 172,000 pupils attended elementary schools (Troebst, 1994: 131). On the association between literacy and nation building, see Gellner (1983).

3. Zotiades (1961) has argued that the geographical definition of Macedonia is meaningless in the sense that Macedonia is a term that should be properly applied only to the territory of the ancient kingdom of Macedonia. No consensus among the different sides involved in this controversy has resulted from the employment of statistics to decide the national identification of the peoples living within Ottoman Macedonia. This is because the Ottomans recorded religious and not national identification (which means that national identification has to be deduced). Moreover, the bitter conflicts of the 1890s and 1900s turned national identity into an issue of international importance.

4. Following 1990, and as a result of the utilization of Serbian nationalism by the Milosevic regime, attitudes have changed. Now, the rump Yugoslavia (Serbia and

Montenegro) is referred to as "Serboslavia" (Loring Danforth, personal communication).

5. In the brief period when this plan was implemented at Pirin Macedonia, communist cadres carried out an extensive Macedonianization campaign (see Nikolov, 2000, and Matzureff, 1978: 170–82 for details). Teachers were sent into Pirin from Yugoslav Macedonia; new textbooks were introduced into the schools; and portraits of Tito and Lazar Kolisevski, premier of the People's Republic and party secretary, were introduced to the Pirin region alongside those of Stalin and Bulgarian Party Secretary Dimitrov (Banac, 1987: 37).

6. On the cultural assimilation of the Slavic minority, see Pribichevich (1982: 237–47), Karakasidou (1993a), Kirjazovski (1990), Poulton (1991), and Peyum (1988).

7. The textbooks constructed a particularly negative image of the neighboring countries. In her study of these textbooks, Vouri (1996b: 199) counts forty-three negative (versus two positive and seven neutral) references for Bulgaria, thirty negative (versus five positive and eleven neutral) references for Greece, twenty negative (versus two positive and neutral) references for Serbia, and ten negative (versus two positive and eight negative) references for Albania.

8. The FYROM government's position was that the Macedonian Slavs just happened to settle in part of the territory of the ancient kingdom of Macedonia. Therefore, the use of the sixteen-ray star was inappropriate as a symbol of present-day Macedonia. Ljupco Georgievski and VMRO–DPMNU were opposed to this particular interpretation (William Dunn, personal communication).

9. See Kofos (1964, 1989a), Perry (1988), Slijepcevic (1958), and Pundeff (1969) regarding views opposite to the "official" Macedonian standpoint. On the linguistic differentiation between Bulgarians and Macedonians, see Friedman (1975, 1985). On interwar and post–World War II developments, see Fischer-Galati (1973), Papapanagiotou (1992), Palmer and King (1971), Vasiliev (1989), Kofos (1974, 1989b), Karakasidou (1993b), and King (1973). In 1978, the Bulgarian Academy of Sciences published a volume titled *Macedonia: Documents and Materials* (Bulgarian Academy of Sciences, 1978). The volume contained a series of historical documents—including reprints of original sources—that aimed to show to the international audience that the Macedonian Slavs were Bulgarians.

10. I owe this point to John Markoff (personal communication). Perhaps the most well-known case of such a break with the original homeland is the case of the former British colonies that became the United States (Lipset, 1963).

11. Troebst (1994: 137) argues that post-1945 Macedonian nation-state building lacked a mythomoteur (Smith, 1986). In his opinion, Macedonian nationalism did not focus initially on a glorious past but on an "equally glorious future." Troebst is correct in arguing that in the first few decades after 1945 Macedonian nation-state building was preoccupied with structuring the local society and establishing a firm identity among the local population. But this changed gradually, and Kolisevki's (1959) statement, quoted in this chapter, is indicative of the growing need of the post-1945 party leadership to eventually develop a national narrative alongside the lines of the Greek and Bulgarian narratives, and to legitimize Macedonian nationalism. The evidence provided in this chapter shows that Troebst's argument is only partially correct—and certainly, it should not be adopted as a blanket statement covering the entire post-1945 period.

12. Despite the efforts of the post-1945 Macedonian historiography to represent Delchev as a Macedonian separatist rather than a Bulgarian nationalist, Delchev himself has stated in his correspondence: " . . . We are Bulgarians and all suffer from one common disease [e.g., the Ottoman rule]" (quoted in McDermott, 1978: 192), and "Our task is not to shed the blood of Bulgarians, of those who belong to the same people that we serve" (quoted in McDermott, 1978: 273).

13. Following Foucault (1984), one could argue that the appropriation of historical legacy is inevitably an arbitrary act. This "strong" thesis might be disputed. But whatever one's position, the substantive issue does not pertain to the ethnic classification of ancient Macedonians, but rather to the beliefs people have on this matter. William I. Thomas's (1928) dictum concerning the "definition of the situation"—that is, "if men define situations as real, they are real in their consequences"—is relevant here.

14. Moreover, Greek historians have countered Macedonian assertions of the existence of a Macedonian minority in northern Greece (to be discussed in Chapter 5) by suggesting that there is a Greek minority in FYROM (Sotiriou, 1991: 109; Vakalopoulos, 1994). The Greek estimates of this minority range between 100,000 and 150,000. These figures are produced by counting as Greeks the majority of the Vlachs of FYROM. However, the Vlachs of FYROM have remained largely apolitical, while maintaining their tradition and their pride as urban people, involved in trade and occupations—in sharp contrast to the majority of the Macedonians who, up until fairly recently, have been predominantly peasants (for details, see Brown, 2000b).

15. From the Greek standpoint, historians consider all Slav-speaking inhabitants of the region to be "Bulgarians" or "Slavophone Greeks." See Dakin (1966), Vakalopoulos (1986, 1987), and Zotiades (1961). Perry (1988) offers an authoritative description of IMRO activities during the 1893–1903 period. He argues that VMRO was striving to create an independent state, but that the majority of the Slav population did not display a strong national identification comparable to that of VMRO leadership.

16. The July 1993 issue of the journal *Makedoniki Zoi* includes a collection of papers by a number of Greek scholars elaborating on the Greek interpretation of VMRO. The journal is among the Greek publications that sponsor cultural cohesion among the Greek diaspora, and its influence is particularly visible among the Greek immigrants abroad (for details on the journal, see Danforth, 1995: 90–93). Lithoxoou (1998: 41) argues that Greek academics—such as Nikolaos Vlachos and Konstantinos Vakalopoulos—have used the archival sources of the Greek foreign ministry in a selective manner. Their goal, he argues, was to conceal the pro-Macedonian character of the Ilinden Uprising and thereby to prevent the open recognition of Macedonian nationalism by Greeks. In his own book, Lithoxoou (1998), using the very same archival sources, provides a description of the Ilinden Uprising that comes close to other scholarly accounts (such as Perry, 1988) and the accounts provided by the Macedonian historians. His account depicts the uprising as a popular peasant revolt against a corrupt Ottoman administration. Suffice to say, the book's thesis contradicts the official Greek line on the Macedonian issue. More specifically, the author gives a rather unsympathetic "heretical" reading of the Greek guerrilla activity in Ottoman Macedonia, considering their activities an "anti-Macedonian" struggle, rather than a "pro-Macedonian struggle." Most of the Greek publishing

houses declined to publish the book, fearful that their business would be adversely affected if they did so.

17. Chronologically speaking, however, Kofos (1964) constitutes the next major work on this issue. Although the book is certainly biased and is heavily influenced by the mentality of the Cold War era (Koliopoulos, 1994: xiv–xv), I think it should be considered a scholarly work and not nationalist propaganda, as Kofos's discussion of the role of communism in the legitimization of Macedonian identity converges with that of other researchers (Barker, 1950; Shoup, 1968; Palmer and King, 1971; King, 1973).

18. Martis's book might be situated within the political context of the period. In 1981, the Greek Socialist Party (PASOK) was successful in obtaining the majority of the votes in the elections and has governed (with a minor interval in 1990–93) the country for the last twenty years. In part, the "revival" of the Macedonian issue served the political interest of the opposition conservative party. This interpretation is meaningful in the context of the early 1980s when PASOK's anti-Americanism was particularly pronounced. But the PASOK government did not really attempt to change the official Greek position on the Macedonian issue—on the contrary, its policy has been rather consistent with that of the conservatives. For a review of the 1980s events (prior to the 1990s public mobilization), see Kostopoulos (2000: 301–09).

19. For an overview of Greek historiography, see Augustinos (1989). The consolidation of the Greek national narrative is also discussed by Dimaras (1985). Perhaps the most comprehensive and explicit analysis of the social construction of modern Greek identity is the one by Herzfeld (1982). For a comprehensive overview of the evolution of cultural nationalism in the 1830–80 period, see Roudometof (2001: 101–29).

20. The most notable deviation from the official line is by the Marxist historian Yannis Kordatos (1991), who argues that the Greek nation was the creation of the eighteenth-century Greek bourgeoisie. The historian Apostolos Vakalopoulos (1961) asserts that the origins of the modern Greek nation are to be sought in the 1204–1453 period, where one can observe the emergence of a "proto-nationalist" sentiment among Byzantine elites. But his argument remains confined within the traditional paradigm since it refers to the origins of the modern Greek nation and not to those of the Greek nation itself. Traditionally, Greek history has been divided into ancient, medieval, and modern. Vakalopoulos's thesis aims to shift the "traditional" date of the modern period from 1453 (the fall of Constantinople to the Turks) to 1204 (the conquest of Constantinople by the Fourth Crusade). For an overview of the 1960s debate on this issue, see Vryonis (1978).

21. See Dimaras (1985: 338–39) and Dimakis (1991). The appropriation of the legacy of ancient Macedonia by the modern Greeks belongs historically to the second half of the nineteenth century. Politis (1993: 40–42) cites fourteen examples from the Greek literature of the 1794–1841 period in which the ancient Macedonians are not considered to be part of the ancient Greek world. Prominent intellectuals like Ioannis Rizos Neroulos and Adamantios Koraes were among those who shared this viewpoint. For a complete listing of all these statements regarding the intellectuals' viewpoint vis-à-vis the Macedonians, see Dimitrakopoulos (1996).

22. See Demetriou (2001) for a useful comparison of the viewpoints held by Paparigopoulos and George Grote. While for Grote Alexander was a deadly enemy

of liberalism, for Paparigopoulos he was a national hero. Underlying these different evaluations are the different political orientations of the two historians.

23. In a 1992 collection of articles dealing with the linguistics of Macedonia (Babiniotes, 1992), 110 out of 275 pages are reprints of two works by G. N. Hatzidakis (dated 1896 and 1911) arguing that the language of the ancient Macedonians was a Greek dialect. The contemporaries' work is based on the same assumptions and repeats the same or similar arguments. This mode of argumentation is meaningful only within the context of the Greek national narrative; it is of limited value when addressing a non-Greek or an academic audience.

24. Kostopoulos (2000: 224–27). The racist, simplistic theories put forward by authors such as Stilpon Kyriakidis (1955) have been thoroughly ridiculed by scholars like Karakasidou (1997: 14–18). The peak of this literature was the wave of publications that coincided with the 1984 eighty-year anniversary of Greek paramilitary warfare in Ottoman Macedonia (Gounaris and Mihailidis, 2000: 120).

25. The first round took place in the aftermath of a lecture delivered by Lazar Kolisevski, the president of the Assembly of the People's Republic of Macedonia, while a second round took place in the aftermath of an interview by the People's Republic Prime Minister A. Grickov in 1961. In both instances, the Macedonian politicians asserted the necessity for Bulgaria and Greece to recognize Macedonian national minorities within their own borders, to allow Macedonians to visit their relatives across the border, and to promote "good relations" with the People's Republic (for details, see Wallden, 1991). These announcements triggered a journalistic fervor around the issue, while the Greek parliamentary opposition did not hesitate to castigate the government's "weak" response to the "provocations" by the "Yugoslav communists." Of course, when in 1965, the opposition (Center Union or *Enosi Kentrou*) became the government, the roles were reversed: Prime Minister G. Papandreou visited Belgrade to promote good Greek-Yugoslav relations while the right-wing opposition (ERE) accused the government of "selling out" Greek national interests.

26. Danforth (1995: 83) cites a popular song sung by Macedonian Greeks as Greek Macedonia's "own national anthem." This is an overstatement. Also, Danforth quotes a recent and cleansed version of the song. His rendering is as follows: "Famous Macedonia, the land of Alexander, you drove out the barbarians, and now you are free." The much more accurate (and older) version of this song refers to "Bulgarians" and not to "barbarians." Indeed, this song was part of the post–World War II nation-building, anticommunist campaign of the Greek government, and identified Greece's adversaries as "Bulgarians" not as "barbarians." The song's reference to Bulgarians is meant as a reminder of the Greek-Bulgarian contest over Macedonia. Because Bulgaria occupied parts of Greek Macedonia during World War II, the song had a contemporary significance even in the recent past. The nameless "barbarians" replaced the Bulgarians of the original version after the government of Constantinos Caramanlis developed its own détente policy toward Bulgaria in the 1970s. Also, Danforth (1995: 82) writes that the diaspora Greeks refer to their homeland as "fatherland" or, in a mixed metaphor, as their "mother fatherland" (*mitera patrida*). His translation is rather hasty; in Greek the word *patrida* (homeland) is a female noun, and therefore it cannot be rendered into a masculine form (e.g., fatherland). *Mitera patrida* is the exact equivalent of "motherland" in English. In Greek, Greece cannot be a "fatherland" without disregarding the fact that Greece (Hellas) is a female

noun. The linguistics are important here because they do shape collective representation. In the popular press and even in political cartoons, Greece (like France) is typically referred to and depicted as a woman (usually a mother).

27. Other regions of Greece, like Crete or the Ionian islands, have their own accents and sometimes their own regional dialects. The written version of the Macedonian Greek accent (sometimes referred to as "Makedonitika") has been immortalized in popular novels about the Macedonian Struggle (1903–8). Penelope Delta's *Sta Mystika tou Valtou* (The Secrets of the Swamp) (1937), a novel glorifying the guerrilla warriors of the Macedonian Struggle, is one of the earlier and most well-known examples of the Greek Macedonians' literary expression. A prominent example of a politician almost instantly recognized as a Greek Macedonian because of his heavy accent was the former prime minister and, later on, president of Greece, Constantinos Caramanlis. For a penetrating analysis of the multicultural origins of Macedonian Greek identity, see Cowan (1997).

Chapter 4

Macedonian National Identity:
An Interpretation

In Chapter 3, I conducted a analysis of the presuppositions of the Macedonian national narrative and traced its consequences for the national narratives of Bulgaria and Greece. I argued that there are good reasons behind the strong Greek and Bulgarian responses toward Macedonian nationhood. In this chapter, I aim to move beyond a critique or a deconstruction of the competing narratives and toward an account of the evolution of Macedonian national identity. In sharp contrast to the prevailing national narratives of the competing sides, I would suggest that, instead of attempting to attribute a national (or ethnic or racial) identity into the peoples of Macedonia, it is more accurate to view such an identity as the product of the region's historical transformation of the last two centuries. Consequently, the conflicting claims of the various sides, the wars, and the state-sponsored policies of ethnic and cultural homogenization contributed to the trajectories followed by different peoples and groups in Macedonia. Furthermore, these long-term structural and cultural factors translated into a variety of strategies for the working people, the peasants, and the urban population of pre-1913 Macedonia. Such strategies were expressed through the ways in which families sought to reproduce themselves, in spite of the numerous external obstacles they faced (for examples, see Karakasidou, 1997). Consequently, family history, international and domestic politics, and state-sponsored strategies of homogenization combined in markedly different ways. Obviously, the complexity of these dynamics precludes an accurate and detailed description at this point in time—largely because obsession with "national history" has detracted from focusing on these much more substantial issues. However, a rough outline of the regional pattern of social and cultural evolution can be ascertained. It is this pattern I aim to describe in this chapter.

My starting point for such a description represents a break with the presuppositions of national narratives. Instead of attributing transcendental existence to the Balkan nations, I suggest that ethnic and national categories should be viewed as products of the larger social and cultural transformation that involved the modernization of the region and its entrance into the modern world of nation-states. This was a belated and cumbersome process in the central region of the Balkan peninsula. Even as late as the nineteenth century, the vast majority of peoples in Bosnia, Macedonia, Greece, Albania, and other parts of the peninsula, still used religious—and not secular—markers for their identity (Roudometof, 2001).

THE ORIGINS OF THE MACEDONIAN QUESTION

Therefore, the development of national identity was the product of a deliberate social construction and not the "natural" realization of a quality inscribed in the people themselves. Over the course of the nineteenth century, the development of national identity in Macedonia was influenced by a variety of factors. Perhaps of central significance for this process was the relative prosperity enjoyed by Ottoman Orthodox merchants in the nineteenth century. This prosperity provided the material basis for the rise of a Bulgarian nationalist intelligentsia. From the 1830s forward, this intelligentsia challenged the foundations of the Ottoman system of confessional association (Palairet, 1997; Roudometof, 2001: 132–39). It was not the first challenge to this system, as the 1821 Greek revolution had already resulted in an increasing awareness of secular distinctions among the Greek-Orthodox Christians of the Balkans (Roudometof, 1998a).

According to the Ottoman confessional system of association (known as the *millet* system), the Greek-Orthodox peoples of the Balkans (Albanians, Bulgarians, Greeks, Vlachs, and so on) all belonged to the same unit (the *Rum millet*), organized under the auspices of the Ecumenical Patriarchate of Constantinople. The eventual "carving up" of Ottoman territory in the 1830s represented a first shift away from this model and toward the model of the ethnically homogeneous nation-state. With the recognition of Serb autonomy (1830) and the creation of the kingdom of Greece (1832), the Ecumenical Patriarchate recognized the necessity for autocephalous ecclesiastical jurisdiction in these units, eventually leading to the establishment of independent national churches in both states. This practice was in line with Orthodox tradition, although the process was by no means free of conflict (for details, see Roudometof, 1998b).

When in 1860 the Bulgarian national movement began its own "church struggle" for the recognition of an autocephalous Bulgarian church, its fundamental claim was on purely ethnological grounds: the Bulgarians were a separate nation, thereby deserving a separate church (Markova, 1985: 41). In itself this premise implied that only ethnic Greeks should be members of the *Rum millet*. Moreover, the Bulgarian crusade for a national church entailed a direct challenge to the whole Ottoman concept of administration, which identified nationality with religious confession. This was because the Bulgarians did not possess a state of their own (at least until 1878), and therefore there was no territorial political unit that could be directly linked to a Bulgarian church. Therefore, it would be necessary to delineate the boundaries of such a church in order to define its jurisdiction. Implicitly, this meant identifying the territorial boundaries of the Bulgarian nation as well.

This was an impossible task. The fundamental issue concerned the degree to which Greek-Orthodox peoples could be defined as "Greek" or "Bulgarian" in a categorical fashion. Such an exercise involved applying national categories into a society that operated (to varying degrees, depending upon the region and the degree of urbanization and secularization) on the basis of pre-national categories of confessional association. The Ottoman census did not record the people's "nationality" but instead their religion alone.

Table 4.1 lists the population of the Ottoman Empire on the basis of the Ottoman registers. The table offers a partial view on this complex question. For example, the Muslim population includes Arabs and Turks. Furthermore, different sources often gave different estimates.[1]

To this problem there was no unanimously accepted answer at the time—and in large part this problem persists in Balkan historiography to this date.[2] A major reason for this lack of reliable information is the political character of the "nationality question" in the late nineteenth and early twentieth century. Therefore, Table 4.1 should be viewed only in the context of providing a general guide to the complexities of the empire's population.[3]

Not surprisingly, the Bulgarian national movement claimed not only Bulgaria proper (that is, today's Bulgaria) but also the adjunct regions of Thrace and Macedonia.[4] But none of these regions (including Bulgaria proper) were inhabited by just one ethnic (or national) group.[5] The Bulgarian movement formed its center between 1821 and 1839 around the regional elites of the Stara Planina towns in central Bulgaria proper. From there, it expanded outward to the rest of the Ottoman Balkan territory, providing a challenge to the Serb and Greek national centers of Belgrade and Athens (Ashley, 1985: 42; Meininger, 1974: 123). This region served as the homeland of almost 50% of Bulgarian intellectuals during the 1835–78 period.

For this nationalist intelligentsia, the issue of ecclesiastical autonomy rose from the desire to gain an institutional outlet for Bulgarian national organization within the context of the *millet* system. In 1856, the Ottoman government's major reform act, the *Hatt-i-Humayun*, ordered *millet* reorganization, a move that paved the way for Bulgarian demands for an independent church. When the Grand Vizier Ali Pasha returned from the 1856 Paris Peace Conference, Bulgarian representatives filed a petition asking

Table 4.1
Population Statistics of the Ottoman Empire, 1885–1914 by Religious Community

Major Religious community	1885	1897	1906	1914
Muslim	12,585,950	14,111,945	15,518,478	15,044,846
Greek-Orthodox	2,329,776	2,569,912	2,822,773	1,729,738
Armenian	988,887	1,042,374	1,050,513	1,161,169
Bulgarian[a]	818,962	830,189	762,754	—
Greek Catholics and Armenian Catholics	150,166	120,479	150,647[b]	130,306[c]
Protestants	36,229	44,360	53,880	65,844
Latin	18,240	22,335	20,447	24,845
Jew	184,139	215,425	256,003	187,073
Maronite	n.a.	32,416	28,726	47,406
Frank	235,690	n.a.	197,700	n.a.
Grand Total (including minor communities)	17,375,225	19,050,307	20,897,617	18,520,016

[a]"Bulgarians" are defined as all the followers of the Bulgarian Exarchate.
[b]The breakdown is 60,597 Greek Catholics and 90,050 Armenian Catholics.
[c]The breakdown is 62,468 Greek Catholics and 67,838 Armenian Catholics.

Source: Shaw (1978: 337), based on Ottoman registrars.

recognition of the Bulgarians as a separate people, different from the *Rum millet*. The Constantinople Bulgarian Society (*Obshtina*) requested all local branches (*obshtinas*) to send petitions to the Porte supporting their original request to Ali Pasha. In 1857, some twenty representatives from Bulgarian towns were assembled in Constantinople; together with forty Bulgarians from the local community they addressed more than sixty petitions and requests to the Porte (Genchev, 1977: 111). But the Ottoman government remained indifferent. Initially, the Russian ambassador Novikov told the Bulgarians that he would not support their mission; but the Russians, afraid of alienating the Bulgarian constituency, mediated to the Patriarchate. In 1858, the Patriarchate responded by making Ilarion Makariopolski, one of the leaders of the Bulgarian movement, bishop *in partibus* (without seat) of the new Bulgarian church in Constantinople. In 1859 the Ecumenical Patriarch himself laid the foundation stone of the new Bulgarian church. Bulgarian communities were also allowed to use Slavic as the church language in regions such as Adrianople and Philipopolis (Nicoloff, 1987: 40–41; Pundeff, 1969: 113–15; Tzvetkov, 1993 vol. 1: 439–52).

By October 1858 a religious council was convoked for dealing with church reforms. The Bulgarian representatives submitted a series of petitions requesting that bishops be elected by the parishioners, that the bishops speak the language of their parishioners, and that their salaries be fixed and misappropriations of funds be stopped. The council concluded its sessions in February 1860. It categorically rejected the Bulgarian demands, declaring them incompatible with church canons. The Bulgarian response to the assembly's decision was a major turning point of the Church question. On Easter Sunday 1860, Bishop Ilarion of Macariopolis, with the general approbation of the Bulgarian community, omitted the name of the Patriarch during the celebration of the liturgy and included instead that of the sultan. This act meant that he no longer recognized the Patriarch as his spiritual chief. The Patriarchate excommunicated Ilarion and his supporters, including Bishop Paisius of Plovdiv (an Albanian) and Bishop Auxentius of Veles (Meininger, 1970: 19–20), and successfully requested that the Ottoman government send them in exile.

The reaction of the Bulgarians to the events of Easter Sunday 1860 was swift. Thirty-three towns petitioned the Sultan expressing their solidarity with Ilarion, as did 734 merchants who were gathered at the Uzundjovo fair. During the 1860s many Bulgarians refused to pay taxes to the Patriarchate, while the towns of Lovech, Samokov, Shumen, Preslav, and Vidin all refused to recognize the Bulgarian bishops who had been appointed by the Patriarch (Crampton, 1983: 14). Still, the Bulgarian movement lacked Russian support of their goals. The Russian diplomats, following their traditional line of being self-proclaimed protectors of the Orthodox Christians, did not wish to see the Bulgarians moving outside the Orthodox faith since this would imply a significant loss of influence for Russia.

In 1864, when Count Ignatiev assumed the post of the Russian ambassador, Russian policy moved toward a reconciliation between Bulgarians and the Patriarchate (McDermott, 1962: 161; Meininger, 1970: 31–97). Ignatiev promoted the recognition of the Bulgarian Church by the Patriarchate (but not by the sultan) and attempted to support fellow Slavs (and Russian foreign policy objectives) without breaking up the unity of the Eastern Church. Ignatiev enlisted the support of Bulgarian nationalists; but it was also among the most extreme nationalists that reaction against his attempts came. In 1867, Patriarch Gregorios VI put forward a provisional plan suggesting such a rapprochement. By that date, most appointed bishops had been expelled from the Bulgarian towns thanks to the actions of the Bulgarian nationalists; hence, the Patriarchate had lost *de facto* control over the Bulgarian dioceses. The Patriarch's plan provided for a Bulgarian ecclesiastical territory extending from the Danube south to the Balkan Mountains. The Bulgarians rejected the plan because it excluded Thrace and Macedonia. Then, the Grand Vizier Ali Pasha developed a compromise plan recognizing ecclesiastical independence and the right of the Bulgarian population to have its own bishops. In 1868, the Ottoman Council of Ministers approved a six-point program that permitted the Bulgarians to elect their own bishops and to retain the churches built at their own expense.

As a result of this decision, the ecclesiastical conflict between Greeks and Bulgarians intensified and the Ottoman government became an important player. The Ottomans manipulated the situation in order to divide the Balkan Christians and negate any future plans of Balkan cooperation (Markova, 1983: 163). The plan worked, and until 1912 the Balkan states were unable to create a coalition to fight the Empire. The "apple of discord" was Macedonia: Bulgarians claimed most of it (and most of Thrace) for themselves on the basis that the population was Bulgarian; whereas the Greeks viewed these claims as assaults on territories they considered to be rightfully theirs. When the Ottoman decree (*firman*) of 12 March 1870 officially established a Bulgarian Exarchate, it further complicated this situation. The *firman* limited the Exarchate's jurisdiction to the Danubian Bulgaria (the area between Danube and Stara Planina mountain); however, it provided (Article 10) that the Exarchate could add additional dioceses if in a plebiscite two-thirds or more of the population voted to join it.[6] By 1878 the Bulgarian Exarchate included eighteen dioceses with approximately 2,000,000 to 2,400,0000 people as its subjects (Markova, 1988: 45–49). Although the initial phase of the Exarchate was short-lived (1870–79), the organization imitated the patriarchal tendency of political support to the Ottoman administration. The newly born Exarchate considered requests for Bulgarian political independence as extremely premature.

The Patriarchate summoned a Council of Orthodox ecclesiastical leaders in order to deal with the unilateral creation of the Exarchate. Despite Ignatiev's plotting against an agreement, on 28 September 1872, the Council members proclaimed the Bulgarian Church schismatic and all its adherents to be heretics. Surrender of Orthodoxy to ethnic nationalism was cited as the major reason for the proclamation of the schism (Meininger, 1970: 189–90; Markova, 1983: 162). From this point on, religious alliances became in effect national alliances; to be a follower of the Exarchate or the Patriarchate was treated as a proclamation of a person's national identity.[7] In the early 1870s Russian policy tacitly supported the Bulgarian Exarchate by influencing the Romanian and Serb Orthodox churches to adopt a favorable stand (Markova, 1983: 169, 175–92).

COMPETING CLAIMS IN OTTOMAN MACEDONIA

As a result of the Eastern Crisis of 1875–78 and the Russo-Turkish War of 1877–78, the Ottoman Empire signed the Treaty of San Stefano, whereby a huge Bulgarian state was created, encompassing most of Macedonia. The diplomatic reactions of the other Balkan states and the Great Powers of the time led to a revision of this initial agreement. In the Treaty of Berlin, most of Ottoman Macedonia was returned to the Ottoman Empire (see Maps 2.1 and 2.2). Instead of the huge Bulgarian independent state, two autonomous principalities were created: that of Bulgaria, which encompassed northern Bulgaria, and that of eastern Romilia, which encompassed what today is southern Bulgaria. The two autonomous principalities were united in a bloodless coup in 1885 (Durman, 1987).

After the 1878 Berlin Treaty, the Exarchate lost authority to regions annexed to Romania and Serbia while a separate synod was set up in Sofia to govern the dioceses within the Bulgarian principality. Despite requests by the Patriarchate to move the seat of the Exarchate to the Bulgarian principality and restrict its authority to the principality, the Bulgarian Exarch continued to reside in Constantinople. Limited autonomy was offered to the Bulgarian bishoprics in Macedonia, which continued to be administered by the Exarchate (Tzvetkov, 1993 vol. 1: 519; Kolev, 1991). In the post-1885 period, Bulgarian nationalists aimed toward the acquisition of the lands granted to Bulgaria by the 1878 San Stefano Treaty—that is, Ottoman Macedonia and Thrace (Todorova, 1995: 77). "Macedonia" meant the three provinces (*vilayets*) of Thessaloniki, Monastir (Bitola), and Kosovo. The region was not called "Macedonia" by the Ottomans, and the name "Macedonia" gained currency together with the ascendance of rival nationalisms (Adanir, 1984–85: 43–44; Wilkinson, 1951).

During the semi-personal regime of Stephan Stambolov (1887–94), Bulgaria's first prime minister, the Bulgarian state used the Bulgarian Exarchate to foster the development of Bulgarian national identity in Macedonia and Thrace (Perry, 1993). This strategy had limited official success: in July of 1890 the Sultan issued permissions (*berats*) for Bulgarian bishops in Skopje and Ohrid. In 1894 the metropolitans of Nevrokop and

Veles also obtained their permissions (Kolev, 1991: 44). This approach reflected the increasingly conservative attitude of the Exarchate leadership, which was hostile to violence and preferred to work with peaceful means to gain peasant support (Markova, 1988: 46–47; Poulton, 1995: 51). The Bulgarian movement benefited greatly by the disarray of the Greek side (Vakalopoulos, 1988: 42–43, 263). Persistent conflicts occurred between Greek nationalist organizations and the local bishops over the control of educational institutions. The venality of the metropolitans and the low quality of the clergy further added to the difficulties faced by the Greek nationalists. By the 1890s, the influence of the Patriarchate had declined in favor of the Bulgarian Exarchate and the Serb church (Lange-Akhund, 1998: 28–33).

The consolidation of a Bulgarian nation-state and calls for its territorial expansion directly threatened the Greek and Serb aspirations in the European territories of the Ottoman Empire. Greek-Orthodox populations were scattered in mostly coastal areas and urban cities in the Ottoman Balkans. Macedonian towns like Monastir (Bitola), Thracian cities like Plovdiv (Philipopolis), or villages like Arbanasi near Turnovo were predominately Greek. In Southern Macedonia in particular, there was no way of clearly drawing ethnic boundaries because Slav-speaking, Greek-speaking, and Vlach-speaking communities were scattered throughout the region. The Greek claims received strong support from Grecophone Vlach populations in Northwestern Macedonia (Vakalopoulos, 1986: 56; Vermeulen, 1984). Perhaps the only meaningful generalization pertained to the presence of a sizable Slavic-speaking (and largely pro-Bulgarian) majority in Northern Macedonia and of a sizable (Slavic-speaking and Greek-speaking) pro-Greek majority in the urban areas and in Southern Macedonia, including coastal areas such as the Chalkidiki peninsula (Tzvetkov, 1993 vol. 1: 442; Vakalopoulos, 1986: 51–57). Between the northern and southern zones lay a wide region where population was mixed, with no clear majority and sometimes without even a clear notion of national identity. In this middle zone, Slavic-speaking populations predominated in numbers, while Greek speakers, being wealthier and more urban, predominated in influence (Vouri, 1992: 47–58). Between 1878 and 1912 the population of this intermediate territory shifted loyalties repeatedly depending upon the success of a particular national propaganda.[8]

The "apples of discord" for Balkan nationalists were, first, the Orthodox Slavic-speaking inhabitants of Ottoman Macedonia who remained loyal to the Ecumenical Patriarchate and, second, the bilinguals. Over the nineteenth century, the increase in the Orthodox population of Ottoman Macedonia led many Macedonian Slavs to move into the urban regions. This population rivaled the established urban groups of Greeks, Vlachs, and Jews. These Slavic speakers or Macedonian Slavs did not display a clear-cut support for any particular side (Lunt, 1984: 108; Adanir, 1984–85). Greeks claimed them because they were Orthodox, while Serbs and Bulgarians declared them as their own on the basis of their Slavic language. Among at least some of the Slavic-speaking population, the word "Macedonia" slowly became a term colored with an ethnic as opposed to a purely regional significance. Among this avant-garde was Grigor Prlichev, whose poem *The Bandit,* written in Greek, won a prize in a competition held in Athens in 1860. Although offered a scholarship, he turned down the offer and went in search of his own ethnic roots. He spent five months in Constantinople learning the "Slavic language" and returned to Ohrid with the intention of teaching it to the local population (Danforth, 1995: 62–63). Needless to say, Prlichev ended up in prison because the local bishop opposed the teaching of any language other than liturgical Greek (i.e., the Byzantine Greek used in church services). Prlichev's story illustrates not only the shifting identity of the local Slavic population, but the extent of bilingualism, too. Bilingualism was widespread among peddlers, merchants, and other peoples who frequently learned more than one language for professional reasons. For example, it was common practice to write Bulgarian commercial correspondence using the Greek alphabet (Todorova, 1990).

For the first part of the nineteenth century, the Bulgarian church movement enjoyed the support of the Macedonian Slavs. In fact, in this period no clear distinction between a Slavic Macedonian and a Bulgarian intelligentsia is possible. Up until the 1870s, however, the development of private schools teaching the Cyrillic alphabet was slow (1843 Prilep, 1859 Ohrid, 1868 Monastir) (Vouri, 1992: 23–24; Friedman, 1985: 33). Bulgarian nationalist activity in Ottoman Macedonia originated in 1845 when the Russian linguist Victor Grigorovic visited Macedonia and came across the teachers Constantin and Dimitri Miladinov. Both were natives of Western Macedonia and had received their education in Greek. Grigorovic had a considerable intellectual influence upon Dimitri Miladinov, who abandoned his pro-Greek orientation and adopted a Bulgarian nationalist outlook. His ideological transformation is manifested in his signatures in various documents: he calls himself Miladinidis in 1840, Miladin in 1846, Miladinos in 1855 and Miladinov in 1857 (Tachiaos, 1974: 33). The Miladinov brothers began teaching in Bulgarian and even published in Zagreb a folk song collection of Bulgarian Macedonian songs in 1861. The collection was published with the help of pro-Yugoslav Catholic bishop Strossmayer, to whom the book was dedicated. The Miladinov brothers were captured by the Ottomans, accused of working for the Roman Catholic Church and imprisoned. While in prison, they died of typhus in 1862.

In the second half of the nineteenth century, Serbs, Greeks, and Bulgarians used educational and religious institutions in order to "convince" the local population that they belonged to the Serb, Greek, or Bulgarian nation. For example, the Serb government adopted in 1878 the *ekavian* dialect as the official language in an indirect attempt to bring the Serb language closer to the spoken vernacular of the Macedonian Slavs (Poulton, 1995: 63). This strategy was a response to the fragmentation of the Bulgarian intelligentsia during the second half of the nineteenth century. The first literary Bulgarian figures wrote in Western Macedonian–Bulgarian vernacular (Todorova, 1990: 444). However, after 1850 it was the Stara Planina towns that served as the nucleus of the national movement. This led to the gradual adoption of the Eastern Bulgarian variant as the standard literary language. In 1836 Vasil Aprilov, the Bulgarian merchant who financed the first secular school in Bulgaria (1835), suggested that the Eastern Bulgarian dialect be adopted as the basis for the literary language. In the post-1856 period, the influential Society for Bulgarian Literature also promoted the Eastern Bulgarian variant as the major literary language (Genchev, 1977: 66; Shashko, 1974: 11; Friedman, 1975: 90).

The victory of the Eastern Bulgarian variant was resented by the Western Bulgarian–Macedonian intelligentsia, and between 1857 and 1880 a total of sixteen textbooks were published in the Western Bulgarian–Macedonian dialect. In the post-1878 period, the emerging Bulgarian educational system gradually led to the codification of the Bulgarian language, a process completed with the introduction of the Drinov-Ivanchev orthography in 1899 (Todorova, 1995: 77). Therefore, the Serb strategy aimed at accelerating the gap between the two variants in order to incorporate the Macedonian Slavs into the Serb nation. After an agreement between the pro-Macedonian activists and the Belgrade authorities (August 1886), the Serb schools proceeded to teach a mixture of Serb and local Macedonian, attempting to develop a middle road between Serb and Bulgarian (Matzureff, 1978: 137; Kostopoulos, 2000: 49–50).[9] This curriculum was followed until 1898, when the Serb schools reverted back to an all-Serb curriculum. When in 1891, Macedonian students in Bulgaria published a periodical (*Loza*) aiming at the creation of a Macedonian literary language, they soon discovered that "Macedonian separatism" was unwelcome.[10] The journal was banned in 1892. In 1894, a new periodical, *Vardar,* which demanded linguistic autonomy for the Macedonian Slavs, appeared in Belgrade (Adanir, 1992: 180).

From the 1870s forward, the Serbs, Greeks, and Bulgarians proceeded to increase their nationalist and educational efforts in Macedonia. By 1876 there were 350 Bulgarian schools in Macedonia alone and their number grew to 800 in 1900 for all Ottoman European territories (Geogreoff, 1973: 153–55; Poulton, 1995: 64–65). Before the Balkan wars of 1912–13 the Bulgarian schools reached their peak: 1,141 schools operated with 1,884 teachers and 65,474 students. The Greek nationalist efforts received a boost only after the 1878 San Stefano Treaty. The realization of an immediate threat to their Macedonian *irredenta* led the Greeks to redefine their goals. The northern part of Ottoman Macedonia was "written off" and attention concentrated in the middle and southern zones (Kofos, 1980: 49, 52–53). Emphasis was put on education, and scholarships for study at the University of Athens were made available to local students. The Athens-based Association for the Propagation of the Greek Letters was initially in charge of these efforts. After 1881, a special governmental committee took over this task. By 1894 there were approximately 907 Greek schools with 1,245 teachers and 53,633 students (Vakalopoulos, 1988: 157, 129–69; Vouri, 1992). Suggestions by Macedonian Greeks to send armed bandits into the region were turned down by the Greek government. Greek guerrilla activity was initiated only after the 1903 Ilinden Uprising—to be discussed later in this chapter.[11]

Slowly the differentiation between Macedonian and Bulgarian intelligentsias led to calls for an autonomous or independent Macedonian state. In 1871, the Bulgarian author Petko Slavejkov wrote in his newspaper *Makedoniya* that those who called themselves *Macedonists* (*Makendisti*) were Macedonians and not Bulgarians (quoted in Slijepcevic, 1958: 116).[12] By 1893 the Macedonian Question was complicated even further with the foundation of the Internal Macedonian Revolutionary Organization (IMRO or VMRO) in Thessaloniki. Of the six founding members, four were teachers who had studied abroad, and three of them had participated in the publication of the journal *Loza*—discussed above (Lange-Akhund, 1998: 36).[13] The VMRO leadership's goal was an autonomous Macedonian state, possibly one that would be part of a broader Balkan federation. The organization created secret means of communication and established branches in the villages. Thanks to its initial small size (fifteen to twenty participants between 1893 and 1896), the group's existence remained a secret to Ottoman authorities up until 1897 (Lange-Akhund, 1998: 42–43).[14]

In Bulgaria, Macedonian Charitable Clubs had been operating since the 1880s. They provided help to refugees from Macedonia and drew attention to their plight. In 1895 the Supreme Macedonian Committee was founded in Sofia. Soon, it developed strong ties with the VMRO leadership. Dominated by people with a military background, the Committee viewed the VMRO as an instrument of Bulgarian policy, thus drawing sharp criticism from the more left-wing and independent-minded VMRO activists. Nevertheless, the VMRO maintained ties with the Bulgarian nationalists (Lange-Akhund, 1998: 44–52; Adanir, 1992: 179; McDermott, 1978).

During the 1899–1903 period, the two groups cooperated with each other, eventually culminating in the 1903 Ilinden Uprising. For a short period of time, the VMRO revolutionaries captured the city of Krusevo and declared Macedonian independence. However, the Ottoman forces acted promptly and crushed the revolt with swift force (for details, see Lange-Akhund, 1998; Perry, 1988). In the aftermath of the bloodshed caused by the revolt, Franz Joseph of Austria-Hungary and Tsar Nicholas II of Russia met in Murzsteg and, with the support of the other European powers, imposed a program of reform on Macedonia.[15] In 1903, simultaneously with the Ilinden Uprising, Kriste Misirkov, a teacher and author from Macedonia, published his book *On Macedonian Matters* in Sofia. Misirkov claimed that the Macedonian Slavs had an identity separate from the Bulgarian one and, as a result, authorities in Sofia proceeded to confiscate copies of the book.[16]

Following the failed Ilinden Uprising VMRO faced a serious crisis. The organization fragmented repeatedly between 1903 and 1908, reflecting the emergence of two wings with distinct ideological profiles and sympathies. On the one side, there were the conservatives, who by 1908 had already developed close ties with the Bulgarian-Macedonian organizations based in Bulgaria. This wing eventually inherited the name of the original VMRO. On the other side, there were the more left-wing members of the organization, who were referred to as the Serres group or the federalists, because they opted for an independent Macedonia in the context of a Balkan federation (Vlassidis, 1997: 69–73; Matzureff, 1978: 72).

Following the Ilinden Uprising, the Greek government decided to sponsor paramilitary activities in Ottoman Macedonia. The resulting Greek-Bulgarian paramilitary confrontation lasted up until the 1908 Young Turk revolution.[17] Following the revolution, all hostilities in Macedonia were suspended. The Young Turk revolution was interpreted as a peaceful way of establishing an alternative democratic system that would allow the various ethnic communities a voice in the Ottoman political system. This interpretation was promoted by the Young Turk leadership—for example, the revolutionary leader Enver Bey proclaimed that "there are no longer Bulgars, Roumans, Jews, Mussulmans; under the same blue sky we are equal, we glory in being Ottomans" (quoted in Miller, 1936: 476).[18] In 1908, following the Young Turk revolution, the (now clearly more pro-Bulgarian) VMRO operated openly as a pro-Bulgarian organization. Soon, however, the promises of a democratic solution evaporated as the Young Turk cabinets proceeded to implement policies of homogenization in the region (for a discussion, see Roudometof, 2001: 92–94). When the Young Turks rejected the more nationalist aspirations of the Greek Orthodox minorities, the VMRO resurfaced once again in 1911 under the leadership of Todor Alexandrov. On the other side, the federalist faction organized the Federalist People's Party in 1908, promoting the idea of a common federation among the Balkan peoples.[19]

The Young Turk assimilatory policies eventually provided a major impetus that broke the Greek-Bulgarian impasse and facilitated the Balkan coalition of 1912. Serbia, Montenegro, Bulgaria, and Greece united and, in the 1912 (first) Balkan War, they conquered most of the European territory of the Ottoman Empire. In the first Balkan war, Serbs and Greeks were able to conquer most of the territory of Ottoman Macedonia—while, in the meantime, the Bulgarian army unsuccessfully pursued Tsar Ferdinand's ill-conceived dream of conquering Constantinople.[20] Bulgarian dissatisfaction with the partition of Macedonia among the victors led to the second Balkan war. The Bulgarians' attempt to reverse the status quo was unsuccessful, and Bulgaria was forced to accept defeat. But the eventual declaration of World

War I provided a further opportunity for Bulgaria to challenge Macedonia's partition. Bulgaria entered World War I on the side of the Central Powers and by 1915 was able to conquer most of the territory of the pre-1913 Ottoman Macedonia. Unfortunately for Bulgaria, World War I eventually led to the victory of the Entente forces, and Bulgaria had to give up all of its conquered territory for a second time.

THE PARTITION AND CULTURAL HOMOGENIZATION OF MACEDONIA

It was only in the aftermath of the two Balkan wars and World War I that Serbs and Greeks were able to effectively govern their newly conquered regions of formerly Ottoman Macedonia. The wars brought with them extensive population transfers—either as a direct result of the warfare or as a result of treaties signed among the parties. In this section, I concentrate on developments in Greek Macedonia mainly because these developments are inexorably tied to the articulation of modern Macedonian identity.

In the aftermath of the population exchanges, the majority of Slavic speakers or Macedonian Slavs were located in Northwestern Greek Macedonia. The thorny issue pertains to estimates of their total numerical strength. Between 1923 and 1945, various Greek and Bulgarian sources, most of them based on surveys or counts of various agencies of the Greek state (including the Greek army and the Greek census), give different figures for this population. Estimates range from 39,242 to 87,068 (statistics cited in Kostopoulos, 2000: 30). Perhaps most important among them is the count undertaken by the *Generale Directorate of Macedonia* (GDM) in 1925—which is a source used by Kostopoulos (2000), Karakasidou (2000a), and Koliopoulos (1999: 38). The Directorate estimated a total of 162,506 Slavic speakers. Table 4.2 lists the GDM results alongside with the results of the official Greek census of 1928. Because these Slavic speakers (or Macedonian Slavs or Slavo-Macedonians or Macedonians, depending upon one's point of view) were claimed by Bulgaria as its own national minority, the Greek state was eager to downplay their numerical strength in the census, thereby avoiding protests by the Bulgarian state. For this reason, it is preferable to view the GDM data as more reliable. Moreover, the GDM data give the highest count of Slavic-speakers, and, therefore, it might overestimate the number of Slavic-speakers. However, because of the lack of reliable data, it is wiser to assume a higher figure for the Slavic-speakers, even if this overestimates the Slavic population.[21]

In any event, Table 4.2 clearly shows that almost half of all Slavic speakers in Greek Macedonia were located in Northwestern Macedonia, and, more specifically, in the prefectures of Florina (where they formed the majority of the population), Kozani, and Pella. Smaller groups were also present in the counties of Paionia, Sintiki, and Langada. This pattern of geographical

Table 4.2
Slavic-Speaking Population in Greek Macedonia

Prefecture	County	1928 Census	1925 GDM Count
Florina	Kastoria	9,678	21,936
	Florina	28,884	45,517
Kozani	Anaselista	257	0
	Grevena	3	0
	Eordaia	3,035	7,931
	Kozani	15	0
Pella	Almopia	5,840	9,230
	Giannitsa	4,847	9,591
	Edessa	8,850	14,827
Thessaloniki	Veroia	1,374	1,828
	Thessaloniki	1,401	8,574
	Kilkis	262	579
	Langada	308	11,465
	Paionia	3,974	6,746
	Pieria	20	30
Chalkidiki	Arnaia	1	0
	Chalkidiki	4	0
Agion Oros	Agion Oros	118	N/A
Serres	Zihni	512	2,471
	Nigrita	558	617
	Serres	2,747	6,500
	Sintiki	3,843	8,270
Drama	Drama	3,148	5,943
	Zirnovo	966	451
Kavala	Thassos	1	0
	Kavala	20	0
	Nestos	1	0
	Paggaion	1	0
TOTAL		80,668	162,506

Source: Kostopoulos (2000: 32).

distribution is corroborated by the information concerning the fate of the Slavic population in the other two parts of Greek Macedonia.[22] Central and eastern Greek Macedonia were the regions where the Greek and Bulgarian armies clashed repeatedly between 1913 and 1919. The Greek army set on fire the pro-Bulgarian villages of Kilkis and the Strumon valley, thereby forcing the villagers to flee into Bulgaria proper. Some 220,000 refugees from Macedonia and Thrace flooded into Bulgaria after the end of World War I

(Lampe, 1996: 152–53). The second wave of Bulgarian refugees took place in the 1920s, following the signing of the Neilly Treaty (1919) concerning the so-called "voluntary" exchange of population between Greece and Bulgaria. Of the 66,126 people from Greek Macedonia who left for Bulgaria, the overwhelming majority was from central and eastern Macedonia, and only approximately 6,000 were from western Macedonia (Lithoxoou, 1992: 60).[23] The refugees who fled to Bulgaria faced great difficulties when attempting to return to Greece, as in most cases the authorities would refuse to allow them to enter the country. In addition, throughout the interwar period, pro-Bulgarian activists were deported to southern Greece and the Aegean islands. Also, the Greek consulates in Florina and Thessaloniki frequently refused to issue passports to Slavic speakers who wished to emigrate because of fear that the émigrés would then campaign against the Greek state (Karakasidou, 2000a: 66–69).

The net result of these population movements was the near extinction of the Slavic population in the rest of Greek Macedonia and the creation of an enclave of Slavic speakers in northwestern Greek Macedonia. This turn of events strengthened Greek rule in Macedonia and significantly weakened the claims of the Bulgarian nation-state in the region. However, the creation of an ethnic Slavic enclave in northwestern Greek Macedonia and the lack of close contact with the Bulgarian state meant that the Slavic speakers of northwestern Greek Macedonia were, in practical terms, on their own. In this context, the relations between the state and the Slavic enclave were characterized by mutual mistrust. Slavic speakers eventually became the Greek nation-state's "Other"—a group stigmatized because of its cultural features. In this marginalization of relations with the state one has to locate the birth of an ethnic (or national) Macedonian identity.[24]

This Slav Macedonian population (or Slavo-Macedonians, as they were referred to in interwar Greece) had to face up to the Greek state and its mechanisms of acculturation. But before discussing this relationship, it is important to explain the reasons that the acculturation campaign of the Greek nation-state—as well as the pre-1913 nationalist acculturation campaigns—had such an uneven impact on Greek Macedonia. As Karakasidou's (1997) study eloquently demonstrated, acculturation into the Greek nation-state was successful in those instances where there was considerable intermarriage between Slavic-speaking and Greek- or Vlach-speaking (and later on refugee) families. Such intermarriage typically took the form of Slavic women marrying Greek men and moving to their household where Greek was the spoken language, thereby breaking down the intergenerational transmission of the Slavo-Macedonian language.

In the areas with a solid economic base, trade, and extensive population movements (such as the village of Assiros studied by Karakasidou) the influx of traders and merchants and the local accumulation of wealth fostered this pattern of intermarriage. On the contrary, in northwestern Greek Macedonia "mountainous terrain, scarcity of resources, insecurity of life and property, and easy access from all directions and particularly from the north have not encouraged the growth of large and important urban centers in the region" (Koliopoulos, 1999: 11). Consequently, the association among economic wealth, intermarriage, and acculturation into the Greek nation produced only limited results. In this region, the traditional extended family of the Slavic population (the *zadruga*) maintained its existence well into the 1930s.[25]

The departure of the Muslim Turks from the region of Florina in the 1920s was followed by the arrival of Greek Orthodox refugees in the region. Following the 1923 Greco-Turkish exchange of populations, 354,647 Muslims left Greece and 339,094 Greeks arrived in Greek Macedonia from Anatolia (Pentzopoulos 1962: 69, 107). The result was a complete change in the ethnic composition of Greek Macedonia. The Slavo-Macedonians, mostly agricultural workers and small farmers, lost the opportunity to take over the property of the Muslims, and now they had to compete with the newcomers for property, fields, and so on. Hence, the assimilationist policy of the Greek state was compounded by the conflict between local Slavs and the often Turkish-speaking Greek refugees who settled in the region. The state's support of the refugees contributed significantly to the delegitimization of the state in the eyes of the local Slavic population (Koliopoulos, 1994: 45).

This economic conflict coincided with the intense conflict between political parties in interwar Greece. The two main political parties, the monarchist People's Party and the nationalist Liberal Party (led by the Cretan politician Eleftherios Venizelos), clashed throughout the interwar period in almost all domains of public life. Given the close connections between the Venizelist Liberal Party and the refugees, the Slavo-Macedonians sided with the People's Party (Mavrocordatos, 1983; Gounaris, 1997b; Mihailidis, 1997).[26] During the interwar period, close to 70% of the Slavic speakers in the counties of Florina, Kastoria, and Pella gave their electoral support to the People's Party (Mihailidis, 1997: 132). In fact, the widespread employment of the Slavo-Macedonian language in Florina was a constant source of worry for Greek nationalists. Local politicians affiliated with the People's Party apparently proceeded to speak the "local language" during electoral campaigns and were harshly criticized by Greek nationalists (Kostopoulos, 2000: 78–87).

In addition to the People's Party, the only other political party that gained support among Slavo-Macedonians was the Greek Communist Party (KKE). To understand the complex relationships between communists and (Slavic) Macedonians, however, it is necessary to adopt a broader regional perspective on Balkan interwar politics. During the interwar period, the VMRO, previously the champion of Macedonian independence, had to face a disastrous situation. Not only had the dreams of an independent Macedonia not materialized in the aftermath of the 1903 Ilinden Uprising, but also, by 1913, Macedonia was divided into three regions, each under the control of a nation-state eager to consolidate its control over its newly conquered region.

In the aftermath of the two Balkan wars and World War I, the conservative (and now firmly pro-Bulgarian) VMRO was reconstituted (1918) under the leadership of Todor Alexandrov, Alexander Protojerov, and Petar Tsaulev. Its initial goal was to help out the war refugees and ultimately to rekindle Bulgarian aspirations in Greek and Serb Macedonia. This conservative VMRO became a powerful player in interwar Bulgarian politics, actively participating in the 1923 coup and the assassination of Bulgarian Prime Minister Alexander Stamboliski (Banac, 1984: 312–23). This (sometimes referred to as a "fascist") VMRO developed an agenda that called for an autonomous Macedonia—for autonomy could provide the legal foundation for a "unification" with Bulgaria proper. From 1919 to 1934 this organization conducted paramilitary warfare in Serb-controlled Vardar Macedonia (with some minor excursions into Greek-controlled Macedonia) (Barker, 1950; Karakasidou, 2000a: 70–73).

In 1924 it approached the Balkan communists in order to attract support for its agenda by the communists in the other countries. In 1920, the communists had already instituted a Balkan Communist Federation (BCF) in Sofia—a subdivision of the Comintern, the international communist organization, consisting of the Greek, Yugoslav, and Bulgarian parties (Matzureff, 1978: 88–95). In 1924, the BCF, the VMRO, the Federalists (to be discussed below), and the Greek and Yugoslav communists signed a joint declaration. The document declared their common goal of an independent Macedonia, which in turn would be possible only with the union of all the Balkan peoples into a single federation (Karakasidou, 1993b: 459; Vlassidis, 1997: 76). While Alexandrov wished that this agreement not be made public, the communists leaked the document to the press, and, just as Alexandrov suspected, the result was internal strife within VMRO itself. In the course of the strife (which included assassinations of each faction's rivals), many of the VMRO leaders were killed, including Alexandrov himself. Ivan Mihailov and Alexander Protojerov, who assumed VMRO's leadership in the wake of Alexandrov's death, retracted their support for an independent Macedonia and moved toward their old position of autonomy. By 1928, Mihailov, who had emerged as the key leader of the group, proposed a new plan, calling for a unification of the pre-1913 Macedonia into a single state that would be autonomous from the Bulgarian state. By 1931, Mihailov, with Italian support, broke his ties with the Bulgarian government and began to operate as a semi-autonomous agent, wishing to create a Macedonian state that would be under his control. Up until 1934, this Bulgarian VMRO remained a potent political force in Bulgarian life and practically a state within a state in Pirin Macedonia (see Map 1.1). In 1934, the Zveno, a group of military officers, overthrew the government in an attempt to "restore order" from the admittedly ineffective parliamentary regime. Virtually its first act was to arrest the VMRO leadership, putting an end to its regime of intimidation and terrorism.

The remnants of the pro-federalist wing of the original VMRO were also reconstituted in 1918. Initially, they formed a single union with pro-Bulgarian organizations, but by 1921 they instituted the Macedonian Federalist Refugee Organization. They cooperated closely with the communists and participated in the failed 1924 attempt to develop a joint program with the conservative pro-Bulgarian VMRO. In 1925, following the debacle of the 1924 rapprochement, the remnants of this faction formed the VMRO-United. Their base was in Vienna, and their stated goal was the implementation of the 1924 joint program of an independent and free Macedonia. Unlike the pro-Bulgarian VMRO, this group did not take up arms but publicized its views through its newspapers, *Le Federation Balkanique* and *Makedonsko Delo*. The group fragmented again in 1931 with a more clearly pro-federalist faction creating a separate organization in Constantinople, thereby leaving the communist faction in charge of the organization's name (Vlassidis, 1997: 81–85; Rossos, 1995: 238–40). Reacting to Mihailov's ideas about an independent Macedonian state, the VMRO-United adopted the platform of an independent Macedonia as well. In 1934 the Soviet Union officially recognized a Macedonian nationality, and the same year the Communist Party of Macedonia was founded. The VMRO-United, which consisted basically of communists at the time, became eventually absorbed into the Communist Party of Macedonia.[27]

These developments have to be placed in the context of the broader policy of the Yugoslav Communist Party (which at the time was closely controlled by the Moscow-based Soviet Communist Party) (Shoup, 1968). Specifically, in the 1920 Yugoslav parliamentary elections, 25% of the total communist vote came from Serb-controlled Vardar Macedonia. But participation was low (only 55%), mainly because the pro-Bulgarian VMRO (Alexandrov's group) organized a boycott against the elections (Lampe, 1996: 140). In the following years, the Yugoslav communists attempted to enlist the sympathies of that faction of the population that supported the pro-Bulgarian VMRO. This was the prime motive behind the failed 1924 agreement. Still, the 1924 suggestion of the international communist organization (the Comintern) that all Balkan communist parties adopt a platform of a "united Macedonia" was not uniformly accepted by the Bulgarian and Greek communists (Papapanagiotou, 1992). Despite individual protests by prominent communists, however, the Greek Communist Party (KKE) did support this goal throughout the 1924–35 period (Karakasidou, 1993b: 458–60; Kostopoulos, 2000: 150–57). The goal was quite simple: just like their Yugoslav counterparts, the Greek communists attempted to raid the popular base of the pro-Bulgarian VMRO, thereby gaining support for their party among Greece's Slavo-Macedonian minority. Indeed, in the Florina district, electoral support for the KKE jumped from 3.96% in June of 1935 to 8.25% in January of 1936.[28] In 1936 the KKE retracted its position in favor of an independent Macedonia, adopting instead a platform of extended autonomy for the Macedonian Slavs (Karakasidou, 1993b: 461). The party's own rationale for the decision was that there were too many Greeks in Greek Macedonia by that time, and the original platform was no longer realistic.[29]

While these international currents have had a significant impact for the articulation of the communists' agenda with regard to the Macedonian Question, it is important to realize that the communists became an important player only during World War II. In contrast, during the interwar period, Greek and Serb authorities were concerned with the revisionist dreams harbored by Bulgarian nationalists (and the pro-Bulgarian VMRO). Local administrators were primarily concerned with the extent to which the Slavic Macedonians were indeed favorably predisposed toward Bulgaria. In her analysis of the reports by the Florina-based Greek administration, Karakasidou (2000a) clearly shows that what preoccupied the administrators was not only the fact that the people were speaking an "alien tongue" but, more important, the fact that many of them harbored anti-Greek or pro-Bulgarian sentiments. The administrators, echoing the worries of the Greek state about Bulgarian revisionism, placed emphasis on the "tints" of the people—that is, whether they were former "Schismatics" (followers of the Bulgarian Exarchate) or "Patriarchists" and whether they displayed a pro-Greek or pro-Bulgarian morale (Karakasidou, 2000a: 62–64). As a matter of fact, even local administrators acknowledged that, in addition to these two categories, there was a third category of people "indifferent to nationality" who called themselves "Macedonians."[30]

The significance of the Bulgarian (as well as Serb) protests for the evolution of Greek policy can hardly be underestimated.[31] The Bulgarian state persistently raised the issue of a Bulgarian minority in Greek Macedonia and asked that Greece keep its obligations in the context of the Neilly treaty (1919) (Founta-Tergali, 1986), the Treaty of Serves (1920), and the Lausanne Treaty (1923). In September 1924 Greece and Bulgaria signed a protocol according to which Greece agreed to accept League of Nations arbitration on matters concerning Bulgarian minorities in its territory (Veremis, 1995b: 20). This led to protests by the Serbs, and by 1925 the Greek authorities faced a two-fold problem. On the one hand, Serbia protested against the possible recognition of a Bulgarian minority in Greece because such recognition would repudiate the official Serb position that all Slavs in Serb-controlled Macedonia were Serbs. According to the Serb diplomats, it would be impossible for Serbia to accept that the Slavs of Serb-controlled Macedonia were Serbs while south of the Greek-Serb border they were Bulgarians. On the other hand, internal reports indicated that if the Slavo-Macedonians of Greece were allowed to ask for Bulgarian schools, it would become evident that many of them were pro-Bulgarian in orientation.

Therefore, the Greek state would have to openly acknowledge that a Bulgarian national minority did in fact exist within the Greek state (Kostopoulos, 2000: 89–96).

Consequently, the Greek state decided to institute in 1925 an educational program in the "local language" and printed a primer (*Abecedar*) for use in minority schools. The primer was an open recognition of the Slavic speakers as a group distinct from Serbs or Bulgarians. Consequently, from the Greek state's point of view, it solved the "problem" of Bulgarian and Serb interference in domestic politics. In this instance, the Greek state, however unwittingly, explicitly promoted a further sense of difference among the Slavo-Macedonians (or Macedonians) of Greek Macedonia. The primer used the Latin alphabet. It is not clear whether this was a deliberate effort to guarantee its rejection by the Slavo-Macedonians or whether it was an attempt to accentuate the difference between the local peoples and the Serbs and the Bulgarians (Danforth, 1995: 70; Kostopoulos, 2000: 99–101). In January 1926, the publication of the primer caused extensive protests in the region of Florina, where Greeks and pro-Greek Slavic speakers staged demonstrations and demanded that the government recant its decision about minority education.[32] These events helped the crystallization of the official Greek position with regard to the Slavo-Macedonian minority: publicly, the Slavic speakers were neither Serbs nor Bulgarians, their difference was confined squarely to linguistic issues, and they were loyal citizens of the state.[33]

During the 1923–36 period, a consistent complaint of Greek nationalists was the fact that the Greek republic was too weak and hesitant in its dealings with the minority, unwilling to adopt harsh measures against the Slavo-Macedonians and force them to acculturate into Hellenism (for examples, see Kostopoulos, 2000: 133–39). Officially, it was the Metaxas dictatorship (1936) that forbade the public speaking of the "alien language" and set up a regime of forceful acculturation against the minority (Kostopoulos 2000: 162–80; Carabott, 1997). Under the dictatorship, the previous attempts at peaceful assimilation were abandoned, and the Slavo-Macedonians were subjected to an intense (and violent) acculturation campaign.[34] The state repression and the humiliations suffered by the people at that time fostered resentment among the minority, leading many of them to abandon any hope of gaining acceptance by the Greek state (Danforth, 1995: 72).

The Slavic population in Vardar Macedonia was also exposed to a similar assimilation campaign by the Serb authorities. The official viewpoint declared Vardar Macedonia to be "Southern Serbia." During the initial Serb occupation (1913–15) and after the return of the region in the Serb-controlled Kingdom of Serbs, Slovenes, and Croats, the Serb authorities proceeded to expel the Bulgarian Exarchist clergy and teachers, removed all Bulgarian signs and books, and dissolved all Bulgarian cultural associations. Additionally, approximately 4,200 Serb families settled in the region by 1940 (Banac, 1984: 318–19). The population's subsequent resentment was registered in the growing support for the Yugoslav communists. Yet, even as late as 1941, the population of Skopje did not hesitate to celebrate the coming of Bulgarian forces to occupy this part of Macedonia. This attitude soon changed as a result of the Bulgarians' misrule: their heavy-handed treatment of the local population and their condescending attitude. During the 1941–44 period, in an ingenious move, the Yugoslav communists were able to appropriate Misirkov's "separatist" viewpoint to turn it into the foundation of the Macedonian homeland (see Shoup, 1968: 144–83 for a description). Undoubtedly, the success of this project was partly due to the local population's alienation from Bulgaria as well as the bad memories of the Serb-dominated administration during the interwar period.[35] Additionally, the Yugoslavs allowed the local Communist Party to assume an exceptionally nationalist position that was at odds with the party's general orientation toward the issue of nationalism in the Yugoslav republics.[36]

In northwestern Greek Macedonia, the growing alienation of the Slavic population facilitated the appeal of German, Bulgarian, and communist propaganda during the 1941–43 period.[37] Of course, not all Slavs supported the occupation forces or the communists; some of them enlisted in the right-wing partisan forces (Karakasidou 1993b: 463; see also, Koliopoulos, 1999). Gradually, as the occupation forces withdrew from the area, the communists were able to attract the Slavo-Macedonians by forming separate units referred to as the Slavo-Macedonian Liberation Front (*Slovenomakedonski Narodno Osloboditelen Front* or SNOF) and promising equal treatment to the minority population.[38] In the areas under the control of the communists, the Slavo-Macedonians set up schools, printed newspapers, and distributed primers for the teaching of the Macedonian language (Kostopoulos, 2000: 190–98; Sfetas, 1995). As a result, the Slavo-Macedonian villagers supported the communist forces during the Greek civil war (1944–49).[39]

In 1945, the Slavo-Macedonian units were formally organized in the National Liberation Front (*Narodnoosloboditelniot Front* or NOF), a semi-independent organization that became a constitutive part of the communist Democratic Army of Greece (DAG). According to Markos Vafiadis, the DAG's general commander, NOF forces accounted for 45% of the entire force of the Democratic Army (Banac, 1987: 45–46). The Greek Communist Party had promised equal rights to the Slavic population but could not openly support the creation of a separate Macedonian state that would include parts of Greek Macedonia (Rossos, 1997; Sfetas, 1995), because such an action would create an upheaval among the local Greek population. At the same time, the Yugoslav communists gained control over Vardar Macedonia, declaring the People's Republic of Macedonia. Close ties soon developed between the Vardar-based communists and their Greek counterparts in Northern Greece.[40] Apparently, Macedonian partisans from Vardar Macedonia did cross into Northwestern Greek Macedonia. From this point on, the Macedonian Question becomes part of a larger and broader topic, that of the Greek Civil War. Suffice to say, historiography has not yet achieved accounts of sufficient depth and detachment with regard to this topic.[41] Part of the reason that the civil war's legacy is so difficult to put aside is the fact that this legacy structured post–World War II political developments in Greece, at least until the collapse of the dictatorship in 1974. The communists who fled to the Eastern Bloc after being defeated in the civil war were able to return to Greece only in the 1980s, when the Socialist government provided an amnesty allowing for "national reconciliation."

To this day, partisanship is an important factor to be dealt with on this topic. Both the Left and the Right blamed each other for the civil war. Also, researchers had to face the general underdevelopment of Greek historical research in the first two decades following World War II as well as the fact that most sources were completely inaccessible for many decades or were carefully edited to fit specific ideological purposes. The political controversies surrounding this issue are closely related to the Macedonian issue. The declaration of the People's Republic of Macedonia was followed almost immediately by calls for the incorporation of the other two regions of Macedonia into the new state (see the proclamations cited in Chapter 2). In fact, the Yugoslav communists were acutely aware that the majority of the Slavs in Vardar Macedonia followed them because of their promises of freedom and national liberation, and not because of ideological reasons. The Macedonian Communist Party undertook a series of purges in the mid-1940s in order to exterminate popular leaders (such as Metodi Andonov, or "Cento") who were not completely under the control of the party hierarchy. Additionally, some 100,000 people were imprisoned in the post-1944 period for violations of the law for the "protection of Macedonian national honor," and some 1,260 Bulgarian sympathizers were allegedly killed (Troebst, 1997: 248–50, 255–57; 1994: 116–22; Poulton, 2000: 118–19).

THE BIRTH OF THE NEW MACEDONIAN QUESTION

The victory of the nationalist pro-Western forces in the Greek Civil War led to the restoration of the pre–World War II boundaries. But the situation remained complicated because part of the remaining Slavo-Macedonian minority of Greece fled to Yugoslavia (Vardar Macedonia) and to other East European countries,[42] while a considerable number of them immigrated to Western countries (mainly Canada and Australia), giving rise to a Macedonian diaspora. The creation of the People's Republic of Macedonia in 1944 officially sanctioned the Macedonian national identity and provided this population with a prospective national homeland.

Of course, some of the Slavo-Macedonians remained in Greek Macedonia. Macedonian sources have claimed that 300,000 Macedonians reside in Greek Macedonia (Popov and Radin, 1989), while Macedonian human rights activists put the number at one million people (Hristov, 1994: 12). Third-party sources estimate approximately 10,000 to 50,000 Slavic-speaking people in Northwestern Greek Macedonia.[43] These are the remnants of the pre–World War II Slavo-Macedonian minority.[44] Although these are more reliable estimates, post–World War II Greek authorities denied the very existence of a Macedonian minority group.

Consequently, during the post–World War II period, the newly born Macedonian nationalism was not contained within the boundaries of the People's Republic of Macedonia. On the contrary, the immigrant communities in Australia, Canada, and the United States were among those who participated, influenced, and were shaped by the post-1945 "affirmation" of the Macedonian nation. This turn of events has had important consequences for regional relations. Unlike the natives of the Macedonian Republic, the immigrants, the Greek Civil War refugees, and their descendants cannot develop an attachment to a homeland that would exclude the regions where their ancestors (or even themselves) were born. The post-1945 generations of Macedonians born in the People's Republic of Macedonia include several thousand refugees who fled into its territory at the aftermath of the Greek Civil War. These refugees became known as "Aegean Macedonians"—a distinct group for whom national affirmation was not achieved in 1945. Many among them had family members, property, and other ties with northwestern Greek Macedonia and could not possibly conceive that their newly constructed national homeland would be defined exclusively as the territory of the People's Republic (e.g., Vardar Macedonia). Consequently, the Macedonian national homeland, the symbolic center of the Macedonian transnational community, does not coincide with the territory of the new Republic of Macedonia but extends to include the Bulgarian and Greek regions of Macedonia (Danforth, 1995: 84).

The existence of these groups provided further reasons for the People's Republic of Macedonia to conceptualize the Macedonian homeland as inclusive of all the regions of the pre-1913 Macedonia (Pirin, Vardar, and Aegean Macedonia)—see Map 1.1 for a representation. Additionally, the ideological elaboration of Macedonian nationhood was bound to follow the pattern provided by the familiar examples of Serbia, Greece, and Bulgaria (Roudometof, 2001: 101–56). All these states stressed nationhood rather than citizenship as their basic component of nation building. They defined a homeland on the basis of cultural and not territorial criteria, and inclusion into (or exclusion from) their respective nation was justified on the basis of people identified with the cultural characteristics of the nation (language, religion, and so on). The constitutional debates concerning the declaration of the post-1991 Macedonian state as the state of the "Macedonian nation" are but a reflection of this trend. This issue is discussed in greater detail in Chapter 6.

Subsequently, in the post-1945 period, the "old" Macedonian Question (that is, whether the inhabitants of Macedonia were Serbs, Bulgarians,

Greeks, or Macedonians) was modified in important ways. First, the Serbs abandoned their claim to the inhabitants of Macedonia, and, despite the presence of a Serb minority in the People's Republic of Macedonia, they have not been among the key contenders. As discussed in Chapter 2, even the nationalist Milosevic regime of the 1990s did not attempt to draw Serbia into a conflict with the People's Republic of Macedonia. Second, the transnational nation-building pursued by FYROM and the Macedonian immigrants gave birth to the "new Macedonian Question" (Pettifer, 1999b). In sharp contrast to the pre-1945 debates, the new conflict centered upon the Macedonians' claim that they are the only indigenous people of Macedonia and that they are the legitimate "owners" of Macedonia's soil (including the cultural legacy of the region). This new turn has had important consequences because the post-1945 "new" Macedonian Question is—at least for all practical purposes—no longer a geopolitical, territorial dispute, at least in the "realist" interpretation of these terms. On the contrary, thanks to the waves of immigrants in Australia, Canada, and the United States, the Macedonian issue has become a transnational symbolic conflict, a conflict involving Australian, Canadian, and U.S. citizens, who do not inhabit the region yet identify with each of the sides involved in the conflict.[45]

Moreover, these immigrant communities are intimately connected to the politics of their home countries. Of course, the long-distance nationalism of these transnational communities is not a phenomenon restricted to the Macedonian case. Examples abound, ranging from the involvement of U.S. Mexicans in Mexican politics to the political projects pursued by the U.S.-based Haitians in the 1990s (Basch et al., 1994). Yet, as critics have argued, these types of ties between immigrants and homelands are not entirely novel. On the contrary, there are plenty of examples of nineteenth- and early twentieth-century immigrants who were active participants in the nationalisms of the Old World. The Macedonian communities of Toronto and Australia (Petroff, 1995; Danforth, 2000) provide good examples of a long-distance nationalism (Anderson, 1993) that predated the arrival of the Internet, cell phones, and other post–World War II technological innovations.

Consequently, what is truly novel in the current phase of transnationalism is the *extent* to which national homelands are conceived as de-territorialized nations—that is, as nations that exist as locales or soils removed from their association to specific places. This feature is an extension of the broader experience of transnationalism as a cultural phenomenon (for further discussion, see Kennedy and Roudometof, 2002a). That is, in the current age of contemporary globalization, the experience of "place" is increasingly removed from its connection to a locale. On the contrary, the very nature of transnationalism assumes the possibility of people experiencing their connection to their place in a de-territorialized fashion. "Greece" or "Haiti" or "Macedonia" exist not only as real places, but also as "de-territorialized" places that can be experienced without physical presence into the specific region (Appadurai, 1995). In this sense, these de-territorialized nations are examples of the manner in which "community" is experienced in the post-modern universe of advanced industrial democracies.[46]

These transnational national communities are today often referred to as diasporas (Safran, 1991; Anthias, 1998)—an age-old term that has gained popularity in contemporary literature. But while the traditional diasporas of world history were groups of people dispersed and with no real prospect of returning to the homeland or connection to a state, the contemporary transnational communities are groups of people committed to the dissemi-nation of their own specific national project. In this regard, they stand in sharp contrast to the pre-modern diasporic communities (Roudometof, 2000b). Today's transnational national communities reflect the continuing importance of nations and nationalism in a globalized world. In sharp con-trast to the earlier projects of nation-formation, however, the transnational nationalism of the new immigrants is a nationalism that does not require a legal bond between the immigrants and their homelands.

In the case of the Macedonian diasporas, there are three distinct groups holding out different images of Macedonia. These are the Greek Macedonians, the Bulgarian Macedonians, and the post-1945 Macedonians (for a detailed presentation, see Danforth, 1995, 2000). This last group is by far the most recent addition to the list, as Greeks and Bulgarians have had transnational communities since the early twentieth century. In the pre-1945 period, the Bulgarian organizations of the United States were able to control the majority of Macedonian immigrants (Matzureff, 1978: 84–86; Mandatzis, 1997: 207–14). In fact, during the interwar period, the Greek government lobbied for the appointment of Athinagoras as the Archbishop of North and South America as a means of limiting the influence of the pro-Bulgarian organizations among the diaspora. The single largest Macedonian community of North America was located in the city of Toronto. It was frag-mented between Macedonians and Bulgarians in the 1930s and 1940s (Petroff, 1995: 147–65). The fragmentation was due to a number of rea-sons, including the Bulgarian government's post-1934 suppression of the VMRO, but also domestic factors, such as growing acculturation into the New World.

CONCLUSIONS

It is necessary perhaps to highlight the extent to which this brief overview of the development of Macedonian national identity should not be viewed as a final statement, but rather as a first attempt to move beyond the political partisanship of the Macedonian Question. I have tried to develop an alter-native narrative, whereby the articulation of national identity is viewed as a process and not as a quality inscribed permanently in the souls of the people. Such a perspective is helpful in providing for a third alternative between the

Greek (and Bulgarian) and Macedonian mutually exclusive viewpoints I reviewed in Chapter 3. In other words, while Macedonian national identity is of recent historical origin—and certainly does not go back to antiquity—its very novelty is not a factor contributing to lack of legitimacy. In this respect, Greek and Bulgarian arguments that assert that Macedonian identity is an "artificial" construction of the communist regime fail to come to terms with the critically important role of these two states in the marginalization of a portion of Macedonia's inhabitants and their eventual transformation into a modern nation. Obviously, my narrative also points out that the assertion that the Macedonians are Macedonia's only "native inhabitants" is also an exaggeration that fails to take into account the fact that only a portion of Slavic speakers in Macedonia identified themselves as Macedonians. Many others chose the Bulgarian or Greek label, and their choice should not be less acceptable because they did not adopt a Macedonian national identity.

The specifics of the narrative I have sought to provide in this chapter should be viewed as a starting point for further discussion and debate among the academic community. I have no doubt that future research will revise, update, and modify parts of the argument developed in this chapter. However, my goal has been to provide an outline that could be useful for future work, and not to provide the final word on this issue. Suffice to say, the persecution of the Slavo-Macedonian population was of central importance for the eventual articulation of Macedonian identity. The state-sponsored strategies of cultural homogenization pursued mainly by the Greek and Serb administrations during the interwar period were counterproductive. They led to the effective marginalization of the Slavo-Macedonians or Macedonian Slavs and to a strongly felt resentment against the state. During the interwar period, Bulgaria attempted to keep alive the pro-Bulgarian sentiments of a number of Slavo-Macedonians—indeed, the strong-arm policies of Greeks and Serbs aimed in many respects to counter whatever pro-Bulgarian sympathies existed among the Slavic population in their parts of Macedonia.

World War II offered the opportunity for yet another failed attempt by the Bulgarian nation-state to conquer Macedonia. Bulgaria was allied with the Axis forces and occupied most of its Macedonian *irredenta*—although a portion of Greek Macedonia remained under Italian and German control. For a second time in the span of only fifty years, control of the region became contested. Germans, Bulgarians, Italians, communist and right-wing partisans all struggled for control over Macedonia. For the Slavic population of Greek- and Serb-controlled Macedonia, it was the partisan forces (mostly, yet not exclusively communist) that eventually claimed the loyalty of the majority of the population.

The victory of the communists in Vardar Macedonia was associated with the proclamation of Macedonian independence and the open assertion of Macedonian national identity. This Macedonian national identity was cultivated in the pre-1945 period through a variety of cultural processes. First, the Bulgarian church struggle of the pre-1878 period raised the awareness of the Slavic Macedonians with regard to their own cultural distinctiveness. Still, the transition from the Ottoman model of confessional association into the model of the modern nation involved a choice among several competing sides. Serbs, Bulgarians, and Greeks all claimed the loyalty of Macedonia's Slavic-speaking inhabitants. Second, the emergence of the original, pre-1913 VMRO was an effort to develop a vehicle that would register the desires of the local peoples. However, the trials and tribulations of the original VMRO reveal the degree to which the solution to the Macedonian Question was colored by partisanship; the more left-wing forces opted for a federation and Macedonian independence, while the more right-wing forces were clearly more pro-Bulgarian. Third, as educational institutions gradually became more important and numerous throughout Macedonia, the significance of language as a cultural marker increased, while the significance of religion steadily declined. Hence, while in the pre-1913 period the Greeks claimed the loyalty of Macedonian Slavs on the basis of their affiliation with the Ecumenical Patriarchate, they were not able to continue to do so in the post-1913 period. Increasingly, language and loyalty to the state became intertwined. The Greek and Serb state-sponsored strategies of cultural homogenization signified the extent to which the two states failed to develop cultural and political models that would be based on civic criteria of inclusion—as opposed to criteria derived from language or culture.

It is clear that even in the pre-1945 period a large segment of Macedonia's Slavs declared themselves to be "Macedonians," although it would be completely premature to assume that this label stood for a national, as opposed to a regional identity. The transformation of the regional into a national label was the consequence of the state-sponsored policies of cultural homogenization pursued by Greece and Serbia. The Serbs' strategy backfired completely and the Yugoslav communists faced little resistance by the Serbs in creating a post-1945 Macedonian Republic. This stands in sharp contrast to the Serb resentment toward the creation of autonomous assemblies in Kosovo and Vojvodina. In contrast, the Greeks' strategy was far more successful, mainly because it involved massive population movements that completely altered the pre-1913 mixture of ethnic groups in post-1913 Greek Macedonia. However, in Northwestern Greek Macedonia a Slavic enclave was created, and the result was a collision between the local Slavo-Macedonians and the Greek state.

The post–World War II political mobilization of the Slavic Macedonians in Vardar and Aegean Macedonia offered the opportunity to express this resentment openly and to claim a separate status as a distinct nation. Still, this process involved the massive displacement of peoples, most of them from Northwestern Greek Macedonia, where the victory of right-wing Greek nationalists led to a massive exodus. The result was the creation of a political constituency for whom personal tragedy became, in effect, national history.

This transformation is reflected in the construction of the post-1945 Macedonian national narrative, already reviewed in Chapter 3. Instead of a territorial definition of the nation, the nation building of the People's Republic of Macedonia followed the very same cultural pattern of the Serbs, Bulgarians, and Greeks. In this fashion, the Macedonian national narrative was able to incorporate the Greek Civil War refugees, while it also made it possible to obtain recruits among the post-1945 diaspora communities.

As a result, the Macedonian saga entered a new phase of claims and counterclaims. However, in this latest round, the roles were reversed. While the cultural distinctiveness of Macedonians was negated in the pre-1945 period, the post-1945 Macedonian transnational nation-building fostered a romantic and nostalgic view of Macedonia, a viewpoint that called for the reunification of the pre-1913 Macedonia into a single state (see Map 1.1). Although the implementation of such a plan is unrealistic, its mere existence has been an important component that facilitated the articulation of Macedonian identity in the post-1945 period. It made it possible to connect people dispersed around the globe into a single transnational imagined community. As I have argued in Chapter 3, the articulation of this national narrative directly clashed with the older Bulgarian and Greek national narratives. Hence, the two states persisted in their formal negation of Macedonian national identity. This issue, however, is not restricted to the purely symbolic realm. The Macedonian nationalists, refugees, and other expatriates have sought to export their post-1945 recognition as a separate people back into interstate Balkan politics. For Greece and Bulgaria, recognition of Macedonian national identity raises the issue of Macedonian national minorities in their respective territories of Macedonia—or, to put it differently, a return to the disastrous interwar situation of claims and counterclaims, already reviewed in this chapter. The minority question will be discussed in detail in the next chapter.

NOTES

1. To cite one example, Abdolonyme Ubicini and Pavet de Courteille, in their *État présent de l'Empire Ottoman* (1876), estimated (among others) 1,000,000 Arabs, 13,500,000 Ottoman Turks, 220,000 Kutzo-Vlachs (Tsinsars), 1,200,000 Albanians, 1,000,000 Circassians, and 220,000 Tartars (quoted in Davison, 1977: 29). The presence of all these groups is confirmed; but the vexing problem is to combine the ethnic and religious breakdown in an accurate manner.

2. For a discussion, see Mihailidis (1998) and Friedman (1996). Friedman (1996: 85) presents a very useful table combining different estimates of the ethnic composition of the population of Ottoman Macedonia, and the table clearly shows the extent to which nationalist biases influenced statistics and related material about the region. As Lithoxoou (1992) argues, with the single exception of the 1905 Ottoman census, all other statistical information should be viewed with great suspicion. Unfortunately, as Lithoxoou admits, there are different published accounts of the

1905 census, thereby raising the issue of whether these results were tampered with at the time.

3. The 1905 Ottoman statistics recorded only two of the three provinces (*vilayets*) of Ottoman Macedonia (see Karpat, 1985: 166–67). Moreover, various statistics produced by Greeks, Serbs, and Bulgarians counted the people of their own "nationality" with mixed criteria. Bulgarians used language because in so doing they maximized the number of "Bulgarians," while Greeks used affiliation with the Ecumenical Patriarchate, thereby producing a "Greek" population. In 1904, following the failed 1903 Ilinden Uprising, the Ottomans conducted a census that did take into account both religion and language. Results published in different sources appear to be inconsistent, see Lithoxoou (1992: 41–44). However, this census was probably the most reliable among the various statistics of Macedonia's ethnological composition published in the first half of the twentieth century. According to the census results, there were more Christians who sided with the Patriarchate than with the Bulgarian Exarchate. However, a large number of the Patriarchists spoke "Bulgarian" as their native tongue. The Greek-speaking population in the three provinces that made up Ottoman Macedonia was approximately 10% of the total population.

4. The discussion in the remainder of this subsection and the next section of this chapter relies heavily on Roudometof (2001: 133–46).

5. Jews and Greeks dominated in many cities. Gagauzes (Turkish-speaking Christians), Circassians, Turks, Pomaks (Bulgarian-speaking Muslims), Armenians, Gypsies, Hellenized Vlachs, Romanian-speaking Vlachs, and Catholic Bulgarians were all present in these territories. Even the province (*vilayet*) of Danube (i.e., northern Bulgaria), where ethnic Bulgarians predominated, was ethnically diverse (Todorov, 1969; Ashley, 1985).

6. Nicoloff (1987: 50–53), Meininger (1970: 129–30) and McDermott (1962: 162–67). On the plebiscites, see Genchev (1977: 117), Tzvetkov (1993 vol. 1: 486), and Kolev (1991: 42). Additional regions occasionally joined the church council; for example, representatives from twenty-two counties and the Nevrokop region attended the 1871 church council, although some of them were still formally under Patriarchal jurisdiction. Initially the Exarchate included sixteen dioceses. Plebiscites held in contested territories (Skopje and Ohrid) in 1874 produced results in favor of the Exarchate, leading to the Ottomans confirming the appointment of Bulgarian bishops in the two towns.

7. As Ivan Mihailov, one of the leaders of the interwar pro-Bulgarian VMRO, has put it: "Until 1878 there existed no Macedonian question; there was only the problem of the Bulgarians as a whole" (Mihailov, 1950: 64).

8. Vakalopoulos (1988: 40–41). See Gounaris (1996) for further discussion on the interplay among class, ethnicity, religion, and support for a particular side. Most foreign observers confirmed that for the majority of the peasantry it was confessional rather than national identity that represented the most significant cultural marker. For some characteristic statements, see Vermeulen (1984), Kofos (1964: 12–13, 24), and Georgeoff (1973).

9. Despite the official Greek and Bulgarian position about the nonexistent status of a Macedonian language, there are a considerable number of intellectuals over the last two centuries who have recognized the Macedonian language as distinct from Bulgarian (for a list, see Kostopoulos, 2000: 37–45). As the Macedonian authors

have insisted, the language described as "Bulgarian" in the *Tetraglosson Lexicon* of Daniil of Moschopolis (1794) is the dialect of Ohrid. This language was described as "Bulgarian" at the time, and the differentiation between the two was impossible up until modern Bulgaria became an autonomous state and began the codification of the Bulgarian language.

10. The editors of the journal were persecuted because their orthographical reforms were deemed suspicious by the Bulgarian authorities. However, the editors protested against this interpretation. They argued that "a mere comparison of those ethnographic features which characterize the Macedonians . . . is enough to prove and to convince everybody that the nationality of the Macedonians cannot be anything except Bulgarian" (quoted in McDermott, 1978: 86).

11. The Greek guerrillas (or *Makedonomachoi* in Greek) became legendary heroes of the struggle for national integration. The officers who fought in Macedonia between 1903 and 1908 were idolized by their contemporaries. For a penetrating analysis, see Basil Gounaris (1997).

12. In 1908, Allen Upward (1908: 204–05) reported that the local peasantry referred to their language as "makedonski"—and not Bulgarian, as his interpreter translated it. Additional examples also abound in the travelers' literature. The employment of a different linguistic label does suggest the initial stirrings of a cultural differentiation. Still, given the general confusion during that period, it is impossible to determine whether the label has a regional or a national connotation. Contemporary Macedonian scholars would invariably decode the statements adopting the latter interpretation, while Bulgarians would decode it adopting the former.

13. Originally, the organization was an offshoot of the Bulgarian national movement and its earliest statute (dating from 1896) refers only to the "Bulgarian population" and stipulates that only a Bulgarian could become a member. By 1902 such qualifications were dropped and the organization begun assuming a more separatist stand (Adanir, 1992: 172–73). For further discussion on the historiography on this subject, see Lange-Akhund (1998: 38–39).

14. It is necessary perhaps to clarify the ambiguities surrounding the concept of autonomy. Autonomy could be interpreted in a two-fold way. On the one hand, it could be self-government within the Empire's framework. On the other hand, it could take the form of establishing an autonomous principality—similar to Eastern Romilia, which was unified with Bulgaria in 1885 thanks to a bloodless coup (Matzureff, 1978: 65). Consequently, Bulgarian nationalists developed the view that an autonomous Macedonia could eventually lead to Bulgaria realizing the boundaries of the 1878 San Stefano Treaty.

15. The nine articles of the agreement are reproduced in Lange-Akhund (1998: 142–43). The reform program introduced international representatives and military officers in Ottoman Macedonia. Their goal was to preserve the peace in the province by modernizing Ottoman administration. Not surprisingly, the Ottomans viewed the program as a further humiliation. Its implementation drew sharp criticism by the Ottoman officers, and it was one of the prime reasons for the 1908 Young Turk revolution.

16. Misirkov was a teacher in the school in Bitola (Monastir), the main commercial town in western Macedonia. After the publication of his book, he dropped his advocacy of Macedonian separatism and wrote pro-Bulgarian articles (Matzureff, 1978: 71). It was only after the end of World War I that Misirkov resurrected the

idea of Macedonian nationality—at a time that it was bound to receive a much more favorable reaction by the public.

17. Dakin (1966) represents the traditional perspective of the Greek historiography. From within this perspective, the Greek military bands protected the Greek villagers from the intimidation and violence of the Bulgarian gangs. For a recently published "heretical" perspective, see Lithoxoou (1998). Lithoxoou turns the traditional Greek perspective on its head, suggesting that the Greek bands were conducting an "anti-Macedonian" struggle (instead of a "Macedonian" struggle as the traditional Greek historiography maintains). Still, it is highly unlikely that these bands of brigands could be classified into "heroes" and "villains." As Koliopoulos (1999: 22) writes, such bands frequently extracted declarations of loyalty through the threat of violence, rendering such statements completely meaningless for any use other than nationalist propaganda.

18. Miller (1936: 476) describes additional examples that illustrate the sudden feelings of unity throughout the Ottoman Empire. In the city of Serres (in Ottoman Macedonia), the president of the Bulgarian Committee embraced the Greek Archbishop. In the neighboring city of Drama the revolutionary officers imprisoned a Turk for insulting a Christian. In an Armenian cemetery, Turks and Armenians listened to prayers offered by their respective priests for the victims of the Armenian massacres of the 1890s. Finally, the Bulgarian and Greek paramilitary bands (in Ottoman Macedonia) were disbanded.

19. For details, see Roudometof (2001: 75–95). The federalists demanded that the Slavic schools be placed outside the jurisdiction of the Bulgarian Exarchate. They recommended that the schools be placed under the control of the local authorities and teach the local (i.e., Slavo-Macedonian or Macedonian) language (Swire, 1939: 112).

20. Following his 1896 visit to Constantinople, Prince Ferdinand—overtaken by romantic nationalism—came to think that one day he might enter Constantinople and become heir to the Byzantine emperors (Constant, 1980: 180). During the first Balkan war (1912), the military (under Ferdinand's control) acted independently from the civilian government. Thus, after its initial victories in Thrace, it followed Ferdinand's plan to conquer Constantinople. But after their initial defeats, the Ottoman forces regrouped in Chataldzha, which was the last line of defense before Constantinople. Ferdinand ordered the offensive against Chataldzha, but poor communications, a cholera epidemic, and Ottoman fortifications proved too much for the Bulgarian army. The attack failed and further peace negotiations were subsequently plagued by the discord between Bulgarian military and civilian authorities. See Hall (1989) on the civil-military conflict; see Constant (1980: 254–74) for Ferdinand's plans and the diplomatic intrigues associated with them; and Crampton (1983: 401–27) for a discussion of the military and diplomatic aspects of the Balkan wars.

21. The Macedonian sources quoted by Rossos (1991: 285) estimate 240,000 Macedonians (for a similar estimate, see Ortakovski, 2000: 94). If this figure provides the Macedonians' interpretation of the statistical data, then it is worth pointing out that Greek and Macedonian estimates are not too far apart—contrary to the conventional wisdom in the literature. The difference between the GDM estimate and Rossos's figures is close to 80,000. Further research and comparison of the different results could help the researchers to reach some kind of unanimity on the

figures—provided that Greek and Macedonian academics decide to cooperate and not to play into the hands of their respective nationalists.

22. Although the total number of this population has been subject to an extensive debate, it is probably correct to assume that, on the eve of the Balkan wars of 1912–13, the total number of Exarchist and Patriarchist Slavic speakers in what became post-1913 Greek Macedonia was close to 250,000 (Koliopoulos, 1999: 28).

23. Koliopoulos (1999: 29–39) provides an overview of the population movements. As with all discussions of this issue it is impossible to have a completely accurate picture, mainly because people crossed state borders repeatedly and warfare led to frequent changes in the borders. Koliopoulos (1999: 35) estimates the Slav Macedonians who left for Bulgaria to be 120,000. This figure in all likelihood includes not just post-1919 migration but also those who fled during the 1910s.

24. As Verdery (1994) suggests, ethnic identities develop from national identities and not the other way around, because the homogenizing efforts of the nation-state enhance the visibility or difference of the nonconforming Other.

25. The pastoral lifestyle of earlier periods was an important factor in all of this. The decline of this lifestyle and the scarcity of resources fostered the enrollment of young men from pastoral nomad families into bands of brigands (Koliopoulos, 1999: 7–8). During the interwar period, Greek sociologist Kostas Karavidas (1931) wrote a penetrating analysis that recognized the importance of the family structure for cultural reproduction. He suggested that institutions such as schools were totally inadequate for the purposes for acculturation. In his view, the necessary ingredient for successful acculturation was the breakdown of the traditional family structure.

26. The local branch of the People's Party was the Macedonian Union of Stathis Gotzamanis. This party gained considerable support among the local people in 1935 and 1936 (Gounaris, 1997b: 104; Kostopoulos, 2000: 158–60). The party's slogan "Macedonia to the Macedonians" had a dual audience as it appealed both to Macedonian Slavs as well as Greek Macedonians who despised the centralized state of Athens.

27. In 1933, the Comintern and the Bulgarian Communist Party adopted formally the line that the Macedonian people were oppressed by the Balkan nation-states and that the solution to the Macedonian national question was the recognition of a separate Macedonian nation (Matzureff, 1978: 109–13).

28. Results reported by Kostopoulos (2000: 152). The Greek Communist Party's position (from 1924 to 1935) in favor of a "united and independent Macedonia" led many young people to identify with the party and hence turn themselves into "voulgarocoumonistes" (Bulgaro-Communists), a "special" category of communists (Koliopoulos 1994: 46–47), oddly combining a pre-1913 enemy (Bulgarians) and a 1930s enemy (communists). To be a communist and a Macedonian Slav implied—almost automatically—that one would be classified as a secessionist, as a local informant told Karakasidou (1993b: 453).

29. The collaboration between communists and Slavo-Macedonians in the interwar period was strengthened by the fact that the two groups were among those persecuted by the state. During the 1928–32 Liberal cabinet, the earlier fear of communism was translated into action through legislation that penalized the open discussion of communist ideas (known as the "Idonymon"). By 1932, the law led to more than 11,000 arrests (Mazower, 1997: 139).

30. The situation was more pronounced in the countryside than in the cities where even in Florina there were enough Greek speakers. In a survey of the ninety-three villages of the Florina prefecture performed by the Perfect of Florina Athanasios Souliotis-Nikolaidis in 1935, Greek speakers populated none of the villages exclusively. On the contrary, 58.7% were populated by Slavic speakers with a "foreign morale" and 41.3% by "foreign speakers" with pro-Greek morale (Lithoxoou, 1992; Karakasidou, 2000a: 88).

31. In 1925, the Slav Macedonian villagers of Meliti asked to become subjects of the Serb king when Greek refugees moved into the village and took over formerly Ottoman lands (Koliopoulos, 1999: 44). This affair led to a short-lived attempt by Serbia to force Greece to recognize a Serb minority in northern Greece. For details, see Mihailidis (1995). A number of families were, as a matter of fact, allowed to move across the border into Serb-controlled Vardar Macedonia. When the Greek government of General Pangalos signed an agreement with the Serb-Croat Kingdom (August 17, 1926), it granted Serbia the much-sought free trade zone on the port of Thessaloniki but also the management of the railroad from Thessaloniki to Belgrade. The agreement also recognized a Serbian minority in Greece. The discontent with the government's decision led to a coup that overthrew Pangalos' government, and in 1927 the Parliament formally refused to ratify the agreement.

32. For an overview of these protests, see Mihailidis (1996: 339). The Abecedar protests also marked a first appearance of right-wing pro-fascist groups in interwar Greece (Kostopoulos, 2000: 104). These groups would grow in strength in the following years and culminate in the state-sponsored organizations of the right-wing semi-fascist Metaxas dictatorship (1936–40). In 1931–32 the rise of right-wing fascist organizations was exemplified by the meteoric rise of the National Union of Greece (*Ethniki Enosis Ellados* or EEE), an organization responsible for the arson of a Jewish neighborhood in Thessaloniki. By 1932 the organization had 7,000 members and nineteen chapters in Greek Macedonia (out of a total of thirty-two chapters nationwide) (Kostopoulos, 2000: 124). In 1933 the EEE members mirrored Mussolini's march to Rome by staging a march of 3,000 members to Athens (Kostopoulos, 2000: 126). The organization included former guerrilla fighters and was strengthened by the combination of anti-communist and pro-nationalist rhetoric. Other organizations, such as the Florina-based association "Aristotelis," were also instituted in the early 1930s. Under the Metaxas dictatorship, other semi-official organizations arose, such as the boy scouts and the National Youth Organization (*Ethniki Organosi Neoleas* or EON).

33. In 1926, the Greek government issued a decree instituting name changes for some 440 villages and municipalities; in 1927 an additional 835 places were given new names; and in 1928, 212 more places assumed their new "Greek" names (Kostopoulos, 2000: 142). Bulgaria and Serbia directly connected this action to the Greek state's desire to deal effectively with their claims, and to display a more ethnically homogeneous image toward the League of Nations.

34. This state oppression and violent tactics of the period have been extensively documented. See Momiroski (1993), Carabot (1997), Karakasidou (1993a; 2000a), Pribichevich (1982) and, for a brief overview, Poulton (1989). See Kostopoulos (2000) for an extremely graphic and thick description of the practices employed at the time. Indeed, Kostopoulos's description coincides with the accounts collected by Danforth (1995) in his interviews with Slavic Macedonians in Australia.

35. In the interwar period, Misirkov's viewpoint began to gain acceptance among young Macedonian intellectuals. See Rossos (1995: 244–47) for a discussion of their activities in the interwar period. Banac (1984: 327) remarks that the Macedonians "were Bulgars in struggles against Serbian and Greek hegemonism, but within the Bulgar world, they were increasingly becoming exclusive Macedonians." Rossos (1995: 251) concurs and points out that the majority of the Macedonian intelligentsia of the period identified with the agenda of the VMRO-United and its call for a united Macedonia in the context of a Balkan federation.

36. According to Troebst (1994: 108), the Yugoslav communists' decision to facilitate Macedonian nation-building was based on the following reasons: first, it facilitated control of the region by Belgrade; second, Bulgarian claims were weakened; and third, it allowed Yugoslav communists to put forward claims vis-à-vis Greek and Bulgarian Macedonia.

37. Between 1942 and 1944 close to 70,000–90,000 people registered with the pro-Bulgarian Club set up in Thessaloniki, although the reasons that motivated the people to do so might range from sincere belief to sheer opportunism (Kostopoulos, 2000: 188). Koliopoulos (1994) suggests that the collaboration of the peasants with the Germans, Italians, and Bulgarians was determined by the geopolitical position of each village. Depending upon whether their village was vulnerable to attack by the Greek communist guerrillas (ELAS) or the occupation forces, the peasants would opt to support the side in relation to which they were most vulnerable. When the Greek communists created the SNOF, many of the former collaborators enlisted in the new unit. In both cases, the attempt was to promise "freedom" (autonomy or independence) to the formerly persecuted Slavic minority as a means of gaining its support. Karakasidou (1993b) also considers the policy of the Greek communists vis-à-vis the minority population in the 1930s and 1940s as opportunistic.

38. There was considerable internal infighting between Yugoslav and Bulgarian communists who competed for the administrative control over the western part of Macedonia. For a review of the specifics, see Matzureff (1978: 117–30).

39. Between 1947 and 1949 the Slavic Macedonian support for the communists was massive; and the majority of the people came from the minority regions of Northwestern Greek Macedonia (Kostopoulos, 2000: 204–5). Still, there were minority members who opted for neutrality and who supported the right-wing pro-Bulgarian VMRO or kept in touch with right-wing diaspora organizations. The Greek communists employed the tactic of guerrilla warfare and were never able to transform their forces into a regular army (Iatrides, 1981b).

40. By 1948, the Yugoslavs had delivered 35,000 rifles, 3,500 machine guns, 2,000 German bazookas, 7,000 antitank guns, and 10,000 field mines to the Greek communist forces. They also provided clothing for 12,000 men and thirty wagons of food (Banac, 1987: 35).

41. For the most recent synthesis, see Koliopoulos (1999). The field is clearly the new frontier of Greek historiography and has attracted growing attention in the last few decades. See Iatrides (1981a), Baerentzen, Iatrides, and Smith (1987), Iatrides and Wrigley (1995), Close (1995), and Mazower (2000). Although closely related to the Macedonian Question, the topic of the Greek Civil War is clearly a different question. Moreover, space considerations clearly suggest that it cannot be addressed in this chapter.

42. According to Perry (1992: 36) there are 80,000 to 100,000 refugees from the Greek civil war in the territory of Skopje. Another estimate gives a more conservative number of 30,000 to 40,000 (Karakasidou 1993a: 12). Writing more than three decades ago, Kofos (1962: 384) also estimated the number of refugees at 30,000 to 35,000. Koliopoulos (1999) lists a wide range of estimates, pointing out that, even at the end of the Greek Civil War, it was impossible for the contemporaries to have an accurate count.

43. See Ortakovski (2000: 178–79) for brief overview of a number of estimates that range from 10,000 to 50,000 (U.S. Department of State, 1991) to 350,000 (by Macedonian nationalists). The U.S. State Department's Country Reports on Human Rights of the last decade (1990–1995) estimate 10,000 to 50,000 people, a figure corroborated by Poulton (1991) and the Minority Rights Group (1990). Poulton (1991) considers the Macedonian minority in Greece as one that has been practically assimilated into Hellenism (Greek Macedonia has more than 2,000,000 inhabitants). Since the Greek censuses do not offer information regarding ethnic affiliation, these numbers are to a considerable extent speculative. The 1991 report was contested by the Greek government, which claimed that such a group (i.e., the Macedonians) does not exist.

44. Despite the active acculturation campaign that persisted for most of the twentieth century, the decline of this minority was eventually due to the gradual dissolution of the extended family structure. While in 1945 the extended families controlled 15.5% of agricultural units in Florina, there is but one such family left in the region in the 1990s (Kostopoulos, 2000: 289).

45. It is important to place these developments within the context of the broader global trends. The construction of Macedonian transnational national communities (Danforth, 1995; Hill, 1989) is a feature closely connected with the articulation of transnationalism as a highly visible facet of the post-1945 phase of contemporary globalization (Albrow, 1997; Held et al., 1999). During the 1990s, transnationalism has become a new frontier of research on international migration (Schiller et al., 1992; Schiller 1995; Smith and Guarnizo, 1999; Portes, 2000). The new research agenda on transnationalism has stressed the extent to which new immigrant communities increasingly maintain ties with their original homelands. They act as intermediaries between host and home societies; they support through their remittances the local economy back home; they also use their own niche in the division of labor to take advantage of opportunities for improving their economic position. These communities provide examples of "globalization from below" and counteract the "globalization from above" (e.g., NAFTA, EU, and the big corporate mergers of the 1990s).

46. Indeed, the transnational national communities of Kurds, Armenians, Palestinians, Greeks, and Macedonians are among the communities reflexively constructed by groups throughout the globe. Other examples include the managerial cosmopolitan groups, tourists, subcultures connected through taste and music, and so on (for examples, see the essays in Kennedy and Roudometof, 2002b).

Chapter 5

The Question of Macedonian Minorities in the Southern Balkans

We, the former child refugees from the Aegean part of Macedonia, present citizens and residents of Australia . . . have been denied the right to return to our homeland by successive Greek regimes on account of the preservation and promotion of our Macedonian identity. We, the innocent victims of that war, look back solemnly to that tragedy in memory of the catastrophe which affected thousands of children, which wrote thousands of sad pages in our national and personal history, in order that it never be forgotten.

> Declaration of the Child Refugees (Association of Refugee
> Children, 1995: 185) proclaimed at the first gathering
> in Australia of the child refugees from the Aegean part
> of Macedonia, Melbourne, Australia, 10–12 January 1992

From the beginning, I approached the Skopje question in its true dimension. . . . What preoccupied me . . . was not the name of this state. . . . The problem was to [avoid the creation of] . . . a second minority issue in the region of western Macedonia. . . . For me, the ultimate target has always been for the Republic [of Macedonia] to declare that there is no Slavo-Macedonian minority in Greece and to agree through international treaties that it will cease any irredentist propaganda against the Greek state. . . . This was the centerpiece of the Athens-Skopje dispute.

> Constantinos Mitsotakis, Greek Prime Minister 1990–93
> (in Mitsotakis, 1995: 3, Greek in the original)

In this chapter, I discuss the dynamics of the minority question in the southern Balkans, and then focus more specifically on the issue of Macedonian national minorities in Greece and Bulgaria.[1] The critically important Albanian question is explored in the next chapter. During the 1980s and 1990s Macedonian human rights activists have been quite vocal in their protests to a variety of international forums and raised the issue of Macedonian national minorities in the two Balkan states. To understand the general context of these issues, it is necessary to explain both the origins of this transnational protest movement, as well as the circumstances surrounding the understanding of the minority question in the Balkans. Quite simply, over the last fifty years the Balkan nation-states have not been among the champions of the international human rights movements and have been consistently suspicious of any kind of "minority talk." In this regard, the Balkan nation-states' rationale has been formulated within the framework of pre–World War II Europe. However, the new post-1945 international movements toward universal human rights and the implementation of international treaties limiting state sovereignty over such matters require that the Balkan nation-states adjust their policies according to the new international standards. This is an ongoing process in states like Bulgaria and Greece—and in many respects it is a necessity for all Eastern European countries that want to become members of the European Union.

But such policies go beyond simple matters of changing bureaucratic rules and making other changes in the formal aspects of legislation. On the contrary, the demand for these changes is closely connected with demands for the establishment of civic ties based on formal membership to a state as opposed to ties based on cultural membership to a nation. The Balkan nation-states have built their public personas on the basis of the discourse of nationhood rather than citizenship (Roudometof, 2001), and therefore they stress cultural rather than civic inclusion as a prerequisite for acceptance into their respective national communities. The contemporary debates on minorities in these states are but a reflection of a debate about broader issues of national self-image and understanding of what it means to be a member of the Greek (or Bulgarian or Serb or Macedonian) nation.

OF ETHNIC GROUPS AND NATIONAL MINORITIES: DILEMMAS OF CONTEMPORARY SCHOLARSHIP

As I have already discussed in Chapter 4, the post–World War II immigration of southeastern European peasantry into the Western democracies of Australia, Canada, and the United States has had a profound effect upon the construction of the post-1945 Macedonian nation. The new immigrants became in varying degrees incorporated into either the Greek-Macedonian or the Macedonian transnational national communities, thereby fracturing communal ties with their former village neighbors and even, in certain cases, with family members (for a review of such cases, see Danforth, 1995: 185–247).

Moreover, the new immigrants were absorbed and incorporated into Western societies at that point in time when acculturation gave way to pluralism—eventually becoming what today is conventionally referred to as multiculturalism (Taylor, 1992). This shift has had important repercussions for immigrant identity because it implied the acceptance of a hyphenated or ethnic identity that would complement their identity as Australians, Canadians, or Americans. Unlike the Balkan context, their ethnic identity was no longer opposed to the civic identity of their host societies. The Macedonians who immigrated into these states could now openly claim their own ethnic identity. Indeed, the "discovery" of Macedonians in Western societies took place in the context of urban ethnography (see, for example, Herman, 1978; Petroff, 1995; Schwartz, 1995, 1997, 2000; Danforth, 1995, 2000). The classification of Macedonians as an "ethnicity" is a prime example of the manner in which particularistic distinctions of class, color, and culture are dealt with in advanced industrial democracies (Hobsbawm, 1996).[2] The effects of continuing acculturation into the Greek (and Bulgarian) nations versus the construction and reproduction of Macedonian ethnicity by New World immigrants created contradictions that cut across families and individual biographies. For example, Petroff (1995: 174) conveys the following story about the family members of Gina Petroff, a Macedonian who immigrated to Canada prior to World War II:

Consider the case of Gina Petroff, one of those brides sent to Toronto after the First World War from the village of Bobista. Her nephews arrived in Toronto well after the Second World War. They were born and raised in her village of origin. As young men, they fulfilled their military obligations in the Greek army. In Toronto, they opened a restaurant and took wives. Gina attended the weddings, which were held in the Greek Orthodox Church. She could not understand the priest but knew the ritual structure. Greek became the working language of her nephews' Canadian households. They spoke Macedonian to their aunt out of courtesy, but also as the only way to communicate with her. They identified themselves as Greek Macedonians, something that Gina continued to find a contradiction in terms. The New World ethnicity created by Gina Petroff and her generation has been superseded by an Old World national identity.

However, the notion of Macedonians as an ethnic group was eventually transferred from the context of the Western societies (such as Canada, Australia, and the United States) back into the Balkan context. This introduction of the ethnic label back into the Balkan context is largely responsible for the characterization of Macedonians as an ethnic group (within Bulgaria and Greece). This classification is not consistent with the manner in which national identity has been received and interpreted within the Balkan context. In particular, the assumption of a multicultural society consisting of a number of different ethnic groups that coexist within a democratic polity is but a reflection of the post-1960 U.S.-inspired multicultural project.

Within the Balkan context, "ethnicity" is frequently considered identical with "nationality," and the two become closely intertwined as state policy consistently conceives of the nation as a single ethnic community. Enshrined in national constitutions (Hayden, 1992b), this generalized belief has achieved the status of canonical truth. For example, until the 1990s, the terms "ethnic" and "national" were routinely conflated in modern Greek. To date, the very employment of the Greek word for "ethnic" (*ethnotikos*) remains confined to intellectuals, ministers, and other members of the elite with sufficient knowledge of the significance of this division.

Macedonian authors are also explicit in their characterization of Macedonians in the neighboring countries as "national minorities"—that is, as members of the Macedonian nation that live outside the Macedonian nation-state's boundaries. For example, Vladimir Ortakovski (2000) refers to Macedonian national minorities in Albania, Bulgaria, and Greece. Ortakovski, professor of Sociology and Criminology at SS Cyril and Methodius University at Skopje, worked in the Ministry of International Affairs (1978–84) and also served as a deputy minister for Science (1993–96). His employment of the term is not a slip of the tongue; rather it is exemplary of a viewpoint shared widely among the peoples and the intelligentsia of the Balkan nation-states.

In contrast, from the 1960s onward, Western democracies (the United States, Canada, Australia) have endorsed multiculturalism as a new means of incorporating unassimilated citizens into their own nations (Taylor, 1992; Walzer, 1994). Although multiculturalism is certainly contested within these states, its institutionalization has meant that "ethnicity" has become increasingly decoupled from citizenship. The post–World War II, UN-sponsored trend toward the standardization of human rights on a global basis offered an opportunity to extend this tendency into the international domain, hence turning it into a late twentieth-century "standard of civilization" (Gong, 1984; Burgess, 1996) according to which peripheral, less advanced societies are judged.

As a result of this gap between global standards and local state-sponsored tradition, anthropological accounts have been sometimes unwillingly misleading. For example, Loring Danforth (1995) describes the situation in northwestern Greek Macedonia as follows:

In the district of Florina, as in other parts of Macedonia, the most important categories people use to classify one another are ethnic categories. Of the 53,000 inhabitants of the district of Florina the largest group, 65 percent according to one Greek estimate, refer to themselves as "locals," or "local Macedonians." In addition to Greek, most of these local Macedonians speak Macedonian. They often refer to this 'other' language not as "Macedonian," but rather as "our language" . . . or the "local language." These are the people Greek scholars refer to as "bilingual" or "Slavic-speaking Greeks." The majority of these local Macedonians has been fully

Hellenized and has a Greek national identity. They say that they are Macedonians *and* Greeks; they are Greek-Macedonians. Some, however, do *not* have a Greek national identity. They have a Macedonian national identity; they say that they are Macedonians and *not* Greeks. (Danforth, 1995: 116–17, emphasis in the original, footnotes omitted)

The above description is highly problematic. But it is not the specifics in the region of Florina that are in any way contested. Rather, it is the manner in which Danforth moves back and forth from generalizations that pertain to the district of Florina to generalizations that pertain to the entire region of Greek Macedonia. With one single blanket statement ("as in other parts of Macedonia"), he alludes that the description of the ethnological composition of Florina is exemplary of the situation in the rest of Greek Macedonia.[3] Moreover, he claims that the "most important categories" in use *throughout* Greek Macedonia are ethnic categories.

What is left outside of this description is the contextual basis of the distinctions people make to differentiate among different groups of people who inhabit the region—already discussed in Chapter 4. That is, Danforth does not mention that the distinction between locals (*dopii*) and refugees is a distinction that emerged in the aftermath of the resettlement of Greek-Orthodox refugees from Asia Minor into Greek Macedonia (Karakasidou, 1997: 152–54). As such, the distinction does not necessarily refer to people of a different "ethnicity." However, Danforth (1995: 7) has lifted the term "locals" from its contextual basis and transformed it into a broader analytical category that he is employing to classify the peoples of Macedonia.[4]

None of this, of course, invalidates Danforth's description of the situation in Florina, where these labels survive to this day and where the distinction between "local" and "refugee" overlaps (to differing degrees) with the distinction between Slavic speakers (or ethnic Macedonians) and Greeks. But this is a feature specific to the district of Florina (and to varying degrees to a few more neighboring districts in northwestern Greek Macedonia). In other words, what is missing from Danforth's description is an acknowledgment and a discussion of the different regional patterns of groups inhabiting throughout Greek Macedonia.[5] As shown in Chapter 4, in the aftermath of all the population movements, the majority of Slavic Macedonians used to inhabit northwestern Greek Macedonia—at least until the Greek Civil War. When the guerrilla fighters withdrew behind the "iron curtain" of the Cold War, they left behind them property, relatives, and their original places of birth. The Greek right-wing nationalist state of the 1950s and 1960s proceeded to confiscate their property, stripped them of their Greek citizenship, and practically took every action possible to make sure that they would never return back to Greece. It should be pointed out that these measures where not aimed exclusively against the Slavo-Macedonians—for the Greek communists were victims of these measures, too (Alivizatos, 1981).

In the literature produced by the people who have been participants in what Danforth (1995) calls the "Macedonian human rights movement," the issue of equal rights for the Macedonians of Greece is routinely confused with the issue of human rights for those who fled Greece in the aftermath of the Greek Civil War (1944–49).[6] Many of these approximately 30,000 to 40,000 refugees, currently residing in FYROM (but also in Canada or Australia), wish to be able to return to their original places of birth in Greece. In 1947 those who had fought against the government in the Greek Civil War and had fled Greece were deprived of their citizenship and their property.[7] When laws were enacted in 1982 and 1985 allowing the civil war refugees in the communist countries to return to Greece and reclaim their property, it was specified that only those who were "Greek by *genos*" (i.e., ethnic Greeks) would be allowed to benefit from this law (Hristov, 1994:9). The Greek state rejects the applications of those who declare themselves to be Macedonians; as a result, family members continue to be separated almost half a century after the civil war. By preventing the return of these refugees, the Greek state avoids the consolidation of a Macedonian national minority in northern Greece. For Macedonian human rights advocates, the existing minority in northern Greece and the refugees who are not allowed to return to their homes are Macedonians whose human rights are violated. As a matter of fact, the 1992 Declaration of the Child Refugees, quoted at the beginning of this chapter, speaks volumes about the feelings of the Australians of Macedonian descent. Not surprisingly, successive Greek governments have refused to accept these demands—and the statement by former Greek Prime Minister Constantinos Mitsotakis reveals the Greek state's preoccupation with this issue.

Recent political and cultural mobilizations by human rights activists aim at gaining recognition of the minority as a Macedonian national minority. The evolution of the pro-Macedonian movement is discussed later on in this chapter. Distinguishing between the refugees and immigrants, on the one hand, and the actual inhabitants of Greek Macedonia, on the other hand, helps clarify some of the confusion created in journalistic accounts and the popular press. However, it is important to note that the question of Macedonian minorities has not been a topic raised exclusively by expatriates. As Danforth (1995) points out in his discussion of the Macedonian human rights movement, a pro-Macedonian minority group does exist in the region of Florina. In 1993, anthropologist Riki Van Boeschoten carried out a survey of ethnic groups among the rural population of Florina. According to the survey, 64% of the rural inhabitants of the region are Slavic speakers—distributed in forty-three Slavic-speaking villages and twenty-nine mixed villages (Van Boeschoten, 2000: 32).

Van Boeshoten (2000: 33–38) highlights the overlapping lines between class and ethnicity. By and large, the Slav speakers are engaged in small-scale agriculture and animal husbandry, and very few of them are employed in the high-status civil sector positions. On the contrary, Vlachs and refugees are much better off, in part because of their access to state employment but also because of their better education. These societal cleavages have to be situated in the context of the regional economy. This district is one of the most isolated and less developed areas of Greece and is quite different from the rest of Greek Macedonia. Van Boeshoten's study documents the remnants of the social cleavages that led to the explosive situation in northwestern Macedonia during the interwar period—reviewed in Chapter 4.

Therefore, reality is at odds with the proclamations of Greek officials and journalists who have been all too eager to declare that not a single Macedonian exists in Greece.[8] Throughout the 1949–74 period, both the right-wing nationalist regime of the post-1945 period and the 1967–74 military dictatorship persisted in denying the existence of a Macedonian minority group.[9] The extent to which this group should be viewed as a "national minority" is a matter of politics—for the term itself is politically laden.

Consequently, in order to avoid the problems associated with the conceptual ambiguities produced by the uncritical employment of labels—such as "local Macedonians," "ethnic groups" or "national minorities"—into contexts quite different from those where these terms originated, it is necessary to define the terms in a careful and less nationalistic fashion. To begin with, I would define a *minority group* as a group using cultural markers (such as language or religion) to distinguish itself from majority outsiders (Barth, 1969). In contrast, a *national minority* establishes itself as such through an identification of its members with cultural symbols that belong to an "imagined community" living outside the boundaries of the particular nation-state the minority inhabits (Brubaker, 1995). Political mobilization is a requirement for the transformation of a minority group into a national minority. The characterization of a minority group as a national minority offers the possibility of outside intervention regarding this group's rights. Defining the terms in this fashion allows one to avoid the errors of assuming a naïvely realist position, namely the thesis that people are "naturally" members of groups and that the issue is merely one of properly recording their affiliation.

In the Balkan context, proclaiming a group to be a "national minority" is viewed as an immediate threat to state sovereignty. This association is routinely made by politicians, journalists, and the public at large—and this association rests in large part on the memories of the interwar period, when the issue of national minorities was employed as a means for territorial revisionism. In contemporary politics, if a minority group views itself as a national minority it is inclined to ask for international recognition of its rights as well as an open acknowledgment of its cultural difference. It thus constrains attempts at ethnic homogenization, especially if the nation-state builds its own public persona as a "cultural" rather than "political" nation (Breuilly, 1993). These issues are particularly important in the Balkan context, and a discussion of Macedonian minorities has to be placed within the broader regional context. The issue of national minorities in the Balkans has a long and turbulent history; it is this history that has a direct bearing upon the general topic of minorities in the region.

COUNTING THE MINORITIES IN THE BALKANS

The Balkan system of states that emerged out of the Balkan wars of 1912–13 and the subsequent World War I (1914–18) formed a *political field* with the issue of national minorities as one of the important factors shaping their interstate and intrastate relationships. As Brubaker (1996) argues, this political field consists of three mutually linked entities: the national minorities, the nation-states that these minorities inhabit, and the external national homelands of these minorities. The interactive processes set in motion by this triadic relationship lead to the vicious circle of mutual animosity. One only needs to recall the motto that proliferated during the disintegration of Yugoslavia in the 1990s: "Why should *I* be a minority in your state if *you* can be a minority in my state?" In the period after World War I but also for most of the twentieth century, no Balkan nation-state was able to incorporate all of its potential nationals into its territory. Minority groups remained scattered in Greece, Bulgaria, Albania, Romania, and the kingdom of Serbs, Slovenes, and Croats. Indeed, the emergence of the so-called "first Yugoslavia" (1917) was an explicit but ultimately futile attempt to manage the complicated cluster of issues surrounding the coexistence of Serbs, Croats, Slovenes, and a host of other smaller southern Slavic groups within the boundaries of a single state (Djilas, 1991; Banac, 1984; Lampe, 1996).

Within this system of states, the completion of nation building required a considerable degree of centralization and homogenization. The concept of the nation-state has been historically linked with the ethnic homogenization of a particular population (McNeill, 1985; Weber, 1976). For the Balkan lands, however, ethnic heterogeneity has been the rule rather than the exception. Although, following World War I, the population exchanges among Bulgaria, Greece, and Turkey helped the ethnic homogenization of these states, they failed to totally solve the issue. Subsequently, during the interwar period, the minority groups in the Balkan nation-states became the subjects of state-sponsored policies of cultural homogenization (for a review of individual cases, see Roudometof, 2002b). In turn, such policies further alienated the minorities from their nation-states, helping the gradual transformation of the minority groups into national minorities. In Chapter 4, I reviewed the interwar policies of ethnic homogenization in Macedonia. It is important to keep in mind that these policies were not isolated instances, but rather part of a broader regional and to some extent European pattern of nation-building during the interwar period (see the essays in Vardy and Tooley, 2002 for further examples).

These policies expressed the conceptualization of the nation-state as a monolithic, culturally integrated community, whereby membership in the nation is defined in terms of cultural membership in an ethnic community (Roudometof, 1999). It is a foregone conclusion that this conceptualization of the nation-state is far from universal. On the contrary, in countries like the United States or even France, citizenship has provided the means for the successful incorporation of generations of new immigrants (Lipset, 1963; Brubaker, 1992). But in Eastern and Southeastern Europe, the absence of a democratic tradition of citizenship rights has been compounded by a strong emphasis on ethnic or collectivist nationalism (Seton-Watson, 1977; Smith, 1986; Greenfeld, 1991). As I have already mentioned in Chapter 1, Eastern European nation-building most often took the form of emphasizing *nationhood*—that is, membership in a nation in terms of religious, linguistic, or ethnic ties—as the most important component of the national idea (Roudometof, 2001).

In this respect, the "ethnic" character of the nation-state provides the basic rationale for policies of cultural homogenization. The application of these policies into the tapestry of minority groups in the Balkans provides a long-term structural predisposition on the part of the minorities to mistrust state authorities. All Balkan states have historically pursued their nation-building process on the basis of what is usually referred to as collectivist or ethnic nationalism.[10] Throughout the nineteenth century, they systematically attempted to enlarge their territory by incorporating as many of their proclaimed "nationals" as possible. Their historical traditions, public institutions, national histories, and literatures all emphasize nationhood rather than citizenship as the single most important component of the nation-state (Roudometof, 1998b).

Under these conditions, a minority group is increasingly put into a position in which its special status—in terms of institutional separation from the majority in the fields of education, religion, and language—is viewed as representing a threat to the very stability of state boundaries. Indeed, as I have already discussed in Chapter 4, the Slavs of Greek-held and Serb-controlled Macedonia were put into such a position. In more general terms, the situation can be formulated in terms of Hirschman's (1970) famous choice between exit and voice. The minority group can attempt to "exit" the state— that is, secede—or it might attempt to cooperate within the state structure— that is, to claim a "voice" within the political system of the nation-state. Hirschman has pointed out the importance of loyalty as a determinant between exit and voice. If the minority group is loyal to the state, it tends to opt for participation, whereas if loyalty is low it might attempt to exit the state through extended autonomy or secession. Loyalty, however, is established with great difficulty when common bonds of solidarity between minority and majority are absent. When ethnic nationalism prevails, the acknowledgment of difference represents hubris to the essential unity of the nation.

Table 5.1 presents an account of the minority groups in Southeastern Europe during the last decade of the twentieth century.

As the reader will observe, reliable counts of the minorities are extremely difficult to obtain because of the local authorities' desire to minimize the official appearance of ethnic fragmentation, but also because of the interplay between ethnicity and religion. That is, the dividing lines between Pomaks and Turks (or between Orthodox Albanians and ethnic Greeks or between Gypsies and Turks) are hazy. In these cases religion establishes a more important link than language, a feature that testifies to the extent that modern Balkan nations trace their origins to the disintegration of the *millet* system of the Ottoman Empire (Roudometof, 2001). Hence, the gradual consolidation of national minorities operates through the identification of some of these "intermediate" groups within one or another national minority.

Moreover, geography plays an important role: if the minority group is not in close proximity with a rival nation-state that can be realistically perceived as an alternative homeland, it is more likely that it will be co-opted within the existing nation-states. A number of minority groups in the Balkans have followed such a fate, with the Vlachs being the most prominent example of successful strategies of assimilation.[11] The Vlachs are mainly pastoral nomads dispersed among the states of Yugoslavia, Bulgaria, Greece, Albania, and Romania. Since they are Orthodox Christians, they have mostly become part of the predominantly Eastern Orthodox nation-states in which they live.[12]

In contrast, minority groups that can look to a highly visible external national homeland (a land perceived as the minority's "natural" fatherland) in close proximity to their own territory are the ones most likely to be transformed into national minorities. This tendency is most often cultivated via school textbooks, religion, language, and political-cultural mobilization. Economic reasons can intensify or inhibit this process as well. Close geographical proximity to an external national homeland makes "exit" a more tenable choice since it "only" requires the alteration of state boundaries.

Of the minority groups located in close proximity to a potential external national homeland, only the Serbs and Croats in Bosnia-Herzegovina were dispersed. In 1991, they constituted 31.4% and 17.3% of the republic's population respectively. Serbs constituted the absolute majority in parts of eastern Bosnia-Herzegovina and the majority or relative majority in parts of western Bosnia. The Croats and Muslims were dispersed throughout the region, with more Croats living close to the coastline and more Muslims living in the interior of the country. In other regions, the pattern of concentration is more pronounced. The Turks of Bulgaria live in the Kardzhali region in southeastern Bulgaria and the Razgrad-Shumen area in northeastern Bulgaria, whereas the Pomaks inhabit the Rhodope Mountain area of

Table 5.1
Minority Groups in the Balkans, ca. 1990–2000

Minority Group	Nation-State	% of Population
Greeks[a]	Albania	8–12
Turks	Bulgaria	8.5
Gypsies[b]	Bulgaria	6.0
Macedonians[c]	Bulgaria	2.75
Muslim Pomaks[d]	Bulgaria	5.0
Serbs[e]	Croatia	11.6
Serbs	Bosnia	32
Croats	Bosnia	18.4

Note: A "minority group" is listed in this table insofar as it constitutes 2% of the population in a state. Smaller groups do exist within the Balkans, but for current purposes they are ignored. Whenever statistical information was contradictory (for example, Greeks in Albania or Turks and Pomaks in Greece), there was an attempt to reconcile different estimates by encompassing the whole range of these estimates.

[a]The total number of Greek-Orthodox Albanians, Greeks, and Vlachs is close to 20% of the population. Greeks routinely consider the approximately 200,000 Vlachs part of the minority, whereas Albanian sources consider them a separate group. Each group (i.e., Orthodox Albanians and Greeks) is estimated between 8% to 12% but, given the significance of religion as a cultural marker and the inadequate knowledge of Greek by many of the ethnic Greeks, it is difficult to accurately differentiate the two groups. For studies of the electoral behavior of the minority and attempts to estimate its numerical strength, see Berholli et al., (1994: 427–34) and Dodos (1994: 115–44).

[b]According to data presented by the Romani leaders, the Gypsies number between 800,000 and 1,000,000 (Simonov, 1990:13). If this estimate is correct, then Poulton's (1991:116) number of 576,926 should be revised.

[c]This figure was reported in the *World Directory of Minorities* (Minority Rights Group, 1990). In all likelihood, it overestimates the Macedonians. See the discussion in the next section of this chapter.

[d]The *World Directory of Minorities* (Minority Rights Group, 1990) estimates 150,000 Pomaks (1.7% of the population) and 900,000 Turks (10% of the population). The Pomaks are Muslim Slavs adhering to Islam in terms of religion, but they are Slav speaking. Poulton (1991:111) reports a figure of 268,971 Pomaks as given by local authorities at the end of 1990. Because of the importance of religion as a cultural marker, it is quite likely that at least some of them might want to consider themselves "Turks." Konstantinov (1997: 33) gives a figure of 220,000.

[e]The Serb population of Croatia lived in eastern Slavonia and the Khin region (the so-called Serb Republic of the Krajina). The Republic included less than 250,000 inhabitants in the early 1990s, and soon its population further diminished because of immigration into Serbia. While the Serbs of Krajina held on to their territory in the first half of the 1990s, they succumbed to the Croatian Army's Operation Flash and Operation Storm in May and August of 1995. Subsequently, this population was ethnically cleansed from their territory and resettled in Vojvodina, Serbia proper, and Kosovo.

Table 5.1 (continued)

Minority Group	Nation-State	% of Population
Albanians	Republic of Macedonia	20
Serbs	Republic of Macedonia	2.2
Gypsies	Republic of Macedonia	2.4
Albanians[f]	Serbia	17.2
"Muslims"[g]	Republic of Macedonia	4.8
"Yugoslavs"[h]	Serbia	3.4
East-Orthodox Albanians	Albania	8–12
Roman Catholic Albanians	Albania	10
Albanians	Montenegro	6.5
Turks/Pomaks[i]	Greece	1–2
Hungarians[j]	Serbia (Vojvodina)	6.1
Hungarians	Romania	8–10

[f]This percentage refers to the Albanian population of Kosovo as part of the Republic of Serbia. Of course, Kosovo was autonomous prior to the late 1980s, and the Albanian population made up close to 90% of the total population of the province. It was the attempt by the Milosevic regime to ethnically cleanse Kosovo of its Albanian majority that prompted the NATO strike against the rump Yugoslavia in the spring of 1999. Subsequently, the majority of the Albanians returned to the region under the protection of the NATO troops. However, the result was a reverse ethnic cleansing whereby the Serb minority had to flee the region or fortify themselves in ethnic enclaves. In most cases, the NATO troops have had to intervene in order to maintain peace and security in the region.

[g]It is unclear how many of the "Muslims" are Turks. According to the 1981 census, there were 86,691 Turks constituting 4% of the population. But these numbers have fluctuated during the last twenty years (in 1953, 203,938 were recorded as "Turks"). More recently, it appears that a number of the people previously declared as "Turks" have switched their identification to "Roma" (Gypsies) or "Albanian" (Petrovic, 1992; also, Poulton, 1991: 91–93).

[h]The category of "Yugoslavs" was created in the 1961 census. The number of people declaring themselves as "Yugoslavs" increased during the last two decades in an uneven pace with significant percentages in Bosnia-Herzegovina, Serbia, and Vojvodina, but small percentages in Slovenia, Kosovo, and Macedonia (Poulton, 1991: 98; see also Gordy, 1999).

[i]According to the Greek government there are only Muslim Greeks (but no Turks). The *World Directory of Minorities* (Minority Rights Group, 1990) gives the estimate of 1% to 2%. It is more likely that the 120,000 people estimated to belong to this category constitute approximately 1.3% of the Greek population recorded officially as "Muslim" (HFDFP's Review, 1992). There are no reliable estimates regarding how many of these are Pomaks.

[j]According to the statistics compiled by Lydanyi (2002), this number has remained stable (around 400,000) for most of the twentieth century. In 1981, there were 385,000, and by 1991 there were 339,000. The Serb population of Vojvodina increased almost three-fold from 382,000 in 1910 to more than a million in 1961. During the later 1990s, Serb authorities began the resettlement of Serb refugees into the region, thereby altering the population ratios in cities that were previously mixed or dominated by the Hungarian minority.

Sources: HFDFP's *Southeastern European Yearbook* (1992), *The Review of Defense and Foreign Policy* (1992, 1999), *World Directory of Minorities* (Minority Rights Group, 1990), Poulton (1991), Lydanyi (2002), Allcock et al., (1998), and Petrovic (1992).

southeastern Bulgaria and the Lovech-Tetever region in central Bulgaria. Most Albanians in the former Yugoslavia were concentrated in Kosovo, while the Albanians in Macedonia live in the western part of the republic, in close proximity to the Albanian state. Also, the Greeks of southern Albania or Northern Epirus live close to the Greek-Albanian border. The situation of the Albanians in FYROM as well as that of Greeks in Albania will be discussed in greater detail in Chapter 6.

Finally, the consolidation of national minorities in the region has been partially influenced by the groups' demographic rates. Over the post–World War II period, the Albanians' high birthrate resulted in their increase from 67.25% of Kosovo's population in the 1961 census to 77.4% in 1981 and almost 90% in 1991 (Cviic, 1991: 67). A high birthrate also helped Albanians in the Republic of Macedonia to increase their numbers from 19.8% of the population in 1981 to 21.0% in 1991. According to the 1994 census this percentage is even higher (see Table 6.1 in Chapter 6). In Bosnia-Herzegovina, the Muslim population also increased from 39.5% in 1981 to 43.7% in 1991 (Petrovic, 1992: 3–24). These high birthrates are not necessarily beneficial for the minority groups. Often, local nationalists portray the minorities as engaged in a demographic warfare whereby a group uses a high birthrate to ensure the ultimate domination of a particular region.

Taking into consideration the factors mentioned in the discussion thus far, Table 5.2 presents an account of the groups most closely resembling national minorities, including the nation-state in which they are located and their potential external national homelands.

Table 5.2
Potential National Minorities in the Balkans*

National Minority	Nation-State	External Homeland
Greeks	Albania	Greece
Turks	Bulgaria	Turkey
Albanians	FYROM	Albania
Albanians	Serbia (Kosovo)	Albania
Serbs	Croatia	Serbia
Serbs	Bosnia	Serbia
Croats	Bosnia	Croatia

Source: Compiled from Table 5.1.

*In this chapter, attention is focused on the minority groups in the southern Balkans (Albania, Macedonia, and Bulgaria). Hungarian minorities within Yugoslavia have been excluded from this discussion. For an analysis of the Hungarian minorities' status, see Lydanyi (2002).

The discussion thus far has focused on the structural factors acting to intensify the minority question in the Balkans. The close proximity between a group's location and a potential external homeland, demographic trends, and the importance of nationhood as a cultural barrier with respect to the incorporation of minorities within the states' political body are all factors that tend to promote "exit" rather than "voice" in the Balkan context. All of these are long-term structural factors leading to the consolidation of the groups listed in Table 5.2 as potential national minorities. Turning these groups into actual national minorities involves attributing political significance to their cultural markers, a feature that is generally absent when cultural differences are used as categories of classification rather than as categories of subjective identification (Rothschild, 1981). In the Balkans, the end of the Cold War offered the opportunity of politicizing ethnic differences.[13] During this mobilization, minority groups became increasingly identified with external national homelands, thus providing the context for the outbreak of ethnic conflict in the peninsula.

This brief overview explains the reasons that local states are extremely sensitive to discussions of national minorities within their borders. The Yugoslav wars of the 1990s revealed the extent to which such issues are indeed explosive. Keeping these broader issues in mind, let us turn to a critical examination of the argument that there are substantial Macedonian *national minorities* in the two neighboring states (Greece and Bulgaria). As the reader will observe, I have not listed such groups as potential national minorities (see Table 5.2). This means that, at least in the foreseeable future, such groups are not likely to be a visible and potent political force in local societies. However, my classification should not be interpreted as suggesting that there are no Macedonian minority groups in these two states. On the contrary, such groups do exist, and organized political activists claim that they represent Macedonian national minorities. In fact, if one had applied different criteria from the ones I have used above, it would be entirely possible to argue that such minorities do exist. Therefore, it is necessary to discuss these issues explicitly and in greater detail.

THE QUESTION OF MACEDONIAN MINORITIES IN GREECE

In the 1990s, the issue of Macedonian national minorities in Greece (and Bulgaria) has become a heated controversy. At the heart of this issue are the claims of Macedonian human rights activists who were successful in attracting international attention in large part thanks to the overzealous persecution addressed against them by Greek (and Bulgarian) authorities (for reviews, see Danforth, 1995; Kostopoulos, 2000; and Koutrovik, 1997). Up until the late 1990s, both Greece and Bulgaria viewed the recognition of

Macedonian minorities as a potential infringement of their territorial sovereignty and as a basis for future Macedonian irredentism.[14] Indeed the proclamations, statements, maps, and textbooks I have reviewed in earlier chapters of this book might serve as documentation of Macedonian latent irredentism. Descriptions of Greek Macedonia as a "colony" of southern Greece (Popov and Radin, 1989), one that remains underdeveloped as part of a deliberate policy, should be seen as just as nationalistic as Greek attempts to convince the public that Macedonian national identity is total fiction.[15]

In Greece, attempts were made to gain cultural rights for the Macedonian minority through the formation of voluntary associations. The first major confrontation among Bulgarian, Macedonian, and Greek sides occurred in the context of the Conference on the Human Dimension of the Council for Security and Cooperation in Europe (CSCE), held in Copenhagen in June 1990. The confrontation had its roots in the utilization of the human rights movement by Macedonian activists, who sought to use the international organizations to pressure Greece into recognizing the Macedonian minority in northern Greece as a national minority. During the conference, Greek, Macedonian, and Bulgarian delegates presented radically different perspectives on the minority question. The mutually exclusive perspectives of the competing sides raised questions with respect to the very definition of Macedonians and made it impossible for the CSCE to subscribe to any particular side's viewpoint. Moreover, the debate raised important conceptual issues regarding the definition of a "national minority" as such (Danforth, 1994).

In 1990 the Multimember High Court in Florina, Greece, refused to register a cultural association called the "Center for Macedonian Culture." In 1991, the court's decision was affirmed by an appellate court in Thessaloniki (United States Department of State, 1991). The court's rationale was that the true goal of the association was to "affirm the idea of the existence of a Macedonian minority in Greece, which contradicts [Greece's] national interests and the law" (quoted in Hristov, 1994: 21). The case made its way to the European Court of Human Rights, and on 10 July 1998 the European Court ruled against the Greek state, because the prohibition violated Article 11 of the European Convention for Human Rights (Kostopoulos, 2000: 326–27). It should be pointed out that competency in Macedonian or its local variant (or dialect) spoken in Florina does not lead to discrimination. Only those individuals who refuse to be assimilated into Greek culture and insist upon maintaining their own separate status as an ethnic group face the sanctions of the local society. Clearly, this is only a segment of the Slavic-speaking population (Hristov, 1994: 17–18). It is debatable whether this group (although a vocal one) is numerically so strong as to warrant the creation of separate educational institutions. According to international standards, a minority population needs to be sufficiently numerous for such a demand to be justified (Stavros, 1995: 6).

In 1991, pro-Macedonian activists founded the Macedonian Movement for Balkan Prosperity (MAKIBE), and in 1993 they successfully held the movement's first congress. The demands put forward included: free repatriation of the refugees; reparations to the "local" Macedonians by the state; and the ability to pursue their cultural activities free from any state interference or harassment (Kostopoulos, 2000: 323). This group published two journals advocating the pro-Macedonian viewpoint. In 1994, this group was renamed Rainbow Coalition (*Ouranio Toxo*) and entered into that year's elections for the European Parliament. The coalition received a total of 7,263 votes (Mihailidis, 1997: 137).[16]

During the post–World War II period, the Greek state considered any political mobilization of ethnic or national minorities as a potential threat to Greece's territorial integrity. This policy grew out of the events of the turbulent 1941–49 period, already reviewed in Chapter 4. Additionally, Greece's position has long been that the only minority group within its boundaries is the Muslim minority in western Thrace. This minority is, for Greece, a religious and not a national minority. This attitude was an outcome of the manner in which the issue of national minorities was used in the first half of the twentieth century and, more specifically, during the interwar period. Greece's official policy and attitude remained largely unaltered in the 1970s, despite the acceptance of the Helsinki accords. Since democracy returned to Greece only in 1974, Greek society spent at least a decade in an effort to consolidate the newly established democratic form of government. In effect, the 1981 electoral victory of PASOK confirmed this consolidation. While the spectrum of a center-left coalition gaining power was one of the reasons that led to the turbulent 1965–67 period and eventually to the 1967 military coup and the 1967–74 dictatorship, the newly reconstructed conservative party (New Democracy) did not react in a similar fashion in 1981. On the contrary, the peaceful change of the guard from New Democracy to PASOK helped the consolidation of democracy (see Karakatsanis, 2001 for a detailed analysis).

It was only in the aftermath of the socialists' 1981 victory (and more specifically in the 1989–91 period) that the connection between human rights and minority rights was explicitly brought to the attention of the Greek government and the majority of the Greek public. In many respects, these issues should be viewed as good test cases for the extent and depth of democratization in post-1974 Greek society. However, just as former prime minister Mitsotakis' statement at the beginning of this chapter makes clear, the "minority question" has geopolitical implications that no Greek government can afford to ignore. For several decades, this particular viewpoint was the dominant perspective in the formulation of Greek policy.

For the post–World War II Greek state, talk of a Macedonian minority was propaganda against Greece's territorial integrity. Given the small size of the minority and the shifting and fluid loyalties of many of its members, the possibility of them representing a real threat to Greece's national security is minimal. But the issue of FYROM-based Macedonian irredentism does not have any necessary connection to the human rights of the Slavo-Macedonian or Macedonian minority within Greek Macedonia (although nationalists on both sides are eager to establish such a connection). Perhaps more important than Macedonian irredentism is Greek society's negative attitude toward this group, which is perpetuated by the systematic blurring of the differentiation between citizenship rights and nationhood. The absence of civil culture in the Balkans has turned disputes over the human rights of linguistic, religious, and ethnic minorities into national disputes.

As the discussion in Chapter 4 has shown, the assimilationist policy of the Greek state in northwestern Macedonia has been counterproductive: it politicized local culture by turning the local Slavic Macedonian population into an undesirable element. Although this strategy was not in complete violation of the pre–World War II international norms, its continuation into the present puts Greece at variance with currently existing international treaties and norms concerning the status of minorities within particular states (see Stavros, 1995). The state is meant to assume a proactive role and to treat non-ethnic Greeks equally with ethnic Greeks. A possible solution could entail the recognition of cultural difference without the concomitant recognition of the minority as a Macedonian national minority. Instead, this group's members could be considered Greeks with a special Greco-Slavic cultural heritage (similar to other Greek ethnic groups like the Pontic Greeks or the Vlachs). Such a reconceptualization would necessitate the clear separation of ethnic from national identity.[17]

However, such a solution raises important conceptual issues concerning the place of civil society, individuality, and human rights within the Greek cultural context. Pollis (1965) argues that Greece's cultural heritage does not allow for the articulation of Western cultural constructs such as the individual or civil society. Although democratic forms might be implemented within the Greek polity, the substance and rationale that accompanies such forms in Western democracies remains absent. Particular manifestations of this trend may be found in the tendency of the judiciary as well as of the Greek Church to sanction Greek state authority uncritically. This tendency has greatly facilitated the operation of nondemocratic regimes throughout modern Greek history. The judiciary and the church have failed to offer adequate protection to dissenting voices, thus promoting state interests (defined in a strictly legalistic manner) over individual rights and liberties.[18] The Greek state is viewed as the guardian of the nation, and the Greek definition of the nation does not encourage the inclusion of linguistic, religious, and other minorities as equal members of the national "imagined community."

The foundation of modern Greek identity rests on the religious and linguistic unity of Eastern Orthodox and Greek-speaking Christians. Traditionally, Eastern Orthodoxy has not created a space in which the notions of natural law and individual freedom can emerge. The organic unity and spiritual character of the *Ekklesia* (religious congregation) have remained primary characteristics of Eastern Orthodoxy. Contrary to the Western conceptualization of the church as an institution apart from society, Eastern Orthodoxy considers the *Ekklesia* to be synonymous with society at large. This lack of differentiation between public institutions and society has been duplicated at the level of Greek national identity. As already discussed in Chapter 3, during the nineteenth century, the fragmentation of the Eastern Orthodox commonwealth—represented by the Ecumenical Patriarchate of Constantinople—led to the creation of the modern Greek nation as a unit that inherited this organic conceptualization of society. The events of the 1941–49 period further strengthened the association between ethnic and national identity. The post-1945 right-wing regimes and the Greek dictatorship thrived on the systematic cultivation of nationalism, setting themselves up as the saviors of modern Greece from the double-headed evil of "Slavo-communism."[19]

In such a cultural context, worldviews and value orientations serve to justify the exclusion of minorities from membership in the Greek nation. Thus, the issue of inadequate protection of minorities is closely related to the employment of cultural rather than civic criteria for such membership. Since Greek nation-building has emphasized national homogeneity, minorities that do not share the ethnic attributes associated with those who are legitimate members of the Greek "imagined community"—that is, with Greek-speaking, Eastern Orthodox Christians—face sanctions from the local society.[20] In the Greek context, citizenship rights are extended to an individual via the person's membership in the Greek nation. Exclusion from membership in the national community *de facto* justifies the curtailment of citizenship rights. For the Macedonian minority, these sanctions are compounded by the suspicion that their loyalty to the state is questionable.

Nevertheless, in the post-1995 period, the Greek government has adopted a new line, which is more consistent with the international standards.[21] First, the Greek Foreign Ministry organized a conference on the topic of Macedonian minorities in 1995—and two years later, the research results were published (Gounaris, et al., 1997), albeit without a reference to the fact that this was a state-sponsored event. Second, Theodoros Pangalos and Georgios Papandreou, the two men in charge of the Greek Foreign Ministry at the time, repeatedly expressed the position that Greek citizens will not be hampered in the exercise of their rights, and, therefore, any private pursuit of cultural mobilization by Macedonian activists was welcome. When Greek Foreign Minister Theodoros Pangalos visited Skopje in 1998 he expressed the Greek official position as follows: "For Greece, there is no Slavic minority in Greek Macedonia," he said. "There might be fifty or a hundred people scattered throughout Greece," he added, who are free to "set up offices, circulate newspapers, learn their language, dance and sing their songs and run in the elections." And Pangalos concluded: "If they think that their rights are violated . . . there is the Court of Human Rights that condemns those who violate human rights" (quoted in Kostopoulos, 2000: 351).

THE QUESTION OF MACEDONIAN MINORITIES IN BULGARIA

A similar pro-Macedonian movement developed among the Pirin Macedonians in Bulgaria during the post-1989 period. The developments in the Pirin region of Macedonia or Bulgarian Macedonia have to be placed in the context of post-1948 Bulgarian-Macedonian relations. As discussed in Chapter 2, following the Tito-Stalin rift (1948), Bulgaria eventually reverted back to the long-held position that all Macedonians are Bulgarians and that the label "Macedonian" is nothing else than a geographical appellation for members of the Bulgarian nation. Despite the new official party line, in the 1965 census a total of 8,750 people from the district of Blagoevgrad declared themselves Macedonians. In the 1960s and 1970s, Macedonian activists were harshly persecuted by the communist state and some of them received prison sentences (Poulton, 2000: 148–51; Ortakovski, 2000: 164–66).

The post-1989 democratization of Bulgaria offered the opportunity to revive pro-Macedonian organizations. As already discussed in Chapter 2, the 1990s witnessed the emergence of numerous Macedonian organizations, including the VMRO-UMCS Bulgarian nationalists, whose power base is in the Pirin region. However, unlike the pro-Bulgarian organizations and parties that claim the Macedonian label, the pro-Macedonian or "separatist" organizations in post-1989 Bulgaria faced open hostility by the state. Just as with Greece, Macedonians' demands for formal recognition of cultural organizations have met the stubborn denial of the Bulgarian authorities. In 1990 the pro-Macedonian organizations formed the unified United Macedonian Organization-Ilinden (OMO-Ilinden). The organization attempted to register with the courts. However, the Blagoevgrad and Sofia district courts, as well as the Supreme Court of Bulgaria (November 1990), rejected its application. The courts claimed that they acted according to the 1949 Persons and Families Law. This law, originally enacted for completely different purposes, is considered obsolete and inadequate to deal with the complex diversity of the emerging civil society in Bulgaria (for a discussion, see Mavrikos-Adamou, 2002). Thus, in the absence of clear legal definitions of "nonprofit" and "partisan" activities, it was left to the judges to decide whether or not an organization can be formally registered.[22] Not surprisingly, Macedonian organizations were denied registration by the courts on the basis of constituting a threat to national security; Macedonian activists were persecuted, harassed by the police, and their passports were confiscated; the Bulgarian police raided a congress of the Macedonian movement (for a review, see Poulton, 2000: 151–60).

Throughout the 1990s, Macedonian activists in Bulgaria stated that autonomy was a long-term goal of their movement. While some defined the desire for autonomy in cultural and spiritual terms, others (those associated with the Macedonian organization OMO-Ilinden), expressed their goal to be that of gaining regional autonomy from the Bulgarian state (Zang, 1991: 83; Perry, 1994b: 50). Numerical estimates of those affiliated with OMO-Ilinden range between 1,000 and 1,500 members—most of whom are located in the Pirin region. Despite the small size of the group, Macedonian separatism within the Bulgarian state continues to be unwelcome. Bulgarians consider Macedonians to be Bulgarians; in fact, there are some thirteen mainstream organizations claiming descent from the legendary VMRO. These groups consider the Macedonian organization OMO-Ilinden as "illegal, anti-state, and anti-Bulgarian" (Perry, 1994b: 51).

The 1999 normalization of relationships between Sofia and Skopje has had an impact on the acceptance of the Macedonian organizations by the state. The Sofia City Court accepted the registration of the Macedonian organization OMO-"PIRIN" as a political party and an officially recognized organization. OMO-"PIRIN" ("PIRIN" is an acronym for Party for Economic Development and Integration of the Population in the Pirin Region) claims to be a Bulgarian party, aiming at the prosperity of the region within the frame of the Bulgarian state.[23] This platform stands in sharp contrast to OMO "Ilinden"-Sandanski, which openly insists on recognition of the specific non-Bulgarian character of the local population and on extending to them autonomy, additional benefits such as the exemption of its young people from conscription into the Bulgarian Military Forces, and the eventual secession of Pirin Macedonia from Bulgaria and its incorporation with the Republic of Macedonia. The recognition of OMO-"PIRIN" prompted reaction by Bulgarian nationalists, and Bulgaria's outgoing Chief Prosecutor Ivan Tatarchev used his last days in office to prepare an appeal against the recognition of OMO-"PIRIN." Later, sixty-one MPs submitted to the Constitutional Court a demand to repeal the recognition on the basis that the organization's true goals are quite different from those stated in its constitution. As one journalist commented, "You state in your Statute, that you will protect the edelweiss in Pirin mountains, but we know that you have something else in your minds."[24]

The bone of contention between the two sides is the (alleged) Macedonian national minority in Bulgaria. The minority is located in Pirin Macedonia (see Map 1.1). Pirin Macedonia comprises two Bulgarian districts, one of which, centered around the city of Blagoevgrad (former Gorna Djumaya), tentatively bears this name. Is there a Macedonian *national minority* in Pirin Macedonia? Are the claims of Macedonian minority advocates in Bulgaria justified? This is a highly politicized question, which requires an answer to another question: How many Macedonians are there in Bulgaria? Any serious discussion of this question must address the problem of the considerable disparity between data from different sources. According to the latest national census (1992), the population of Pirin is 96.0% Bulgarians. This is the highest ratio of ethnic homogeneity in the whole country: the national average percentage of ethnic Bulgarians is only 85.8%. The other groups in the Pirin region include 2.1% Gypsies or Roma (concentrated mainly around Kyustendil), 0.2% to 0.3% Turks (who average 9.7% nationwide), and 2.6% of "others," a relatively high share since the national mean for this category is 1.1%. Of the Pirin population, only around 6,000 to 7,000 inhabitants identified themselves as Macedonians. As this category did not appear on the census forms, those who chose to do so should be considered active members of the Macedonian cause in the region (Bozhikov, 1993: 48).

According to the Minority Rights Group (1990), the self-identified Macedonians in Bulgaria are somewhere between 2.5% and 3.5% of the population (see Table 5.1 in this chapter). However, in a 1991 survey carried out by an independent organization, only 4.4% of the population in the Blagoevgrad region (Pirin Macedonia) identified themselves as Macedonians.[25] Inevitably, the contradictory numerical figures reveal the extent to which the underlying issues have more to do with complex and fluid dynamics of identity and less with obtaining an accurate count of a solid identity. The mere mention of Macedonians in Bulgaria poses an important problem for Bulgarian political culture. In 1990s Sofia, dissenters within the intelligentsia have broken with the sacred taboo of considering all Macedonians to be Bulgarians. Their argument has been that the people living in the region around the Vardar River (the territory of the Republic of Macedonia) are different from the Bulgarians—or at least, they consider themselves a different nation today. However, Bulgarians at large do not doubt that the population of Pirin Macedonia is purely Bulgarian.

Indeed, close relatives from different sides of the border claim to be of different ethnicities. Officially, during the post–World War II period, Sofia and Skopje have agreed on only one thing: that there is one and the same population residing on both sides of the border. Certainly, they all speak the same language, which is comprehensible to people from other areas of Bulgaria as well—although those from eastern Bulgaria, who generally speak more softly than their counterparts in the west, may experience some difficulties. In some rural areas of Bulgaria far more complicated dialects are spoken, making understanding difficult, even for native speakers coming from outside. However, ease of communication between ordinary people does not imply any mutual understanding between officials. On the contrary, the opposite seems to be the case.

Although Bulgaria often claims to have been the first foreign state to extend diplomatic recognition of independent Macedonia after the 1991 dismantling of the Yugoslav Federation, this recognition was accompanied by a statement that Bulgaria recognizes the state alone, not the Macedonian people and their language as defined in the Macedonian Fundamental Law. Colorful events on both sides of the border testify to the intense difficulties created by such a policy. In Skopje, a fashionable pop folk song devoted to Struma and Vardar, the sister rivers, one on each side of the border, was banned. In Tetovo, a music competition awards ceremony was delayed for hours while organizers frantically tried to contact Skopje and waited for permission from the Ministry of Culture to award the prize to Bulgarian performers—who also sang in the unrecognized Macedonian language. A Bulgarian TV correspondent, born in Skopje, was severely condemned in Bulgaria for making a comment on Macedonian TV in the Macedonian language (or the Skopje dialect as it is called). Later, Macedonian border guards prevented him from entering the Republic of Macedonia because he was allegedly included on the notorious list of Bulgarian citizens not welcome in the republic. At the top of this list is none other than Ivan Tatarchev, who was Bulgaria's Chief Prosecutor until 20 February 1999. He is a close relative (uncle) of Hristo Tatarchev, a member of the VMRO leadership in the early 1900s, who has a street in Skopje named after him. In Bulgaria, every year riot police are mobilized around the Rozhen Monastery to prevent people calling themselves Macedonians from laying flowers on the tomb of Yane Sandanski, one of the pre-1913 VMRO leaders.

To untangle the issue of Macedonians in Bulgaria it is necessary to go beyond mere statistical description. Given the wide discrepancy between different estimates, a standard feature in the literature dealing with the Macedonian Question (Mihailidis, 1998), it is more appropriate to look more closely at the labeling process involved in ethnic identification. This process is closely related to the local states' efforts to achieve national homogeneity, but it has been further complicated by the turbulent twentieth-century history of the region.

For most Bulgarians in their everyday speech, a "Macedonian" is simply a Bulgarian whose origins are in the geographic area of Macedonia and who is generally accepted in the same way as a Bulgarian from Plovdiv, Varna, or any other region. Moreover, between 1870 and 1950, refugees from throughout Macedonia, now divided between Bulgaria, Macedonia, and Greece, resettled all over the country, and they do not appear to be considered "foreigners," as are other neighboring or more distant groups (Turks, Greeks, Romanians, Serbians, Russians, Poles, etc.). The labeling ambiguity between "Macedonians" defined as part of the Bulgarian nation and "Macedonians" defined as citizens of the Republic of Macedonia is acutely reflected among the public. In a 1999 nationwide survey of 1,009 individuals by ACG Ltd., the question "When someone is called 'A Macedonian,' what is the first thing that comes to your mind?" was answered in the following fashion: 24.5% replied that it means a person from Pirin Macedonia; 15.8% that it means a citizen of the Republic of Macedonia; 19.6% that it means both of the above; and 35.6% that it means a Bulgarian from Macedonia (with the remaining 4.6% providing "other" answers).

Consequently, the numerous competing pressures applied by various sides over the last century have led to a situation whereby members of a single family might come to consider themselves of different ethnic backgrounds.[26] It is worth pointing out that such pressures have not been confined to Bulgaria, but were, rather, part of the very process of nation building in the Balkans (Roudometof, 2002b). In her study of Assiros, a village in Greek Macedonia, Karakasidou (1997: 126–32) brings forward some remarkable examples that illustrate the fluid nature of "ethnicity" and the instrumentalist employment of various labels by the local peasantry. The tale of one of her informants, an elderly woman called Paskhalina, is worthy of a brief recitation, as it illustrates both the fluid nature of ethnic identity and the ability of social actors to shift their identity in a strategic manner. When first approached by the anthropologist, Paskhalina recounted a tale of suffering during the Balkan Wars of 1912–13. During the Battle of Kilkis (21 July 1913) the Bulgarian army picked up her brother and sister and took them to Bulgaria in its retreat. Her siblings eventually stayed in Bulgaria: they were united only in 1957, but correspondence proved difficult as Paskhalina wrote in Greek while her sister could read only Bulgarian. Growing up in interwar Greece, Paskhalina was repeatedly referred to by her fellow peasants as "Bulgarian" ["voulgharoudha"]. During the 1960s, she finally went to court to force one of her female neighbors to stop calling her by that name. In court, she showed her Greek identity card and told the judge that had she been a Bulgarian her son would not have been able to join the Greek air force (an elite group). She won her case, the district judge ruling that the neighbor should not repeat the "slanderous" remark.

However, Karakasidou discovered later that this was only half the story. When, after some time, she gained the trust of the elderly woman, Paskhalina recounted a second tale, with substantive differences from the first one. In this account, the local people of Ambar-Koy had a Bulgarian church and a Bulgarian school, and it was the Greek army (not the Bulgarian) who burnt down her village. Her elder brother and sister were not prevented from returning home, but simply did not want to do so. The rest of the family, ashamed at the turn of events, made up a story of abduction to account for the exile of her two siblings. Interestingly enough, her brother ended up in Serbia and her sister in Bulgaria. Paskhalina's native tongue was "Bulgarian"—yet not identical to that spoken by her sister. The tale of Paskhalina is instructive because it acts as a reminder to overzealous researchers that local people are active participants in the politics of ethnicity.[27]

Hence, even before counting how many individuals identify themselves as Macedonians, the most important issue is to gain conceptual clarity with regard to the meaning of the Macedonian label. The examples cited above act as a guide for approaching the issue of identity in Pirin Macedonia. They

illustrate that words and their meaning lie at the very heart of identity formation. In 1992 Bulgarian ethnologist Bonka Stoyanova–Boneva (1996,
1998) carried out a study on the meaning of Macedonian identity in the town
of Petrich, in the far southwestern part of Bulgaria, which had then a population of 27,662. Interviews were conducted with twenty-two Petrichans,
using a quota sample. The tape-recorded interviews were then transcribed,
yielding around 120 standard pages of text, which was subsequently con-
tent-analyzed. In that research, because of the peculiarities of ethnic identity formation in Pirin, an indirect approach to self-identity was indispensable.
As the discussion in this section has demonstrated, the "Macedonian" identity has for a long time been an object of ruthless manipulation in the region. Consequently, it is reasonable to expect a considerable degree of
ambiguity regarding the term "Macedonian." The study outlined three main
social representations of "Macedonian."

The first social representation is that "all so-called Macedonians are in fact
Bulgarians, even those in the Republic of Macedonia." The respondents
supporting this representation claim that "only twenty to thirty people in
the whole town, and even less than that, consider themselves Macedonians."
In their view, "less than 5% of the Petrich population consider themselves
Macedonian," but "these are actually Bulgarians like us." Underlying this
social representation is the idea of a Greater Bulgaria. "If it were Great Bulgaria, economically prosperous, and not in economic crisis as it is now," then,
the story goes, "Bulgaria would for sure have acted as a centrifugal force for
all those who more or less recognize themselves as being in fact Bulgarians"
(i.e., the Macedonians, the Bessarabian Bulgarians, etc.).

The second social representation is that "we are Macedonians, different
from the Bulgarians, and part of the Macedonian nation." The respondents
supporting this representation strive for a united Macedonia or a Macedonian
state including Pirin and Greek Macedonia. They argue that "80% of the
population in Pirin Macedonia think like us." When asked what is common
to both Macedonians and Bulgarians, the answers cluster around two attitudes: "We are all Slavs," and "We are like relatives," with the additional
remark that "a Macedonian [in the Republic of Macedonia] is like a brother
to me," while the "Bulgarian is my cousin." One-third of the respondents
supporting this social representation demonstrate very strong loyalty and
emotional ties to the Republic of Macedonia and its own Macedonians. The
content analysis shows that the Republic of Macedonia is mentioned much
more frequently than Bulgaria in their interviews and often with much greater
appreciation, as evidenced by statements like "Macedonia is in our blood,"
or "when we speak of Macedonia and of Bulgaria, we hold Macedonia more
dear."

The third social representation can be defined in the following way: "Although we are called Macedonians, the population in the Pirin region are
all Bulgarians. We are different from the people who live in the Republic of

Macedonia, who are the real Macedonians." The respondents supporting this representation are indifferent toward being categorized as Macedonians: "I don't care if they call me Macedonian. In the town I have not met anybody who truly considers themselves Macedonian. . . . We are all Bulgarians." It appears that there is a strong economic motive in the process of ethnic identification. As a number of Petrichans emphasized: "Macedonia [i.e., the republic] has no natural resources, no wealth. . . . It is economically worse off than Bulgaria. Why [should I] call myself [a] Macedonian?" Bulgarian citizenship motivates a priority of belonging for these respondents: "We are citizens of the Republic of Bulgaria, so we are Bulgarians; those who are citizens of the Republic of Macedonia are Macedonians," they say. It should be pointed out, however, that only a very small proportion of the respondents (four out of twenty-two) supported this particular representation.

The Center for the Study of Democracy's 1991 survey data shed additional light on these findings. In this representative survey of the Blagoevgrad (Pirin) region (Center for the Study of Democracy, 1992), the younger generation (18–25 age group) supported the second representation: "Pirin Macedonians, as all Macedonians all over the world, belong to the Macedonian nation." However, the older generation (46 and over) supported the first one: "All Macedonians are mere Bulgarians, even those in the Republic of Macedonia." At the same time, it is important to emphasize that the largest proportion of respondents who identified themselves as Macedonians were in the 46-and-over age group. They made up 66.6% of those who selected this identity. In the other two age groups, the distributions were as follows: among the 18–25-year-olds, 10.3% identified themselves as Macedonians and 12.6% as Bulgarians; while among the 26–45 age group 23.1% identified themselves as Macedonians and 38% as Bulgarians.[28] In this regard, the evidence would seem to suggest an acculturation into the broader Bulgarian culture of the post-1945 period. In other words, Macedonian identity seems to be strong among those who have had a memory of the World War II and the pre–World War II situation.

A few of the respondents came close to rationalizing the complexity of ethnic identity in the town, wording it quite precisely: "The very propaganda that we have something Macedonian about us has been imposed on us for so long, that we cannot but think of ourselves as Macedonian." As one of the respondents put it: "It is much easier for the Turks as well as the Gypsies [in Bulgaria]; because for the Macedonians it is not easy to [find] their identity. The Macedonian is truly confused, whether to continue to be a Macedonian or not." The difficulty of clearly drawing the boundaries between Macedonians and Bulgarians is exacerbated by the lack of traceable differences between the cultural reality in Pirin Macedonia and that in the Republic of Macedonia ("We speak the same language, have the same religion"). All the respondents had relatives in the ex-Yugoslav republic, those sometimes being their own parents or siblings. They visit and maintain active communication through watching Macedonian TV and through effective business relations.

For those respondents who claimed loyalty to a Bulgarian identity (the third social representation: "Although some call us Macedonians, all those who live in Pirin Macedonia are in fact Bulgarians"), the meaning of "being Bulgarian" was sought through the question: "What does 'Bulgaria' mean to you?" The answers clustered around three meanings: first, Bulgaria is "the name of the nation I belong to"; second, it is "the state of Bulgaria within its borders"; and third, it is "my country of birth." Still, more than half the respondents in this category admitted that they would not mind being ruled by a government of another nationality, provided they lived well. This may be indicative of a detachment from ethnic loyalties and a shift of priorities toward economic success and material prosperity. In fact, we can see here the subtle interplay between ethnic identity and economic concerns. As one respondent put it, "To most people here it does not matter what ethnicity they are. What matters is to live a good life, then, they won't care whether they are Macedonians or whatever." Ethnicity, as any type of belonging to a group, is not something given, once and for all. It is constantly re-created and changed in the context of powerful social, political, and cultural factors (for discussions, see Smith, 1979; Gellner, 1983).

According to the pro-Macedonian activists in Pirin Macedonia, fear of the nationalist post-1989 Bulgarian VMRO-UMCS (already discussed in Chapter 2) is the main reason for the region's extremely low percentage of people identifying themselves as Macedonian. However, this "conspiracy theory" should be considered as equally valid as its counterpart—namely that Pirin Macedonia plays host both to those who interpret their Macedonian identity as a facet of Bulgarian identity, as well as to those who conceive the two identities to be mutually exclusive.[29] Occupying the middle ground between the two extremes, there are those who accept a sense of regionalism, yet they steer away from transforming this regionalism into a full-fledged rival identity. While most respondents agreed that "the pie [Macedonia] was already cut into pieces in 1912" (alluding to the tripartite division of Macedonia among Greece, Bulgaria, and Serbia), others believed that "these pieces" can be redistributed anew. Such an agenda calls for the "unification" of geographical Macedonian into a single state—and is typically interpreted by official Greece and Bulgaria as Macedonian irredentism vis-à-vis Greek and Bulgarian Macedonia.

In conclusion, the evidence presented in this section would seem to suggest a tripartite division among the local people—a division that echoes the profiles of Macedonians in northwestern Greek Macedonia (Karakasidou, 2000a). In other words, people's attitudes tend to cluster into three relatively well-defined categories: those who acculturate into the national culture, those who maintain a sense of distinction, and those who reject all acculturation. In the case of Pirin, the process of cultural differentiation is even harder to articulate because of the absence of clear-cut cultural cleavages.[30]

CONCLUSIONS

In this chapter, I have reviewed in some detail the claim that Greece and Bulgaria house substantial Macedonian national minorities. As the discussion has shown, Macedonian communities, activist organizations, and small groups of people who identify themselves as Macedonians do exist in both states. However, this does not mean that there are substantial, compact, and culturally coherent communities, certainly not to the extent that they should warrant the vague and politically laden term "national minorities." In many instances, estimates of the numerical size of these groups have been based on self-reporting by individual activists, who were all too eager to provide numbers that would increase their visibility and importance. More careful research on both states confirms that the actual numbers of Macedonians are considerably less than the inflated figures reported by human rights activists.

This should not detract from the fact that, in both states, individual activists and other people who identify themselves as Macedonians have been subject to mild or extreme forms of discrimination and sometimes even malicious persecution. In this regard, it is important to highlight these cases, to publicize them, and to make sure that the freedoms of expression, speech, and association are observed in both states. This issue represents a good test for Greece and Bulgaria's consolidation of their democracies. In the long run, guaranteeing these rights is a responsibility these two states have assumed under the rules of the European Union (EU). In the 1990s, the two state bureaucracies appear to have realized the importance of coordinating their internal laws and practices with the new legal standards of the international community. The 1999 Sofia-Skopje agreement and the post-1995 Greek policy should be interpreted as (belated, yet welcomed) attempts by the two states to harmonize their minority policies in a manner consistent with EU standards.

However, a sharp distinction ought to be made between individual and collective rights. In its current phase (Miall, 1994), the emerging transnational European regime on minorities does not draw an explicit distinction between the two. Consequently, the two issues have been intermingled in public discourse. Still, there are important differences between individual and collective rights. The rights guaranteed to a specific person are not necessarily identical to the rights granted to collectivities. While in the first instance we may speak of human rights of individual people, in the second instance we are talking about rights granted to specific groups, to "national minorities." The difference between the two types of rights is strongly reminiscent of the post-1960 U.S. debate on the nature and implementation of affirmative action policies. While individual discrimination is against the law, policies that would eradicate discrimination through the imposition of quotas have met with considerable opposition (and indeed, have been declared unconstitutional by the U.S. Supreme Court).

As I have argued in this chapter, invoking the concepts of "group rights" and the ill-fated term "national minorities" only serves as a reminder of the discrimination, revisionism, and nationalism that plagued interwar European politics. National minorities are a social construct produced by the interactive processes set forward by states claiming groups as their co-nationals, by individual activists who promote such a conception, and by the policies of states that aim to acculturate a population into a single cultural community (Brubaker, 1995). As I have described in Chapter 4, the pursuit of such policies during the interwar period had disastrous consequences in Macedonia—just as it did for the rest of Europe. Not surprisingly, the concepts of collective rights and national minorities receded in the post–World War II period. Emphasis was placed on individual and not collective rights, with the ultimate goal of avoiding the poisonous disputes of the pre–World War II period (Pearson, 1983; Musgrave, 1997).

The revival of the collective rights discourse in the post-1989 period ought to be refuted. The tragic consequences of this logic in Bosnia, Croatia, and Kosovo have become evident throughout the 1990s, and, certainly, extending this logic to the Macedonian Question is detrimental to regional stability. In spite of Macedonian protests, there would be little to be gained from forcing Bulgaria and Greece to recognize Macedonian national minorities. On the contrary, it is a foregone conclusion that if the international community acted in such a fashion it would cause a nationalistic and anti-Western backlash in both countries. Moreover, the resolution of some of the demands put forward by Macedonian human rights activists—such as compensation for the property of post–World War II refugees—depends on the degree that the Greek state would be satisfied that the territorial status quo is respected.

The sheer presence of such activists and the employment of human rights discourse has some unintended consequences—namely the fact that the activists explicitly raise issues of nondiscrimination, democratization, observance of UN-sanctioned international standards, and so on. Raising these issues into the international community does help the long-term process of democratization for the Greek and Bulgarian societies. However, raising these issues has also invited the backlash of committed nationalists, who see all such talk as nothing else than pretense to justify FYROM-sponsored Macedonian irredentism. Indeed, it is possible to find individuals who support such a view among Bulgarians, Macedonians, and Greeks. In many respects, then, these controversies provide an extremely important test for the evolving international human rights regime and, more specifically, for the extent to which human rights have to be conceived in terms of individual rights or whether such rights should be considered as group rights. Indeed, for a long period of time, the UN and United States have insisted on the individual nature of human rights, especially because it was a discussion of group rights that was used to justify Nazism and Fascism in the mid-twentieth century. It remains to be seen whether the international institutions of the twenty-first century will be able to deal effectively with these challenges.

NOTES

1. One also finds a small Macedonian minority in Albania (Hill, 1999). However, this group has attracted limited attention. Albania officially accepted the existence of this minority in the 1991 CSCE meetings. It also allowed Macedonians from Albania to visit their relatives on the other side of the border.

2. The Macedonians of Australia have been quite explicit in admitting the close relationship between multiculturalism and the assertion of Macedonian ethnicity. In its 1992 Declaration, the Association of Refugee Children states: "Let Australia's policy of multiculturalism, which has created conditions in which we, the former child refugees, are able to preserve and develop our rich Macedonian culture, serve as a shining example to Greece, Bulgaria, and Albania" (1995: 188).

3. Not surprisingly, Danforth's (1995) initial statements produced a wealth of criticism by Greek scholars (see, for example, Agelopulos, 1997; Koliopoulos, 1997) who argued that his interpretation was quite false. Reacting to these criticisms, Danforth (2000: 52–53) has clarified his original interpretation by adding that his statements on the existence of different ethnic groups in Greek Macedonia should not be interpreted as statements about the numerical strength of the different groups.

4. Accordingly, Danforth's theoretical position is practically derived from the descriptions of the Macedonians of Florina, who, quite correctly, pointed out that they (the "locals") are a group quite distinct from the refugees. But this description simply fails to mention the fact that the label "local" is not an ethnic category. This label has been applied throughout Greek Macedonia to differentiate between all of the people who lived there before the refugees arrived and the refugees themselves. Therefore, it is not exclusive to the Macedonians of Florina.

5. There is also an argument to be made with regard to the identification of the "local language" as Macedonian. Namely, the older generations of the people who spoke the "local language" did not speak a language that was identical with the language spoken in FYROM. They spoke one of the several southern Slavic dialects that are present throughout the southern Balkans. The post-1945 standardization of these dialects into what became the official Macedonian language brought changes into the various dialects. In due course of time, and thanks to the influence of radio broadcasting and contact with their neighbors on the other side of the border, many of the Slavic speakers have adopted the more recent version of Macedonian spoken in FYROM today (Ioannidou, 1997). This phenomenon is observed practically wherever nation-state building brings with it the standardization of language. It simply points out the extent to which language should not be conceived as a "natural" indication of national identity.

6. According to the 1951 census the total number of those who declared "Slavic" as their mother tongue was 41,167. Of them, 14,476 were in the county of Florina

and 9,353 in the county of Pella (National Statistical Service of Greece, 1951). Post–World War II informal estimates reported by Kostopoulos (2000: 222–27) are higher. However, it is likely that such informal estimates express the siege mentality of the Cold War in the 1950s and 1960s.

7. Between 1948 and 1963 the Greek state officially deprived 22,266 people of their Greek citizenship (Kostopoulos, 2000: 219). A portion of this figure includes Slavo-Macedonians—the rest were Greek communists who had fled to Eastern Bloc countries.

8. It is indicative of the strong feelings involved that even the existence of commercial ties with the Macedonians of FYROM leads to a resurfacing of the old passions. In 1990–92 Florina was the beneficiary of cross-border trade with FYROM, whereby many Macedonians would cross the border on regular intervals and shop in the 500 shops of the city. This trade amounted to 150–200 million drachmas on a weekly basis and was quite important for the local economy. Despite the obvious benefits, local nationalists (and the local bishop) strongly protested against the cross-border trade, because they were afraid that regular contact with the Macedonians from FYROM would lead to a revival of the Macedonian language in the district (see Kostopoulos, 2000: 294).

9. In the 1950s and early 1960s, a variety of measures were undertaken. These included official declarations (under oath) whereby peasants declared that they are not going to speak again the "alien tongue"; the building of kindergartens to acculturate the next generation of Slavic speakers; as well as intimidation by the police and the army. Indirect funding of associations and other groups by the Greek secret agencies was also extensively used to finance a variety of activities aiming at Hellenization (for details, see Kostopoulos, 2000: 222–82).

10. For accounts of the emergence of the Balkan nation-states in the nineteenthth century, see Stavrianos (1958), Jelavich and Jelavich (1977) and Jelavich (1983). On the importance of nationhood as a defining characteristic of these states, see Smith (1986), Kitromilides (1983), and Roudometof (1998b). The relationship between religion and nationalism in Yugoslavia is explored in Ramet (1989: 299–327).

11. For more detailed discussions on the acculturation of the Vlach population, see Poulton et al. (1989: 29–36), Poulton (1991: 95–96, 189–92) and the Minority Rights Group (1990: 130–31). For the history of the Vlachs, see the classic study by Wace and Thompson (1914) and the more recent work of Winnifrith (1987).

12. The Gypsies (or Roma) are another group that is most often identified with the Muslims or Turks. There is a movement toward the opposite direction as well. In 1993, Macedonia's Roma political party addressed a letter to the UN calling for the creation of a separate "nation" (see Troxel, 1992; Poulton, 1991: 90–93; Ilchev and Perry, 1993: 35–41). Additionally, a number of Muslim Roma, apparently desiring to disassociate themselves from the Turks, have formed an association proclaiming Egypt as their historical homeland and asking for recognition of their minority group as "Egyptians." It is not surprising, that this declaration came from the Macedonian Roma, who are the most prosperous group among the Balkan Gypsies. The high rates of illiteracy, the relative absence of educational systems in the Romany language, the migratory lifestyle, and their dispersion make it unlikely the Roma will be able to transform themselves into an influential constituency.

13. Some Western observers have confused ethnic conflict among peoples with feelings of prejudice or animosity on an individual basis. Such feelings were certainly

absent in the Yugoslav case. See the survey research results cited by Gordy (1999: 2–6).

14. Legislation enacted throughout the 1980s followed this rationale. According to Law 1268/82 the Greek state does not recognize the degrees of students who attended universities where the language of instruction is "not widely recognized." The administrative interpretation of this regulation was that the only university included in this category was the SS Cyril and Methodius University of Skopje (Kostopoulos, 2000: 300). The goal of the legislation was to prevent Greek students from studying in the university and learning the Macedonian language.

15. Scholarly publications relying on information provided mainly by Macedonian human rights advocates are prone to exaggeration—but, unfortunately, third parties often unwittingly repeat such statements. For example, Hill's statement that "Macedonian is still today the second language of everyday communication in northern Greece" (1999: 23) is without any corroboration. Given the large numbers of Albanian immigrants and Pontic Greeks in northern Greece, it is more accurate to argue that Albanian and Russian supersede Macedonian as a language of everyday communication.

16. In the 1996 national elections, the Rainbow Coalition joined left-wing fringe groups and this led to a lower number of votes compared to their performance in the 1994 elections. The result is rather typical of all small parties in Europe whereby voters are able to use the elections for the European parliament to register their "protest vote" against the major political parties. In contrast, in the national elections, voters usually support one of the main contenders, because casting a vote for smaller parties is in itself inconsequential to the election's final outcome.

17. Karakasidou (2000a: 82–83) suggests a tripartite division among the Slavic population that, she argues, has been in place since the 1920s. First, there are those who possess an internalized sense of their Greekness and consistently express it in public and in private. These are the people Danforth (1995) refers to as "Macedonian Greeks." Second, there are those who possess a continuing sense of their distinctiveness and express it openly. They form the activists of Danforth's (1995) Macedonian human rights movement. Third, there are those who are oriented toward the Greek state at least externally—but they are not oriented toward the Greek nation. Identifying with neither of the two other categories, they are left homeless. Solutions that would clearly differentiate between civic and ethnic identity would be welcome for this third group, but it is rather unlikely that they would have a positive effect upon the orientations of the other two groups.

18. Also see Pollis (1987, 1993) on Eastern Orthodoxy's relationship to human rights and the role of the legal system in failing to become a counteracting force to the state's pervasive domination over Greek social life.

19. The celebrations of 26 October (St. Demetrius Day) and 28 October (the commemoration of Greece's entrance into World War II) were fused in northern Greece, becoming a single ethno-religious occasion that confirmed the Greekness of Macedonia. The date of 26 October is also the anniversary of the liberation of Thessaloniki by the Greek forces in the first Balkan war of 1912. See the analysis of Karakasidou (2000b) for further details and description. On the impact of the civil war, see also, Tsoukalas (1981), Mazower (1997), and Alivizatos (1981).

20. Pollis (1992) has addressed the issue of religious minorities (Protestant sects, Catholics, and Jehovah's Witnesses) who face the sanctions of the Greek state as well

as those of the local society. Her description of the general attitude concerning minority rights is directly relevant to the issue of minority rights for linguistic and cultural groups as well.

21. As early as 1991, Evangelos Kofos, who served for many years as an advisor to the Greek Foreign Ministry, expressed the urgency that Greek policy toward the Macedonian issue adapt into the new international norms. See Kofos's memorandum to the Foreign Ministry dated 29 April 1991, quoted in Kostopoulos (2000: 319).

22. When various minority cultural organizations are involved, there is also another important obstacle—the explicit ban imposed by the Bulgarian Fundamental Law of "political organizations based on ethnic or religious divisions," which led to a very complicated and prolonged procedure of registration for organizations of Bulgarian Turks, Romas, Karakachans, Vlachs, etc. In comparison, organizations of Bulgarian Jews, Armenians, and other groups faced much less trouble.

23. In July 1998, the European Commission for Human Rights accepted a lawsuit by OMO-Ilinden against the Republic of Bulgaria. The lawsuit claimed that Bulgaria was guilty of continuous violation of Article 11 of the European Convention for the Protection of Human Rights and Fundamental Freedoms (Ortakovski, 2000: 167–68). The 1999 recognition of OMO-Ilinden by the Sofia courts prevented the continuation of the legal case—and it might have been prompted in part by the Bulgarians' desire to show the country's willingness to conform with European legal standards.

24. *Trud Daily* 16 February 1999, No. 44 (15900), pp. 1–2; Sv.Vasileva, "We Legitimized an Anti-Bulgarian Party," *Trud Daily* 17 February 1999, No. 45 (15901), p. 8; see also same issue and page for an interview with the leader of the OMO-PIRIN Party; and on p. 9 Nenka Ivanova, "In Our Country a Fascist Party could be Registered."

25. Center for the Study of Democracy (1991 Survey of the Blagoevgrad Region, 1992, unpublished manuscript). This survey gives slightly different figures: in the Blagoevgrad region 79.7% of the population identify themselves as Bulgarians, 8.4% as Bulgarian Moslems, 4.4% as Macedonians, 3.6% as Gypsy/Roma, 1.2% as Turks, and 0.5% as Bulgarian Macedonians.

26. As Albert Londres, a French author from the beginning of the century, wrote: "We knew many families, where one of the brothers did identify himself to be a Serb, another a Bulgarian, and if there was a third one, then the third one leaned to the Greeks" (Londres, 1996: 43).

27. It is not surprising that Karakasidou (1997: 136) suggests that simplistic theories suggesting the existence of coherent ethnic communities in early twentieth-century Macedonia are theoretically and empirically unsound. In his study of Macedonian and Greek immigrants in Australia, Loring Danforth (1995) points to a similar process: families fragment over the issue of identity, with siblings opting for opposite identities. In Danforth's analysis, it is the ability of local people to craft identities for themselves that makes it possible for the same mother to give birth to a Greek and a Macedonian.

28. Certainly, there are significant historical, political, and social reasons for such a confusion in the region. On the other hand, in principle, ethnicity cannot easily be rationalized (Glazer and Moynihan, 1975). The same difficulty is observed among the pro-Macedonian minority press in Greece. For a discussion and analysis of this discourse see Hotzidis (1997: 143–70).

29. There is nothing surprising in the fact that some more or less closely related peoples have been transformed successfully into nations and reached the status of nation-states, while others have split into two or more separate nations. The case of Romania and the former Soviet republic of Moldova—where there is an almost complete absence of doubts and rebuttals about the common nature of the two nations—indicates how difficult an apparently "natural" reunification and accommodation may prove to be in fact (on Moldova, see Crowther, 1997; for further details, see the 1998 special topic issue of *Nationalities Papers*).

30. The analysis presented in this section explicitly seeks to go beyond the naïve or realist position that people's identities are simply a question of recording them. Given the fluid boundary between Bulgarians and Macedonians, the analysis has sought to articulate those characteristics that can produce a solid profile for different groups. In his review of an earlier version of this chapter, Eminov (2001) has argued that the sample for this study is too small. Suffice to say, the goal of qualitative analysis is different from that of quantitative analysis. The sample of twenty-two interviews is within the well-established parameters for social research—for the goal of the research is to tease out the meaning people ascribed to concepts, and not to provide evidence for the numerical strength of a particular group. Of course, this is not the first time that critics have conveniently blended the two types of research. Anastasia Karakasidou's (1993a) essay on the Slavic Macedonian minority in northern Greece was subject to this type of misinterpretation. It is important that academics display more refinement and rigor in their critiques and avoid using political criteria for the evaluation of social scientific research.

Chapter 6

The Albanian Question in the Southern Balkans

In the earlier chapters, I have discussed the articulation of Macedonian nationhood and its implications in modifying the centuries-old Macedonian Question. I argued that the conflict among Bulgaria, Greece, and FYROM is a symbolic struggle to define Macedonia and appropriate the cultural legacy of the territory (both in terms of ancient Macedonia as well as in terms of the medieval history of the region). Although Greek opposition to FYROM's recognition was an important obstacle in the international recognition of the post-1991 Macedonian state, this issue did not rise to the level of a real, as opposed to symbolic, conflict. The issue is substantively different when it comes to the Albanians of the southern Balkans.

First of all, unlike the Greek-Macedonian-Bulgarian symbolic conflict over Macedonia, the Albanian issue has sparked armed confrontation. Both the 1999 Kosovo Crisis and the 2001 Albanian-Macedonian strife have been extensively covered by the media and raised the status of the Albanian question to a topic of concern for the United States, the EU, NATO, the UN, and a host of other international associations. Second, the Albanian Question is not an interstate diplomatic issue. The FYROM and Kosovo Albanians lack statehood and, consequently, their representation in international forums is incomplete. Third, the entire radicalization of the Albanian movement is not determined by a national center and should not be viewed as an expression of an irresistible trend toward unification. In many respects, the Albanian state is important for symbolic reasons; it is the only state that is the official national homeland of Albanians. But the actual political trajectories of Albanians in FYROM and Kosovo have been determined not by the Tirana-based Albanian governments, but rather by the complex relationship among Albanians, Macedonians, and Serbs (and to a considerable extent, the international community).

All of the above shape the Macedonian Question in important and still largely unanticipated ways. First, the success of the radicalized Albanian movement in Kosovo has provided an example for the Macedonian Albanians to emulate. Second, the Albanian movement toward a Greater Albania has a bearing on Greek-Albanian relations. Both states have had territorial claims on each other's territory, and the future success of Albanian separatism in Kosovo and FYROM could provide the impetus for a collision between Greek and Albanian nationalisms. Finally, in the context of contemporary regional geopolitics, the disassociation of Macedonian Albanians from FYROM will undoubtedly weaken FYROM, raise questions about its sovereignty, and cause concern about FYROM's viability in the long term. Indeed, FYROM might end up as a new Bosnia, a state united in theory (but not in practice). Such a turn will strengthen Bulgarian claims for "unification" of Bulgarians and Macedonians—and it can be safely predicted that the Bulgarian VMRO-UMCS will be in favor of such a move. FYROM's alliance with Turkey sets forward the well-known (yet not too likely) scenario where FYROM calls upon Turkey for assistance in its dispute with Serbia or Bulgaria or Greece. Turkey's entrance into the arena transforms the conflict into a broader geopolitical dispute between Bulgaria, Greece, and Turkey.

It is therefore clear that the Albanian national question has become a central geopolitical issue in the southern Balkans. In this chapter, I describe the dynamics of the Albanian Question in terms of three separate, but interrelated, sets of issues. First, there is the set of issues involving Greek-Albanian relations. These issues range from the situation of Albanian immigrants in Greece to the fate of the Greek Orthodox minority in Albania to Albanian irredentism vis-à-vis the Greek territory of Epirus. Second, there is the Kosovo issue, a topic that has been discussed extensively in the popular press. In the aftermath of the 1999 Kosovo Crisis and the transformation of Kosovo into an international protectorate, the Kosovo issue appears to have been "solved" in terms of its *de facto* separation from Serbia. However, its long-term status remains uncertain. Although the fall of the Milosevic government removed Serbia from the list of international pariah states, it should be noted that the post-Milosevic governments are not likely to allow the formal separation of Kosovo from Serbia. Third, there is the issue of the Macedonian Albanians and their relationship to the Slavic Macedonian majority. This issue has come to the forefront of the international media in 2001 as civil war broke out between the Albanians of the self-declared National Liberation Army and Macedonian armed forces. However, the overview of Albanian-Macedonian relations in this chapter concludes with the 1999 Kosovo Crisis. The post-1999 events are discussed in the Postscript.

GREEK-ALBANIAN RELATIONS AND THE MINORITY QUESTION

The Albanians are divided into two groups, the Geghs of the north (who tend to be Muslim with a minority that is Catholic) and the Tosks of the south (who also are predominately Muslim, but include a substantial number of Orthodox as well). Additionally, the Geghs (who live in northern Albania and Kosovo) are less urbanized than the Tosks and, traditionally, have been more conservative. The 1913 declaration of Albanian independence was rather rhetorical since the country soon fell into anarchy, and during World War I (1914–18) Serb and Greek forces occupied its northern and southern parts.

The origins of the minority question in Greek-Albanian relations are directly linked with the drawing of the boundary between Albania and Greece. Following the 1912–13 Balkan Wars, the Great Powers, the Balkan states, and the Ottoman Empire negotiated the final territorial gains that the Balkan states would get from the defeated Ottoman Empire. In these negotiations, Greece was offered a choice between territory in southern Albania and the Aegean Islands. The Greek government chose the Aegean Islands. Consequently, the international committee responsible for finalizing the boundary between Greece and Albania did not satisfy Greek claims and included a contested region of the south into the Albanian state. Subsequently, the Greeks in the regions of Gyrogaster (Argyrokastro) and Korce (Korytsa) revolted and asked for Greek troops to intervene. To avoid a direct confrontation, the parties signed the Protocol of Corfu (1914), which granted autonomy to the Greek minority. By 1914, following the declaration of World War I and with encouragement by the Entente, Greek forces returned to the region and occupied it militarily. It was during this period that the Greek army conducted a survey of the region and published in 1919 a map of the southern part of Albania where the region is officially called "Northern Epirus." Subsequently, the term was adopted into Greek discourse, in spite of the fact that the survey was (obviously) biased.[1] In 1920, an international committee set out to redraw the new state's boundaries. The committee's final decision left a portion of the Greek population within Albanian territory and, likewise, a portion of the Albanian population within Greek territory. The former region became known as Northern Epirus, while the latter region, home to approximately 20,000 Albanians, became henceforth known as Chameria (Thesprotia in Greek).[2] Map 6.1 provides a basic guide to the region—including the ill-defined territories of Chameria and Northern Epirus.

The "minority question" was a concern for Theodoros Pangalos, whose coup d'état took place on 25 June 1925. Pangalos considered himself a friend of Albania, spoke Albanian, and was proud of his half-Albanian origin. Under his regime, the two states moved decisively to normalize relations in a

Map 6.1
Political Map of Albania, Including Chameria and Northern Epirus

whole range of topics, from commercial relations to citizenship laws. Indeed, the two countries agreed on mutually accepted guidelines and regulations whose goal was to sort out who was Albanian and who was Greek. This was a vexing question because there was no clear-cut way of differentiating between the two. The two states established mutually accepted rules according to which people had to make a choice within a certain period with regard to their preferred citizenship.

Albanian-Greek relations took a negative turn in 1927, when the administration of the Greek Ministry of Agriculture realized the consequences of the original agreement regarding the compensation of land originally owned by Albanian landlords that had been expropriated by the Greek state. These

Albanian land properties were estimated to be around one million *stremmas* (1 *stremma* = 0.10 hectares). The amount of money required for compensation was deemed exuberant and, consequently, the initial Greek-Albanian agreement was never ratified by the parliament (Mihalopoulos, 1987: 66–71).

The resulting impasse led to a new round of Albanian complaints in 1928. The complaints raised two issues: the land question and the treatment of the Chams. With regard to the Chams, the Albanian government complained that the Greek government was persecuting the minority. There was little evidence of direct state persecution, but the Albanians insisted that the Greek state open minority schools for the Chams, which the Greek side firmly opposed. Also, the Albanian government complained that the Chams' property was expropriated and given to Greek refugees from Anatolia. The Greek government replied that this was done in consultation with the local religious authorities of the Albanian community, and it concerned solely the necessity to find temporary accommodation for the refugees (Mihalopoulos, 1987: 95–97). Over time the list of complaints was extended to the Chams' effective denial of their right to get elected in local elections. The reports of a League of Nations committee and the reply by the Greek government reveal that part of the bone of contention concerned the change in the status of the local Albanian landlords. In Ottoman times, the overlords received revenues from neighboring villages. But the peasants refused to pay tribute after their land was occupied by the Greek state and in this case they "expropriated" what the Albanian overlords considered to be their property (Mihalopoulos, 1987: 108–9). In June 1928, the League of Nations turned down the Albanian petition against Greece. The compensation for land properties had not been paid until 1933; and when it was paid it fell short of Albanian expectations.[3] As a result of these Greek-Albanian confrontations, the Chams were viewed with suspicion by the Greek state authorities.

The Italian attack on Greece in 1940 took place through Albanian territory; this led to Greece declaring war on Albania. The formal state of war existed until the late 1980s. When Greece entered into war against Italy in October 1940, the Greek authorities disarmed 1,800 Champ conscripts and put them to work on local roads, while the next month they deported all remaining Albanian males to camps or to island exile (Mazower, 2000: 25). In 1941, in the aftermath of the German occupation of Greece, the Albanian government at the time submitted a report to the Italian government where it spelled out the Albanian demands on Greece. These included territorial demands on the Greek province of Epirus, which was deemed by the Albanians to be populated by a majority of Albanians.

During World War II, the Italians who occupied Albania in the post-1939 period organized the creation of a Greater Albania in an effort to attract Albanian support for their occupation (Fischer, 1999: 61–88). Indeed, the Albanian government asked for the "unification" of Chameria, Kosovo, and western Macedonia into a single Albanian state (Mihalopoulos, 1987: 161–62). This instance is among the few open declarations of Albanian irredentism in the twentieth century. During the occupation of Yugoslavia by the Axis powers, the Italian government arranged to have Kosovo united with Albania (Malcolm, 1998: 291). On this occasion, Albanian schools were opened in Kosovo for the first time since the 1910s (Logoreci, 1977: 69–70). When Italy surrendered to the Allies, the Germans took over from the Italians and followed a similar policy of fostering Albanian independence and nationalism in Kosovo. They set up a second League of Prizren, named after the first League of Prizren (1878), the first Albanian nationalist organization. They also armed close to 15,000 Kosovo Albanians (Malcolm, 1998: 305).

During the occupation of Greece by the Axis powers, the Albanian minority in Chameria campaigned for the annexation of the region into the Albanian state and enrolled in armed units sponsored by the Italians. Additionally, several hundred Chams enrolled in the anti-communist and nationalist movement *Balli Kombetar* (to be discussed later on in this chapter). From 1943 the armed Chams joined the German forces in burning Greek villages (Mazower, 2000: 25; Antonopoulos, 1999: 102–3). With the withdrawal of the German forces in 1944, the Greek right-wing guerrilla forces of the National Republican Greek League (*Ethnikos Dimorkatikos Ellinikos Syndesmos*), commanded by Napoleon Zervas, made an offer to the Chams to join them against the communist guerrilla forces of ELAS. When the Chams turned down this offer, Zervas ordered a general attack against the Chams, an action supported by the peasants whose villages had been burned down by the Chams and who were all too eager to extract revenge. Many of the Chams' villages were burned and most of the Chams (around 18,000) fled to Albania.[4]

During World War II, three military guerrilla movements developed in Albania. The first was organized by the pro-royalist forces of Abas Kupi, a former officer of the germanderie under the reign of King Zogu. Its power base was in the northern part of the country. The second movement was the *Balli Kombetar* (National Front), under the leadership of distinguished writer, diplomat, and scholar Midhat Frasheri. This was a republican movement and it supported a program of social, political, and agrarian reforms. Frasheri, its leader, was the son of Abdul Frasheri, one of the three legendary Frasheri brothers who were the protagonists of the post-1878 Albanian national movement. The organization's program included the unification of all Albanian areas; this coincided with the Italian-sponsored Greater Albania.[5] The third movement was the communist guerrilla movement that developed in close association with the Yugoslav Communist Party. Eventually, civil war broke out, and in the course of the 1943–44 period, the communists were successful in eradicating all resistance by the other two movements (Logoreci, 1977: 72–80; for details, see Fischer, 1999).[6]

After World War II, Albanian communist leader Enver Hoxha was angered by Greek claims that Albania should be placed on the side of the Axis allies. Both sides sought retribution from each other. Because neither side would cede, the formal state of war between the two states remained in effect for several decades. With the end of World War II, the right-wing Greek government felt that Greece was entitled to Northern Epirus as compensation for Greece's participation in World War II on the side of the Allies. The Greek government also invited British troops to enter the country and help the government deal with the Greek communists, who, in the aftermath of the German withdrawal from Greece, held control over large parts of the state. The Albanian communists were afraid that the British troops that had landed in Greece in 1944 could invade Albania proper (Logoreci, 1977: 90). More important, members of the Greek minority even took up arms in an effort to promote their cause to the Allies. Hoxha, on the other hand, did not hesitate to support the Greek communists in the Greek Civil War (Xhudo, 1995: 117–20). In the context of the emerging Cold War, the Greek claims vis-à-vis southern Albania (or Northern Epirus) received a favorable ear by the United States, and commissions were set up to inquire into the Greek claims. The end result was Hoxha's policy of isolation from the West, which persisted for several decades.[7]

Greek-Albanian relations improved only after Hoxha's death in 1985 and the collapse of communism in Albania during the 1990s. The two events that have shaped Greek-Albanian relations in the 1990s are the immigration wave of Albanians into Greece and the revitalization of the Greek minority organizations and their entrance into Albanian post-communist political life. The Albanian immigration wave was a reflection of the poor economic conditions in the country. Between 1989 and 1992 Albania's GNP fell by more than 50%, while industrial production declined by 60% and agricultural production by 30% (statistics reported by Biberaj, 1998: 188). By mid-1991 Albania had a budget deficit of approximately U.S. $580 million, a balance of payments deficit of U.S. $400 million and a foreign exchange deficit of U.S. $170 million (Xhudo, 1995: 125). These poor economic conditions led to a mass immigration wave directed mainly toward Greece (and to lesser extent, Italy). The Greek response to this immigration wave was belated, and it took several years for the Greek authorities to develop a coherent administrative plan to register the immigrants. Initially, the Greek state's reaction was shaped by attempts to provide a preferential treatment for the Greek minority. When in December 1990 the first wave of immigration began, the Greek consulates initiated a policy of providing visas to members of the Greek minority with Orthodox Albanians next and Muslim Albanians last (Vihou et al., 1995: 70). The result of this policy was that the overwhelming majority of the labor force from the ranks of the Greek minority ended up in Greece. Subsequently, the numerical strength of the minority—in terms of the persons actually residing in southern Albania—declined significantly in the 1990s. The main issue that has preoccupied Greek research on the minority concerns the minority's lack of adequate education in communist Albania, as well as the biases in the textbooks used in minority education.[8]

The political mobilization of the Greek minority was made possible only with the collapse of the communist regime in the 1990s.[9] Although Greece and Albania resumed diplomatic relations in 1971, the state of war between the two countries was formally maintained until 1987 (Veremis, 1995a: 35). During the communist regime's rule, the Greek minority was isolated and subjected to harsh repression by the authorities, especially with respect to religious practices. By the mid-1980s the regime's attitude had softened and there was the possibility of relatives visiting their compatriots on the other side of the border. But before discussing the minority issue in the 1990s, it is necessary to provide a brief overview of the Albanian political institutions in the 1990s.

The democratization of Albanian society produced two main rivals, the former communist People of Labor Party (PLA or Socialist Party) and the Democratic Party of Albania (DPA) led by Sali Berisha. Although the PLA won the first free elections in 1991, the persistent criticism of the opposition eventually led to the DPA winning the 1992 elections with a record 66.7% of the vote. It is important to highlight the degree to which the two parties relied on the preexisting ethnic or tribal loyalties—the Socialists gaining support by the Tosks; the Democrats gaining the support of the Geghs, who had been marginalized and persecuted by the communist regime (Blumi, 1997).

The Berisha government (1992–97), however, suffered from a number of growing pains typical of post-communist Eastern European regimes.[10] Throughout the 1990s, unemployment remained around 15% of the active labor population. Moreover, favoritism, fear of outsiders, persecution of the opposition, a tendency to use the government for the party's benefit, and willingness to flirt with extreme nationalism all characterized the regime, which, in this respect, resembled more the post-1989 Russian version of "democracy" than Western democracies. Berisha expelled members of the opposition from the parliament, purged moderate members of his party, and even tried to discredit the PLA by refusing to distribute international food aid in the towns with mayors from the PLA. State security harassed members of the opposition, and PLA members (like Fatos Nano, who later became prime minster) were jailed (Biberaj, 1998: 158–61).

The Berisha government instituted privatization policies sponsored by the IMF and World Bank—but whatever economic improvement the people experienced in the 1990s was largely the result of remittances sent back home by the immigrant workers dispersed in Greece, Italy, Germany, and a few other countries.[11] By 1995, the remittances from Albanian immigrants alone accounted for 25% of Albania's GNP. The post-1995 normalization of the status of Greece's illegal Albanian immigrants is likely to help the preservation of this important financial source. The so-called liberalization of the economy led to a variety of economic schemes ranging from money laundering to pyramid-deposit schemes.[12] From 1991 on, approximately twenty "banks" were set up in Albania and were able to attract the investment of numerous Albanians with promises of huge returns (30% to 40%). The so-called investment schemes absorbed close to 1.2 billion U.S. $ or around 50% of the country's GNP (Antonopoulos, 1999: 230). In early 1996 new pyramid schemes (Xhaferi and Poppulli) offered 15% to 100% interest to prospective investors for a three-month deposit in such pyramid schemes. This enticed people to invest and soon the total number of investors reached two million (out of a population of close to 3.5 million). Some of the people involved in these schemes maintained close ties to the DPA, while it is also rumored that the Al-Qaeda also participated in the schemes.[13] The pyramid schemes collapsed in the first half of 1997, triggering widespread riots throughout the country (Emadi, 2000). The country soon plunged into anarchy, and the riots led to close to 2,000 deaths. In the end, the people rose up, took to the streets, and looted the army depots, with thousands of guns ending up in the hands of citizens. Eventually, the Berisha government lost the next elections (1997), and, despite vocal protests, Berisha agreed to assume the post of the opposition leader and step down. Many of the weapons (Kalashnikov automatic guns, grenades, and other small weapons) that people seized during this turbulent period eventually ended up in Kosovo and FYROM.[14]

Following the collapse of the communist regime, the Greek minority was organized in the *Omonia* (Harmony) party and attempted to compete in the first free elections. The party's organization was the result of mobilization among the minority's intelligentsia with little or no contact with the émigré associations on the other side of the border or any ties to the Greek government. The Ministry of Justice attempted to restrict parties that organized themselves according to an "ethnic" basis (Vihou et al., 1995: 63–70), but *Omonia* was successful in electing five deputies to the new Albanian Parliament. Following this electoral success a law was passed barring the formation of parties based on ethnicity. Soon afterwards, however, the more nationalistic-oriented individuals of the minority, assisted by Greek émigré organizations, set up the Movement of Human Rights. This party was formulated on an explicitly non-ethnic basis, thereby making it eligible to participate in the 1992 nationwide elections. Despite some problems, the party was able to participate in that year's elections, and its performance registered the dispersion of the Greek minority throughout Albania (including those regions not recognized as "minority zones" by the Albanian government).[15]

In addition to the issue of the Greek minority's political participation, Greek-Albanian relations in the 1990s were also influenced by the post-communist reorganization of the Albanian Orthodox Church.[16] The church suffered extensively during the communist regime, and in the course of the official persecution of its personnel many priests and bishops died (including Archbishop Chistophoros in 1958). The 1950 Church Constitution was abolished with the 4,337 decree dated 13 November 1967 (Georgoulis, 1995: 154–55). This abolition was reiterated and strengthened during the 5th Congress of the Albanian Communist Party and officially sanctioned with the 1976 constitution that declared Albania to be an atheist state. Therefore, following the collapse of the communist regime, the Orthodox Church had to begin rebuilding its institutional structure from ground zero. In the 1990–92 period, because of lack of an approved constitution, the church operated solely on the basis of its canons. On 24 July 1992 the Ecumenical Patriarchate of Constantinople (Istanbul) elected Anastasios—a Greek citizen—as the new head of the Albanian Church and ordered that no other church organization (including the U.S.-based Albanian Orthodox Church) had jurisdiction on Albanian soil (Georgoulis, 1995: 155). The church reorganization triggered protests by the U.S.-based Albanian Orthodox Church, which lost the opportunity to extend its influence into the home country.

On 25 June 1993, the Albanian authorities deported Archimandrite Chrysostomos Maidonis, a Greek clergyman working with the Orthodox archbishop, to Greece on grounds of his alleged "nationalist propaganda" against the Albanian state. President Berisha also declared that only Albanian nationals should occupy posts with the Albanian Orthodox Church, thereby raising the possibility that the archbishop himself (who is a Greek citizen) might be deported as well. In this context, it is important to note that the boundaries differentiating Orthodox Albanians from Greeks are unclear. Many members of the Greek minority have only an elementary knowledge of Greek and look to the Orthodox Church as the basic cultural marker for their own cultural differentiation from the rest of the population. Hence, an emphasis on the "Greek" character of the Albanian Orthodox Church can be seen as an attempt to "acculturate" members of the Albanian Orthodox community into Hellenism. The deportation was accompanied by protests by the Greek minority and clashes between the Albanian police and the demonstrators (Antonopoulos, 1999: 129). The minority rallied behind the archbishop, whereas the Albanian authorities treated the situation as a nationalist provocation. On the other side of the border, the Greek authorities were quick to react.

In the days following the Archmandrite's deportation, some 5,000 Albanians were deported to Albania.[17] Given the inadequate control of the border, there was little doubt that most of them would be back within a few days, but the purpose of these actions was to "remind" Albania of its financial dependence on the income coming from Albanian workers in Greece. In an interview in the Greek journal *Economic Review* (19 August 1993), Greek Premier Costantinos Mitsotakis made clear that Albania could not afford to react to the deportations of Albanians from Greece since its weak economy made the state dependent upon the remittance of Albanians from Greece. In the aftermath of this affair, Mitsotakis declared that the status of the Greek minority in southern Albania (or Northern Epirus) should be equated with that of the Albanian population in Kosovo, and if autonomy was given to them, then the same should apply to the Greeks in Albania. The post-1993 socialist governments abandoned this approach, and relations between the two states have improved.

However, another round of political confrontation was initiated on 10 April 1994, when an Albanian military post near the Greek border was attacked and unidentified armed men killed two soldiers. The Albanians blamed the attack on the extremist "Northern Epirus Liberation Front" (*Metopo Apeleutheroseos Voreiou Ipirou*, or MAVI) and argued that the Front had received assistance by minority members and the Greek Special Forces. The Albanians' suspicions were confirmed when, in 1995, Greek authorities discovered and successfully prosecuted the members of MAVI (Antonopoulos, 1999: 159). However, the Albanian president, Berisha, did not hesitate to accuse Greece of "state terrorism" and to suggest a parallel between Athens and Belgrade in terms of their regional policy (quoted in Biberaj, 1998: 243). Berisha's charges that Greece had "expansionist goals" led to the Albanian police investigating and eventually arresting five members of the Greek community, who were accused of having assisted in the attack. The Albanian authorities charged these five former members of the *Omonia* group with plotting an armed insurrection against the Albanian government. All of them were found guilty in a kangaroo trial that caused protests by international associations (Papoudakis, 1996). Within months of their imprisonment, however, economic and diplomatic pressure from Greece led to their release.[18]

As this brief overview suggests, Greek-Albanian relations remained precarious throughout the 1990s. Minor incidents or police matters frequently led to political confrontations between the two sides. However, it is important to highlight the extent to which the Greek and Albanian economies have grown interdependent, and eventually this factor prevents the recurrent disputes from becoming major obstacles in interstate relations. For example, Greek exports to Albania increased from $12.2 million in 1991 to $221 million in 1994 (Giannaris, 1996: 58). Moreover, the Greek state instituted in 1997 a green card program that allowed the majority of illegal immigrants to register, thereby making it possible for them to stay in the country legally and work without fear of prosecution. According to the latest reports of the Greek Unemployment Agency (OAED), the total number of people who registered with the green card program is close to 800,000, and authorities estimate that close to 75% of them are Albanian immigrants (reported in the newspaper *Ethnos*, 16 August 2001).

In the long run, economics has solved the Greek minority issue in southern Albania. Given the large difference in the standards of living between the two countries, it is unlikely that most of the Greek minority who immigrated into Greece in the 1990s will be moving back to their original homes in the near future. On the contrary, it is far more likely that both ethnic Albanian immigrants as well as minority immigrants will choose to remain in Greece. In this respect, the relations between the two states are greatly influenced by the discrimination against the Albanian immigrants by Greeks and the sub-sequent resentment Albanians feel against Greeks. The unstable geopolitical situation of the 1990s (involving Kosovo and FYROM) further complicated matters. Still, the successful incorporation and inclusion of the Albanian immigrants by Greece should aid significantly in the development of better relations between Athens and Tirana.[19] Currently, this is perhaps the most important challenge facing the two countries.

The extent to which the state and the broader Greek society succeed in dealing with this challenge will determine the long-term relations between Athens and Tirana, as well as the economic development of the two countries. In 2000 and 2001, Greek conservative critics have campaigned against various forms of Albanian incorporation into Greek society—and it is important that the Greek state stays the course with regard to its policy of inclusion. For example, Albanian students have enrolled in Greek schools, and some of them have received honors, thereby becoming eligible for participating in the school parades during the Greek national holidays and carrying the Greek flag. Conservative Greek critics consider such activities to be inappropriate, thereby provoking a fierce debate on the Albanian immigrants' future incorporation into twenty-first century Greek society.

THE ALBANIAN QUESTION IN THE FORMER YUGOSLAVIA

The Kosovo issue played an important role in post-1945 communist Yugoslavia. In the 1940s and 1950s, it was among the most important is-sues in Albanian-Yugoslav-Soviet relations. In the 1970s and 1980s, it be-came an important site for the resurgence of nationalism in Yugoslavia. The resurrection of Yugoslavia by the communist partisans of General Tito en-tailed the recognition of different nations of Yugoslavia as equal partners. This was a reflection of the communists' desire to stress the degree to which their new state was substantively different from the interwar, Serb-controlled, Kingdom of Serbs, Slovenes, and Croats.

The Yugoslav communist leadership took specific steps to improve the conditions of Albanians in Kosovo.[20] But it also opposed the annexation of Kosovo to Albania. In fact, Tito's high profile among southeastern Euro-pean communists and his control over the Albanian Communist Party in the 1940s prevented the Albanian leadership from even raising this issue in public. Bowing to Tito's directives, between 1945 and 1948 the policy of the Albanian communists explicitly rejected "Albanian unification" and opted for the creation of a larger Balkan federation that would include Albania as one of the partners (Malcolm, 1998: 319). In fact, the influence Tito held over neighboring communist countries was perhaps the most important factor responsible for the Tito-Stalin rift of 1948 and the expulsion of Yugoslav communists from the international communist organization (Banac, 1987: 29).

In 1950s Yugoslavia, the communist regime instituted a program of Yugoslavism, whose goal was to construct a single Yugoslav people from the different ethnic groups and nations of the federation. This program fostered resentment among non-Serbs, leading to its eventual modification after the 1966 dismissal of the Minister of the Interior Aleksandar Rankovic, who served as the mastermind of the original pro-Yugoslav program.[21] During the 1950s, this campaign involved the suppression of all manifestations of Albanian nationalism, as well as the forced emigration of some 195,000 Albanians into Turkey (Vickers, 1998: 157). After 1966, Yugoslavia enjoyed a less oppressive atmosphere that fostered the expression of (Croat, Bosnian, and Albanian) "separatism" (i.e., nationalism). During this period, the Kosovo Albanians demanded equal rights and even called for a Kosovo republic in 1968 (Malcolm, 1998: 324–26; Sfetas and Kentrotis, 1995: 85). The Yugoslav authorities allowed the Kosovo Albanians to fly the Albanian flag as their own national symbol. More important, however, was the Albanians' demand for better education in their own language. The Yugoslav authorities responded to this demand by setting up the University of Prishtina in 1970. Approximately 200 teachers from Albania were brought to teach in the university, whose population soon reached a total of 30,000 students. This dramatically improved the proportion of the Kosovo Albanians' student population, which jumped from 38% in 1968 to 72% in 1978. The result was a partial reversal of the traditional overrepresentation of Serbs and Montenegrins in the civil sector.

In an attempt to provide a more comprehensive solution to the national tensions among the Yugoslav republics, the 1974 constitution fractured the federal structure even more by expanding the autonomy of the provinces of Vojvodina and Kosovo. In fact, the constitution stopped just one step short of turning them into full-fledged republics. The reason for not doing so had a lot to do with the general framework of Titoist Yugoslavia. The standard classification of peoples included a legal distinction between "nations" (*narod*) and "nationalities" (*narodnost*) or what has been rendered as "minorities" in Western discourse. The nations were a potentially state-forming unit. Their national homelands (Croatia, Slovenia, Serbia, Macedonia) were full-fledged members of the federation, and they had, at least in theory, the right to secede. Of course, this was rhetorical because the communists had a monopoly over the political institutions of all the republics, thereby preventing any real exercise of state sovereignty. In contrast to the Yugoslav "nations," the "nationalities" did not have their national homelands in federal Yugoslavia (e.g., Albania and Hungary) (Malcolm 1998: 328; Simic, 1998: 189–91). The autonomy of the provinces was first established in 1947, but the 1974 constitution expanded this autonomy and established assemblies in both Vojvodina and Kosovo. This was viewed as a "carving" of the Serb territory and served as a first basis for Serb grievances in the next decades (Ramet, 1992: 73–78; Dragnich, 1989; Vickers, 1998: 183).

During the 1970s, both Macedonian Albanians and Kosovo Albanians lived under similar conditions. However, the two communities' trajectories became differentiated during that decade. In large part, this was the result of the Albanians dealing with different adversaries in the two regions. The recognition of Kosovo's autonomous status led to a proliferation of nationalist activity that took the form of organizations, literature, etc., spreading over its territory. This new wave of nationalist activity was directly related to the rise of a new generation of local intellectuals, who replaced the traditional authority of the elders of the Albanian clans (Vickers, 1998: 173–74). In 1981, Albanian nationalism expressed itself in a series of demonstrations, arson, and clashes with the police. The University of Prishtina—with a population of approximately 37,000 students—served as the principal site for the nationalist activity. Through the blatant use of military force, the Yugoslav armed forces crushed the protests.

Malcolm (1998: 337) highlights the extent to which grievances about discrimination in employment in the public sector were intermingled with nationalism. The nature of the Albanian complaints is clarified when one takes into account the fact that only some 178,00 people out of a population of 1.5 million had jobs in the public sector. Of them, Serbs and Montenegrins held some 30% of the positions. The socioeconomic analysis performed by Yugoslav communist leaders in the aftermath of the 1981 protests highlighted this situation. But nothing was done to rectify it. While public investment in Kosovo was among the highest in Yugoslavia's republics, it did not lead to an amelioration of the dreadful conditions in the labor market.[22] Most investment was capital-intensive rather than labor-intensive, thereby preventing the absorption of surplus workforce in industry. The 1981 suppression of the protests did not put an end to nationalist activity—although such activity did not imply a desire for unification with Albania proper (Vickers, 1998: 202–5). Throughout the 1980s a number of underground organizations were uncovered, and, during the 1981–87 period, the local authorities brought criminal charges against thousands of Albanians (Ramet, 1992: 195–98; von Kohl and Libal, 1997: 73–75).

In the People's Republic of Macedonia, despite the post–World War II Yugoslav rhetoric, Albanians and Macedonians continued to live largely separate lives, mainly due to the limited intermarriage between Muslim Albanians and Orthodox Macedonians.[23] Albanian nationalist activities proliferated in the 1970s, including underground organizations, such as the National Party of Labor created in 1979 by Macedonian Albanians in Tetovo. The party aimed at the secession of the Albanians who inhabited the western part of the People's Republic (Clement, 1998: 363). The Macedonian Albanians also supported the 1981 student uprising in Kosovo and issued statements calling for equal treatment in political representation, education, and language (Sfetas and Kentrotis, 1995: 99).[24] The result was a deterioration of inter-ethnic relations and a further distancing between the groups. However, the Macedonian Albanians' methods were less confrontational than the methods employed by their counterparts in Kosovo. Reacting to the Albanians' demands, the Macedonian authorities proceeded to harden their stance in the 1980s.

Already in 1981, the Pedagogical Council of the Republic stated that there were "weaknesses in the educational content, programs, textbooks, and reference books used by the Albanian nationality in Macedonia" and stressed that "the publishers were not careful enough to prevent the penetration of Albanian nationalist, irredentist, and counter-revolutionary tendencies" in the Albanian-language publications (quoted in Ortakovski, 2000: 279–80). During the 1980s, the Macedonian authorities abolished measures taken to ensure the Albanians' proportional representation in state affairs, including the use of the Albanian language in state institutions and education. In 1986, 4,346 parents, largely Albanians, were fined because they sent their children to religious schools instead of the state-run institutions (Perry, 2000a: 275–77). In an effort to prevent the spread of Albanian "religious nationalism," the state forbade in 1987 the instruction of the Koran to children under the age of 15. In 1987 the state authorities canceled Albanian language classes in the middle schools, and in 1988 Albanian schools were converted into bilingual schools. In the process, the state sacked some 155 Albanian teachers who were accused of fostering Albanian nationalism.

The situation of Albanians in Macedonia became more complicated in the 1980s as many Kosovo Albanians, fearful of the post-1981 Serb repression, settled in the Albanian-inhabited regions of the People's Republic of Macedonia, thereby increasing the Albanian majority in these areas. Macedonian Albanians, trained in Saudi Arabia, organized religious seminars and built mosques. In the course of the 1980s, Albanian nationalist organizations demanding the independence of the Albanian-inhabited western provinces of the People's Republic emerged once again (Poulton, 1991: 26; Sfetas and Kentrotis, 1995: 103–4). The authorities reacted by forbidding land sale to Albanians in the western part of the republic as a way of preventing more land from falling into Albanian hands. The deterioration of interethnic relations was reflected in the 1989 constitutional revision, according to which the People's Republic was declared the "state of the Macedonian people" (thereby excluding all non-ethnic Macedonian groups, such as the Albanians). The specifics of the post-1989 evolution in Albanian-Macedonian relations are discussed in the next section. In the remainder of this section, let us conclude with an overview of the Albanian-Serb confrontation in Kosovo.

The Kosovo issue played a central role in the disintegration of Yugoslavia in the 1990s. Up until the mid-1980s, Yugoslavia appeared to be stable because the threat to centralization was coming from "peripheral" republics and not from the center (Serbia). In fact, the possibility of fragmentation remained rather remote given the control of the Communist Party over the federal apparatus and its commitment to the federal idea.[25] Through the 1970s and '80s economic conditions worsened, causing a widening of the economic gap between the country's rich northern provinces and the south (Rusinow, 1988; Woodward, 1995). While the country was facing dire economic conditions in the 1980s, Serb resentment against the 1974 constitutional arrangement was openly expressed in the Draft Memorandum prepared in 1985 by a working group of the Serbian Academy of Sciences under the chairmanship of Antonije Isakovic, one of the country's prominent writers. The Serb complaints against the government argued for discriminatory policy vis-à-vis Serbia in the economic field; for the partition of Serbia proper into three parts under the 1974 constitution (Serbia proper and the autonomous provinces of Vojvodina and Kosovo); and for the allegedly anti-Serb policy pursued in Kosovo by Albanian "separatists" (Cviic, 1991: 65). In January 1986, 200 prominent Belgrade intellectuals signed a petition accusing the authorities of committing national treason and "genocide" against the Serb minority in Kosovo (Poulton, 1991: 19).[26] The intensification of nationalist feelings with respect to the Kosovo Serbs was also greatly facilitated by the attitude of the Serb Orthodox Church. The church added a religious element to the conflict since it had allied itself with those opposing the Serb "genocide" within the province (Ramet, 1999: 99–116).

Slobodan Milosevic, a rather unknown Communist Party apparatchik in the 1980s, successfully exploited the Albanian "threat" to build popular support for the Communist Party. In the spring of 1987 Milosevic paid a visit to Kosovo to take part in the celebration of the battle of 1389, the most important national holiday of Serbia. Milosevic played out the national themes with reference to the contemporary situation. He promised Kosovo Serbs that "nobody would ever beat them again." Within a few months, he used their alleged suffering to attack the previous leadership in Serbia and carried out a purge of his opponents throughout Serbia. In October 1987, more federal police units were dispatched in Kosovo. Milosevic staged a number of protests and demonstrations that led to the fall of the local governments in Vojvodina and Montenegro (in 1988 and 1989) bringing the control of these regions under the auspices of his followers.

On 3 February 1989, Serbia's National Assembly passed a series of amendments that brought Kosovo's security, judiciary, finance, and social planning under Serb control. The Albanians protested that this action violated the provisions set forth in the 1974 constitutions (Vickers, 1998: 235). In

Kosovo, a general strike in February 1989 led to military oppression that crushed the Albanian protests within a week, claiming a reported number of twenty-four deaths. On 23 March 1989 Kosovo's Assembly, ringed by Yugoslav army tanks, gave its consent to the constitutional changes demanded by Belgrade (Cviic, 1991: 67–68). On 28 March 1989 Serbia's Assembly adopted them, giving the Serb authorities in Belgrade control over Kosovo's police, courts, and territorial defense (a similar strategy was followed in Vojvodina as well). In the aftermath of this coup, the Serb authorities proceeded to fire some 115,000 Albanians from their public sector positions (Maliqi, 1998: 230). This figure represented the majority of Albanians working in the civil sector (altogether coming to approximately 170,000). When the Serb authorities assumed control over Kosovo in the early 1990s, they proceeded to ship much of Kosovo's hardware into Serbia proper. The Serbs also assumed control over the bankrupt Bank of Kosovo, leading to the loss of 66,000 individual accounts in foreign currency, worth an estimated $98 million. The money was confiscated by the state-controlled *Jugobanka* in Belgrade, which simply refused to honor the local bank's obligations toward its clients (Vickers, 1998: 249). In search of jobs and money, scores of Albanians immigrated to Western countries in the 1990s; their remittances, alongside the local underground economy (including the black market in drugs, fuel, and women), have been largely responsible for sustaining the local Albanians throughout the 1990s.[27]

The reestablishment of direct Serb control over Kosovo raised Milosevic's popularity to unprecedented heights and resulted in his election as president of Serbia in December 1990. Milosevic appeared to be the protector of all Serbs within Yugoslavia. The Kosovo affair—and to a lesser extent the similar developments in Montenegro and Vojvodina—acted as warnings for Croatia and Slovenia that the Serb program of "centralized democratization" meant the return of Serb supremacy. As pluralism within and outside the Communist Party lines came to the forefront of politics during the late 1980s, politicians in both countries used the national question as a means for attracting the votes of the population. Eventually, Slovenia's attempt to disassociate itself from the Yugoslav federation set the stage for the collapse of Yugoslavia (Hayden, 1992a). Yugoslavia soon became engulfed in the flames of war, first in Croatia and, later on, in Bosnia-Herzegovina (for an overview, see Cohen, 1993).

In the meantime, the Kosovo Albanians' reaction to the suppression by the Serb state was to set up an illegal parliamentary session. Assembled on the steps of the parliamentary building, they proclaimed, on 2 July 1990, the sovereign Republic of Kosovo and voted for secession from Serbia. The Serbs proceeded to dissolve the assembly three days later. The Albanians responded with a general strike on 7 September 1990 (Vickers, 1998: 245). On the same, some 111 Turkish, Albanian, and Muslim members of the dissolved Parliament gathered at Kacanik, a small town bordering the People's

Republic of Macedonia. They adopted the "Kacanik Constitution" (September 1990) (Babuna, 2000: 74). While Yugoslavia was collapsing and international attention was focused on the conflict between Slovenia, Croatia, and the Serbs, the now illegal Kosovo Parliament approved a resolution declaring Kosovo's independence and sovereignty (22 September 1990). The decision was approved in a clandestine referendum held between 26 and 30 September, in theory illegal, yet tolerated by the Serb authorities (Vickers, 1998: 251). On 24 May 1992 new presidential and parliamentary elections were also held, in which twenty-two political parties participated (Babuna, 2000: 74). Ibrahim Rugova, the leader of the peaceful nonviolent movement of Kosovo Albanians, was elected president with a 99.5% of the vote, while his Democratic League of Kosovo (DLK) won 75% of the seats in the (illegal) Kosovo Parliament.[28] In 1991, following the initial declaration of Kosovo's independence, the Albanian government recognized the clandestine Kosovo Republic.[29] The DLK proceeded to establish ties with Albania proper and, more specifically, with Berisha's Democratic Party (Biberaj, 1998: 134). For the better part of the 1990s, the two parties maintained a virtual monopoly over the Kosovo issue (Nesho, 1998). Prime Minister Berisha used the Kosovo issue as a diversion in order to establish his own semi-authoritarian regime and avoid democratic reforms in Albania.[30] Rugova's DLK received high praise for its insistence on peaceful means of protests, but did not receive sufficient support by the international community. In fact, in 1995, the United States excluded representatives of the Kosovo Albanians from the Dayton negotiations. The Dayton Accord signaled to the Kosovo Albanians the necessity for armed struggle as a means to force the international community to hear their demands.

In 1995, following the expulsion of Croatian Serbs from Croatia, the Serbs proceeded to resettle close to 20,000 Serb refugees from Bosnia and Croatia into Kosovo, thereby adding oil into the fires of ethnic confrontation (Gavrilis, 1996: 285). Following the 1995 Dayton Accord, the Kosovo Albanians moved toward more radical (and less peaceful) solutions. Their vehicle was the elusive Kosovo Liberation Army (KLA or UCK in Albanian). KLA's initial stirrings can be traced to the early 1990s. The first armed attack took place in May 1993 in Glogovac, killing two Serb policemen and wounding five more (Hedges, 1999). It is not entirely clear, however, whether the early military units were identical with the post-1995 KLA (Vickers, 1998: 278). Albanian military forces drew their strength from a few clans in Kosovo alongside the Albanian diaspora.[31] The Albanian recruits came mainly from the ranks of 5,000 ethnic Albanians who had fought against the Serbs on the Croat side during the Serbo-Croat war of the early 1990s.[32] Others were recruited from the local gangs involved in black market activities. In the post-Dayton period, the KLA grew in importance, gaining support from Rugova's DLK. The organization was a coalition among the descendants of the right-wing clans who supported the Axis forces during

World War II and left-wing pro-communists (former Stalinists) (Babuna, 2000: 78).[33] Despite the lack of any ideological common ground, the KLA was united in its determination to fight against Serb rule and did not hesitate to use money earned from the international drug trade to purchase supplies and weapons (Chossudovsky, 1999).

The KLA's first organized operations took place in 1995–96, and its popularity increased in the aftermath of the Dayton Accord and the Serb post-1995 colonization program (Vickers, 1998: 290–92). The 1997 riots in Albania were a turning point in the group's ability to obtain guns and explosives—and a number of guns and ammunition ended in KLA hands. By 1998, KLA forces were successful in their strategy of inviting Serb reprisals; these reprisals provided the impetus (or pretext) for the United States' military intervention (Chomsky, 1999: 30–35). The KLA provided an outlet for the frustration of the local population. In many instances, local clan leaders took the initiative without truly being members of the KLA organization, thereby adding a glow of popular representation that contributed to the KLA's mythological status (Babuna, 2000: 78).

However, there was little support from the post-1997 Albanian government. On the contrary, on 4 November 1997, in a joint statement, the new Albanian Prime Minister Fatos Nano and then Serb President Slobodan Milosevic agreed to upgrade the level of diplomatic contacts between the two states. On this occasion, Nano also suggested that his government was in favor of autonomy for Kosovo, and, therefore, he was opposed to armed conflict (Antonopoulos, 1999: 326). This attitude stood in sharp contrast to the more aggressive attitude of the former Berisha government (1992–97) that had endorsed (and recognized) the outlawed shadow Albanian government of Kosovo. Following Nano's resignation in the autumn of 1998, the new Albanian Prime Minister Pandeli Marko quietly assumed a more pro-independence stance, reversing Nano's policy and restoring channels of communication between Kosovo Albanians and Tirana. Still, Tirana's message was that a solution to the Kosovo issue should take place through dialogue and cooperation instead of violence. In February 1999, the Albanian government invited Adem Demaci, the KLA's representative, to Tirana, in an attempt to bring some unity among the different Kosovo Albanian factions. In the aftermath of the visit, the KLA agreed to participate in the Rambouillet meeting (Vickers, 2001: 33–35). When the talks collapsed, events took a downward turn, as NATO and the United States signaled gradually that force was indeed going to be used in order to prevent the Serb armed forces from expelling hundreds of thousands of Albanians from Kosovo.

The subsequent events in Kosovo have been too well publicized to warrant repetition.[34] In the aftermath of the NATO-led campaign, Kosovo was turned into an international protectorate whereby the Albanians won freedom from Serb domination, yet without an open international recognition of Kosovo's sovereignty. The Serb minority became the target of reprisals, prompting the intervention of NATO forces to protect them. But, the most important consequence of the NATO intervention in the region was the message delivered to Macedonian Albanians—that is, that armed insurrection could, under certain conditions, receive the endorsement of the international community. Still, the situation in the post-1991 Macedonian Republic was quite different from the conditions in post-1989 Kosovo.

ALBANIANS AND MACEDONIANS IN THE 1990s

The 1991 declaration of independence by the People's Republic of Macedonia added a further twist in Albanian-Macedonian relations. The emergence of VMRO-DPMNU (already mentioned in Chapter 2) fostered Macedonian nationalism at the expense of the inclusion of the Macedonian Albanians as equal partners into the new state. This was but another twist in the Albanian complaints that had originated in the 1980s. Already, the 1989 revised Macedonian Constitution defined the republic as the "the state of the Macedonian people and the Albanian and Turkish minorities," thereby delegating Albanians to the status of a "nationality" (i.e., minority) and not to that of a constitutive nation of the new state (Perry, 2000a: 277). In 1990, Albanian activists organized demonstrations in the city of Tetovo in which they openly called for a Greater Albania. Moreover, governmental inaction to solve the long-standing complaints of the Albanians concerning discrimination in the People's Republic led to calls for boycotting the original independence referendum in September 1991.

In the winter months of 1991–92 several Albanian politicians from the Tetovo region declared the creation of the so-called Republic of Illirida. Illirida turned out to be a hoax rather than a real republic, but the declaration had obvious political ramifications. In January 1992, a watered-down referendum was held in FYROM's western part, where Albanians comprise a majority (see Map 1.2). Of the 92% of eligible voters who participated in the referendum, a reported 74% voted for territorial autonomy (Buck, 1996: 253–54). In 1993, in connection with this affair, state authorities arrested and tried five Albanian members of the ruling coalition government. They were accused of fomenting a *coup d'état* orchestrated by the so-called "All Albanian Army" (AAA), a paramilitary force allegedly consisting of 21,000 armed men, aiming to create the Republic of Illirida as a base for a Greater Albanian state (Clement, 1998: 370).

As discussed in Chapter 2, in the early 1990s, VMRO-DPMNU was promoting "Macedonian unification" or what Greece and Bulgaria considered to be territorial aspirations against their own regions of Macedonia. Against the VMRO-DPMNU nationalists stood President Gligorov's reformed League of Communists in Macedonia. Although VMRO-DPMNU won 33 out of 120 seats in the first open elections, it was a coalition between the League of Communists and the Albanian ethnic parties that eventually became the new state's government. The ruling coalition, under the name of the Social Democratic Union of Macedonia, included an alliance of the former communists with two Albanian parties, the Albanian Party for Democratic Prosperity (PDP) and the People's Democratic Party (NDP), which together captured twenty-three seats in the assembly (Buck, 1996: 249). Of the two parties, the PDP was by far the most popular one.[35]

In 1992, the constitutional debates about the nature of the new state illustrated the growing gap between Albanians and Macedonians. The constitution initially recognized the Albanians as a mere minority, similar to the Turks, Vlachs, and other groups in the state. The Macedonian nationalists of VMRO-DPMNU wanted to define the new republic as the "national state of the Macedonian people." In contrast, moderate Macedonians and Albanians wanted to define the republic as a civil state for all its citizens. Unable to resolve their differences, the two sides opted for a mixed formula where in the preamble of the constitution the republic is defined as the "the national state of the Macedonian people," whereas in the body of the constitution itself it is referred to as an independent, sovereign, democratic, and welfare state of equal citizens (Ramet, 1996: 216).

The Albanians protested their lack of inclusion as a constitutive nation in the new republic. In 1992, they successfully collected 150,000 signatures in support of a constitutional revision (Sfetas and Kentrotis, 1995: 122). Throughout 1992–93 the Council on Security and Cooperation in Europe (CSCE) also pressured the government to grant more rights to Albanians. Yet, it took more than a year of negotiations to reach an agreement on a new citizen-based constitution. The revised constitution would omit references to the Macedonian Orthodox Church and recognize the Albanian language as one of the two official languages of the state, alongside Macedonian. In 1994, the former communists tried to have the new constitution accepted by the Parliament, but were unable to overcome the opposition of VMRO-DPMNU. In the 1994 elections, the VMRO-DPMNU called for a boycott after a report of the CSCE observers that suggested electoral irregularities (Buck, 1996: 252). As a result of the boycott, President Gligorov's former communists won 110 out of 120 seats. Although this outcome suggested the possibility of solving the impasse concerning the Albanian demands, it was not so. The two Albanian parties won only fourteen seats and bitterly complained about the process of district redrawing initiated by Gligorov's party. Four of the fourteen Albanian deputies belonged to a more radical Albanian faction who were upset with the low pace of reforms, refused to cooperate with Gligorov, and accused the moderate Albanians of being mere puppets of the government.

A key event in the further radicalization of the Albanian movement took place in 1993 when PDP representatives claimed that they were prevented from meeting with the then Turkish President Ozal by Macedonian authorities. This set off internal strife among the Albanians with the more radical

wing accusing the moderates of being soft. The Berisha government supported the more radical Albanians, thereby causing the bitter complaints of
the Macedonian government that it interfered with FYROM's domestic
politics (Biberaj, 1998: 240–41). The formal split took place in February
1994. Arben Xhaferi, a Belgrade-educated philosophy graduate, and his followers upstaged the moderates of the PDP, the main Albanian party. For a
time it appeared that both factions would use the label of the PDP. But by
April 1994 Xhaferi's faction established the Party for the Democratic Prosperity for Albanians, or PDP-A. This party amalgamated in 1997 with the
smaller radical People's Democratic Party to form the Democratic Party of
Albanians, or DPA (Poulton, 2000: 195–99). The main difference seems to
have been over tactics rather than strategy. The PDP continued to be part
of the ruling coalition while the more radical DPA appealed to the younger
Albanians, in a way that mirrored the success of the Macedonian nationalist
party VMRO-DPMNU. Although Xhaferi has publicly made comments that
would seem to support Albanian separatism, the DPA 1998 electoral platform included demands for a binational Macedonian state; a consociational
model of democracy for the state; the institution of an Albanian deputy head
of state; and the affirmation of Albanian culture by educational, cultural, and
other national institutions.

   In opinion polls conducted in 1993 and 1994, the majority of the Albanians felt discriminated against by the Macedonians (Gaber, 1997: 111). Not
surprisingly, the Albanians consider that, in order for them to be on equal
footing, they need to be considered a co-founding nation, as opposed to a
mere minority. The issue is directly related with the politically laden issue
of the Albanians' numerical strength. An important factor in the Albanians'
complaints was the fact that current citizenship requirements exclude from
citizenship (and also from the census) all Albanians who once lived in other
parts of Yugoslavia and who returned to FYROM in the aftermath of
Yugoslavia's breakup in the 1990s. The Albanians boycotted the 1991 census.
Consequently, the bureau of statistics proceeded to provide estimates for the
boycotted communities based on statistical projections from the 1981 census,
natural population growth, migration, and similar indicators.

   Before the final census results were published in 1991, the Macedonian
Albanians initiated an international campaign, arguing that the census underestimated them and that the Albanian population was close to 40% of the
new republic's total population. The Albanians protested that the 1991
census did not include scores of Macedonian Albanians who worked and lived
in other former Yugoslav republics and who, in the aftermath of the disintegration of Yugoslavia, returned back to their original homeland. On 11
November 1992 the Macedonian Parliament passed the new Law on Citizenship. Although, according to the new law, close to 90% of the republic's
inhabitants became overnight legal citizens of the new state, the law also
postulated that only those born in the republic and those who were ethnic

Macedonians were considered Macedonian citizens.[36] Regular naturalization is possible only when the person submitting the request is at least 18 years old; has had continuous residence in the republic for the previous fifteen years; is of good physical and mental health; maintains a residence in the republic, has a permanent source of income, and no criminal record; has terminated any prior citizenship; knows the Macedonian language; and finally, granting citizenship to the petitioner will not endanger the security and defense of the republic (regulations quoted in Petrusevksa, 1998: 169–71).

The Albanians demanded the lowering of the residency requirement for Macedonian citizenship from fifteen to five years. The entire issue aroused the interest of the international community and eventually led to the 1994 "European" extraordinary census, conducted under the auspices of European organizations. According to Trajkovska (1998: 189), between 1992 and 1998 a total of 120,000 petitions for acquisition of Macedonian citizenship were filed with the Department of Public Administration. Of them, a reported 95.4% were approved, although the process did take several months to conclude. However, the situation was not resolved—on the contrary, by 2001 Albanian sources estimated that close to 110,000 ethnic Albanians lacked proper documentation.[37]

Table 6.1 shows the ethnic distribution of FYROM's population throughout the post–World War II period—including the 1991 and 1994 census results. A simple comparison of the estimates from the 1991 census with the 1994 census results would seem to suggest that the Albanians' complaints were largely—although not entirely—misplaced. Still, the issue is more complicated. The Albanian complaints about the census were closely connected to the law on citizenship requirements. However, despite Albanian protests, the Macedonian government refused to change the law, thereby leading to accusations that even the 1994 census (see Table 6.1) was biased because it did not count those "newer" members of the Albanian community as citizens, thereby undercounting the Albanian population by 10% or more.[38]

To this issue it is necessary to add the problem of providing higher education in Albanian language institutions. The centrality of this issue for Albanians is clearly revealed by the educational statistics. In 1989–90, of 71,505 pupils continuing into higher education only 2,794 were Albanians. Of 22,994 university students in 1991–92, only 386 were Albanians (Poulton, 2000: 184). The key reason for the Albanians' lack of advancement is that most Albanians receive their elementary education in Albanian, but they need to switch to Macedonian to continue their education. The issue became more acute in the 1990s, after the Serb authorities closed down Prishtina University in Kosovo, the only higher institution where the language of instruction was Albanian. In FYROM, the SS Cyril and Methodius University in Skopje provided higher education. However, the language of instruction was Macedonian and not Albanian, thereby leading Albanian students to avoid applying to the school even though the authorities set aside some 10% of

Table 6.1
The Population of FYROM According to the Census Declaration of National Affiliation

Ethnic Group	1953	%	1961	%	1971	%	1981	%	1991	%	1994	%
Macedonians	860,699	66	1,000,854	71.2	1,142,375	69.3	1,279,323	67	1,328,187	65.3	1,401,389	66.5
Albanians	162,354	12.5	183,108	13	279,871	17	377,208	19.8	441,987	21.7	484,228	23
Turks	203,938	15.6	131,481	9.3	108,552	6.6	86,591	4.5	77,080	3.8	82,976	3.9
Roma	20,462	1.5	20,606	1.5	24,505	1.6	43,125	2.3	52,103	2.6	47,363	2.3
Vlachs	8,668	0.7	8,046	0.6	7,190	0.4	6,384	0.3	7,764	0.4	8,730	0.4
Serbs	35,112	2.7	42,728	2.8	46,465	2.8	44,468	2.3	42,775	2.1	40,972	1.9
Others	13,111	1	19,180	2.3	38,350	2.3	72,037	3.8	84,068	4.1	41,006	2
TOTAL	1,304,514	100	1,406,003	100	1,647,308	100	1,909,136	100	2,033,964	100	2,106,664	100

Note: The 1994 census results were adjusted to include persons that lived abroad for more than a year, and exclude persons that have approved residence for a period for less than a year. The original 1994 census did not count these categories of people. Friedman (1996: 90) reports the original raw results of the 1994 census. However, because the pre-1994 censuses included these categories of people that were excluded in the 1994 census, the census results cannot be compared to the pre-1994 census. Moreover, because of the differences in the classification schemes between the 1994 census and the pre-1994 censuses, the total number of inhabitants recorded in the 1994 census was less than the number of inhabitants recorded in the 1991 census. Milosavleski and Tomovski (1997) adjusted the 1994 census results in order to allow for a comparison with the pre-1994 censuses. The above table reflects this adjustment and the census results reported in the table are comparable.

Source: Milosavleski &Tomovski (1997: 293–94).

the available slots for Albanians. Consequently, the Macedonians argued that higher education was available to all citizens (including the Albanians), but it was the Albanians who failed to take advantage of the educational opportunities (Perry, 2000a: 279).

In 1994 and 1995 the Albanians began setting up an Albanian University in Mala Recica, near the city of Tetovo. The authorities attempted to shut it down forcefully, leading to the persecution of the Albanian faculty members as well as the death of one Albanian protester.[39] Taking advantage of the new constitutional guarantees about the individuals' right to free association, on 17 December 1996, the local assembly of the city of Tetovo decided to sponsor the clandestine Albanian university (Biberaj, 1998: 259; Clement, 1998: 385, note 32; Sfetas and Kantriotis, 1995: 130–32). The Macedonian authorities considered the new university illegal, but its operation met with the approval of practically all of FYROM's Albanian political parties, as well as the Berisha government in Albania. Most of the teachers of the university came from the University of Prishtina, thereby leading the Macedonian authorities to suspect that the institution's main goal had to do more with Albanian separatism than education. The university continued to operate in private houses, following the model of the Kosovo "underground" parallel system of administration, claiming that some 4,000 students were enrolled, taking classes from 260 teachers. In practice, classes were held wherever possible (Poulton, 2000: 185; Perry, 2000a: 280).[40]

The 1997 fall of the Berisha government in Albania also led to a change in international relations between Skopje and Tirana. While, up to 1997, Tirana employed demands for a better treatment of Macedonian Albanians as a precondition for improvement of interstate relations, the post-1997 Socialist government of Fatos Nano declared that Albanian demands in FYROM should be satisfied in accordance to European standards and within the institutions of the state, not by disloyalty toward the state or by civil disobedience (Otrakovski, 2000: 285). The 1998 elections signaled a further turn in FYROM's complicated politics of ethnic confrontation and coexistence. The elections gave a majority to the VMRO, which proceeded to organize a coalition government with the smaller Democratic Alternative Party of Vasil Tupurkovski. In a surprise move, the Macedonian side invited Xhaferi's DPA to become a member in the governmental coalition, and Xhaferi accepted the offer (Perry, 2000a: 284–85). This coalition was in place at the time of the 1999 Kosovo Crisis. The Kosovo Crisis brought an influx of some 200,000 to 250,000 Albanian refugees into FYROM's own territory (Otrakosvki, 2000: 290). The large number of refugees led to a rather cool reception by Macedonian authorities, who were less than enthusiastic about a possible further increase of the Albanian population in the state.

Although the majority of the refugees eventually returned to Kosovo, the 1999 Kosovo Crisis (and NATO's military involvement) led to a further polarization between Macedonian Albanians and their Slav counterparts.

While the Macedonians correctly foresaw that NATO's intervention could potentially destabilize "their" state and threatened even the republic's very existence, the Macedonian Albanians were enthusiastic in their support for the intervention. Therein lies the origin of the Macedonians' perception that NATO and the United States are protecting and sheltering Albanian nationalism at the expense of FYROM's stability and territorial integrity (Drezov, 2001). In this context, it is necessary to highlight the degree to which, throughout the 1990s, NATO, the UN, and the United States did not hesitate to deploy their armed forces in FYROM's territory as a means of safeguarding the new state's territorial integrity, security, and stability.[41] Before the 1999 Kosovo Crisis, close to 1,000 U.S. and UN troops were already stationed in FYROM, while Western observers from numerous EU and UN organizations have had an extensive presence throughout the 1990s (and the 1994 international census aptly illustrates their clout). The original UN-sponsored military presence was terminated in early 1999, when China vetoed its extension in retaliation for Skopje's recognition of Taiwan. However, the 1999 Kosovo Crisis led to close to 30,000 NATO troops entering the country, thereby, relegating the 12,000-strong Macedonian military to a secondary place for the duration of the operation.

CONCLUDING REMARKS

In this chapter, I have provided an overview of the development of the Albanian Question in the southern Balkans. Although Albanians are dispersed throughout the region, it is important to keep in mind that, with the exception of a brief period of time during World War II, the Albanians were never united into a single state. Consequently, the evolution of the different Albanian communities in the southern Balkans has been greatly impacted by their relations with neighboring peoples. It is at best naïve to accept the argument of an inevitable Albanian movement toward unification into a single state as somewhat derived from primordial ties.[42] On the contrary, the dynamics of the Albanian Question—and the reactions of the neighboring states—have played a critically important role in shaping, strengthening, and modifying the direction of the Albanians' political mobilization.[43]

Although the issues of Kosovo and western Macedonia have almost monopolized international public attention in the 1990s, it is also important to remember that the Albanian nation-state has long been involved in a series of claims and counterclaims with regard to the Greek minority in southern Albania and the by now defunct Albanian minority of the Chams in Greece. In contemporary politics, the minority issue resurfaced once again after the collapse of the communist regime in Albania during the early 1990s. It contributed significantly to mutual suspicion and antagonism between Tirana and Athens. Eventually, however, the two states seem to have succumbed to the economic logic of mutual interdependence. With hundreds of thousands of Albanian immigrants in Greece, both states have everything to gain from preventing the escalation of conflict with regard to the minority issue. Most important, the majority of the Greek minority have also become economic immigrants themselves, and, therefore, the only remaining issues between the two sides concern the extent to which minority members should have equal rights with the rest of the Albanian citizens as well as issues of property and ecclesiastical autonomy for the Greek Orthodox Church of Albania. Although the magnitude of these issues should not be underestimated, the real issue lies elsewhere. The modern Greek nation-state is currently entering the twenty-first century as a host country of immigrants. This is the first time in its history that Greece has been transformed from a country of emigration to a country of immigration. The real challenge concerns the successful incorporation and coexistence of the immigrants (and their descendants) into modern Greek society. The extent to which such incorporation is effective will determine the shape and future direction of Greek-Albanian interstate relations.

In sharp contrast to the issues that have preoccupied Athens and Tirana for most of the twentieth century, the problems faced by the Albanians in the former Yugoslavia were substantively different. In the post-1945 communist Yugoslavia, the Albanians became one of the new state's "nationalities" (i.e., national minorities). Their national affirmation remained incomplete, and they were never acknowledged as one of the "nations" whose union constituted the so-called second Yugoslavia. The long-term consequences of the Albanians' status as a "minority" continue to be felt throughout the region to this day; and they shaped the pattern of mobilization among the Albanian population. A second major factor that shaped the evolution of Albanian political mobilization was the relatively low degree of social development among the Albanians of the former Yugoslavia. Unlike their counterparts of (mainly southern) Albania, the Albanian tribal culture of the Kosovo plateau and western Macedonia remained alive for most of the twentieth century. It began to crumble over the post–World War II period—and in many respects, the modernization of the local societies and their transition from a traditional into a modern cultural *milieu* is largely responsible for the effective and persistent political mobilization of the Albanians in both regions. After all, some of the issues that preoccupied the Kosovo Albanians were practical, economic issues that are shared among citizens in all modern societies: popular representation, equal access in employment, use of the Albanian language, schooling and higher education in Albanian-language institutions, and access to state resources directed toward regional development.

However, in both western Macedonia and Kosovo, the Albanians' rising demands for inclusion into government and access to resources were frustrated by Serbs and Macedonians. In Kosovo, the Albanians were able to enjoy a brief period of equality and inclusion in the 1970s. In light of their progress in the 1970s, it might be surprising that the end result was the 1981 protests and the subsequent Serb repression of the 1980s. In this regard, it is important to realize that, just as numerous other Third World regions, Kosovo experienced a rapid population explosion that eroded whatever gains the Albanians received in the 1970s. In western Macedonia, the Albanians had to compete against the newly institutionalized Macedonian nationalism of the People's Republic of Macedonia. The post-1945 communist regime was successful in providing some minor steps toward equality; however, its main focus remained directed toward Macedonian nation building. The effect of the 1981 protests in Kosovo was dramatically felt in the People's Republic of Macedonia. Fearful of resurgent Albanian nationalism, the Macedonian authorities attempted to restrain and control the Albanian population. The Macedonians' gradual trend toward stressing the ethnic character of the Republic of Macedonia only fueled the Albanians' own desire to be considered a "co-founding" nation and not a mere "minority."

In the 1990s, however, the two communities followed largely different patterns. Following the post-1989 Serb oppression against the Kosovo Albanians, the nonviolent movement of Ibrahim Rugova was able to sustain a nonviolent strategy for several years. However, the lack of international attention to the plight of Kosovo Albanians and their exclusion from the 1995 Dayton Accord led to further radicalization, thereby strengthening the Albanian radicals who formed the KLA. The ultimate result of the Albanian-Serb confrontation in the region was the NATO military strike and the transformation of Kosovo into a protectorate whose status remains unsettled to this day. In sharp contrast to Kosovo, however, the Macedonian Albanians were successful in participating in the post-1991 political system of the Republic of Macedonia and thereby registered their concerns in the open, gaining a voice that was indeed heard by the international community (as the 1994 extraordinary census illustrates). Despite what outsiders considered a success story, however, the Macedonian Albanians failed to gain the constitutional guarantees and other concessions that would affirm their status as a co-founding nation (as opposed to a mere minority). On the contrary, in a variety of issues, ranging from the thorny issue of the Albanians' numerical strength to the institution of an Albanian-language university in Tetovo, the Macedonian Albanians had to compete against a rising Macedonian nationalism, perhaps best represented by the nationalist VMRO-DPMNU. Albanian politics were consequently tilted toward radicalism, and the 1998 coalition government between the Albanian radicals and the VMRO-DPMNU was widely viewed as a marriage of convenience that would be short-lived. The 1999 Kosovo Crisis changed this prediction, as it placed the entire political situation in limbo—at least for close to a year. It was only after the Kosovo situation was stabilized that the Albanian-Macedonian dispute returned to . the forefront of the political agenda. The post-1999 events are discussed in Chapter 7's postscript.

Finally, tribal membership is an important factor influencing attitudes toward possible "unification" of Kosovo and western Macedonia with Albania proper. That is, the majority of Kosovo and Macedonian Albanians are Geghs—similar to the Geghs of northern Albania. Hence, national unification will upset the relations between Geghs and Tosks in Albania, leading to Gegh dominance (Biberaj, 1998: 205–6). Such a turn of events is bound to raise suspicion among the Tosks, who traditionally have been more urbanized, prosperous, and "modern" than the Geghs and who have long dominated the intelligentsia of the Albanian state. Therefore, the possibility of unification does not necessarily bring stability to the region, but it is likely that it could promote further tribal competition among the Albanians.

The evolution of Tirana's attitude during the 1999 Kosovo Crisis illustrates Tirana's concern regarding this issue, while it also dramatically demonstrates the extent to which ethnic or tribal loyalties play a crucial role in contemporary Albanian politics. It is not accidental that former President Berisha's party—whose membership comes predominantly from the northern Geghs—has been consistent in its support of Albanian nationalism in Kosovo and Macedonia. On the eve of the Rambouillet conference, the pro-Berisha daily *Albania* hailed the meeting with the headline "Albanians on the Eve of Their Future Destiny" (quoted in Vickers, 2001: 35). According to the newspaper, the meeting was an opportunity to revise the Balkan maps of 1913–15 and restore Albanian territorial integrity. On the other hand, the Tirana-based Tosk government did not dare to intervene or stop the cooperation between the Geghs of northern Albania and their Kosovo counterparts.

NOTES

1. For a discussion of the original survey, see Kallivertakis (1995: 32–34). For a brief overview of the diplomatic negotiations in the 1910s, see Xhudo (1995: 113–16). According to an ethnological survey of this region conducted in the early 1990s, past Greek claims do not represent the reality of the rather complex situation regarding groups and boundaries in Albania. In addition to the Orthodox Tosks who form the majority of Albanians in the southern part of the state, there are Serbs, Macedonians, Vlachs, and Greeks. Hence, counts of the "Greek minority" that include all Orthodox Christians are misleading. This reason accounts for the lack of an accurate count (see Table 5.1 in Chapter 5). While the Albanian side estimates the minority to be around 60,000, third parties (such as Noel Malcolm) agree with Greek scholars and church leaders in estimating the minority to be around 100,000 (and no more than 150,000) (Malcolm, 1992, cited in Georgoulis, 1995: 163; Kallivertakis, 1995: 42–44).

2. According to the League of Nations the total number of Chams in 1925 was 20,160. Of them, 2,993 became part of the Greek-Turkish exchange of population by declaring themselves Turks rather than Albanians. The 1928 Greek census recorded 17,008 Chams. In the 16 October 1940 census their number declined further to 16,890, but in 1941 the Italian occupation administration recorded a total

of 28,000 (all statistics from Kallivertakis, 1995: 37–38). Initial plans for their deportation to Turkey were canceled after protests by the Albanian side (Mihalopoulos,
1985). The original region referred to in Greek as "Chamouria" (or Chameria in
English) was divided between Greece and Albania in 1920. Henceforth, the term
"Chams" referred only to the Albanians left on the Greek side of the border.

3. The extent to which national labels were superimposed onto the people at
the time was revealed when the League of Nations sent a committee to collect information on the Albanian minority. According to the committee, although the
majority of Muslims did not wish to go to Turkey, they did not appear to have a
clear-cut understanding of their own "national affiliation" and tended to consider
themselves as simply "Muslims" when asked about it (Mihalopoulos, 1987: 37).
Furthermore, minority members made rather opportunistic use of their affiliation,
declaring themselves Turks, Muslims, or Albanians depending upon the context.

4. The Cham refugees set up associations and clubs. These have been revital-
ized after the collapse of the communist regime in Albania. According to the local
officials they claim that the original Chams were 30,000 to 35,000 and that today
their descendants number close to 170,000 (Kallivertakis, 1995: 50). Biberaj (1998:
15) mistakenly reports that, in the aftermath of World War II, "the Greeks expelled
some 30,000 Albanians (Chams) from Chameria in northern Greece, accusing them
of having collaborated with Nazi invaders." The figure of 30,000 is adopted from
the Cham associations without checking the other sources used in the discussion in
this chapter. Also, the Chams' collaboration with the Germans is a fact, not an
accusation.

5. The movement capitalized on the lack of the communists' engagement with
the Albanian national question. The Albanian Communist Party was hardly in existence in 1941 and displayed a submissive attitude toward Moscow. Their directives
clearly suggested that Kosovo was to be dealt with by the Yugoslav Communist Party
(Malcolm, 1998: 302–4).

6. In early August 1943, the communist-controlled National Liberation Front
and *Balli Kombetar* held a meeting. The two sides came close to an agreement, but
when the communist representatives agreed to a call for Albanian unification, Hoxha,
the Albanian communist leader, stepped in to assure the collapse of an agreement
between the two sides. Hoxha's policy followed the directives from Moscow and de-
ferred the status of Kosovo to Tito (Malcolm, 1998: 303; Vickers, 1998: 130–35).

7. Despite its many weaknesses, the Hoxha regime was successful in liquidating
the large estates and distributing the land among the peasantry. It also increased the
total amount of agricultural land from a mere 10% of the Albania's total geographical
area to close to 50% (Emadi, 2000).

8. According to Paschalis (1998: 198–212) during the post–World War II period,
the quality of textbooks in minority schools declined steadily. A comparison of these
textbooks over time reveals an increase in mistakes in word choice, verb use, and
other related issues dealing with proper syntax and grammar. Paschalis (1998: 209)
suggests that the decline in Greek language use in the post–World War II period is
largely the consequence of Albania's social isolation from its neighbors. Not surprisingly, the image of Greece in the textbooks used in the minority schools is particularly negative—with heavy emphasis placed upon the negative consequences of the
Greek military occupation of southern Albania during the two World Wars. Moreover, keeping in step with the textbooks in the rest of the Balkans, the Ottoman

Empire is presented in a quite negative light, while the role of the communist-led partisan movement is exalted. The Greek minority's self-image is connected with Albanian independence. The minority exists only after the creation of the Albanian state, and heavy emphasis is placed on presenting local minority literature, written almost exclusively by pro-communist authors who belong to the minority (for details, see Paschalis, 1998: 278–315). According to Kapsalis (1996: 32–33), some of the more recent history textbooks that were to be used in the Greek minority schools were so heavily biased against Greece that the authorities never distributed them to the schools.

9. Fear of Albanian claims into the Greek region of Epirus has provided a renewed interest in Albania and the Albanian region of Northern Epirus (or southern Albania). It is characteristic of this interest that Alexandros Papadopoulos, an Epirote Socialist MP, wrote a brief overview of Greek-Albanian relations including reviews of the Northern Epirus question (Papadopoulos, 1992). Two editions of the book were issued within a few months, just an indication of Greek renewed interest in Albania.

10. See Pano (1997: 285–352) and Biberaj (1998) for overviews of Albania's transition to democracy. Biberaj's book is the most comprehensive account; however, the author is biased in favor of the Berisha government and fails to provide an even-handed treatment of the regime. Additionally, he fails to even discuss the interplay between tribal affiliation (Geghs versus Tosks) and political orientation (Socialist versus Democratic). Biberaj (1998: 16) concedes that Geghs and Tosks have "alternated in dominating Albanian politics" and that "communist policies widened the gap in the educational and economic levels between north and south." He writes that "many Geghs resented what they saw as political, economic, and cultural domination by the more prosperous southerners." But he fails to connect the regional and tribal influences to the support for the two main political parties. Berisha's Democratic Party was supported mainly by Geghs. In contrast, the Tosks were more supportive of the Socialists. It is impossible to analyze the evolution of Albanian politics without taking into account the regional and tribal factors. Support for the two parties is partly a reflection of these regional loyalties and is not determined by ideological considerations. As Blumi (1997) argues, the post-1945 communist regime successfully persecuted Gegh leadership and promoted Tosk domination over the institutions of the state. In this regard, it is not surprising that the post-1990 Albanian "democrats" attracted the support of the previously persecuted Geghs.

11. For a largely favorable overview of Berisha's efforts to stabilize the economy, see Biberaj (1998: 188–201). Even Biberaj has to concede that attempts to attract foreign investors failed and that "the economy remained highly dependent on external financial factors," that is, "continued foreign assistance, foreign investment, and remittances from Albanian refugees in Greece" (Biberaj, 1998: 199–200). According to Biberaj, the remittances were likely to decrease in the future, but this prediction has not come true. On the contrary, the legalization of the Albanian immigrants' status in Greece has had the opposite result.

12. The initial round of the pyramid schemes involved large companies—such as VETA, Gjallica, and Kamberi—that had substantial real investments. They were widely believed to have been involved in smuggling of goods into the former Yugoslavia during the international embargo of the early 1990s (Jarvis, 2000).

13. There was a noticeable revival of Islamic institutions in post-1989 Albania (for

a review, see Trix, 1995). The Berisha government cultivated strong ties with Muslim nations, attempting to gain financial support for the Albanian nation-state from its newly-found religious allies.

14. Accurate figures are difficult to obtain. However, Ortakovski (2000: 201) considers the number of guns to be close to one million plus 20,000 tons of explosives. Judah (2000: 22) also corroborates the figure of one million Kalashnikovs that went to market for $16 each.

15. The party's ascent represented the victory of more radical groups. These groups include émigré associations and Orthodox associations affiliated with the Archbishopric of Jannina (Vihou et al., 1995: 73–75).

16. The Albanian Orthodox state church was established by decree in 1922. The church was declared autocephalous in a unilateral manner that violated the canons of the Eastern Church (in this respect very similar to the manner in which the Greek state-sponsored church was created in 1833). The Ecumenical Patriarchate officially recognized the autocephaly of the Albanian Church in 1937 (Georgoulis, 1995: 150; Biberaj, 1998: 209).

17. Biberaj (1998: 247) gives the rather exuberant figure of 30,000 as deported to Albania. Biberaj (1998: 247) recognizes that many Albanian citizens (both members of the Greek minority and ethnic Albanians) fled to Greece "for economic reasons," that is, "in search of jobs and a better life in Greece." Unfortunately, Biberaj consistently refers to the Albanian illegal immigrants as "refugees"—a term that invites confusion. Refugees flee for fear of persecution while immigrants are in search of jobs. It is indicative of the author's biases that while Albanian illegal immigrants are referred to as "refugees," the Greek minority members are not.

18. Biberaj (1998: 162) reports that Greece used the incident as a "pretext to deport some 70,000 illegal Albanian refugees" (that is, immigrants, see note 17 in this chapter). However, deportation of illegal immigrants is a legal action and does not need any "pretexts." What Biberaj really means is that, during the 1990–95 period, the Greek governments used to equate the Greeks' treatment of Albanian illegal immigrants to the Albanians' treatment of the Greek minority. Because of the absence of a legal framework to accommodate the wave of illegal immigration, Greek authorities could turn a blind eye toward the Albanian immigrants or to enforce the law. The post-1995 Greek government eventually developed legislation to normalize the Albanian immigrants' status, and this contributed significantly to better Greek-Albanian relations. See the discussion in this chapter for details.

19. Countering such trends, the organization of "liberation armies" by Albanians in FYROM and Kosovo only fuels the revisionist dreams of the descendants of the Chams, who would like to see a Greater Albania that would include a good portion of the Greek region of Epirus (where the original Chameria is located). The Greek authorities have confiscated considerable amounts of ammunition and guns in Epirus (reported in *Expresso*, 1 June 2001), and KLA leaders in Switzerland are reported to favor such plans. But the Albanian state's leaders have not endorsed such actions, and their appeal seems to be limited at this point in time.

20. In fact, in the spring of 1945 Tito issued a provisional decree banning the return of Serb colonists to Kosovo. The decree was later modified and 4,829 colonists were allowed to assume their fields while 5,744 lost some property. Only 595 Serbs lost everything (Malcolm, 1998: 318). Between 1922 and 1941, 12,000 Serb and Montenegrin families (around 60,000 people) were settled in Kosovo (Simic,

1998: 184). According to the 1948 Yugoslav census some 750,483 Albanians were illiterate. The Yugoslav communists promoted the creation of cultural societies under their control, and by 1950 Kosovo had 258 societies with 3,150 members (all statistics quoted in Vickers, 1998: 152–53).

21. The complicated issues surrounding the meaning of Yugoslavism and its gradual abandonment by the Yugoslav communist leadership cannot be discussed in this chapter. For a useful overview, see Budding (1997), and for a more detailed discussion, see Rusinow (1977).

22. Between 1952 and 1987 the level of investments in Kosovo was 67.3% higher than the average for Yugoslavia as a whole (Blagojevic, 1998: 253). However, the result was the creation of largely inefficient enterprises that were not competitive (see von Khol and Libal, 1997: 50–51). On the other hand, this public investment did not always take the form of economic development. Blagojevic (1998: 253) reports that in the 1980s, 10% of all employed persons were teachers, while 20% were classified as "experts." According to Vickers (1998: 223) between 1981 and 1989 unemployment in Kosovo rose from 25% to 57%.

23. In a 1974 sociological survey, a reported 95% of Albanian and Macedonian and 84% of Turkish heads of households would not let their sons marry a woman outside their own ethnic group (Poulton, 2000: 132).

24. The post-1981 situation of Albanians in the People's Republic of Macedonia is captured in the ethnic statistics about their representation. Even in Tetovo, by all accounts a predominantly Albanian town, the Albanians held less than 50% of the seats in the 1982 city council—despite the fact that they accounted for more than 70% of the city's population. In the 1986 parliament the Albanians had only 17 out of a total of 250 deputies (Sfetas and Kentrotis, 1995: 102).

25. It would be obviously naïve to blame just one of the Yugoslav "nationalities" for the disintegration of the Yugoslav federation. As Pavkovic's (1997) overview of the nationalist mobilizations in the 1980s aptly illustrates, the Serbs were not the only ones who promoted ideologies that placed their own "national interests" above the interests of the federation. The same pattern is observed among Albanians, Croats, and Bosnian Muslims.

26. Despite Serb complaints about alleged "genocide," most outsider researchers, including Vickers (1998) and Malcolm (1998), blame Serb emigration on the poor economic conditions of the province rather than persecution of Serbs by the local Albanians. For a brief overview of the evidence concerning this topic, see Von Kohl and Libal (1997: 65–70).

27. The Albanian Foreign Ministry estimated that some 300,000 Albanians left Kosovo between 1991 and 1995 (Kofos, 1998: 72). Vickers (1998: 272) reports that a total of 400,000 Albanians had left Yugoslavia for Western Europe by 1993. Obviously, the Albanian migration was a response to the harsh economic conditions. It was intensified in the post-1989 period, but it was not spearheaded by Serb oppression alone. In the Yugoslavia of the 1990s, the informal economy ("black market") accounted for close to 40% of the GNP (Blagojevic, 1998: 242). In Kosovo, this figure was considerably higher than the national average.

28. The DLK was founded in 1989 as a Yugoslav organization with branches in Slovenia, Croatia, Bosnia, and Montenegro. The Macedonian Albanians, after consultations with the DLK, organized their own organization, the Party for Democratic Prosperity or PDP. The collapse of Yugoslavia in 1989–90 changed the initial

plans for a Yugoslav organization. Instead, DLK developed ties with the Albanian diaspora (Maliqi, 1998: 223). The party claimed a membership of 700,000, but the actual number of people affiliated with the party was probably half that number.

29. In November 1992 in Vlore, Albanian president Berisha attended ceremonies marking the eightieth anniversary of Albania's independence. Rugova was invited to these ceremonies, and Berisha seized the moment to declare: "The soul unites us because the nation is like an individual. You can break its body into pieces, but you can never break the soul" (quoted in Gavrilis, 1996: 284). The implication was that although Albanians are divided, they are, nevertheless, united in their sense of belonging to a single Albanian nation.

30. It was not until 1995 that the Albanian Socialists developed ties with their counterparts in Kosovo. On the contrary, relations between the Socialists and the DLK were not particularly warm. In addition to his pro-Rugova stance, Berisha's government also fostered the development of ties with Islamic organizations, such as the Al Qaeda (i.e., the Osama Bin Ladin group) (Antenna satellite TV news, 20 September 2001; see also Chossudovsky, 1999: 20–22). The information was corroborated a few days later by the Macedonian security agencies.

31. In terms of geographic dispersion, most of the Kosovo Albanian immigrants are located in Germany (around 100,000) and Switzerland (around 120,000) with smaller groups in Belgium and Denmark (Antonopoulos, 1999: 356). The U.S.-based Albanians are estimated to be 350,000 to 400,000, but this number includes both older (pre-1945) and new generations of immigrants. See Vickers (1998: 272) for similar (yet not identical) estimates.

32. The Jashari family was rumored to have provided the leadership of the KLA—at least according to Hedges (1999), the first Western journalist to interview them in 1997. The Jashari brothers were killed later on in that year; however, this did not halt KLA operations. According to Hedges (1999) and Judah (2001: 23), by killing the brothers, the Serb forces turned them into martyrs.

33. According to Judah (2001: 20), even as late as 1997, the KLA did not number more than 200 fighters. The organization originated as a militant political group in the post-1989 period. It advocated armed struggle and held its first meetings in 1992 and 1993. However, its appeal was strengthened significantly after the 1995 Dayton Accord. It was at that point in time that the organization's leadership was able to convince the Albanians of the diaspora to finance their enterprise by shifting the 3% "informal tax" reserved for Rugova's DLK to the KLA. The informal "tax" was used to finance the Albanians' "parallel system" of administration in post-1989 Kosovo.

34. See Campbell (1999) and Judah (2000) for two accounts that cover the critical period that led to NATO intervention. The Kosovo issue goes beyond the scope of the book, and, therefore, it is not addressed in detail here. It is relevant only to the extent that developments in Kosovo have been influential in the regional geopolitics and the relations between Albanians and Macedonians in FYROM. For further bibliographical sources on Kosovo, see the compiled bibliography in Eslie (1997).

35. The party was founded by Nevzat Halili, a teacher of English from Tetovo, and, despite the fact that its initial orientation was as a party inclusive of other groups, it soon became the main vehicle for ethnic Albanians. Its emergence was surrounded by all kinds of rumors that it was an appendix to Rugova's DLK and it supported Albanian nationalism (Poulton, 2000: 133–35).

36. Of course, there are the obvious exceptions that regulate naturalization in the cases of an individual born by Macedonian parents outside the republic's borders, as well as the typically complex situation that pertains to the alien spouses of citizens of the republic. These and related cases are analyzed by Petrusevska (1998).

37. Albanian officials reported this estimate to the International Crisis Group. See International Crisis Group, *The Macedonian Question: Reform or Rebellion* (Skopje/ Washington/Bruseels: ICG Balkans Report No. 109, 5 April 2001), p. 10. According to the Macedonian officials, the real number of Albanians lacking proper documentation was 11,151.

38. According to Macedonian Albanians, the Albanians excluded from the 1991 and 1994 census amount to approximately 200,000 people (Biberaj, 1998: 258–59), most of whom were immigrants who used to work in other regions of Yugoslavia and who, in accordance with the new citizenship legislation, are deprived from Macedonian citizenship. For an excellent and insightful discussion of the politics of the 1994 "European" census in FYROM, see Friedman (1996). As Friedman argues, the issue of getting an accurate count of the Albanians was not a mere question of conducting a bureaucratic routine survey. On the contrary, the census and the related issues of representation had been politicized long before the 1994 census.

39. The project of an Albanian University outraged Macedonian nationalists. In December 1994, some 2,000 Macedonian students demonstrated in Skopje against its establishment (Babuna, 2000: 81). Another event increasing tension between the two sides was the flying of Albanian flags at the municipal buildings in Tetovo and Govistar. When, on 9 July 1997, the Macedonian police attempted to take down the flags, the Albanians protested, leading to clashes that left three Albanians dead and many more wounded.

40. In response to the founding of Tetovo University and to international pressure, the Macedonian authorities instituted Albanian language teaching in the Pedagogical Faculty over the protests of the Macedonian students. Such protests caused great anger among the more radical Albanians, and Poulton (2000: 192) reports that they give rise to references to the "so-called Macedonian people," thereby alluding to the Macedonians' recently institutionalized status. In turn, such comments further fuel the Macedonians hard-core attitudes.

41. Initially, 700 UN peacekeeping troops were deployed in FYROM. On 11 May 1993, the United States unilaterally declared its desire to send U.S. forces into the republic's territory. In an interview on the *McNeill-Lehrer News Hour* (PBS, 13 May 1993), Stevo Crvenkovski, FYROM's Minister of Foreign Affairs, denied any prior knowledge of the United States' intentions. Finally, on 10 June 1993, the United States and FYROM reached an agreement allowing the deployment of the troops in the new state's territory. In addition to the American troops, there were 1,000 UN Protection Forces (UNPROFOR) troops (Perry 1994b: 31).

42. Biberaj (1998: 263) cites two statistical surveys carried out by the U.S. Information Agency in the 1990s that confirm the novelty of plans for "national unification." In the 1993 survey 55% of Albanians said they would not help Kosovo Albanians militarily, but in the 1996 survey 61% believed that Albania should provide military support to Kosovo Albanians in case of a Serb attack. The results reflect the success of Berisha's pro-nationalist agenda among the Albanian population.

43. From a historical-comparative perspective, religion does not appear to be the major factor contributing to either Albanian solidarity or to ethnic hatred. It was only in the 1990s that religion became one of the major factors contributing to the rift between the Albanians and Macedonians in FYROM (Babuna, 2000: 84). However, these attitudes are the result of Macedonians considering Orthodoxy to be a facet of Macedonian national identity—similar in this respect to the other Balkan nations (Roudometof, 2001). Macedonian nationalists are in a position to exploit the religious component of the people's national identity by promoting the "myth" of a Muslim "conspiracy" aimed against an "endangered Orthodoxy." Similar trends have been observed in other neighboring countries such as Greece and Serbia.

Chapter 7

Conclusion: The Macedonian Question Never Dies

In this final chapter, I synthesize the arguments developed in this book's chapters and discuss the relationship between collective memory and national identity in the southern Balkans. Collective memory plays an important role in the manner in which Bulgarians, Greeks, and Macedonians conceptualize their relationship to Macedonia's soil. The national narratives of each party allow little room for mutual accommodation and therefore provide the raw material used by nationalists for the construction of mutually exclusive viewpoints. The end result is a saga with no end in sight—hence the title of this final chapter.

The situation in the southern Balkans is further complicated by the presence of a sizable Albanian population living outside the borders of the Albanian state. Indeed, it is the Albanian national question that has held the spotlight in the international arena. This issue provides an important, almost indispensable geopolitical component to the entire minority situation in the region. The recent guerrilla war between the Albanian liberation army (NLA) and the Macedonian armed forces aptly illustrated the significance of the Albanian minority for regional geopolitics and for the future stability of the Macedonian Republic. It is therefore necessary to address it here in order to avoid a partial or misleading treatment of the region.

The analysis I have pursued in this book rests on a pragmatic distinction between the "symbolic" struggle for Macedonia and the "actual" real, ethnic conflict between Albanians and Macedonians. While Greeks and Bulgarians have been quite hostile toward the recognition of the Macedonians as a separate nation, their reluctance does not invariably imply territorial claims—although committed nationalists would no doubt raise such claims. The international community or even the academic audience has not always appreciated the distinction between the two types of struggle. On the contrary, speculation on Greek and Bulgarian military involvement has been a persistent feature of commentators on the Macedonian issue throughout the 1990s.

THE POLITICS OF COLLECTIVE MEMORY

From the perspective adopted in this book, the Macedonian Question is a paradigmatic example of the significance of collective memory in the people's sense of belonging and the way they negotiate their relationship to the nation's soil as well as with their neighbors. The reproduction of collective memory has attracted the attention of historians and social scientists who have sought to describe the various mechanisms that shape our understanding of the past. In the modern world, there is a multitude of such mechanisms, including schools, official holidays, textbooks, public lectures, journalism, pictorial representations, photographic and phonographic reproductions of various kinds (movies, documentaries, exhibitions, etc.), scholarly works, and so on.[1]

Indeed, scholars of collective memory feel compelled to draw a distinction between *history* and *commemoration* as a means of separating the mythological interpretation of the past from the historical record (Connerton, 1989: 7; Schwartz, 2000: 9–12). Such a distinction is valid to the extent that history is sufficiently professionalized and differentiated from the state and related institutions. Not surprisingly, it is the advanced industrial democracies of Western Europe and North America where this separation is most pronounced. As I have sought to show in Chapter 2, this is not the case with regard to the Macedonian saga. On the contrary, the involvement of a variety of constituencies—ranging from diasporic communities to politicians and academics—has contributed to the production of rival identities. Underneath these differences lie the deep, important socioeconomic and cultural differences between the Balkans (and other less-developed regions) and the advanced capitalist countries. Subsequently, in order to pursue this topic from a sociological perspective, it is necessary to integrate the pattern of scholarly production with the production of collective memory.

Had I undertaken the conventional task of providing an account of the celebrations, textbooks, and other forms of representation responsible for the perpetuation of the mutually exclusive interpretations of "Macedonia," this book would have been several hundred pages. The study of such cultural reproduction is a valuable exercise that has the potential of significantly contributing to the social-scientific knowledge of identity formation and reproduction. However, I set myself a different task, a task pursued with less rigor in the literature, yet one that helps shed light on the social significance of collective memory. My intention has been to trace not the reconstruction of the past in the present, but rather the consequences of the past (real or imaginary) into the lives of the contemporaries (Schudson, 1997). To effectively accomplish this task I have developed and employed throughout the book the concept of a *national narrative*. My argument rests on the thesis that behind the volumes of pages, lectures, and other forms of cultural representation lies a specific cultural logic, a mode of organizing and structuring the mountains of archival information. It is this logic that I have sought to inquire into. This logic provides the premises and structure of a general narrative, what I have referred to as a *national narrative*. Public commemorations and other forms of cultural reproduction operate according to the logic of the national narrative. They aim to illustrate, highlight, and expand upon the national narrative; they respond to the narrative by enriching it with additional names, places, and actions or by seeking to modify or redefine it in ways commensurable with the contemporaries' values, beliefs, and predispositions. The national narrative emerges out of our forgetting of possible or alternative pasts and constructing a past that is meaningful in the present context.

In Chapter 2, I surveyed the international and domestic politics of the post-1989 Macedonian Question. The goal of this survey was two-fold. On the one hand, the overview of the contemporary symbolic struggle for Macedonia illustrates the importance of this issue for international politics, alongside the importance of memory and history for the production and reproduction of each side's national narrative. On the other hand, this overview illustrates the extent to which the contemporary political, cultural, and diplomatic struggle over "Macedonia" (the name and the cultural legacy associated with the region) is a struggle undertaken from within the premises of particular national narratives. Hence, this overview establishes this topic's factual basis and the necessity for an overview and comparison of the competing national narratives.

Substantively, the recent resurrection of the Macedonian saga caught many among the international audience by surprise. During the post–World War II period, Western researchers, scholars, and journalists came to believe that the Macedonian saga was a thing of the past, a nasty political dispute confined to history books. Yet, the proclamation of independence by the People's Republic of Macedonia led to a decade-long (and still unresolved) dispute between Greece and FYROM over the use of the world "Macedonia." Greece and Bulgaria worry that the recognition of FYROM as Macedonia would lead to demands for minority rights for Macedonians inhabiting these two states. Such a turn would delegitimize each side's carefully crafted national narrative and question the historical canvas upon which the modern national identities have been constructed.

It is for this reason that the Macedonian Question has become a terrain of intellectual contestation, where the local intelligentsias (the journalists, the amateur historians, and the local leaders of various communities, alongside academics from a bewildering variety of disciplines and perspectives) are active participants. The involvement of academics and intellectuals in the Macedonian saga dates back to the nineteenth century (Gounaris and Mihailides, 2000). Yet, after almost an entire century, the intellectuals' participation has led to no mutually acceptable solutions. This is not the outcome of intellectual poverty, but rather a consequence of the fundamentally political character of the Macedonian Question.

The official recognition of Macedonian nationality by the Yugoslav communists and the post-1945 Macedonian nation-building gave birth to what Pettifer (1999a) has referred to as the "new Macedonian Question"—as opposed to the "old" pre-1945 Macedonian Question. This classification is indeed a valid one to the extent that there are distinct issues where the "old" and the "new" questions clearly depart from each other. Obviously, from a world-historical perspective the two issues are linked because both of them refer to the identity of Macedonia's inhabitants. But this does not mean that there are no important differences between the Macedonian Question in the pre-1945 period and the Macedonian Question as it has evolved in the post–World War II period.

First, during the pre-1945 period, the Macedonian Question was in many respects a debate about the extent to which the inhabitants of pre-1913 Macedonia should be described as Greeks, Serbs, or Bulgarians and, therefore, should become united with their fellow nationals. Although the pre-1903 VMRO championed Macedonian independence, its agenda did not win overwhelming popular support, institutional assistance, or international recognition. In sharp contrast, during the post-1945 period, the Macedonian Question consists of the extent to which the Macedonian national narrative would gain legitimacy and acceptance both in the eyes of the international community and scholarly audience as well as in the eyes of the Bulgarian and Greek nation-states.

Second, there is a marked difference with regard to the key players in the politics of the Macedonian Question. During the pre-1945 period, the key players were Serbia (and post-1917 Serb-dominated Yugoslavia), Bulgaria, and Greece. In sharp contrast, during the post-1945 period, the key players are Greece, Bulgaria, the People's Republic of Macedonia, and (during the pre-1989 period) the Yugoslav communists. Being sheltered within the context of the second Yugoslavia, Macedonian nationalism had to take into account the policy of the Belgrade federal government and, more specifically, Belgrade's desire for good relationships with its neighboring Greece and Bulgaria. In addition to the local states, over the post-1945 period, international organizations (such as Helsinki Watch or Amnesty International) and voluntary organizations (such as the immigrant Macedonian and Greek organizations in North America and Australia) have become important players in the Macedonian saga.

Third, during the post-1989 period, the issue attracted the attention of the EU, UN, OSCE, United States, Russia, and so on. This is not an entirely new phenomenon since the Great Powers have been involved in the politics of the Macedonian Question since the second half of the nineteenth century (Glenny, 2000). However, in the pre-1945 period, geopolitics played the central role in determining state policy among the rivaling Great Powers. More specifically, Russia's long-standing efforts to gain a foothold on the Mediterranean were opposed by Great Britain. France, Germany, and the Habsburg Empire also intervened in this geopolitical rivalry, each with its own agenda. The Habsburgs' long-standing policy consisted of efforts to expand their sphere of influence into the Balkans. Germany inherited the same fundamental tendency, and this provided for alliances between the Central Powers (in World War I) and the Axis (in World War II) and Bulgaria. On the contrary, France typically tended to oppose the expansion of Germany in the region, by supporting the Serbs or the Greeks.

Although geopolitical rivalries have not completely disappeared, things are quite different in the post-1945 period. For almost forty years, the Cold War divided the Balkans quite neatly into communist states (Albania, Romania, Bulgaria), pro-Western states (Greece, Turkey), and nonaligned states (Tito's Yugoslavia). This classification reflected the importance of the United States in regional as well as European politics. But it is not only the number of players that has changed—it is also the principles according to which public policy is pursued. U.S. foreign policy is not solely determined by geopolitically defined national interests, but it is (to varying degrees) also determined by moral imperatives, such as the responsibility to promote democracy, human rights, free markets, and so on. In addition to the United States, the emergence of the EC/EU has meant that the European core states have to negotiate among themselves in order to be able to formulate a coherent policy vis-à-vis the region. Of course, this is the ideal—and it is far from being the reality. On the contrary, the difficulties surrounding the EU decision-making process reflect the fact that the old geopolitical games among France, Germany, and Russia are not a thing of the past but continue to play an important role in contemporary politics (Lavdas, 2002). Although journalists and public policy analysts thrive on drawing analogies between the pre-1945 geopolitical rivalries and the post-1989 return of Great Power competition in the region (see, for example, Kennan, 1993), it is important to highlight the extent to which this competition is only one of the elements of the contemporary international arena.

In Chapter 3, I sought to illustrate the dynamics of the current, post-1945 "new Macedonian Question" by providing a critical overview of the relationship between the Macedonian and Greek national narratives. The construction of a national narrative is a political enterprise, one that is full of contestation, argument, and debate. In many respects, controlling and defining a specific past allows the contemporaries to dictate moral imperatives for future social action. This association among past, present, and future is well understood by the local intelligentsias who have been active participants in the cultural politics of the Macedonian Question. Therefore, the national narrative is not an objective description of the past; it is rather an act of selection, appropriation, and proliferation of selected features from a people's past. Therefore, it stands at the crossroads of power and knowledge (Foucault, 1980). The national narrative rests upon a gaze that seeks to establish continuities across time and space. These continuities function as the means of establishing links between the contemporaries and their past, thereby allowing the contemporaries to appropriate the legacy and the achievements of their (presumed) ancestors and, of course, to lay claim upon the territory occupied (or alleged to have been occupied) by these glorious ancestors. In other words, the exercise rests upon "reading history back-wards," that is, reading pre-national history from within nationalist lenses.

Chapter 3 consists of a preliminary attempt at an "archaeology" (Foucault, 1972) of the Macedonian Question. This archaeology is to be understood as a deliberate deconstruction of the official interpretations advocated by the Greek and Macedonian national narratives. It is an inquiry into the contra-dictions of these narratives—and the connections between the pattern of intellectual production and regional geopolitical competition over Macedonia. In this sense, my goal was not to provide a straightforward narrative of the historical record; such an enterprise cannot be undertaken without analyzing the already present perspectives on the Macedonian Ques-tion. Hence, my analysis sought to provide an account of the production of the mutually exclusive national narratives about Macedonia, as well as to show the gaps, inconsistencies, half-truths and other ruptures present in the na-tional narratives of Macedonians, Bulgarians, and Greeks. Because Greece has been the most important adversary of Macedonian national affirmation in the 1990s, my discussion focused mainly on the juxtaposition and criti-cal analysis of the narratives put forward by Athens and Skopje. According to the analysis provided in Chapter 3, the Macedonian national narrative fractures the unity of the Greek national narrative by suggesting a gap be-tween antiquity and modern Greece. The Macedonian side is not claiming that the ancient Macedonians were the genealogical forefathers of contem-porary Macedonians, an argument that cannot possibly be sustained on bio-logical or racial grounds. After all, contemporary Macedonians are a Slavic people. However, what is important in the Macedonian thesis is the sugges-tion that the ancient Macedonians were not ancient Greeks. This suggestion allows for the contemporary Macedonians to appropriate the cultural legacy of ancient Macedonians.

The consequences of this interpretation for the Greek side are quite sig-nificant, especially since the Greek nation-state has spent more than a cen-tury carefully constructing and promoting a national narrative based on the thesis of 3,000 years of unbroken cultural continuity. Indeed, this continu-ity is part of the ancient Greeks' legacy, and this legacy has been absorbed into modern Greek identity as one of the major elements of national pride, whereby Greece is the land of "civilization." In the post-1945 period, the Greek and Macedonian contenders have pursued their respective national narratives, thereby producing radically opposed interpretations of geography, history, archaeology, ethnology, linguistics, and so on. To this disagreement it is necessary to add the Macedonian-Bulgarian contestation, a contest of similar nature yet one that has been less visible in the eyes of the international community. While in the case of the Greek-Macedonian dispute, the bone of contention is the status of ancient Macedonians, in the Macedonian-Bulgarian dispute, the bone of contention is the interpretation of the recent past, the extent to which the Slavs of Macedonia were (or still are) better described as Bulgarians rather than as Macedonians. Indeed, both Greeks and Bulgarians converge in their respective arguments when they point out that the label Macedonian is fundamentally a geographical appellation, not a national one.

I need to stress the partial nature of the deconstructionist project pursued in Chapter 3. Moreover, it is necessary to highlight the degree to which such an enterprise invariably assumes a value-neutral position—that is, there are no *a priori* decisions made about the quality, credibility, and factual accuracy of the different narratives under examination. The goal is to analyze their relationships, to trace their gaps and contradictions, and to reveal their novelty and their origins in the political projects of nation building and irredentism. In accordance with postmodernist interpretations, it would be tempting to argue that all there is in the Macedonian saga is a series of rival narratives, all of equal importance as the next one, and that all of them are valid as representations of the people's beliefs. Of course, this is the case, and the statements and other forms of popular mobilization overviewed in Chapter 2 testify to the degree to which the impact of national narratives on the public and the diasporas of the Balkan nation-states cannot be summarily dismissed. Still, in order to advance our conceptual understanding of the Macedonian Question, it is necessary to develop an analysis that goes beyond mere critique of particular national narratives, beyond the perspectives of Greek, Bulgarian, or Macedonian "national history," and toward a third perspective that recognizes Macedonian national identity as such—albeit without assuming that Macedonian national identity predated the modern world. On the contrary, the formation of modern Macedonian national identity is to be sought in the dynamic interplay among the contenders of Macedonia over the post-1860 period.

THE SOCIAL CONSTRUCTION OF THE MACEDONIAN QUESTION

This enterprise is undertaken in Chapter 4. My analysis and synthesis of the historical record is only a first attempt, a point of departure for future work, and should not be interpreted as the final word on this issue.[2]

Methodologically speaking, my approach is based on the thesis that national identity is socially constructed, fluid, situational, and modified through encounters and interaction with other groups, thereby fostering the necessity for boundary preservation and the exaggeration of cultural difference. Macedonia's historical record offers an exceptionally rich research site where these processes have fostered the appeal of different national identities among the multiplicity of ethnic and religious groups inhabiting the region during the pre-1913 period. Accordingly, the development of national identity in the region that came be referred to as "Macedonia" was a belated phenomenon that was shaped by a multitude of factors, including the socioeconomic transformation of the Ottoman state in the nineteenth century, the waves of immigration and urbanization in the same time period, the nationalist propagandas of the Greek, Serb, and Bulgarian states, the voluntary and forceful population exchanges of the early twentieth century, as well as the impact of secularization in the local society.

Any attempt to decipher the Macedonian Question has to place this issue in the broader context of the social transformation of the Balkans in the course of the nineteenth century (Roudometof, 2001). The Macedonian Question is simply one of the instances where regional nation building has produced ethnic or national rivalry (other well-known cases include Bosnia, Croatia, Kosovo, and Cyprus). Throughout the last two centuries, the export of the national idea from Europe to the Balkans led to the geopolitical reconfiguration of the human geography of the region. Indeed, the very term "Balkans" came into currency in many respects as a corollary of the rivalries produced by the national question in the European part of the Ottoman Empire. The employment of the word "Macedonia" was simultaneous with the political projects advanced by the Bulgarian, Greek, and Serb political and cultural organizations as well as the revolutionary conspirators of the International Macedonian Revolutionary Organization (VMRO). For the pre-1912 European part of the Ottoman Empire, "Macedonia" came to be a rather ill-defined region that practically encompassed the overwhelming majority of the European territories, especially since the dispersion of the Albanians in the western Balkans as well as their belated national movement meant that Albanian national aspirations lacked the visibility of the claims set forth by the other states, let alone the support of a state apparatus (like the Serbs, Greeks, and post-1878 Bulgarian nationalists) (Roudometof, 2001: 147–51).

Not surprisingly, then, the 1913 partition of Ottoman Macedonia failed to resolve the conflict over possession of "Macedonia." It left Bulgarian nationalists bitter and disappointed, thereby providing an incentive for the participation of Bulgaria in World War I on the side of the Central Powers. This involvement did not bring the much-sought conquest of Macedonia by the Bulgarian nation-state, and the post–World War I boundaries remained close to the original 1913 demarcation lines. These large-scale geopolitical rivalries and military confrontations have had a strong impact upon the population of Macedonia (including warfare, the destruction of homes and property, violent ethnic cleansing by the opposing armies, and so on).

Since the 1890s, the presence of paramilitary units, anarchists, and terrorist autonomist movements (VMRO) meant that the inhabitants of Ottoman Macedonia were pressured by all sides to pick a church affiliation, either on the side of the Ecumenical Patriarchate or on the side of the Bulgarian Exarchate or, later on, on the side of the Serb Church. They were further pressured to send their children to the schools operated by one of these competing sides. The end result was an instrumental use of religion and political affiliation. Contemporary observers pointed out the tendency of different members of the same family to align themselves with different sides, hence securing the family unit against any possible outcome. In itself, this observation indicates both the absence of strongly felt beliefs on behalf of the common folk, as well as the degree to which such "national attachments" cannot be treated as voluntary declarations, but rather as family strategies of resistance, circumvention, and adaptation.

A further point worth mentioning here is the extent to which Ottoman Macedonia was a tapestry of ethnic, religious, and national groups. There is no way to provide precise numerical estimates for the different groups, especially since each side has had the opportunity to manipulate the statistics for its own benefit. It is nevertheless well known that the population of Ottoman Macedonia ranged from Ottoman Muslims (one of the largest constituencies) to Hellenized or Latin-speaking Vlachs (claimed by the Romanians as their own nationals) to Greeks, Albanians, Pomaks (Bulgarian-speaking Muslims), Jews (mainly concentrated in the cities of Thessaloniki and Kavala), and other minor Turkish-speaking groups. To this tapestry of groups, it is necessary to add the Slavic-speaking population, a population that by all accounts represented a significant segment of the population of Ottoman Macedonia. This population was mainly rural, consisting of peasants working in their own fields or in the Ottoman estates. It was the ethnic composition or national allegiance of this group of peoples that became bitterly contested in the course of the twentieth century.

To begin with, neither the Slavic-speakers nor the other groups listed above should be viewed as "naturally affiliated" with any particular side. Plenty of examples exist suggesting that people switched sides on various occasions and on the basis of opportunism rather than national identity. For the Slavic-speaking population, the fundamental division produced by the creation of the Bulgarian Exarchate (1870) and the subsequent excommunication of the Bulgarian Church by the Ecumenical Patriarchate (1872) was one between Patriarchists and Exarchists (considered to be Schismatics by the Patriarchists). Although this distinction was treated as a declaration of national affiliation (the Patriarchists on the side of the Greeks and the Exarchists on the side of the Bulgarians), it would be misleading to suggest that the

peasantry had a full understanding of the issues involved, let alone a prefer-
ence based on national identity.[3] Rather, the construction of Greek or Bulgarian national identity in the region operated through church affiliation and
the operation of schools sponsored by each side.

To further complicate matters, from the 1870s forward, the Serb state
expanded its national propaganda in the region. The impetus for this move
was two-fold. On the one hand, the Serbs wished to be in a position to conquer Kosovo, the brethren of Serb nationalism. On the other hand, the
Habsburg occupation of Bosnia-Herzegovina (1878) meant that Serb geopolitical designs for the western Balkans had to face up to a formidable adversary. Hence, Ottoman Macedonia represented an alternative direction.
The Serb intelligentsia attempted rather successfully to capitalize on the linguistic divisions between what was referred to as eastern versus western
Bulgarian dialects, in order to suggest that the Macedonian Slavic population were not Bulgarians, but rather lacked a coherent national identity and
therefore they could be claimed by the Serb state (for a brief summary of
the positions advocated by the various sides, see Gounaris, 1996).

The foundation of the original VMRO (1893) further complicated the
situation. The VMRO was a fourth agent (Greece, Bulgaria, and Serbia being the other three) and therefore added to the general confusion. In large
part because of the already existing crowded space, the VMRO was far less
successful in gaining popular support. It is this lack of support that has led
to an entire discussion on whether there was a Macedonian national
independence movement in pre-1912 Macedonia. The articulation of
Macedonian national identity was strongly influenced by the failure of
Bulgaria to conquer the majority of Macedonia in the 1910s and the subsequent harsh acculturation campaigns of Greeks and Serbs in their respective parts of Macedonia.

In Chapter 4, I discussed in detail the interwar situation in northwestern
Greek Macedonia. There are several reasons for this choice. First, the
Macedonian enclave in Greek Macedonia was forcefully isolated from other
compact Slavic populations, and this intensified their sense of difference.
Additionally, unlike other Slavic speakers in Macedonia who, over time, developed a Greek national identity, the Slavo-Macedonians of northwestern
Greek Macedonia were mainly poor peasants, who came in direct conflict
with the Greek refugees who settled in the region. State-sponsored discrimination, conflict over resources, and cultural exclusion all provided more than
sufficient reasons for the Slavic inhabitants of the region to assert their regional identity as an ethnic label. The electoral support of the Slavo-
Macedonians went to the People's Party—just a reflection of the manner in
which national politics were determined by the regional conflict between
refugees and "local" Slavo-Macedonians. The post-1936 harsh repression
propagated by the Metaxas dictatorship only intensified the feelings of isolation and alienation from the Greek state.

World War II and the organization of guerrilla units by the communists offered the opportunity to transform the affinity of the Slavo-Macedonians into a more consistent support. Throughout the interwar period, the communists had been eager to use the plight of the Slavo-Macedonian population in order to gain electoral support for their parties both in Yugoslavia and Greece. In Vardar Macedonia, the communists were able to claim the loyalty of a large portion of the local population, and this led to the foundation of the People's Republic of Macedonia and the affirmation of the Macedonian nation. In Greek Macedonia, however, the Slavo-Macedonians of northwestern Macedonia had to join the Greek Communist Party, fighting alongside the Greek communists in the Greek Civil War (1944–49). When the communists were defeated, scores of Slavo-Macedonians fled to Vardar Macedonia. Others emigrated to Canada, Australia, and the United States in the 1950s and 1960s. The result was that only a few tens of thousands of Slavo-Macedonians remained in Greece. But the dispersion of this group did not put an end to the Macedonian saga.

On the contrary, post-1945 Macedonian nation-building assumed a transnational character, whereby the immigrants and their descendants became members of a transnational Macedonian imagined community that currently lives in Canada, Australia, and the United States. The incorporation of the immigrants into the Macedonian nation helped the legitimization of the post-1945 Macedonian nation-building. But it also created the necessity for a cultural or geographical definition that would allow those immigrants from Greek (Aegean) and Bulgarian (Pirin) Macedonia to include themselves in the new imagined community. Subsequently, the national homeland of the Macedonian nation became identified as the pre-1913 Macedonia—in spite of the fact that the Macedonians are no longer the dominant national or ethnic group in this region and in spite of the fact that such a definition would be detrimental to regional stability. The post-1989 transnational struggle for Macedonia has aptly illustrated the significance of the immigrant constituencies for the international relations of the countries in the region.

THE CULTURAL CONTRADICTIONS OF NATION-STATE BUILDING

It is with these broader considerations in mind that one has to approach the question of Macedonian national minorities in neighboring countries— a task pursued in Chapter 5. In sharp contrast to the claims of Macedonian nationalists, the numerical strength of minority groups who identify with the Macedonian nation is quite limited. This does not mean that there are no people and organized groups in the two states who have such an allegiance and who have been the subject of extensive harassment and persecution. But this should not be interpreted as an indication of the presence of a large minority population, let alone of the presence of a "national minority," an ill-fated term that implies the identification of a minority with a national homeland that lies outside the boundaries of the nation-state that is inhabited by a particular national minority (Brubaker, 1996).

From the Macedonians' viewpoint, the recognition of Macedonian national minorities by Greece and Bulgaria has represented an important step in the process of the global legitimization of Macedonian national identity, as well as a *de facto* recognition that the Greek and Bulgarian occupation of their respective parts of Macedonia has been based on force rather the loyalty of the people. Not surprisingly, such recognition has been fiercely denied by both states. During the post–World War II period, both Athens and Sofia considered such an assertion to be nothing less than a front for Macedonian territorial claims against their own regions of pre-1913 Macedonia. This reaction has to be placed in the context of the minority question in the region and (pre-1945) Europe at large. In Chapter 5, I have provided a brief overview of the status of minority groups in the southern Balkans. As my review shows, the existence of minority groups in the region is viewed as a geopolitical "weakness" and not as a bridge between nations. This is the legacy of the turbulent interwar period, during which minority groups throughout the region suffered extensively by aggressive policies of cultural homogenization (Roudometof, 2002a).

Consequently, the entire issue of Macedonian minorities in the neighboring states is but an illustration of the power of national narratives. In contrast, other minority groups in the region are far more numerous and do hold out the potential of secessionist movements, like the Turks of Greece, or the Muslims and Turks of Bulgaria, or the Albanians of Kosovo and FYROM. Hence, the impact of the Macedonian minority discourse is of limited importance in terms of the numerical strength of the people affiliated with such groups. This does not mean that this issue has been inconsequential in regional geopolitics. On the contrary, the sheer mention of Macedonian minorities has contributed significantly to poor relations between FYROM, Greece, and Bulgaria. From the viewpoint of the post-1945 Macedonian Republic, the partition of Macedonia was a national disaster that divided Macedonians among the different nations of the Balkans and led to forced acculturation into the Serb, Bulgarian, and Greek nations. The establishment of the People's Republic of Macedonia offered the opportunity for national self-assertion and affirmation. The next step should be the recognition of Macedonian national minorities by Greece and Bulgaria.

Still, the issue of the recognition of the people's individual rights is conceptually distinct from the issue of collective rights. While the post-1945 international human rights movement and evolving international regime concerning the inviolability of people's rights around the globe has provided a useful terrain for Macedonians to assert their rights both in Greece and

Bulgaria, it would be at best naïve to consider these issues independently from the post-1945 Macedonian national narrative and the latent irredentism that accompanies it. This does not mean that Greece and Bulgaria should interfere in the people's right to express themselves openly, to form organizations, and to pursue the free expression of their cultural identity. In the post-1989 period, the continuation of past practices put the two states at odds with the evolving European human rights regime. Eventually, the two states realized the shortcomings of their practices and adopted a more open policy toward Macedonian organizations. In this regard, these developments indicate the willingness of the two states to align themselves with EU policies on these matters. The degree to which Macedonian organizations operate without harassment and persecution by local authorities is a good indicator of the extent of the two states' deepening democratization. However, demands that the local states adopt a policy of *actively promoting* the articulation of Macedonian identity within their boundaries go beyond mere protection of human rights—and it is certain that such policies would cause a nationalist backlash that could threaten the transformation of the "symbolic" battle for Macedonia into an actual one.

Indeed, there are two sets of issues that converge on FYROM's territory. The first issue concerns the symbolic conflict over legitimate ownership of "Macedonia." The second issue concerns the political (and to varying degrees, also military) movement for Albanian self-assertion and self-determination. The first issue is in many regards an issue of domestic politics for Greece, Bulgaria, and FYROM, as well as a hot topic for regional foreign policy debates. Therefore, the international community has the opportunity to monitor, pressure, and intervene in order to promote regional peace and security. The second issue is largely an issue of domestic politics in Albania, Kosovo, and FYROM. In sharp contrast to the first issue, international pressure is of limited value. The fragmentation of Albanians into three distinct regions, each with its own problems and historical trajectory, has meant that there is not a single central authority and certainly no single state that can control the actions of the KLA "freedom fighters" or those of other minor rival groups that might emerge in the future.

This observation plays a central role in interpreting the evolution of the Albanian national question in the southern Balkans. In my review in Chapter 6, I argued that this topic has to be conceptually separated into three distinct, yet interrelated subtopics. First, there is a set of Greek-Albanian issues that have been the topic of debate and negotiation between Athens and Tirana. More specifically, the Albanian nation-state has to contend with two issues of importance for Greek-Albanian relations. The first issue is the question of the Greek minority in southern Albania and the concomitant residual feelings of irredentism about this region, traditionally referred to as Northern Epirus by the Greeks. It is worth pointing out that it is not only Greek nationalists who harbored delusions of territorial expansion. Albanian nationalists have traditionally claimed a portion of the Greek region of Epirus and have raised the issue of the Albanians who used to live in the region of Thesprotia (Chameria). The second issue refers to the conditions of the sizable Albanian immigrant population who descended upon Greece in the post-1989 period. The negative image of the Albanian immigrants among the Greek public is a factor that colors Greek perceptions of Albania and contributes to the resentment felt by the Albanians, who rightly feel that the Greek public has treated them very poorly. The two issues are interrelated and necessitate a continuing dialogue between Athens and Tirana.

While this topic can be (and has been) dealt with in interstate negotiations between Athens and Tirana, the other two subtopics are more difficult to tackle. These two subtopics include the Albanian question in Kosovo and the Albanian question in FYROM. They are also closely linked because the evolution of the status of Kosovo has provided an example for the Macedonian Albanians to emulate. In this regard, NATO and the United States have played an important role because the lack of clearly defined policy guidelines has contributed to the proliferation of aspirations (and violence) among the Albanians in both regions. The Kosovo issue has practically been resolved after the 1999 NATO-led strike against Yugoslavia. The end result of the strike was to create an international protectorate that did not allow the open declaration of the province's independence but in practice has meant the removal of Serb administrative control over the Albanian population. The difficult task of constructing a viable political authority is lagging behind, and if Bosnia provides a model for postwar NATO-led reconstruction, it will be a task that will take several years. In practice, the NATO war led to the creation of a largely Albanian province, because the remnants of the Serb population either fled or barricaded themselves into a few municipalities.

The lesson from this intervention was clear: NATO will support Albanian national movements for self-determination, even if these are violent ones. The Albanian-Macedonian civil war of 2001 can be attributed to the influence of the Kosovo affair into Albanian-Macedonian relations in FYROM (see the postscript at the conclusion of this chapter). It should be noted that the radicalization of the Kosovo Albanians was the product of a long period of suppression by the Serb authorities, and that this radicalization occurred only when it became quite clear that the peaceful movement of Ibrahim Rugova had not produced the desired results. Most troublesome of all, however, is the sense that the NATO-led intervention in Kosovo and the establishment of an international protectorate over the province delivered a rather misleading message to the minority population of the various Balkan nation-states. It would be no exaggeration to suggest that the lesson delivered was that armed insurrection pays off, provided that the rebels would be able to provoke sympathy, hold their ground, and depict their enemy in a negative light.[4]

It is important to highlight the extent to which the Albanian question has been quite different in Kosovo and FYROM. In Kosovo, the Albanian population has been the majority for a considerable period of time, and the suppression of its political rights has a history reaching back more than twenty years. In sharp contrast, the Macedonian Albanians have had the opportunity to participate in government, organize their own parties freely, and certainly enjoy more freedom than their counterparts in pre-1999 Kosovo. In addition, the Macedonian Albanians are clearly a minority within FYROM; therefore, it is more difficult for them to argue for national self-determination on purely ethnic grounds. It would be reasonable to argue that no logical inevitability exists that would dictate a long-term trend toward a Greater Albania. Yet, this is precisely where the future appears to be moving.

THE FUTURE NOW

Throughout this book's chapters I argued that the Macedonian Question is a symbolic conflict that centers on the construction (or production) of conflicting ethnocentric national narratives. These narratives shape the construction of collective memory on each side, thereby producing an everlasting saga. Commentators and public policy analysts have raised the issue of the extent to which the symbolic conflict over Macedonia might be transformed into actual conflict. As I have alluded to in Chapter 1, fear of such a potential conflict was invoked by U.S. President Bill Clinton as one of the reasons that dictated the U.S.-led NATO war against the rump Yugoslavia in 1999. The Albanian-Macedonian guerilla war of 2001 has further amplified such worries.

Is the formation of a Greater Albania a historical inevitability? Indeed, the question might be posed in broader terms with respect to the entire region: Would it be better for the international community to accept the premise that nation-state formation in the Balkans would lead to the reconstruction of state borders? Would it be wiser to move through this phase as soon as possible in order to resolve the national rivalries of the region and then be able to deal with the more pressing issues of economic and social development? To the extent that this book might shed some light into these "hot questions," I would argue that the regional disputes that appear to be the outcome of incomplete projects of national unification are in reality produced by the national narratives of different nation-states. The Macedonian Question is a paradigmatic case of a dispute that has thankfully mutated into a more symbolic conflict over the cultural legacy of Macedonia. The fact that this dispute refuses to die—even though very little can be gained from it in sheer geopolitical terms—aptly demonstrates the power of national narratives in determining the predisposition of the public in different states and the degree to which state policies have to take into account public opinion, thereby rendering difficult (if not impossible) the successful resolution of the Macedonian saga.

In a brief but insightful article, historian Gale Stokes (1999) has put forward an interpretation that runs parallel to some of the arguments developed in this book. Stokes's interpretation rests on the thesis that ideas and institutions are at least as important as social configurations in generating and framing political affairs. His interpretation of the Balkan crises rests on three interrelated points: first, that nationalism in Europe can be understood as a set of powerful mobilizing ideas dating back to the French Revolution; second, that nationalist consolidation on the basis of ethnic homogenization has always been violent; and third, that Europeans are currently in the process of constructing mechanisms that will lessen the chances of future outbursts like the Yugoslav crises of the 1990s.

All three arguments are indeed valid to differing degrees but fail to incorporate sufficiently the very concepts invoked by the author.[5] As I have argued in my *Nationalism, Globalization, and Orthodoxy* (2001), the Ottoman Empire faced considerable difficulties in its attempt to become such a "modernizing" state. In the end, this task of modernization was pursued by the Balkan nation-states that inherited the empire's European territory, as well as by the Republic of Turkey. It is indicative of the necessity for a turn away from Ottoman structures that even the Turkish nationalists led by Kemal Ataturk felt that a clear-cut distinction ought to be drawn between Turkey and the former Ottoman Empire. The key issue confronted by the Balkan societies over the last two centuries did not have much to do with absolutism (Stokes, 1999: 5), as was the case in Western and Central Europe. On the contrary, the key issues for the Ottoman (and, to some extent, for the Habsburg) Empire was the nature of the system that would supersede the imperial form of social organization.[6]

Stokes (1999: 5–6) correctly points out the three legacies of the 1789 French Revolution, that is, the principles of equity and political sovereignty as well as the proposition that states ought to be nation-states. Indeed, the central conceptual question that preoccupied the Balkans in the course of the nineteenth century was precisely the interpretation and contextualization of these principles in the light of the Balkan cultural experience (Roudometof, 1999). As Stokes himself points out, these lofty ideas left the peoples of the world with the difficult task of defining the criteria according to which people are awarded legitimate membership to the nation. However, Stokes does not discuss the theoretical conundrum created by the proclamation of equality, sovereignty, and national self-determination.

I would argue that ethnic fragmentation and violent homogenization is but one of the possible solutions for the application of these principles; they are far from an inevitable outcome, as Stokes seems to suggest. It is, of course, true that forced cultural homogenization has been the reality for much of twentieth-century Europe (Vardy and Tooley, 2002). But it is one thing to accept historical reality as a fact; it is quite different when this historical reality is clothed in the rhetoric of historical inevitability (or sociological determinism).[7] Stokes's argument relies all too heavily on the Eastern European experience and does not compare the differences in trajectories between North American, postcolonial British nation-states (or even Western European states like France) and the Eastern (and Central) European nation-states (including pre-1945 imperial Germany).

Such a comparison would be consistent with his thesis that ideas are just as important as social configurations, and it would also give his analysis a more global frame of reference. Although I do not wish to resurrect the misleading distinction between Western and Eastern nationalisms (Plamenatz, 1976), I believe that it is important to highlight the different principles of governmentality (Foucault, 1991) as they were applied to different regions of the globe, or what I have referred to as the discourses of nationhood and citizenship (Roudometof, 1999). Institutionalized in the United Kingdom and its former colonies, but also in commercial states like the Netherlands, and later on France, the discourse of citizenship proclaimed that all citizens of the state are equally members of the nation. It is worth recalling in this regard the degree to which "nation" and "state" are used almost interchangeably in English (hence, we refer to the United Nations instead of the more accurate United States). The operation of the discourse of citizenship on a global basis reveals the global foundation of the national idea and does not misinterpret nationalism as a purely European phenomenon (Anderson, 1991; Lipset, 1963, 1997; and for Eastern Europe in particular, Ingrao, 1999).

It is critical to recall that even in the United States the discourse of citizenship does not operate in isolation from its conceptual adversary, the discourse of nationhood. In contrast to citizenship, the discourse of nationhood proclaims that the bonds uniting the peoples of a particular nation are located at the cultural level, that is, as a genealogical or cultural (ethnic, religious, or linguistic) tie connecting every member of this cultural community with his or her fellow nationals. In the United States, this discourse has been confined to the margins, under the rubric of "race and ethnicity," or in discussions about the role and significance of the Confederate flag, the degree of school segregation, and other public policy issues, including the everlasting American debate about immigration.

But in Eastern Europe, this type of cultural intolerance became the central foundation for the construction of nation-states. I do not wish to inscribe historical inevitability to this outcome. As I have explained elsewhere (Roudometof, 2001), this outcome was the product of the interaction among a variety of factors. Most important, the discourse of citizenship failed to take root in the Ottoman Empire, mainly because of the absence of crosscutting cleavages that would allow democracy and parliamentarism to enjoy strong popular support.[8] On the contrary, over the second half of the nineteenth and early twentieth century, the social structure of the Ottoman state became more and more polarized, with the urban strata and the economy coming under the control of the Ottoman minorities (mostly Greeks and Armenians), while, at the same time, the Ottoman administration became more and more Ottoman Muslim. While groups within both camps tried to build civic ties among the empire's diverse population, such policies did not really have a clientele among the Ottoman Muslim peasantry.

On top of this already quite difficult situation, the Ottoman state had to defend its territory against the nationalist propaganda of the Serb, Bulgarian, and Greek nation-states, all of them obsessed with dreams of national unification and territorial expansion into the European part of the Empire. It was from within these nation-states that the discourse of nationhood spread over the European territories of the Ottoman Empire (including Kosovo, Bosnia, Macedonia, Albania, and Thrace). The peoples of the "central zone" of the Balkans (Albanians, Macedonians, and other minor groups) were caught up in a maelstrom of political pressure where they had to face competing nationalist propagandas and, at least for the Albanians, to organize militarily and politically in order to avoid the complete carving up of their land among the Balkan nation-states. The Albanians were partially successful, in large part thanks to the support of Italy and the Habsburg Empire. On the other hand, the Macedonian separatist movement (organized by the Internal Macedonian Revolutionary Organization [VMRO]) was less successful in finding a strong protector; hence, Ottoman Macedonia was eventually divided among Serbia, Greece, and Bulgaria (Roudometof, 2001: 131–55).

Throughout the twentieth century, the Balkan nation-states attempted to make reality conform to the ideal standards set out by the discourse of nationhood. In other words, their population ought to be "made" into a single cultural community adhering to the nation-state. We know that this project led to a great deal of suffering, murder, and warfare—ranging from the Ustasa campaigns of terror during the World War II to the Greek Civil War and, of course, the more recent, post-1989 wars of the Yugoslav disintegration. The pattern that I have sketched in the preceding paragraphs suggests that the current predicament of the Balkans is not the inevitable outcome of trying to make state borders conform to ethnic distribution, as Stokes (1999: 8–10) suggests. Such an argument fails to take into account the simple fact that there is more than one route to centralization, homogenization, and nationalization. On the contrary, my analysis in this book is very much in favor of Ingrao's (1999: 296) thesis that for the Balkans—as well as for Eastern Europe at large—"multiethnicity is the solution, not the problem." It is at best naïve to attempt to make reality conform to ethnic boundaries, for these "ethnic boundaries" do not really exist in "nature" but, on the contrary, they are the product of national narratives. To escape the vicious logic of the local national narratives it is necessary to reverse the cultural logic inherent in the Balkan national narratives—whether Albanian, Bulgarian, Serb, or Macedonian. Accomplishing such a goal requires the institutionalization and conscious promotion of the discourse of citizenship as the foundational principle for the organization of the local societies and interethnic relations. The simple fact that the Balkan nation-states have not followed this route does not entail a historical inevitability that makes the local societies inherently incapable of developing such principles. Such a thesis simply transforms the product of human social action (e.g., history) into a "social law" that humans are incapable of changing or transforming.

The Balkan nation-states certainly have had (and still do have) the option of making the discourse of citizenship their fundamental social principle of cultural organization. This is not a theoretical proposition, but it does provide for concrete public policy strategies. For example, the suggestion should be that all people of a given state are equal members of the nation and that any form of discrimination, either by individuals or by state agencies, is illegal. It is not as if these recommendations are alien to the Balkan nation-states. On the contrary, such provisions have to be adopted in order for the states to conform to EU normative standards or other international human rights treaties.

Moreover, the ethnic or national rivalries in the region are the product of the cultural logic of nation building, that is, of the attempt to apply the discourse of nationhood into public policy and make reality conform to this fiction. It is not that peace can be established if only all the people end up within the "right" borders. Given the ethnic intermixing of the Balkans, as well as the fact that international mobility has tremendously increased over the post-1945 period, it is extremely unlikely that any of the Balkan nation-states would ever approach anything resembling national homogeneity. Consequently, to uncritically accept the discourse of nationhood as the natural consequence of nation building is a recipe that dissolves moral and ethical responsibility from the observer, while it simultaneously justifies inaction at the international level.

NOTES

1. See Lowenthal (1985, 1996), Spillman (1997), Zelinski (1988), and O'Leary (1999) for some examples of studies dealing with the relationship between national identity and collective memory. The bewildering variety and interdisciplinary nature of the field does not allow memory studies to coalesce around specific paradigms. Moreover, for the purposes of this book, literature dealing with the cognitive aspects of social memory has been ignored—it is only the social aspects of collective

memory, and more specifically, those aspects that have a bearing on the construction and reproduction of national identity that are relevant to this book's subject matter.

2. The line of argument pursued in Chapter 4 is closely related to Danforth's (1995) interpretation of the Macedonian controversy. However, there are some important differences between the interpretation set forward in Chapter 4 and Danforth's interpretation. First, the discussion of the historical record is much more extensive and takes into account sources hitherto underutilized. Second, in accordance with the sociological perspective of this book, attention is paid not solely to the existence of Macedonians as such, but also to the numerical strength of the Macedonians and the patterns of geographical dispersion throughout post-1913 Macedonia. In this regard, the discussion might be viewed as a useful update and improvement upon Danforth's initial interpretation of the evolution of the Macedonian saga.

3. It is worth recalling that even in France, the peasantry did not display strong national attachments up until the late nineteenth century—as Weber's (1976) groundbreaking study has demonstrated.

4. There is, of course, nothing new to this strategy, which, as a matter of fact, dates back to the eighteenth- and nineteenth-century revolutions and insurrections. The 1821 Greek revolution incited a wave of Philhellenism across Europe, and this wave facilitated changes in the foreign policy of the European powers, eventually leading to their military involvement in the conflict. In turn, this involvement led to the Navarino battle of 1827 and paved the way for the creation of independent Greece. Echoing this strategy, the 1876 failed April Uprising of the Bulgarian national movement was successful in invoking harsh Ottoman reprisals that tilted European opinion toward the Bulgarian cause and was among the contributing factors that led to the Russo-Turkish War of 1877. In the aftermath of the war, Bulgaria became an independent principality, gaining statehood eventually in 1908. Similarly, the 1903 Ilinden Uprising attempted to duplicate the same strategy, but this time it fell on deaf ears, since the international community was not ready for yet another territorial change in the Balkans (for details, see Anderson, 1966; Jelavich, 1991; Sumner, 1962).

5. Stokes argues that Continental states (Russia, Prussia, the Habsburg Empire) predated capitalism and nationalism and were central agents of public policy and social transformation. This is the case, but Stokes further argues that these were rationalizing states. However, his own examples come almost exclusively from Western Europe (Stokes, 1999: 4). Indeed, it is quite debatable whether the empires of the eastern part of Europe (Habsburg, Ottoman, and Russian) can be described as "rationalizing states" at all (see Ingrao, 1999). Throughout their history, these empires employed a variety of different administrative systems that frequently maintained local customs, practices, or even legal codes. They united a patchwork of different regions by imposing administrative oversight on certain important areas, such as conscription, taxation, and submission to central authority.

6. Ingrao (1997a) puts it quite succinctly in his theses that the "East is different" (from the West) and that, in Eastern Europe, "the nation-state is the problem not the solution" to the issues of ethnic conflict in the region. Contemporary discussions frequently accept the wishful thinking of diplomats and other Eastern

European cultural workers who strive to represent their societies as "inherently European." Such arguments are extensions of Eastern European nationalist mobilization and rhetoric, according to which each nation is "closer to the West" while its neighbors to the East are "Orientals" (Mestrovic, 1993; cf. Todorova, 1997).

7. Ingrao (1999: 300) correctly points out that Eastern Europe (including the Balkans) continues to this day to be plagued by the legacy of the post–World War I treaties and their effects in determining the state boundaries in a fashion that bred resentment and revisionism among the World War I losers.

8. As Lipset (1960) argues, the distribution of ethnic and racial groups across the entire range of the socioeconomic spectrum is a critically important factor contributing to the preservation of U.S. democracy. When ethnic and racial solidarities are not fragmented by class position, the final outcome is the production of social solidarity along ethnic or national lines. While the United States has been able to avoid such an outcome, the Ottoman Empire failed to develop an Ottoman Muslim urban class that would counteract the Greek-Orthodox domination of trade, the professions, and other middle-class occupations. It also failed to incorporate Greek-Orthodox peoples in the administration of the state. Hence, the peoples of the empire failed to achieve the much-sought "identity of interests" that would have allowed the empire to survive (see Roudometof, 2001: 75–99).

Postscript: Macedonia 2000+

Look what is happening. Albanians want territory. Macedonian people are getting thrown out. The only way [to reverse the trend] is through the army.

Unnamed 63-year-old woman in Tearce.
Quoted in the *New York Times,* 30 July 2001.

In the aftermath of the 1999 Kosovo Crisis, and as this book was being-crafted, events in FYROM took a negative turn, with the Albanian National Liberation Army (NLA) engaging in guerrilla war against the Macedonian army. The civil strife continued throughout 2001 and was eventually settled through international intervention. The events will undoubtedly continue to unravel; consequently, any account is bound to be partial and incomplete. However, it would be negligent to fail to include a summary of the more recent developments—especially because these developments illustrate the critical importance of some of the issues analyzed in this book.

As I have already discussed in Chapter 6, the 1999 Kosovo Crisis and the military involvement of NATO in Kosovo delivered the implicit message that armed insurrection can indeed provide a mechanism for bringing the long-held grievances of FYROM's Albanian population to the attention of the international community (and in particular NATO, EU, and the United States). Prior to the Kosovo Crisis, the 1998 elections in FYROM led to the overturn of the socialist government. The alliance between the VMRO-DMPNU and its centrist partner, the Democratic Alternative (DA), was successful in capturing 59 of 120 parliamentary seats—while the Albanian parties received a total of 25 seats (Perry, 2000b: 130). Amid concerns about growing regional instability in Kosovo, the winners turned to Arben Xhaferi, leader of the Democratic Party of Albanians (DPA), who agreed to join the government. This coalition was in place during the Kosovo Crisis of 1999. Despite the influx of refugees during the Kosovo Crisis, FYROM's economic situation improved with the GNP increasing by 3% in 1999 and 5% in 2000.

In the fall of 1999, presidential elections were also held. The presidency does not hold special powers since FYROM has a parliamentary system and power rests in the hands of the prime minister. However, the presidential elections were important because Macedonian President Kyro Gligorov was not among the candidates. Gligorov, an elder statesman, held the office since 1991, and his leadership was crucial in the early years of Macedonian independence. In addition, he served as the leader of the socialist party (e.g., the former communists), but his party already had been defeated in the 1998 elections. The 1999 elections provided the opportunity for a crucial contest between the Socialists and the VMRO-DPMNU nationalists. The socialists supported Tito Petkovski, and the nationalists supported Boris Trajkovski. The two emerged as the major contenders as DA's candidate, Vasil Tupurkovski, came in third and dropped out of the race after the first round of presidential elections in October 1999. The critically important Albanian vote went against the nationalists in the first round, but in the second round Trajkovski won 53% of the vote and was elected president—albeit in the midst of allegations that some 200,000 ballots had been falsified (for details, see Perry, 2000b).

The strong polarization between the socialists and the nationalists revealed the extent to which the Albanian vote played an important role in domestic politics. Moreover, the two parties attempted to win over the electorate by suggesting that each was the more "true" to the cause of Macedonian nationalism than the other—an unfortunate situation that only increased Albanian mistrust. Still, the VMRO-DPMNU was successful in developing and maintaining an alliance with the DPA. Its electoral success in the 1999 presidential elections was due to the fact that the DPA was able to deliver a bloc of Albanian votes in favor of Trajkovski.

While the 1999 Kosovo Crisis held the spotlight for some time, the Albanian-Macedonian relationship did not deteriorate. Although the Macedonians were fearful of the large number of refugees who fled from Kosovo into FYROM, the presence of an Albanian party in the government seemingly suggested that FYROM could escape the ethnic confrontations that plagued the other post-Yugoslav republics in the 1990s. By virtue of being one of the parties participating in the government, the DPA was able to win some symbolic victories. For example, the party secured the release of two party members jailed for civil disobedience; it secured a more visible profile for ethnic Albanians working in the public sector; it also secured more hours of Albanian language programming on public radio and television; and it attempted to push forward the issue of Albanian-language higher education.

Still, none of the fundamental issues—reviewed in Chapter 6—were resolved. The Albanians' demand for a bi-national state was not satisfied, and complaints persisted with regard to Albanians who were not properly registered as citizens of the state. Given this situation, NATO's intervention in Kosovo could potentially signal a willingness by the international community to intervene in interethnic strife within the boundaries of a Balkan state—and commentators pointed out that such a message could have disastrous consequences for FYROM's future (Schmidt, 1998; Clement, 1999; Drezov, 2001). The future turn of events unfortunately confirmed these predictions.[1]

It is important to highlight the extent to which nationalist mobilization is intertwined with the operation of the underground economy, involving the smuggling of goods, drugs, and women (who are usually forced to work as prostitutes). In Chapter 6, I referred to the proliferation of the underground economy in Kosovo. This is not a phenomenon isolated to this province but extends to neighboring Albania, Serbia, Montenegro, and Bulgaria (and to a lesser extent in Greece, as well). FYROM's Prime Minister Georgievski has stated that close to twenty-seven firms—mainly involved in alcohol, oil, steel, cigarette, and chemical production—had close connections to the Milosevic regime and were involved in money laundering; while many local banks had opened nonresident accounts allowing Serbian assets to enter the country for transfer to third countries.[2] In this respect, the deterioration of economic conditions in the region throughout the 1980s and 1990s has provided the context for a synergy between illegal activities and armed confrontation. It is also worth pointing out that the local political parties—including both VMRO-DPMNU and the Albanians' DPA—have been the beneficiaries of this rather loose approach toward the law. The parties are shareholders in companies and have, by most accounts, committed collusion with local businessmen. Moreover, political appointees do not hesitate to treat public companies as party properties, setting off mechanisms of political patronage toward their local clientele.[3]

Although the above do not excuse armed confrontation, they provide an indispensable component for understanding the specifics of FYROM's social milieu. On 2 April 2000 four Macedonian soldiers were captured by what the government described as "Kosovo militants" who asked for the release of Albanian Xhavit Hasani from the Skopje jail. Hasani, allegedly a former KLA leader, had been ordered to demolish his house because it was built without a permit, and, in response, he shot at an official from the Ministry of Urban Planning and Reconstruction. Hasani was eventually released and the soldiers returned home. Prime Minister Ljubco Georgievski initially denied the event, but later he confirmed the exchange between the government and the kidnappers.

Border incidents persisted throughout the remainder of the year, and the government even deployed the Wolves, a Special Forces unit of the army, in an effort to curb what seemed to be gang activity. In 2000, the village of

Tanusevci became a transit point for weapons bound for Albanian insurgents in the Presevo Valley of southern Serbia, some thirty kilometers to the northeast. Tanusevci eventually became the first region where open warfare erupted; therefore, it is worthwhile to briefly elaborate on the specifics of the village. Tanusevci lies within earshot of the border with Kosovo, about twenty-four kilometers from Skopje, but nearly double that distance over winding roads. With no bus service to Skopje, the nearest school and clinic are in the town of Viti in southern Kosovo, about an hour away on foot. The border in this mountainous region was never marked, and as long as the former Yugoslavia existed it was nothing more than an administrative boundary. Most residents considered themselves Kosovo Albanians. The post-1989 breakup of Yugoslavia had little immediate impact on Tanusevci. However, in the late 1990s, and because of its close geographical proximity to Kosovo, the village became a funnel for arms to the KLA. The situation changed as FYROM and Serbia agreed on 28 February 2001 to the final demarcation line between the two countries, including the borders between Kosovo and FYROM.

Rumors suggested that the Kosovo-based KLA had established groups aiming to export the "national liberation" from Kosovo to the neighboring region.[4] Accordingly, two groups were established: the Liberation Army of Presevo, Medvedje, and Bujanovac; and the National Liberation Army of Macedonia. The first of these groups assumed operations in the border region between Serbia and Kosovo in 2000. The result was a joint operation of the Serb forces with the local NATO troops that sought to cut off the lines of communication between the two sides of the border. The existence of the second group was not altogether clear during 2000. However, in the autumn of that year FYROM's Albanian political parties hinted that unless they achieved quick concessions from the Macedonians concerning their national rights, rebel forces could take matters into their own hands—or what was referred to as "Plan B" or the "undemocratic plan," in contrast to "Plan A" or the "democratic plan" for recognizing and affirming Albanian rights in FYROM.

In September 2000 Macedonian military vehicles were fired upon near Tanusevci, and the Macedonian police later went to the village and checked the identity cards of residents. Those without proper documentation were told to leave.[5] The first open terrorist activity by the National Liberation Army took place on 22 January 2001 when a self-propelled rocket grenade hit the police station in Tearce, an ethnically mixed village between the city of Tetovo and the Kosovo border. On 23 January 2001 the National Liberation Army claimed responsibility for the attack in a statement titled Communiqué No. 4, sent to the newspaper *Dnevnik*.[6]

In February 2001, the police went to Tanusevci to investigate a report that a Skopje television news team had been surrounded by armed Albanians, some in uniform, who confiscated their equipment and ordered them to leave. Those in uniform wore patches with the letters UCK—the initials standing no longer for the officially disbanded Kosovo Liberation Army but rather for the National Liberation Army ("Kombetar" is Albanian for "National").[7] On 4 March 2001, three Macedonian policemen were killed around Tanusevci, near the border between FYROM and Kosovo, and the Macedonian authorities blamed the NATO-led peacekeeping force in Kosovo for failing to secure the border from what they called "armed Albanian infiltrators."[8] But the turn of events did not at all conform to this interpretation. On the contrary, the NLA declared its goals on 5 March with a fax to *Deutsche Welle*'s Albanian Service. They said they were fighting for the equality of ethnic Albanians in Macedonia. On 7 March, Macedonian Interior Ministry spokesman Stevo Pendarovski estimated the rebels to be around 300 armed men—most of them recruited in the neighboring Kosovo town of Viti. The Macedonian authorities initially considered the rebels to be a mixture of UCK veterans, criminals, and smugglers and did not believe that the rebels could find support among the population. The Macedonian security forces deplored a force of 3,000 to 4,000 men in an effort to isolate the rebels, but, within days, the rebellion spread to neighboring villages. Some 500 residents of Tanusevci, mainly women and children, crossed into Kosovo in order to get themselves out of the crossfire between the two sides.

On 13 March, another group of rebels began firing at the Macedonian police officers in the city of Tetovo from high positions in the Shar Mountains around the city. Tetovo, the unofficial Albanian capital, was long associated with the struggle for Albanian rights in FYROM, and opening a front in the city increased the visibility and support for the NLA. The conflict accelerated unexpectedly, with a breathtaking speed that caught most observers and politicians by surprise. It became apparent that the National Liberation Army (NLA or UCK) was not a small gang of criminals or some freebooters who sneaked in from Kosovo. The movement was well organized, well equipped, and supported by many Macedonian Albanians.[9] The conflict soon brought further polarization between Albanians and Macedonians— with the Albanians siding with the rebels or at least expressing their sympathy and the Macedonians eager to fight against a possible secessionist movement. Albanian political leaders denounced the violent confrontation with FYROM's authorities.[10]

The press soon capitalized on the emerging conflict, adding to interethnic tensions. On 23 March, the Macedonian-language weekly newspaper *Makedonija-Europe* described the guerrillas as "the black plague," printed in huge letters on its front page. The daily also referred to snipers, who shot at policemen in Skopje, as "monsters." Furthermore, the paper included the rubric "War in Macedonia," in which it sought to sensationalize the violence. In a similar fashion, the Albanian diaspora daily *Bota Sot* of 24 March wrote that a particular district of Tetovo "is standing in flames," a dramatic description that was probably an exaggeration. The daily clearly misrepresented a well-documented incident in which Macedonian police officers shot and killed two Albanians at a checkpoint. According to police sources, one of the victims attempted to throw a grenade at the police seconds before he was killed. The grenade was clearly recognizable in various press photos taken on the spot. Some ethnic Albanian media and politicians, however, hardly gave any credibility to the police claims and presented the incident as the "execution" of a man who was about to throw his mobile telephone. Thus *Bota Sot* wrote that the two men killed were "Albanian victims of . . . Macedonian terror." There was little evidence, however, to suggest that the Macedonian authorities pursued a policy of "ethnic cleansing" or arbitrary killings against ethnic Albanians. On the contrary, the refugees from the neighboring villages fled areas that were immediately affected by fighting or that were close to the areas in which the guerrillas were operating.

In an interview on 22 March 2001 former Macedonian President Kiro Gligorov claimed that the Albanians already had sufficient rights and that there was no need for the Albanian language to be declared an official language in areas where few Albanians live. He warned the international community against insisting on a peaceful solution to the crisis, adding that no government can allow others to shoot at its forces without returning fire. Gligorov stressed that the way to end the insurgency was by "nipping it in the bud" militarily.[11] But this was not the case. First, the rebels were able to retreat and regroup under pressure by government forces. Second, the Macedonian army arrested scores of Albanians, and this incited discontent by local Albanians and by Albanian politicians who urged the government to find an alternative solution.

The rebels' demands surfaced slowly in the spring of 2001. They were, more or less, identical to the demands put forward by the Albanian political parties: changes in the constitution, including the preamble; official recognition of Albanian language; and removal of references to the Macedonian Orthodox Church in the constitution. The rebels denied the cliché accusation that theirs was a secessionist movement. In an interview with BBC's Paul Wood they said that they did not wish to achieve a Greater Albania. Their goal was a "new Macedonian constitution, better rights for Albanians, and international mediation."[12] Although these demands have been on the Albanian political parties' agenda for nearly a decade, the rebels' demands received a very cold response by the Macedonian side, which eventually bowed not to the local Albanian requests, but rather to the growing international pressure. Moreover, the NLA soon gained a more public profile by developing a political front. By May of 2001, Ali Ahmeti emerged as the political leader of NLA. Ahmeti was involved with the KLA in the early 1990s, and allegedly he was responsible for a series of terrorist attacks.[13] Throughout the spring of 2001, NATO forces in Kosovo tightened their patrols and extra KFOR troops were sent into the Kosovo-FYROM border. But, contrary to Macedonian wishes, the alliance did not assume a more proactive role. Fueled by Prime Minister Georgievski's original address to the nation on 20 March 2001, public opinion viewed the role of NATO and the United States with growing suspicion. Rumors suggested that NATO supported the Albanian insurgents and failed to protect FYROM's borders and sovereignty.[14] Riots broke out in some towns—for example in Bitola—while Macedonians protested against the weak U.S. response. Prime Minister Geogrievski found himself in an uncomfortable position because every statement he made to reassure his nationalist voters undermined his ability to make concessions and vice versa.

The protracted guerrilla warfare also produced a wave of refugees—a majority of whom were (Slavic) Macedonians who fled the predominantly Albanian western region of FYROM. The United Nations High Commission on Refugees (UNHCR) estimated that the refugees, or "internally displaced persons," came to around 70,000 in the first half of 2001. In the fall of 2001, there remained still some 26,000 ethnic Albanian refugees from Macedonia in neighboring Kosovo. Most of these refugees were likely to stay there over the winter. In addition to the Albanians who fled the country altogether, the Macedonian Red Cross speaks of about 44,500 internally displaced persons, 60% of whom are ethnic Macedonians.[15]

In mid-July 2001 the international negotiators were able to achieve a ceasefire that was followed by a proposal for constitutional changes. These also received a cold reception by the Macedonian side; however, persistent international pressure succeeded in formalizing the agreement between the Albanian political parties and the Macedonian coalition government (which was formed in the spring of 2001 to deal with the crisis). The agreement became known as the Ohrid accord and contained some specific provisions whose goal was to satisfy Albanian demands for official recognition of their status as equal partners in the state. Specifically, the agreement included a proposal for a constitutional amendment that would allow any language (other than the official Macedonian recognized in the constitution as the language of the state) spoken by at least 20% of the population to be an administrative language as well, in its respective alphabet. In units where at least 20% of the population spoke this language, this language—alongside the official Macedonian—would be used and official documents that refer to speakers of this language would be published both in Macedonian and this language. Every person could use this language to communicate with the central administration. This proposal specifically aimed at providing the Albanians with a guarantee that their language would be officially recognized as such by the central administration. On the other hand, the Macedonians reacted strongly to these provisions because the Albanians gained what Macedonian minority groups have asked for in the neighboring countries, where such demands have fallen on deaf ears (see Chapter 5).

In addition to the issue of the Albanian language, the agreement also included a provision for hiring Albanian police officers and for developing a framework for greater regional autonomy of local municipalities. Following the Ohrid agreement, NATO forces moved in, assuming the leadership role in what became known as "Operation Harvest"—the disarmament of the NLA forces. The operation concluded on 26 September 2001 with 3,875 weapons and more than 397,000 pieces of ammunition collected.[16] In spite of what on the surface appears to be a success story, it is important to note that the Macedonians viewed the entire operation as a sham—for the numbers of guns and ammunition in the region is so high that the operation did not truly lead to a practical reduction of arms in the region. According to estimates circulating in Balkan and Western ministries, the total of weapons in Albania, Kosovo, and FYROM is as follows: 280,000 Kalashnikov automatic weapons, 1 million antitank missiles, 3.1 million hand grenades, 1 billion rounds of ammunition, and 24 million machine guns.[17]

When the Ohrid peace accord was signed in Skopje on 13 August by the leaders of the main Macedonian and ethnic Albanian political parties and the Macedonian president, few observers believed that it could be implemented easily.[18] Indeed, throughout the fall of 2001, events confirmed the conventional wisdom about the difficulties surrounding the implementation of the peace accord. First of all, the tight timetable for the various steps of the implementation—including disarmament of the NLA, the ratification of the agreement by FYROM's parliament, and the constitutional amendments— did not allow for delays. Second, while NATO forces assumed the implementation of NLA disarmament, the parliamentary process faced delays that threatened to derail the process. Prime Minister Georgievski nearly brought the peace process to a standstill with a demand for a referendum on the Ohrid agreement. As international pressure against a referendum mounted, the Parliament delayed a vote on it. Third, the issue of amnesty for the former guerrilla rebels led to lengthy discussions as to whether the restricted amnesty proclaimed by a cabinet decree on 8 October 2001 would be sufficient to protect NLA members from criminal prosecution. The Albanians wanted a broad amnesty approved by the Parliament.

For those familiar with VMRO-NPMNU this turn of events was hardly a surprise. Georgievski and other Macedonian politicians—including the Parliament's Speaker Stojan Andov and Minister of the Interior Boskovski— flirted with the idea of revising the territorial boundaries by allowing the "unification" of the Albanians of the western part of FYROM with Kosovo if FYROM would get some territorial concessions from Albania.[19] The Macedonian nationalists' reaction to the Ohrid peace accord is closely related to their advocacy of FYROM as an "ethnic" state of the Macedonians, a view that is radically opposed to turning FYROM into a "civic" state, to be ruled as a "consociational democracy."[20] In this regard, the Ohrid agreement might be viewed largely as an expression of the policy position advocated in Chapter 7.

In order to provide for the practical implementation of these principles, the agreement proposes scaling down central authority by ceding both administrative power and legislative authority to the municipalities and by granting Albanians a quasi-veto over the choice of judges, laws on local government, culture, use of language, education, documentation, and use of national symbols. The agreement also surrenders all preferences toward Macedonians in the public sector and education and erodes the supremacy of Macedonian national symbols by allowing the open display of Albanian national symbols. Macedonian nationalists view this agreement as forcing them to give up the ethnic character of their state. For example, changing the preamble of the constitution is viewed as nothing less than a symbolic "erasure" of Macedonian distinctiveness.[21] Macedonian nationalists correctly point out that they are asked to take the first step toward a "civic state," while their neighboring states of Serbia, Bulgaria, and Greece maintain their "ethnic" character—and in the Macedonians' view, they deny such recognition to Macedonian national minorities.

Consequently, recent and future political developments in FYROM are going to reveal the degree to which Albanians and Macedonians conceive of the political game as a "zero sum game," where one side's gains are the other side's losses. Needless to say, participating in political life by these rules is not likely to contribute to FYROM's viability. For example, in late autumn of 2001 the Macedonian Parliament was supposed to pass a new law on local self-government—a key element of the Ohrid peace agreement. Thanks to this law and a number of additional measures, the centralized state administration was expected to be decentralized. The municipalities were to be given far-reaching rights in the spheres of budgeting, culture, education, urban planning, and basic health care.[22] On 6 December, parliamentary speaker Stojan Andov adjourned the session after ethnic Albanian deputies refused to show up in the chamber to vote. This was their protest against some amendments to the law proposed by ethnic Macedonian parliamentarians. The Albanian legislators explained their unwillingness to accept any major changes to the draft law by citing the Ohrid peace agreement. For the Macedonian lawmakers, the amendments were necessary to avoid the federalization or "cantonization" of the country. This could have resulted from a provision in Article 61 of the draft law, which allowed municipalities to form common administrations with neighboring municipalities. This, the opponents of the law say, could lead to the introduction of an intermediate level of administration, which neither the constitution nor the peace accord foresees. These intermediate administrative bodies could then be set up on an ethnic basis and later grow into ethnically based cantons (along the lines of the Bosnian experience).

Whether (and how) this particular issue will be resolved is obviously less important than the underlying rationale responsible for producing the

perception of a "zero sum game" that makes it inherently difficult to negotiate and ultimately to secure the viability of a consociational democracy. In
turn, contemplating this issue brings us back to the broader issues of national
identity construction and the production of national narratives that have been
the main issues addressed in this book. In a recent report, for example, the
International Crisis Group correctly raises the issue of FYROM's international
recognition and the necessity of finding a solution to the long-standing
Athens-Skopje dispute. However, the particular policy recommendations are
rather shallow and fail to engage with the underlying problems that have been
the focus of this book.[23]

I would therefore dare to suggest that the fault in the solutions currently
proposed in FYROM does not rest in the proposed "civic" nature of the
state—including the possibility of a *de facto* "cantonization" of the country.
On the contrary, as I have argued in Chapter 7, the fault lies in the absence
of a regional strategy of strengthening civic ties within the population of the
southern Balkan states. It is a complete chimera to expect a single state (and
a rather weak one) to lead the way without a regional agreement that would
establish shared rules about the inviolability of borders and the treatment
of minority groups. Such rules can be developed on the basis of the EU and
UN resolutions, but it will be necessary for the local states to establish the
mechanisms and provisions that would be applicable to the specific context
of the local societies. Only a region-wide plan would provide the international community and capital with the reassurance that the interethnic disputes of the region would not be likely to resurface in the future. In the long
run, only such a strategy has the potential of bringing the Balkans out of
their socioeconomic decline and toward inclusion into the common European home.

In practical terms, this means that the international community has to
include other parties in the region (including Serbia, Albania, Greece, and
Bulgaria) to play a more active role in the resolution of regional disputes.
In the recent past, many of these states have been unwilling or unable to
play a constructive role in the regional crises. However, a long-term solution to the national rivalries in the region can only be borne out of the local
states agreeing to develop and respect a common set of rules, including viable
and mutually acceptable mechanisms for dispute resolution.

NOTES

1. In the summer of 2000, rumors and journalistic reports suggested the existence of a secret "Albanian National Army." However, these rumors quickly faded
away, while the Albanian political leaders suggested that the entire affair was a ploy
by Macedonian nationalists who wished to depict Albanians as traitors to the state.
See International Crisis Group, *Macedonia's Ethnic Albanians: Bridging the Gap*
(Skopje/Washington/Brussels: ICG Balkans Report No. 98, 2 August 2000).

2. Reported in the newspaper *Dnevnik*, 23 February 2001, quoted in International Crisis Group's report, *The Macedonian Question: Reform or Rebellion* (Skopje/Washington/Brussels: ICG Balkans Report No. 109, 5 April 2001), p. 12. The following paragraphs rely heavily on this report.

3. For additional examples, see Ulrich Buechsenschuetz, "Macedonia Divided," *RFE/RL Balkan Report,* 4 May 2001. Vol. 5, No. 33.

4. A U.S. KFOR intelligence officer in Viti told a RFE/RL reporter in June that KFOR was monitoring the movement of weapons just across the border in northern Macedonia but, beyond informing the Macedonian authorities, lacked a mandate to respond.

5. According to FYROM officials, Tanusevci had some 750 inhabitants before the 1999 Kosovo crisis; however, after the war, that number was further reduced to around 300. It is quite likely that the population remained around 750, with only half of the inhabitants actually registering with Macedonian authorities.

6. Rumors suggested that the group was an offshoot of the Kosovo Liberation Army—established simultaneously with the Liberation Army of Presevo, Medvedje, and Bujanovac, another offshoot of the KLA that assumed operations in the border region between Serbia and Kosovo in 2000. The result was a joint operation of the Serb forces with the local NATO troops that sought to cut off the lines of communication between the two sides of the border.

7. Ethnic Albanian Professor Bexheti, a member of the Party of Democratic Prosperity and former minister for transportation and communications, told a RFE reporter that the situation was the result of the village's isolation from the rest of the country. He said that it is understandable why the villagers resorted to arms. "I fully excuse their bid to establish their own fundamental civic rights for the simple reason that for the last fifty years, all their educational, health and business affairs were with Viti, a town in Kosovo rather than with Skopje, from which unfortunately they were isolated due to wholly inadequate transportation and [communications]" (Naegele, 2001). According to Bexheti, the villagers were never provided with Macedonian identity papers and also failed to register their births with FYROM authorities. The professor predicted that "it is possible that [these] problems will spread to other parts of Macedonia. There are some who [believe] that the current situation in Macedonia regarding the constitutional and legal status of Albanians will result in [something like] what is happening now [but on a broader scale]. We must think seriously about changing the constitutional and legal status [of Macedonia] from a nation-state to one with a civic character—that is, to establish a civil or bi-national state of Macedonians and Albanians, embracing the two main ethnic groups that live here and together make up 93% of all the citizens."

8. Jolyon Naegele, "The Tanusevci Story." *RFE Balkan Report,* 9 March 2001, Vol. 5, No. 18. In his address to the nation on 20 March 2001 Prime Minister Georgievski said that the armed rebellion was "a long-planned aggression of Kosovo toward Macedonia. . . . You can convince no one in Macedonia that the U.S. and German governments are unfamiliar with the identity of chiefs of rebel gangs invading Macedonia today and that had they implemented a much stricter policy, the aggression of these against our country would have been thwarted." Quoted in "The Macedonian Question: Reform or Rebellion," p. 9.

9. Patrick Moore, "Going for Broke."*RFE/RL Balkan Report,* 9 March 2001.

Vol. 5, No. 18. See the National Liberation Army's Web site www.tetovari.com for a presentation of the rebels' viewpoint.

10. Arta Dade, the Albanian Socialist Party's foreign affairs secretary, suggested that the problems in Macedonia should be settled by political means and added that ethnic Albanians and Macedonians must cooperate in implementing a "high degree" of minority rights in order to contain the conflict. Dashamir Shehi, the secretary of the opposition New Democratic Party, also said that the crisis in Macedonia should be settled by dialogue. He dismissed the notion of a "Greater Albania," arguing that "we do not need to aspire to the unification of all Albanians [in one state]. But something that all Albanians need is . . . the idea of belonging to a single people." (Fabian Schmidt, "Albanian Parties Denounce Violence in Macedonia," *RFE/RL Balkan Report,* 20 March 2001).

11. Patrick Moore, "Macedonia's Gligorov: Hit Rebels Hard," *RFE/RL Balkan Report,* 27 March 2001. Vol. 5, No. 23.

12. Paul Wood, "The Rebels' Agenda," BBC News, Sunday 11 March 2001. http://news.bbc.co.uk/hi/english/world/europe/newsid_1213000/1213887.stm.

13. For a profile, see Ulrich Buechsenschuetz, "Ali Ahmeti—and a number of new faces," *RFE/RL Research Report,* 1 June 2001. Vol. 5, No. 38.

14. As is conventional in these cases, various articles published in the European press provided support for these conspiracy theories—with the CIA being named as one of the culprits. See Patrick Moore, "A Spooky Campaign in the Balkans?" *RFE/RL Balkan Report,* 31 July 2001. Vol. 5, No. 53. In response to the proliferation of these reports, the U.S. Office of Public Affairs in Prishtina issued a statement on 10 August reaffirming the U.S. commitment to peaceful solution.

15. "Estimated Number of People Uprooted from their Homes in Macedonia Since March 2001" (Chart, UN High Commissioner for Refugees, 2001) and "Mid-Year Country Report: Macedonia," U.S. Committee for Refugees, September 2001. http://www.refugees.org/world/countryrpt/europe/mid_countryrpt01/macedonia.htm.

16. Regional Headquarters Allied Forces Southern Europe Operation Essential Harvest—Achievements, 1 December 2001. http://www.afsouth.nato.int/operations/skopje/ACHIEVEMENTS.htm.

17. Figures reported in International Crisis Group's report, *The Macedonian Question: Reform or Rebellion,* p. iv.

18. Ulrich Buechsenschuetz, "Macedonia Stumbles on the Road to Peace." *RFE/RL Balkan Report,* 23 October 2001. Vol. 5, No. 69. For details, see Patrick Moore, "Expectations in the Balkans." *RFE/RL Balkan Report,* 21 August 2001. Vol. 5, No. 59; Ulrich Buechsenschuetz, "Peace or War for Macedonia?" *RFE/RL Balkan Report,* 21 August 2001. Vol. 5, No. 57. For the specifics of the Peace Accord, see Ulrich Buechsenschuetz, "The Macedonian Peace Agreement Part III." *RFE/RL Balkan Report,* 21 August 2001. Vol. 5, No. 59.

19. International Crisis Group, *Macedonia's Name: Why the Dispute Matters and How to Resolve It,* ICG Balkans Report No.122 (Skopje/Washington/Brussels, 10 December 2001), pp. 3–5.

20. In this respect, the Ohrid agreement is an attempt to reverse the trend of the 1995 Dayton Accord. While Dayton bowed into the principle of ethnic division, the Ohrid agreement is an effort to establish an alternative model. For multiethnic or

multinational states, the long-standing position is that it is possible to maintain the unity of the state if all groups receive a veto power and enough real power within the state apparatus to give them an incentive to participate in the political process and govern the state along the lines of developing a consensus over policy matters. This is the model of a number of Western European states. For a discussion of the "consociational democracy" thesis see the works of Arend Lijphart (1975 and 1977).

21. International Crisis Group, *Macedonia's Name*, p. 8.

22. Ulrich Buechsenschuetz, "The Macedonian Game Goes On." *RFE/RL Balkan Report*, 11 December 2001. Vol. 5, No. 82.

23. See *Macedonia's Name*, especially pp. 11–24, where the authors provide a very brief recapitulation of the Macedonian Question and proceed to draft policy recommendations for a compound name solution. The recommendations do not take into account the perspectives of Sofia and Athens—and it is extremely unlikely that they could lead to a political settlement, let alone to a real, substantive resolution of this issue. Future policy recommendations should take into account the issues discussed in the chapters of this book, otherwise they are going to fail to produce solutions that are likely to receive popular support by the Greek and Bulgarian public.

Bibliography

Adanir, Fikret. 1984–85. "The Macedonian Question: The Socio-Economic Reality and Problems of Its Historical Interpretation." *International Journal of Turkish Studies* 3 (1): 43–64.

Adanir, Fikret. 1992. "The Macedonians in the Ottoman Empire 1878–1912." Pp. 161–92 in A. Kappeler (ed.), *The Formation of National Elites: Comparative Studies on Governments and Non-dominant Ethnic Groups in Europe, 1850–1940* Vol. 6. New York: New York University Press.

Agelopulos, Giorgos. 1995. "Perceptions, Construction, and Definition of Greek National Identity in Late 19th–Early 20th Century Macedonia," *Balkan Studies* 36 (2): 247–63.

Agelopulos, Giorgos. 1997. "Marital Exchanges in Culturally Mixed Agricultural Communities of Macedonia: Their Significance for Defining and Separating Groups." Pp. 103–22 in Vassilis Gounaris, Giorgos Agelopulos, and Iakovos Mihailidis (eds.), *Identities in Macedonia*. Athens: Papazisi [in Greek].

Albrow, Martin. 1997. *The Global Age*. Stanford, CA: Stanford University Press.

Alivizatos, Nicos. 1981. "The 'Emergency Regime' and Civil Liberties, 1946–1949." Pp. 220–28 in John O. Iatrides (ed.), *Greece in the 1940s: A Nation in Crisis*. Hanover, NH: University Press of New England.

Allcock John B., Marko Milivojevic, and John J. Horton (eds.). 1998. *Conflict in the Former Yugoslavia: An Encyclopedia*. Denver, CO: ABC-CLIO Press.

Alter, Peter. 1989. *Nationalism*. Translated by Stuart McKinnon-Evans. London: Edward Arnold.

Analytical Creative Group ACG Ltd. 1999. *Unpublished Nationwide Survey of the Bulgarian Population,* Sofia: ACG LTD.

Anderson, Benedict. 1991. *Imagined Communities: Reflections on the Origin and Spread of Nationalism*. London: Verso (2nd edition).

Anderson, Benedict. 1993. "The New World Disorder." *New Left Review* 193 [May–June]: 3–14.

Anderson, Matthew Smith. 1966. *The Eastern Question: A Study in International Relations*. New York: St. Martin's Press.

Andrejevich, Milan. 1990a. "Macedonia on the Eve of the Elections." *Report on Eastern Europe,* [30 November]: 25–31.

Andrejevich, Milan. 1990b. "The Election Scoreboard of Serbia, Montenegro, and Macedonia." *Report on Eastern Europe,* [21 December]: 37–39.

Andriotis, Nikolaos. 1992. *The Federated State of Skopje and Its Language*. Athens: Trohalia [in Greek]. (First published in 1960.)

Angelou, Alkis. 1999. *The Underground School: Chronicle of a Myth*. Athens: Hestia [in Greek].

Anthias, Floya. 1998. "Evaluating 'Diaspora': Beyond Ethnicity?" *Sociology* 32 (3): 557–80.

Antonopoulos, Ilias. 1999. *Greece, Albania, Kosovo 1912–1998*. Athens: Okeanida [in Greek].

Apostolski, Michailo and Haralampie Polenakovich (eds.). 1974. *The Socialist Republic of Macedonia*. Skopje: Macedonian Review.

Apostolski, Michailo, Dancho Zografski, Aleksandar Stoyanovski, and Gligor Todorovski (eds.). 1979. *A History of the Macedonian People*. Skopje: Macedonian Review.

Appadurai, Arjun. 1995. "The Production of Locality." Pp. 204–25 in R. Fardon (ed.), *Counterworks: Managing the Diversity of Knowledge*. London and New York: Routledge.

Armenakis, A., Th. Gotsopoulos, N. Dermetzis, R. Panagiotopoulou, and D. Charalambis. 1996. "Nationalism in the Greek Press: The Macedonian Question in the December 1991-April 1993 Period." *Epitheorisi Koinonikon Ereunon: The Greek Review for Social Research* 89–90 (A–B): 172–231 [in Greek].

Armstrong, John A. 1982. *Nations Before Nationalism*. Chapel Hill, NC: University of North Carolina Press.

Ashley, S. 1985. "Minority Populations and the Nationalist Process in the Bulgarian Lands (1821–1876)." In *Proceedings of the Anglo-Bulgarian Symposium,* London, July 1982, edited by L. Collins, 41–64. Vol. 1, History. London: School of Slavonic and East European Studies.

Association of Refugee Children From the Aegean Part of Macedonia. 1995. "Declaration of the 'Child Refugees.'" Pp. 185–88 in Victor Bivell (ed.), *Macedonian Agenda*. Marrickville, New South Wales, Australia: Southwood Press Pty Ltd.

Augustinos, Gerasimos. 1989. "Culture and Authenticity in a Small State: Historiography and National Development in Greece." *East European Quarterly* 23 (1): 17–31.

Babiniotes, Giorgos. 1998. "The Persecution of the Words," *Vima,* May 31, Section B [in Greek].

Babiniotes, Giorgos (ed.). 1992. *The Language of Macedonia*. Athens: Olkos [in Greek].

Babuna, Aydin. 2000. "The Albanians of Kosovo and Macedonia: Ethnic Identity Superseding Religion." *Nationalities Papers* 28 (1): 67–92.

Baerentzen, L., J. O. Iatrides, and O. L. Smith (eds.). 1987. *Studies in the History of the Greek Civil War*. Copenhagen: Museum Tusculanum Press.

Balalovski, Risto. 1995. "Australian Law, International Treaties and the Government's 'Slav' Prefix." Pp. 215–22 in Victor Bivell (ed.), *Macedonian Agenda*. Marrickville, New South Wales, Australia: Southwood Press Pty Ltd.

Banac, Ivo. 1984. *The National Question in Yugoslavia: Origins, History, Politics*. Ithaca, NY: Cornell University Press.

Banac, Ivo. 1987. *With Stalin against Tito: Cominformist Splits in Yugoslav Communism*. Ithaca, NY: Cornell University Press.

Barker, Elisabeth. 1950. *Macedonia: Its Place in Balkan Power Politics*. Hertfordshire: Royal Institute of International Affairs.

Barth, F. 1969. "Introduction." Pp. 9–38 in F. Barth (ed.), *Ethnic Groups and Boundaries: The Social Organization of Cultural Difference*. Boston: Little, Brown.

Basch, Linda, Nina Glick Schiller, and C. Szanton Blanc. 1994. *Nations Unbound: Transnational Projects, Postcolonial Predicaments and Deterritorialized Nation-States*. New York: Gordon & Breach.

Bauman, Zygmunt. 1987. *Legislators and Interpreters: On Modernity, Post-Modernity, and the Intellectuals*. Ithaca, NY: Cornell University Press.

Belia, E. D. 1993. "The Balkan Wars in History Textbooks." In *Greece of the Balkan Wars, 1910–1914*, 279–98. Athens: ELIA [in Greek].

Bell, John D. 1997. "Democratization and Political Participation in 'Post-communist' Bulgaria." Pp. 353–402 in Karen Dawisha and Bruce Parrott (eds.), *Politics, Power, and the Struggle for Democracy in Southeast Europe*. Cambridge: Cambridge University Press.

Ben-Yehuda, Nachman. 1995. *The Masada Myth: Collective Memory and Mythmaking in Israel*. Madison, WI: University of Wisconsin Press.

Berholli, Arqile, Seifi Protara, and Kristaq Prifti. 1994. "The Greek Minority in the Albanian Republic: A Demographic Study." *Nationalities Papers* 22 (2): 427–34.

Bhabha, Homi K. 1996. "Culture's In-Between." Pp. 53–60 in Stuart Hall and Paul De Gay (eds.), *Questions of Cultural Identity*. London: Sage.

Bhabha, Homi K. (ed.). 1990. *Nation and Narration*. New York: Routledge.

Biberaj, Elez. 1998. *Albania in Transition: The Rocky Road to Democracy*. Boulder, CO: Westview Press.

Billig, Michael. 1995. *Banal Nationalism*. London: Sage.

Bivell, Victor. 1995. "A Political Strategy for the Macedonian Diaspora." Pp. 204–12 in Victor Bivell (ed.), *Macedonian Agenda*. Marrickville, New South Wales, Australia: Southwood Press Pty Ltd.

Blagojevic, Marina. 1998. "Kosovo: In/Visible War." Pp. 239–310 in Thanos Veremis and Evangelos Kofos (eds.), *Kosovo: Avoiding Another Balkan War*. Athens: ELIAMEP.

Blumi, Isa. 1997. "The Politics of Culture and Power: The Roots of Hoxha's Postwar State." *East European Quarterly* 31 (3): 379–98.

Boneva, Bonka Stoianova. 1996. "Ethnicity in Pirin Macedonia: Blurred Categories, Emergent Minority." *Balkanistica* 9: 156–65.

Boneva, Bonka Stoianova. 1998. "Ethnicity and the Nation: The Bulgarian Dilemma." Pp. 80–97 in C. B. Paulston and D. Peckham (eds.), *Linguistic Minorities in Central and East Europe*. Philadelphia: Multilingual Matters Publishers, LTD.

Bourdieu, Pierre. 1977. *Outline of a Theory of Practice*. Cambridge: Cambridge University Press.

Bourdieu, Pierre. 1989. "Social Space and Symbolic Power." *Sociological Theory* 7/1 (Spring): 14–25.

Boyarin, Jonathan. 1994. "Space, Time and the Politics of Memory." Pp. 1–38 in Jonathan Boyarin (ed.), *Remapping Memory: The Politics of TimeSpace*. Minneapolis, MN: University of Minnesota Press.

Bozhikov, P. 1993. "Ethnodemographic Characteristic of the Bulgarian Population." *Bulgarian Sociological Review* 3: 47–53.

Breuilly, John. 1993. *Nationalism and the State*. Manchester: Manchester University Press (2nd edition).

Brown, Keith S. 1994. "Seeing Stars: Character and Identity in the Landscapes of Modern Macedonia." *Antiquity* 68: 784–96.

Brown, Keith S. 2000a. "A Rising to Count On: Ilinden Between Politics and History in Post-Yugoslav Macedonia." Pp. 143–72 in Victor Roudometof (ed.), *The Macedonian Question*. Boulder, CO: East European Monographs.

Brown, Keith S. 2000b. "In the Realm of the Double-Headed Eagle: Parapolitics in Macedonia 1994–1999." Pp. 122–39 in Jane K. Cowan (ed.), *Macedonia: The Politics of Identity and Difference*. London: Pluto.

Brubaker, Rogers. 1992. *Citizenship and Nationhood in France and Germany*. Cambridge, MA: Harvard University Press.

Brubaker, Rogers. 1995. "National Minorities, Nationalizing States and External National Homelands," *Daedalus* 22 (2): 107–32.

Brubaker, Rogers. 1996. *Nationalism Reframed: Nationhood and the National Question in the New Europe*. Cambridge: Cambridge University Press.

Buck, Thomas. 1996. "Fear and Loathing in Macedonia: Ethnic Nationalism and the Albanian Problem." Pp. 243–62 in John S. Migel (ed.), *State and Nation Building in East Central Europe: Contemporary Perspectives*. New York: Institute on East Central Europe, Columbia University.

Budding, Audrey Helfant. 1997. "Yugoslavs into Serbs: Serbian National Identity, 1961–1971." *Nationalities Papers* 25 (3): 407–26.

Buechsenschuetz, Ulrich. 2001. "Ali Ahmeti—and a number of new faces." *RFE/RL Research Report* 5 (38) [1 June].

Buechsenschuetz, Ulrich. 2001. "Macedonia Divided." *RFE/RL Balkan Report* 5 (33) [4 May].

Buechsenschuetz, Ulrich. 2001. "Macedonia Stumbles on the Road to Peace." *RFE/RL Balkan Report* 5 (69) [23 October].

Buechsenschuetz, Ulrich. 2001. "The Macedonian Game Goes On." *RFE/RL Balkan Report* 5 (82) [11 December].

Buechsenschuetz, Ulrich. 2001. "The Macedonian Peace Agreement Part III." *RFE/RL Balkan Report* 5 (59) [21 August].

Buechsenschuetz, Ulrich. 2001. "Peace or War for Macedonia?" *RFE/RL Balkan Report* 5 (57) [21 August].

Bulgarian Academy of Sciences. 1978. *Macedonia: Documents and Materials*. Sofia: Bulgarian Academy of Sciences.

Burgess, Adam. 1996. "National Minority Rights and the 'Civilizing' of Eastern Europe." *Contention* 5 (2): 17–36.

Burke, Peter. 1997. *Varieties of Cultural History*. Ithaca, NY: Cornell University Press.

Campbell, Greg. 1999. *The Road to Kosovo: A Balkan Diary*. Boulder, CO: Westview Press.

Carabott, P. 1997. "The Politics of Integration and Assimilation vis-à-vis the Slavo-Macedonian Minority of Inter-war Greece: From Parliamentary Inertia to Metaxist Repression." Pp. 59–78 in Peter Mackridge and Eleni Yannakakis (eds.), *Ourselves and Others: The Development of a Greek Macedonian Identity Since 1912*. Oxford: Berg.

Center for the Study of Democracy. 1992. *1991 Survey of the Blagoevgrad Region*. Unpublished manuscript. Sofia: Center for the Study of Democracy.

Cerulo, Karen A. 1995. *Identity Designs: The Sights and Sounds of a Nation*. New Brunswick, NJ: Rutgers University Press.

Chomsky, Noam. 1999. *The New Military Humanism: Lessons from Kosovo*. Vancouver: New Star Books.

Chossudovsky, Michael. 1999. "Kosovo 'Freedom Fighters' Financed by Organized Crime." *Covert Action Quarterly* 67 [Spring/Summer]: 20–26.

Clement, Sophia. 1998. "Macedonian Albanians and Kosovo Albanians: Toward the Bosnian Model?" Pp. 357–88 in Thanos Veremis and Evangelos Kofos (eds.), *Kosovo: Avoiding Another Balkan War*. Athens: ELIAMEP.

Clement, Sophia. 1999. "The Regional Implications of the Kosovo Crisis." *The International Spectator* 34 (3): 55–66.

Close, David H. 1995. *The Origins of the Greek Civil War 1945–1949*. London and New York: Longman.

Cohen, Leonard J. 1993. *Broken Bonds: The Disintegration of Yugoslavia*. Boulder, CO: Westview Press.

Connerton, Paul. 1989. *How Societies Remember*. Cambridge: Cambridge University Press.

Connor, Walker. 1990. "When Is a Nation?" *Ethnic and Racial Studies* 13 (1): 93–103.

Connor, Walker. 1994. *Ethnonationalism: The Quest for Understanding*. Princeton, NJ: Princeton University Press.

Constant, S. 1980. *Foxy Ferdinand, Tsar of Bulgaria*. New York: Franklin Watts.

Council for Research into Southeastern Europe, Macedonian Academy of Sciences and Arts. 1993. *Macedonia and Its Relations with Greece*. Skopje: Macedonian Academy of Sciences and Arts.

Cowan, Jane K. 1997. "Idioms of Belonging: Polyglot Articulations of Local Identity in a Greek Macedonian Town." Pp. 153–74 in Peter Mackridge and Eleni Yannakakis (eds.), *Ourselves and Others: The Development of a Greek Macedonian Identity Since 1912*. Oxford: Berg.

Cowan, Jane K. (ed.). 2000. *Macedonia: The Politics of Identity and Difference*. London: Pluto.

Crampton, R. J. 1983. *Bulgaria 1878–1918: A History*. New York: East European Monographs.

Crowther, William. 1997. "The Construction of Moldovan National Consciousness." Pp. 39–62 in Laszlo Kurti and Juliet Langman (eds.), *Beyond Borders: Remaking Cultural Identities in the New East and Central Europe*. Boulder, CO: Westview Press.

Cviic, Christopher. 1991. *Remaking the Balkans*. London: Royal Institute of International Affairs.

Dakin, Douglas. 1966. *The Greek Struggle in Macedonia 1897–1913*. Thessaloniki: Institute for Balkan Studies.

Danforth, Loring M. 1994. "National Conflict in a Transnational World: Greeks and Macedonians at the Conference on Security and Cooperation in Europe." *Diaspora* 3 (3): 326–47.

Danforth, Loring M. 1995. *The Macedonian Conflict: Ethnic Nationalism in a Transnational World*. Princeton, NJ: Princeton University Press.

Danforth, Loring M. 2000. "Ecclesiastical Nationalism and the Macedonian Question in the Australian Diaspora." Pp. 25–54 in Victor Roudometof (ed.), *The Macedonian Question*. Boulder, CO: East European Monographs.

Davison, R. H. 1977. "Nationalism as an Ottoman Problem and the Ottoman Response." Pp. 26–56 in W. W. Haddad and W. Ochsenwald (eds.), *Nationalism in a Non-National State: The Dissolution of the Ottoman Empire*. Columbus, OH: Ohio State University Press.

De Bray, Reginald George Arthur. 1980. *Guide to the South Slavonic Languages*. Columbus, OH: Slavica.

Deletant, D. and H. Hanak (eds.). 1988. *Historians as Nation-Builders: Central and Southeast Europe*. London: Macmillan.

Delta, Penelope. 1937. *Sta Mystika tou Valtou*. Athens: Hestia [in Greek].

Demertzis, Nicolas, Stylianos Papathanassopoulos, and Antonis Armenakis. 1999. "Media and Nationalism: The Macedonian Question." *Harvard International Journal of Press Politics* 4 (3): 26–50.

Demetriou, Kyriakos N. 2001. "Historians on Macedonian Imperialism and Alexander the Great." *Journal of Modern Greek Studies* 19 (1): 23–60.

Dimakis, Ioannis. 1991. *The Constitutional Change of 1844 and the Issue of Autochnonous and Eterochnonous Greeks*. Athens: Themelio [in Greek].

Dimaras, K. Th. 1977. *Modern Greek Enlightenment*. Athens: Ermis [in Greek].

Dimaras, K. Th. 1985. *Greek Romanticism*. Athens: Ermis [in Greek].

Dimaras, K. Th. 1986. *Constantinos Paparrigopoulos*. Athens: National Bank of Greece [in Greek].

Dimitrakopoulos, Fotis. 1996. *Byzantium and the Modern Greek Intelligentsia in the Middle of the 19th Century*. Athens: Kastaniotis [in Greek].

Djilas, Aleksa. 1991. *The Contested Country: Yugoslav Unity and Communist Revolution, 1919–53*. Russian Research Center Studies, vol. no. 85. Cambridge, MA: Harvard University Press.

Djordjevic, Dimitrije. 1970. "Projects for the Federation of South-east Europe in the 1860s and 1870s." *Balkanica* 1: 119–46.

Dodos, Dimosthenis Ch. 1994. *Electoral Geography of Minorities: Minority Parties in the Southern Balkans, Greece, Bulgaria, Albania*. Athens: Exantas [in Greek].

Dragnich, Alexis N. 1989. "The Rise and Fall of Yugoslavia: The Omen of the Upsurge of Serbian Nationalism." *East European Quarterly* 26 (2): 183–98.

Dragona, Th. 1997. "When National Identity Is Threatened: Psychological Strategies of Coping." Pp. 72–105 in Th. Dragona and A. Frangoudakis, *"What's Our Motherhood?" Ethnocentrism in Education*. Athens: Alexandria [in Greek].

Drezov, Kyril. 2001. "Collateral Damage: The Impact on Macedonia of the Kosovo

War." Pp. 59–70 in Michael Waller, Kyril Drezov, and Bulent Gokay (eds.), *Kosovo: The Politics of Delusion*. London: Frank Cass.

Dunn, William. 1994. "Macedonia: Europe's Finger in the Dike." *Christian Science Monitor,* 9 May, p. 19.

Durman, K. 1987. *Lost Illusions: Russian Policies Towards Bulgaria 1877–1887.* Stockholm: Almqvist and Wilksell International.

Emadi, Hafizullah. 2000. "The 'New World Order' and Albania's Convoluted Route to Transition in a Free Market Economy." *East European Quarterly.* 34 (3) [Sept. 2000]: 61–79.

Eminov, Ali. 2001. "Review of *The Macedonian Question,*" *Slavic Review* 49 (3) (Fall): 631–32.

Eslie, Robert (ed.). 1997. *Kosovo: In the Heart of the Powder Keg.* Boulder, CO: East European Monographs.

"Estimated Number of People Uprooted from their Homes in Macedonia Since March 2001." 2001. Chart, UN High Commissioner for Refugees.

Fallmerayer, Jacob Philip. 1830. *Geschichte der Halbinsel Morea wahrend des Mittelalters: ein historischer Versuch.* Stuttgart and Tubingen: Cotta'schen.

Fischer, Brend J. 1999. *Albania at War 1939–1945.* West Lafayette, IN: Purdue University Press.

Fischer-Galati, Stephen. 1973. "The Internal Macedonian Revolutionary Organization: Its Significance in 'Wars of National Liberation.'" *East European Quarterly* 6 (4): 454–72.

Foucault, Michel. 1972. *The Archaeology of Knowledge.* New York: Pantheon.

Foucault, Michel. 1980. *Power/knowledge: Selected interviews and other writings, 1972–1977.* New York: Pantheon Books.

Foucault, Michel. 1984. "Nietzsche, Genealogy, History." Pp. 76–100 in Paul Rabinow (ed.), *The Foucault Reader.* New York: Pantheon.

Foucault, Michel. 1991. "Governmentality." In Graham Burchell, Colin Gordon, and Peter Miller (eds.), *The Foucault effect: studies in governmentality: with two lectures by and an interview with Michel Foucault.* Chicago: University of Chicago Press.

Frangoudakis, Th. and A. Dragona (eds.) 1997. *"What's Our Motherhood?" Ethnocentrism in Education.* Athens: Alexandria [in Greek].

Friedman, Victor A. 1975. "Macedonian Language and Nationalism during the Nineteenth and Early Twentieth Centuries." *Balkanistica* 2: 83–98.

Friedman, Victor A. 1985. "The Sociolinguistics of Literary Macedonian." *International Journal of the Sociology of Language* 52: 31–57.

Friedman, Victor A. 1996. "Observing the Observers: Language, Ethnicity, and Power in the 1994 Macedonian Census and Beyond." Pp. 81–105 in Barnett R. Rubin (ed.), *Toward Comprehensive Peace in Southeastern Europe: Conflict Prevention in the South Balkans.* Report of the South Balkan Working Group of the Council on Foreign Relations, Center for Preventive Action. New York: The Twentieth Century Fund Press.

Gaber, Natasha. 1997. "The Muslim Population in FYROM (Macedonia): Public Perceptions." Pp. 103–14 in Hugh Poulton and Suha Taji-Farouki (eds.), *Muslim Identity and the Balkan State.* London: Hurst.

Gavrilis, George. 1996. "The Making of a Greater Albania?" Pp. 279–96 in John S. Migel (ed.), *State and Nation Building in East Central Europe: Contemporary*

Perspectives. New York: Institute on East Central Europe, Columbia University.

Gellner, Ernest. 1983. *Nations and Nationalism.* Ithaca, NY: Cornell University Press.

Genchev, N. 1977. *The Bulgarian National Revival Period.* Sofia: Sofia Press.

Georgeoff, P.J. 1973. "Educational and Religious Rivalries in European Turkey Before the Balkan Wars." Pp. 143–70 in *American Contributions to the Seventh International Congress of Slavists.* Paris: Mouton.

Georgoulis, Stamatis. 1995. "Orthodoxy in the Modern Albanian State: A Historical Review." Pp. 147–82 in Th. Veremis, Th. Couloumbis, and I. Nikolakopoulos (eds.), *The Hellenism of Albania.* Athens: Sideri [in Greek].

Giannakos, Symeon A. 1992. "The Macedonian Question Reexamined: Implications for Balkan Security." *Mediterranean Quarterly* 3 (3): 26–47.

Giannaris, N. V. 1996. *Geopolitical and Economic Changes in the Balkan Countries.* Westport, CT: Greenwood.

Gills, John R. (ed.). 1994. *Commemorations: The Politics of National Identity.* Princeton, NJ: Princeton University Press.

Glazer, N. and D. P. Moynihan (eds.). 1975. *Ethnicity: Theory and Experience.* Cambridge, MA: Cambridge University Press.

Glenny, Misha. 2000. *The Balkans: Nationalism, War and the Great Powers 1804–1999.* New York: Viking.

Gligorov, Kiro. 1999. "The Unrealistic Dreams of Large States." Pp. 96–104 in James Pettifer (ed.), *The New Macedonian Question.* New York: St. Martin's Press.

Gong, G. W. 1984. *The Standard of "Civilization" in International Society.* Oxford: Clarendon Press.

Gordy, Eric D. 1999. *The Culture of Power in Serbia: Nationalism and the Destruction of Alternatives.* University Park, PA: Pennsylvania State University Press.

Gounaris, Basil C. 1989. "Emigration from Macedonia in the Early Twentieth Century." *Journal of Modern Greek Studies* 7: 133–53.

Gounaris, Basil C. 1993. "Defining Ethnic Identity in Hellenic Macedonia: Remarks on Anastasia Karakasidou, 'Politicizing Culture: Negating Ethnic Identity in Greek Macedonia.'" *Balkan Studies* 34 (2): 309–14.

Gounaris, Basil C. 1997. "Social Gatherings and Macedonian Lobbying: Symbols of Irredentism and Living Legends in Early Twentieth-Century Athens." Pp. 99–112 in Philip Carabott (ed.), *Greek Society in the Making, 1863–1913: Realities, Symbols and Visions.* Aldershot: Ashgate.

Gounaris, Vassilis. 1996. "Social Cleavages and 'National Awakening' in Ottoman Macedonia." *East European Quarterly* 29 (4): 409–26.

Gounaris, Vassilis. 1997a. "Recycling Traditions: Ethnic Identities and Minority Rights in Macedonia." In Vassilis Gounaris, Giorgos Agelopoulos, and Iakovos Mihailidis (eds.), *Identities in Macedonia.* Athens: Papazisi [in Greek].

Gounaris, Vassilis. 1997b. "The Slavophones of Macedonia." Pp. 73–118 in K. Tsikelidis and D. Christopoulos (eds.), *The Minority Issue in Greece: A Contribution of The Social Sciences.* Athens: Kritiki [in Greek].

Gounaris, Vassilis and Iakovos Mihailidis. 2000. "The Pen and the Sword: Reviewing the Historiography of the Macedonian Question," pp. 99–142 in Victor

Roudometof (ed.), *The Macedonian Question: Culture, Historiography, Politics.* Boulder, CO: East European Monographs.

Gounaris, Vassilis, Giorgos Agelopulos, and Iakovos Mihailidis (eds.). 1997. *Identities in Macedonia.* Athens: Papazisi [in Greek].

Greenfeld, Liah. 1991. *Nationalism: Five Roads to Modernity.* Cambridge, MA: Harvard University Press.

Guibernau, Maria Montserrat. 1999. *Nations Without States: Political Communities in a Global Age.* Oxford, MA: Blackwell Publishers.

Gupta, Akhil and James Ferguson. 1992. "'Beyond Culture': Space, Identity, and the Politics of Difference." *Cultural Anthropology* 7 (10): 6–23.

Halbwachs, Maurice. 1992. *On Collective Memory,* edited by Lewis Coser. Chicago: University of Chicago Press.

Hall, R. 1989. "Civil-Military Conflict in Bulgaria During the Balkan Wars," *East European Quarterly* 23 (3) [September]: 293–303.

Hall, Stuart. 1992. "The Question of Cultural Identity." In Stuart Hall, David Held, and Tony McGrew (eds.), *Modernity and Its Futures.* Cambridge: Polity Press.

Hall, Stuart and Paul De Gay (eds.). 1996. *Questions of Cultural Identity.* London: Sage.

Handler, Richard. 1994. "Is 'Identity' a Useful Cross-Cultural Concept?" Pp. 27–40 in John R. Gills (ed.), *Commemorations: The Politics of National Identity.* Princeton, NJ: Princeton University Press.

Harris, Marshall Freeman. 1999. "Macedonia: The Next Domino?" *National Interest* 55 (Spring): 42–46.

Hatzidimitriou, Constantine G. 1993. "Distorting History: Concerning a Recent Article on Ethnic Identity in Greek Macedonia." *Balkan Studies* 34 (2): 315–51.

Hayden, Robert M. 1992a. *The Beginning of the End of Federal Yugoslavia: The Slovenian Amendment Crisis of 1989.* Pittsburgh, PA: Carl Beck Series in Russian and East European Studies, Center for Russian and East European Studies, University of Pittsburgh.

Hayden, Robert M. 1992b. "Constitutional Nationalism in the Formerly Yugoslav Republics." *Slavic Review* 51 (4): 654–73.

Hechter, Michael. 1975. *Internal Colonialism: The Celtic Fringe in British National Development, 1536–1966.* Berkeley, CA: University of California Press.

Hedges, Chris. 1999. "Kosovo's Next Masters?" *Foreign Affairs* 78 (3) [May/June]: 24–42.

Held, David, A. McGrew, D. Goldblatt, and J. Perraton. 1999. *Global Transformations: Politics, Economics and Culture.* Stanford, CA: Stanford University Press.

Hellenic Foundation for Defense and Foreign Policy (HFDFP). 1992. *Southeastern European Yearbook.* Athens: ELIAMEP [in Greek].

Hellenic Foundation for Defense and Foreign Policy (HFDFP). 1992 and 1999. *Review of Defense and Foreign Policy.* Athens: ELIAMEP [in Greek].

Helsinki Watch/The Fund for Free Expression. 1993. *Greece. Free Speech on Trial: Government Stifles Dissent on Macedonia* 5 (9), July.

Herman, Harry Vjekoslav. 1978. *Men in White Aprons. A Study of Ethnicity and Occupation.* Toronto: Peter Martin.

Herzfeld, Michael. 1982. *Ours Once More: Folklore, Ideology, and the Making of Modern Greece.* Austin, TX: University of Texas Press.

Hill, Peter. 1989. *The Macedonians of Australia*. Carlisle, Western Australia: Hesperian.

Hill, Peter. 1999. "Macedonians in Greece and Albania: A Comparative Study of Recent Developments." *Nationalities Papers* 27 (1): 17–30.

Hirschman, Albert O. 1970. *The Passions and the Interests: Political Arguments for Capitalism Before Its Triumph*. Princeton, NJ: Princeton University Press.

Hobsbawm, Eric J. 1990. *Nations and Nationalism since 1780: Programme, Myth, Reality*. Cambridge and New York: Cambridge University Press.

Hobsbawm, Eric J. 1996. "Ethnicity and Nationalism in Europe Today." Pp. 255–66 in G. Balakrishnan (ed.), *Mapping the Nation*. London: Verso.

Hobsbawm, Eric J., and T. Ranger, (eds.). 1983. *The Invention of Tradition*. Cambridge: Cambridge University Press.

Holevas, Ioannis K. 1991. *The Greek Slavophones of Macedonia*. Athens: Risos [in Greek].

Holevas, K. 1993. "Does the Recognition of Skopje Raise a Border Issue?" *Oikonomoikos Tachidromos* [8 April]: 14–15 [in Greek].

Hopken, W. 1996. "History Education and Yugoslav (Dis-)Integration." Pp. 99–124 in W. Hopken (ed.), *Oil and Fire? Textbooks, Stereotypes, and Violence in Southeastern Europe*. Hannover, Germany: Verlag Hahnsche Buchhandlung.

Horne, Donald. 1984. *The Great Museum: The Re-presentation of History*. London: Pluto.

Hotzidis, Angelos. 1997. "Articulation and Structure of the Minority Discourse: The Cases of Molgenon and Zora." Pp. 143–70 in Vassilis Gounaris, Iakovos Mihailidis, and Giorgos Agelopulos (eds.), *Identities In Macedonia*. Athens: Papazisi [in Greek].

Hristov, Alexander. 1971. *The Creation of Macedonian Statehood (1893–1945)*. Skopje: Kultura.

Hristov, Alexander. 1994. *Denying Ethnic Identity: The Macedonians of Greece*. New York: Human Rights Watch.

Huntington, Samuel P. 1996. *The Clash of Civilizations and the Remaking of World Order*. New York: Simon and Schuster.

Hutton, Patrick H. 1993. *History as an Art of Memory*. Hanover and London: University Press of New England.

Iatrides, John O. (ed.). 1981a. *Greece in the 1940s: A Nation in Crisis*. Hanover, NH: University Press of New England.

Iatrides, John O. 1981b. "Civil War 1945–1949 National and International Aspects." Pp. 195–219 in John O. Iatrides (ed.), *Greece in the 1940s: A Nation in Crisis*. Hanover: University Press of New England.

Iatrides, J. O. and Linda Wrigley (eds.). 1995. *Greece at the Crossroads: The Civil War and Its Legacy*. University Park, PA: Pennsylvania State University Press.

Ignatieff, Michael. 1994. *Blood and Belonging: Journeys into the New Nationalism*. New York: Farrar, Straus, and Giroux.

Ilchev, Ivan and Duncan M. Perry. 1993. "Bulgarian Ethnic Groups: Politics and Perceptions," *RFE/RL Research Report* 2 (12) [March 19]: 35–41.

Ilievski, Done. 1973. *The Macedonian Orthodox Church: The Road to Independence*. Translated by James M. Leech. Skopje: Macedonian Review.

Iliou, P. 1993. "School Textbooks and Nationalism: The Approach of Dimitris Glinos." Pp. 259–78 in *Greece of the Balkan Wars, 1910–1914*. Athens: ELIA [in Greek].

Ingrao, Charles. 1999. "Understanding Ethnic Conflict in Central Europe: An Historical Perspective." *Nationalities Papers* 27 (2): 291–318.

International Crisis Group. 2000. *Macedonia's Ethnic Albanians: Bridging the Gap*.
Skopje/Washington/Brussels: ICG Balkans Report No. 98 [2 August].

International Crisis Group. 2001. *The Macedonian Question: Reform or Rebellion*.
Skopje/Washington/Brussels: ICG Balkans Report No. 109 [5 April]: 12.

International Crisis Group. 2001. *Macedonia's Name: Why the Dispute Matters and
How to Resolve It*. Skopje/Washington/Brussels: ICG Balkans Report No.122
[10 December]: 3–5.

Ioannidou, Alexandra. 1997. "Slavic Dialects in Greece: Linguistic Approaches and
Political Departures." Pp. 89–102 in Vassilis Gounaris, Giorgos Agelopulos,
and Iakovos Mihailidis (eds.), *Identities in Macedonia*. Athens: Papazisi [in
Greek].

Jacobson, D. 1996. *Rights Across Borders: Immigration and the Decline of Citizenship*. Baltimore, MD: John Hopkins University Press.

James, Paul. 1996. *Nation formation: towards a theory of abstract community*. Thousand Oaks, CA: Sage.

Janev, Igor. 1999. "Legal Aspects of the Use of a Provisional Name for Macedonian
in the United Nations System." *American Journal of International Law* 93
(1) [January]: 155–60.

Jarvis, Christopher. 2000. "The Rise and Fall of Albania's Pyramid Schemes."
Finance & Development 37 (1) [March]: 46–47.

Jelavich, Barbara. 1983. *History of the Balkans* (2 vols.). Cambridge: Cambridge
University Press.

Jelavich, Barbara. 1991. *Russia's Balkan Entanglements 1806–1914*. Cambridge:
Cambridge University Press.

Jelavich, Charles and Barbara Jelavich. 1977. *The Establishment of the Balkan
National States, 1804–1920*. History of East Central Europe, vol. 8. Seattle:
University of Washington Press.

Judah, Tim. 2000. *Kosovo: War and Revenge*. New Haven: Yale University Press.

Judah, Tim. 2001. "The Growing Pains of the Kosovo Liberation Army." Pp. 20–
24 in Michael Waller, Kyril Drezov, and Bulent Gokay (eds.), *Kosovo: The
Politics of Delusion*. London: Frank Cass.

Kallivertakis, Leonidas. 1995. "The Greek Community of Albania from the View-
point of Historical Geography and Demography." Pp. 25–58 in Th. Veremis,
Th. Couloumbis, and I. Nikolakopoulos (eds.), *The Hellenism of Albania*.
Athens: Sideri [in Greek].

Kaplan, Robert D. 1991. "History's Cauldron." *Atlantic Monthly*, June, pp. 93–104.

Kaplan, Robert D. 1993. *Balkan Ghosts: A Journey Through History*. New York: St.
Martin's Press.

Kapsalis, Georgios D. 1996. *The Education of the Greek Albanian Minority*. Athens:
Gutenberg [in Greek].

Karakasidou, Anastasia. 1993a. "Politicizing Culture: Negating Ethnic Identity in
Greek Macedonia." *Journal of Modern Greek Studies* 11: 1–28.

Karakasidou, Anastasia. 1993b. "Fellow Travelers, Separate Roads: The KKE and the
Macedonian Question." *East European Quarterly* 27: 453–77.

Karakasidou, Anastasia. 1994. "Sacred Scholars, Profane Advocates: Intellectuals
Molding National Consciousness in Greece." *Identities: Global Studies in
Culture and Power* 1 (1): 35–61.

Karakasidou, Anastasia. 1997. *Fields of Wheat, Hills of Blood. Passages to Nationhood in Greek Macedonia 1870–1990*. Chicago: University of Chicago Press.

Karakasidou, Anastasia. 2000a. "Transforming Identity, Constructing Consciousness: Coercion and Homogeneity in Northwestern Greece." Pp. 55–98 in Victor Roudometof (ed.), *The Macedonian Question: Culture, Historiography, Politics*. Boulder, CO: East European Monographs.

Karakasidou, Anastasia. 2000b. "Protocol and Pageantry: Celebrating the Nation in Northern Greece." Pp. 221–46 in Mark Mazower (ed.), *After the War Was Over: Reconstructing the Family, Nation, and State in Greece, 1943–1960*. Princeton, NJ: Princeton University Press.

Karakatsanis, Neovi. 2001. *The Politics of Elite Transformation: The Consolidation of Greek Democracy in Theoretical Perspective*. Westport, CT: Praeger.

Karavidas, K. 1931. *Agrotika*. Athens: National Press [in Greek].

Kargakos, S. 1993. "Hellenism and Cannibalism." *Oikonomoikos Tachidromos,* [Economic Review] [1 July]: 44–45 [in Greek].

Karpat, Kemal H. 1973. *An Inquiry into the Social Foundations of Nationalism in the Ottoman Empire*. Princeton, NJ: Center for International Studies.

Karpat, Kemal H. 1985. *Ottoman population, 1830–1914: demographic and social characteristics*. Madison, WI: University of Wisconsin Press.

Katardzhiev, Ivan. 1973. "The Internal Macedonian Revolutionary Organization." Pp. 47–60 in *The Epic of Ilinden*. Skopje: Macedonian Review.

Katardzhiev, Ivan. 1980. *The Macedonian Uprising in Kresna*. Skopje: Macedonian Review.

Katsoulakos, Th. and K. Tsantinis. 1994. *Historiographic Issues in the School Textbooks of the Balkan Countries*. Athens: Ekkremes [in Greek].

Kazamias, Alexander. 1997. "The Quest for Modernization in Greek Foreign Policy and Its Limitation." *Mediterranean Politics* 2 [Autumn]: 71–94.

Kedourie, Elie. 1971. "Introduction." Pp. 1–152 in Elie Kedourie (ed.), *Nationalism in Asia and Africa*. New York: Meridian.

Kedourie, Elie. 1985. *Nationalism*. London: Hutchinson.

Kennan, G. F. 1993. "Introduction." In *The Other Balkan Wars: A 1913 Carnegie Endowment Inquiry*. Washington DC: Carnegie Endowment for International Peace.

Kennedy, Paul. 1970. "The Decline of Nationalistic History in the West, 1900–1970." *Contemporary History* 77–100.

Kennedy, Paul and Victor Roudometof. 2002a. "Introduction: Transnationalism in a Global Age." Pp. 1–26 in Paul Kennedy and Victor Roudometof (eds.), *Communities Across Borders: New Immigrants and Transnational Cultures*. London: Routledge.

Kennedy, Paul and Victor Roudometof. (eds.). 2002b. *Communities Across Borders: New Immigrants and Transnational Cultures*. London: Routledge.

King, Robert R. 1973. *Minorities under Communism: Nationalities as a Source of Tension Among Balkan Communist States*. Cambridge, MA: Harvard University Press.

Kirjazovski, Zlatko. 1990. "The Struggle of the Macedonians from Aegean Macedonia for the Use of Standard Macedonian." *Macedonian Review* 20 (3): 186–203.

Kirkos, Leonidas. 1993. *The Dead End Road of Nationalism*. Athens: Themelio [in Greek].

Kitromilides, Paschalis. 1978. *Tradition, Enlightenment, and Revolution: Ideological Change in Eighteenth and Nineteenth Century Greece*. Ph.D. dissertation, Department of Political Science, Harvard University.

Kitromilides, Paschalis. 1983. "The Enlightenment East and West: A Comparative Perspective on the Ideological Origins of the Balkan Political Traditions." *Canadian Review of Studies in Nationalism* 10 (1): 51–70.

Kitromilides, Paschalis. 1990. *The French Revolution and Southeastern Europe*. Athens: Dhiatton [in Greek].

Kofos, Evangelos. 1962. "The Making of the Yugoslavia's People's Republic of Macedonia." *Balkan Studies* 3 (2): 375–96.

Kofos, Evangelos. 1964. *Nationalism and Communism in Macedonia*. Thessaloniki: Institute for Balkan Studies.

Kofos, Evangelos. 1974. *Macedonia in the Yugoslav Bibliography*. Thessaloniki: The Society for Macedonian Studies [in Greek].

Kofos, Evangelos. 1980. "Dilemmas and Orientations of Greek Policy in Macedonia, 1878–1889." *Balkan Studies*. 21 (1): 45–55.

Kofos, Evangelos. 1986. "The Macedonian Question: The Politics of Mutation." *Balkan Studies*. 27: 157–72.

Kofos, Evangelos. 1989a. "National Heritage and National Identity in the Nine-teenth- and Twentieth-Century Macedonia." *European History Quarterly* 19: 229–68.

Kofos, Evangelos. 1989b. *The Balkan Dimension of the Macedonian Question During the Occupation and Resistance*. Athens: Dhodhoni [in Greek].

Kofos, Evangelos. 1994. *The Vision of the Greater Macedonia*. Thessaloniki: Museum of the Macedonian Struggle [in Greek].

Kofos, Evangelos. 1998. "The Two-headed 'Albanian Question': Reflections on the Kosovo Dispute and the Albanians of FYROM." Pp. 43–98 in Thanos Veremis and Evangelos Kofos (eds.), *Kosovo: Avoiding Another Balkan War*. Athens: ELIAMEP.

Khol, Christine von and Wolfgang Libal. 1997. "Kosovo, the Gordian Knot of the Balkans." Pp. 3–104 in Robert Elsie (ed.), *Kosovo: In the Heart of the Powder Keg*. Boulder, CO: East European Monographs.

Kolev, J. 1991. "The Bulgarian Exarchate as a National Institution and the Posi-tion of the Clergy (1878–1912)." *Etudes Balkaniques* 2: 40–54.

Koliopoulos, Ioannis. 1994. *Plundered Feelings: The Macedonian Question in Occu-pied Western Macedonia 1941–1944 Vol. 1*. Thessaloniki: Vanias [in Greek].

Koliopoulos, Ioannes and I. Hasiotis, eds. 1992. *Modern and Contemporary Macedonia: History, Economy, Society, Culture*. Thessaloniki: Papazisi-Paratiritis [in Greek].

Koliopoulos, John. 1997. "The War Over Identity and Numbers of Greece's Slav Macedonians." Pp. 39–58 in Peter Mackridge and Eleni Yannakakis (eds.), *Ourselves and Others: The Development of a Greek Macedonian Identity Since 1913*. Oxford: Berg.

Koliopoulos, John. 1999. *Plundered Loyalties: World War II and Civil War in Greek West Macedonia*. New York: New York University Press.

Kolisevski, Lazar. 1959. *The Macedonian National Question*. Belgrade: Jugoslavija.

Kondis, Basil, K. Kentrotis, S. Sfetas, and Yannis D. Stefanidis, eds. 1993. *Resurgent Irredentism: Documents on Skopje 'Macedonian' Nationalist Aspirations (1934–1992)*. Thessaloniki: Institute for Balkan Studies.

Konstantinov, Yulian. 1997. "Strategies for Sustaining a Vulnerable Identity: The Case of the Bulgarian Pomaks." Pp. 33–53 in Hugh Poulton and Suha Taji-Farouki (eds.), *Muslim Identity and the Balkan State*. London: Hurst.

Koraes, Adamantios. 1971. "Report on the Present State of Civilization in Greece." Pp. 153–88 in Elie Kedourie (ed.), *Nationalism in Asia and Africa*. New York: Meridian. (Speech originally delivered in 1804.)

Kordatos, Yannis. 1991. *The Social Dimension of the 1821 Revolution*. Athens: Epikerotita [in Greek]. (First published in 1924.)

Korobar, Pero. 1987. *The Macedonian National Culture in the Pirin Part of Macedonia*. Skopje: Macedonian Review.

Kostopoulos, Tasos. 2000. *The Forbidden Language*. Athens: Mavri Lista [in Greek].

Koutrovik, Gianna. 1997. "Justice and Minorities." Pp. 245–80 in K. Tsikelidis and D. Christopoulos (eds.), *The Minority Issue in Greece: A Contribution of The Social Sciences*. Athens: Kritiki [in Greek].

Krapfl, James. 1996. "The Ideals of Ilinden: Uses of Memory and Nationalism in Socialist Macedonia." Pp. 297–316 in John S. Migel (ed.), *State and Nation Building in East Central Europe: Contemporary Perspectives*. New York: Institute on East Central Europe, Columbia University.

Kyriakidis, Stilpon. 1955. *The Northern Ethnological Boundaries of Hellenism*. Thessaloniki: Society for Macedonian Studies [in Greek].

Lampe, John R. 1996. *Yugoslavia as History: Twice There was a Country*. Cambridge: Cambridge University Press.

Lange-Akhund, N. 1998. *The Macedonian Question, 1893–1908: From Western Sources*. Boulder, CO: East European Monographs.

Lape, Ljuben. 1973. "The Republic of Krusevo." Pp. 117–32 in *The Epic of Ilinden*. Skopje: Macedonian Review.

Larrabee, F. Stephen (ed.). 1994. *The Volatile Powder Keg: Balkan Security After the Cold War*. Washington, DC: American University Press.

Lavdas, Kostas. 2002. "Institutionalized Restraint as Policy: The European Union and the Distintegration of Yugoslavia." In George Kourvetaris, Victor Roudometof, Kleomenis Koutsoukis, and Andrew Kourvetaris (eds.), *The New Balkans: Disintegration and Reconstruction*. Boulder, CO: East European Monographs, forthcoming.

Le Goff, Jacques. 1992. *History and Memory*. New York: Columbia University Press.

Lefebvre, Stephane. 1995. "Bulgaria's Foreign Relations in the Post-Communist Era: A General Overview and Assessment." *East European Quarterly* 28 (4): 453–70.

Leigh Fermor, Patrick. 1992. "A Clean Sheet for Paeonia." *Spectator,* 12 September, pp. 24–26.

Lewis, Martin W. and Karen E. Wigen. 1997. *The Myth of Continents: A Critique of Metageography*. Berkeley, CA: University of California Press.

Liakos, Andonis, Angelos Elefantis, Andonis Manitakis, and Damianos Papadimitropoulos. 1993. *The Janus of Nationalism and the Greek Policy in the Balkans*. Athens: Politis [in Greek].

Lijphart, Arend. 1975. *The Politics of Accommodation: Pluralism and Democracy in the Netherlands.* Berkeley, CA: University of California Press.

Lijphart, Arend. 1977. *Democracy in Plural Societies: A Comparative Exploration.* New Haven: Yale University Press.

Lipset, Seymour Martin. 1960. *Political Man; the Social Bases of Politics.* Garden City, NY: Doubleday.

Lipset, Seymour Martin. 1963. *The First New Nation.* New York: Basic.

Lipset, Seymour Martin. 1997. *American Exceptionalism: A Double-Edged Sword.* New York: W. W. Norton.

Lithoxoou, Dimitris. 1992. *Minority Issues and National Consciousness in Greece: Insolence of Greek Historiography.* Athens: Leviathan [in Greek].

Lithoxoou, Dimitris. 1998. *Greek Anti-Macedonian Struggle.* Athens: Megali Poreia [in Greek].

Logoreci, Anton. 1977. *The Albanians: Europe's forgotten survivors.* Boulder, CO: Westview Press.

Londres, A. 1996. *Komitadzii. Terorizmot na Balkanot.* Skopje: Kultura.

Lowenthal, David. 1985. *The Past is a Foreign Country.* Cambridge: Cambridge University Press.

Lowenthal, David. 1994. "Identity, Heritage, and History." Pp. 41–60 in John R. Gills (ed.), *Commemorations: The Politics of National Identity.* Princeton, NJ: Princeton University Press.

Lowenthal, David. 1996. *Possessed by the Past: The Heritage Crusade and the Spoils of History.* New York: Free Press.

Lukacs, John. 1985. *Historical Consciousness or The Remembered Past.* New York: Schocken Books.

Lukic, Renio and Michael Brint (eds.). 2001. *Culture, Politics and Nationalism in the Age of Globalization.* Burlington, VT: Ashgate.

Lunt, Horace G. 1984. "Some Sociolinguistic Aspects of Macedonian and Bulgarian." Pp. 83–132 in Benjamin A. Stolz, I. R. Titunik, and Lubomir Dolezel (eds.), *Language and Literary Theory.* Ann Arbor, MI: University of Michigan Press.

Lydanyi, Andrew. 2002. "The Fate of Hungarians in Vojvodina." In Steven B. Vardy and Hunt Tooley (eds.), *Ethnic Cleansing in 20th Century Europe.* Boulder, CO: East European Monographs, forthcoming.

MacDonald, Sharon and Gordon Fyfe (eds.). 1996. *Theorizing Museums: Representing Identity and Diversity in a Changing World.* London: Blackwell Publishers/ The Sociological Review.

Mackridge, Peter and Eleni Yannakakis (eds.). 1997. *Ourselves and Others: The Development of a Greek Macedonian Identity Since 1913.* Oxford: Berg.

Mahon, Milena. 1998. "The Macedonian Question in Bulgaria." *Nations and Nationalism* 4 (3): 389–408.

Malcolm, Noel. 1992. "The New Bully of the Balkans." *Spectator,* 15 August, pp. 8–10.

Malcolm, Noel. 1998. *Kosovo: A Short History.* New York: HarperCollins.

Maliqi, Shkizen. 1998. "A Demand for a New Status: The Albanian Movement in Kosova." Pp. 207–38 in Thanos Veremis and Evangelos Kofos (eds.), *Kosovo: Avoiding Another Balkan War.* Athens: ELIAMEP.

Malkii, Lisa. 1992. "National Geographies: The Rooting of Peoples and the Territorialization of National Identity Among Scholars and Refugees." *Cultural Anthropology* 7 (1): 24–44.

Mandatzis, Christos. 1997. "Immigration and Identity: The Case of Macedonian Greek Immigrants." Pp. 197–228 in Vassilis Gounaris, Giorgos Agelopulos, and Iakovos Mihailidis (eds.), *Identities in Macedonia*. Athens: Papazisi [in Greek].

Markova, Z. 1983. "Russia and the Bulgarian-Greek Church Question in the Seventies of the Nineteenth Century." *Etudes Historiques* (11): 159–97.

Markova, Z. 1985. "The Church Question in the Bulgarian National Revolution." *Bulgarian Historical Review* 13 (3): 38–51.

Markova, Z. 1988. "Bulgarian Exarchate, 1870–1879." *Bulgarian Historical Review* 16 (4): 39–54.

Martis, Nikolaos. 1983. *The Falsification of the History of Macedonia*. Athens: Evroekdotiki [in Greek].

Matzureff, George D. 1978. *The Concept of "A Macedonian Nation" as a New Dimension in Balkan Politics*. Unpublished doctoral dissertation. Washington, DC: American University.

Mavrikos-Adamou, Tina. 2002. "The Development of Civil Society in Southeastern Europe." In George Kourvetaris, Victor Roudometof, Kleomenis Koutsoukis and Andrew Kourvetaris (eds.), *The New Balkans: Disintegration and Reconstruction*. Boulder, CO: East European Monographs, forthcoming.

Mavrocordatos, George Th. 1983. *Still Born Republic: Social Coalitions, and Party Strategies in Greece 1922–1936*. Berkeley, CA: University of California Press.

Mazarakis-Aenian, John C. 1992. *The Macedonian Question and the Birth of the New Macedonian Question*. Athens: Dhodhoni [in Greek].

Mazower, Mark. 1996. "Introduction to the Study of Macedonia." *Journal of Modern Greek Studies* 14 (2).

Mazower, Mark. 1997. "Policing the Anti-Communist State in Greece, 1922–1974." Pp. 129–50 in Mark Mazower (ed.), *The Policing of Politics in the Twentieth Century*. Oxford: Berghahm Books.

Mazower, Mark. 2000. "Three Forms of Political Justice: Greece 1944–1945." Pp. 24–41 in Mark Mazower (ed.), *After the War Was Over: Reconstructing the Family, Nation, and State in Greece, 1943–1960*. Princeton, NJ: Princeton University Press.

McDermott, Marcia. 1962. *A History of Bulgaria, 1396–1885*. New York: Praeger.

McDermott, Marcia. 1978. *Freedom or Death: The Life of Gotse Delchev*. New York: Journeyman Press.

McNeill, William H. 1985. *Polyethnicity and National Unity in World History*. Toronto: University of Toronto Press.

Meininger, Thomas A. 1970. *Ignatiev and the Establishment of the Bulgarian Exarchate, 1864–1872: A Study in Personal Diplomacy*. Madison: State Historical Society of Wisconsin, University of Wisconsin.

Meininger, Thomas A. 1974. *The Formation of a Nationalist Bulgarian Intelligentsia*. Ph.D. dissertation, Department of History, University of Wisconsin.

Mestrovic, Stjepan Gabriel with Slaven Letica and Miroslav Goreta. 1993. *Habits of the Balkan heart: social character and the fall of Communism*. College Station, TX: Texas A&M University Press.

Miall, Hugh (ed.). 1994. *Minority Rights in Europe: Prospects for a Transnational Regime*. New York: Council on Foreign Relations Press.

"Mid-Year Country Report: Macedonia," U.S. Committee for Refugees, September 2001. http://www.refugees.org/world/countryrpt/europe/mid_countryrpt01/macedonia.htm.

Mihailidis, Iakovos. 1995. "Traditional Friends and Occasional Claimants: Serbian Claims in Macedonia Between the Wars." *Balkan Studies* 36 (1): 103–16.

Mihailidis, Iakovos. 1996. "Minority Rights and Educational Problems in Greek Interwar Macedonia: The Case of the Primer 'Abecedar,'" *Journal of Modern Greek Studies* 14 (2): 329–43.

Mihailidis, Iakovos. 1997. "Slavophones and Refugees: Political Factors of an Economic Conflict." Pp. 123–42 in Vassilis Gounaris, Giorgos Agelopulos, and Iakovos Mihailidis (eds.), *Identities in Macedonia*. Athens: Papazisi [in Greek].

Mihailidis, Iakovos. 1998. "The War of Statistics: Traditional Recipes for the Preparation of the Macedonian Salad." *East European Quarterly* 32 (1): 9–21.

Mihailidis, Iakovos. 2000. "On the Other Side of the River: The Defeated Slavophones and Greek History." Pp. 68–84 in Jane K. Cowan (ed.), *Macedonia: The Politics of Identity and Difference*. London: Pluto.

Mihailov, Ivan. 1950. *Macedonia: A Switzerland of the Balkans*. St. Louis, MO: Pearlstone.

Mihalopoulos, Dimitris. 1985. "The Moslems of Chameria and the Exchange of Population Between Greece and Turkey," *Balkan Studies* 26 (2): 303–13.

Mihalopoulos, Dimitris. 1987. *Greek-Albanian Relations 1923–1928*. Thessaloniki: Paratiritis [in Greek].

Mihalopoulou, Aikaterini, Paris Tsartas, Maria Giannisopoulou, Panagiotis Kafetzis, and Evdokia Manologlou. 1998. *Macedonia and the Balkans: Xenophobia and Development*. Athens: Alexandria [in Greek].

Miller, William. 1936. *The Ottoman Empire and Its Successors, 1801–1927, With an Appendix 1927–1936*. Cambridge: Cambridge University Press.

Milosavleski, Slavko and Mirche Tomovski. 1997. *Albanians in the Republic of Macedonia 1945–1995 Legislative, Political Documentation, Statistics*. Skopje: NIP Studentski Zbor.

Minority Rights Group. 1990. *World Directory of Minorities*. London: Longman.

Misirkov, Kriste. 1974. *On Macedonian Matters*. Skopje: Macedonian Review (originally published in 1903).

Mitsotakis, Constantinos. 1995. "Introduction." Pp. 1–6 in Th. Skylakakis, *In the Name of Macedonia*. Athens: Elliniki Evroekdotiki [in Greek].

Mojsov, Lazar. 1979. *The Macedonian Historical Themes*. Belgrade: Jugoslovenska Stvarnost.

Momiroski, T. 1993. "Nasite Granici: Macedonian Group Boundaries, 1900–1945," *Journal of Intercultural Studies* 14 (2): 35–52.

Moore, Patrick. 1992. "The 'Albanian Question' in the Former Yugoslavia." *RFE/RL Research Report* 1 (14) [3 April]: 7–15.

Moore, Patrick. 2001. "Expectations in the Balkans." *RFE/RL Balkan Report* 5 (59) [21 August].

Moore, Patrick. 2001. "Going for Broke."*RFE/RL Balkan Report* 5 (18) [9 March].

Moore, Patrick. 2001. "Macedonia's Gligorov: Hit Rebels Hard," *RFE/RL Balkan Report* 5 (23) [27 March].

Moore, Patrick. 2001. "A Spooky Campaign in the Balkans?" *RFE/RL Balkan Report* 5 (53) [31 July].

Mosse, George L. 1975. *The Nationalization of the Masses: political symbolism and mass movements in Germany from the Napoleonic wars through the Third Reich.* New York: H. Fertig.

Mosse, George L. 1990. *Fallen Soldiers: Reshaping the Memory of the Two World Wars.* New York: Oxford University Press.

Musgrave, Th. D. 1997. *Self–Determination and National Minorities.* Oxford: Clarendon Press.

Naegele, Jolyon. 2001. "The Tanusevci Story." *RFE Balkan Report* 5 (18) [9 March].

National Center for Public Opinion Research (NCIOM). 1997. *Obstestvenoto mnenie* (Public Opinion) Newsletter, Ch. 8 Public Opinion and the VMRO Vol. 8: 108–12.

National Statistical Service of Greece. 1951. *Results of the Census of April 7, 1951.* Athens: National Statistical Service of Greece [in Greek].

Nationalities Papers. 1998. "Moldova: The Forgotten Republic." Special Issue 26 (1), edited by Michael F. Harm.

Nedeva, Ivanka and Naoum Kaytchev. 1999. "IMRO Groupings in Bulgaria after the Second World War." Pp. 167–83 in James Pettifer (ed.), *The New Macedonian Question.* New York: St. Martin's Press.

Nesho, Agim. 1998. "Political Developments after 22 March 1992 and the Albanian National Question." Pp. 311–28 in Thanos Veremis and Evangelos Kofos (eds.), *Kosovo: Avoiding Another Balkan War.* Athens: ELIAMEP.

Nicoloff, A. 1987. *The Bulgarian Resurgence.* Cleveland, OH: n.p.

Nikolov, Stephan. 2000. "Perceptions of Ethnicity in Bulgarian Political Culture: Misunderstanding and Distortion." Pp. 207–36 in Victor Roudometof (ed.), *The Macedonian Question: Culture, Historiography, Politics.* Boulder, CO: East European Monographs.

Norra, Pierre (ed.). 1984–92. *Les Lieux de memoire.* 3 vols. Paris: Gallimard.

Novick, Peter. 1989. *That Noble Dream: The "Objectivity Question" and the American Historical Profession.* Cambridge: Cambridge University Press.

Oestergaard, Uffe. 1991 "Denationalizing National History." Pp. 9–31 in Uffe Oestergaard (ed.), *Britain: Nation, State and Decline.* Copenhagen: Academic Press.

O'Leary, Cecilia Elizabeth. 1999. *To Die For: The Paradox of American Patriotism.* Princeton, NJ: Princeton University Press.

Olick, Jeffrey K. and Joyce Robbins. 1998. "Social Memory Studies: From 'Collective Memory' to the Historical Sociology of Mnemonic Practices." Pp. 105–40 in John Hagan and Karen S. Cook (eds.), *Annual review of sociology,* Vol. 24. Palo Alto, CA: Annual Reviews Inc.

Ortakovski, Vladimir. 2000. *Minorities in the Balkans.* Ardsley, NY: Transnational Publishers.

Palairet, Michael. 1997. *The Balkan Economies c. 1800–1914: Evolution without Development.* Cambridge: Cambridge University Press.

Palmer, Stephen E., Jr. and Robert R. King. 1971. *Yugoslav Communism and the Macedonian Question.* New York: Archon Books.

Panagiotopoulou, Roy. 1996. "The Manufacturing of National Stereotypes by the Press in the Case of the Macedonian Question." *Epitheorisi Koinonikon Ereunon: The Greek Review for Social Research,* Vol. 89–90 (A–B), pp. 232–274v [in Greek].

Panagiotopoulou, Roy. 1997. "Greeks in Europe: Antinomies in National Identities." *Journal of Modern Greek Studies* 15 (2): 349–70.

Pandevski, Manol. 1979. *Macedonia and the Macedonians in the Eastern Crisis.* Skopje: Macedonian Review.

Pano, Nicholas. 1997. "The process of Democratization in Albania." Pp. 285–352 in Karen Dawisha and Bruce Parrott (eds.), *Politics, Power, and the Struggle for Democracy in Southeast Europe.* Cambridge: Cambridge University Press.

Papadopoulos, Alexandros. 1992. *Albanian Nationalism and Ecumenical Hellenism.* Athens: Livani [in Greek].

Papakonstantinou, Mihalis. 1992. *Macedonia After the Macedonian Struggle.* Athens: Ermias [in Greek]. (First published in 1985.)

Papapanagiotou, Alekos. 1992. *The Macedonian Question and the Balkan Communist Movement, 1918–1939.* Athens: Themelio [in Greek].

Paparrigopoulos, Constantinos M. 1878. *Histoire de la civilisation hellénique.* Paris: Hachette.

Paparrigopoulos, Constantinos M. 1865–74. *History of the Greek Nation.* Athens: Passare [in Greek].

Papoudakis, Photini. 1996. "The Omonia Five Trial: Democracy, Ethnic Minorities and the Future of Albania." *Sudosteuropa* 45 (4–5) [Jhg]: 342–58.

Paschalis, Athanasios. 1998. *The Post–World War II Textbooks of the Greek Minority in Albania.* Athens: Gutenberg [in Greek].

Pavkovic, Aleksandar. 1997. "Anticipating the Disintegration: Nationalisms in Former Yugoslavia, 1980–1990," *Nationalities Papers* 25 (3): 427–40.

Pearson, R. 1983. *National Minorities in Eastern Europe 1848–1945.* New York: St. Martin's Press.

Pentzopoulos, D. 1962. *The Balkan Exchange of Minorities and Its Impact Upon Greece.* Paris and The Hague: Mouton.

Perry, Duncan M. 1988. *The Politics of Terror: The Macedonian Liberation Movements 1893–1903.* Durham, NC: Duke University Press.

Perry, Duncan M. 1992. "Macedonia: A Balkan Problem and a European Dilemma." *RFE/RL Research Report* 1 (25) [19 June]: 35–45.

Perry, Duncan M. 1993. *Stephan Stambolov and the Emergence of Modern Bulgaria, 1870–1895.* Durham, NC: Duke University Press.

Perry, Duncan M. 1994a. "Macedonia." *RFE/RL Research Report* 13 (6) [22 April]: 83–86.

Perry, Duncan M. 1994b. "Crisis in the Making? Macedonia and its Neighbors." *Sudost Europa* 43: 31–58.

Perry, Duncan M. 2000a. "Conflicting Ambitions and Shared Fates: The Past, Present, and Future of Albanians and Macedonians." Pp. 259–300 in Victor Roudometof (ed.), *The Macedonian Question: Culture, Historiography, Politics.* Boulder, CO: East European Monographs.

Perry, Duncan M. 2000b. "Macedonia's Quest for Security and Stability." *Current History* (March): 129–36.

Petkovski, Mihail, Goce Petreski, and Trajko Slaveski. 1992. "Stabilization Efforts in the Republic of Macedonia." *RFE/RL Research Report* 2 (3) [15 January]: 34–37.

Petroff, Lillian. 1995. *Sojourners and Settlers: The Macedonian Community in Toronto to 1940*. Toronto: University of Toronto Press.

Petrovic, Ruza. 1992. "The National Composition of Yugoslavia's Population, 1991." *Yugoslav Survey* 33 (1): 3–24.

Petrovski, Trayan. 1981. "Macedonian Emigration to the USA." *Macedonian Review* 11 (1): 102–10.

Petrusevska, Tatjana. 1998. "Legal Grounds for the Acquisition and Termination of Citizenship in the Republic of Macedonia: The Possibility of Multiple Citizenship and Statelessness." *Croatian Critical Law Review* 3 (1/2): 153–86.

Pettifer, James (ed.). 1999a. *The New Macedonian Question*. New York: St. Martin's Press.

Pettifer, James. 1999b. "The New Macedonian Question." Pp. 15–27 in James Pettifer (ed.), *The New Macedonian Question*. New York: St. Martin's Press.

Peyum, Naum. 1988. "The Assimilatory Policy of Greece in Aegean Macedonia." *Macedonian Review* 18 (2): 117–26.

Plamenatz, John. 1976. "Two Types of Nationalism." Pp. 22–37 in Eugene Kamenka (ed.), *Nationalism: The Nature and Evolution of an Idea*. London: Edward Arnold.

Politis, Alexis. 1993. *Romantic Years: Ideology and Mentality in Greece 1830–1880*. Athens: E.M.N.E.-Mnimon [in Greek].

Pollis, Adamantia. 1965. "Political Implications of the Modern Greek Concept of Self." *The British Journal of Sociology* 16: 29–47.

Pollis, Adamantia. 1987. "The State, the Law, and Human Rights in Modern Greece." *Human Rights Quarterly* 9: 587–614.

Pollis, Adamantia. 1992. "Greek National Identity: Religious Minorities, Rights, and European Norms." *Journal of Modern Greek Studies* 10: 171–95.

Pollis, Adamantia. 1993. "Eastern Orthodoxy and Human Rights." *Human Rights Quarterly* 15: 339–56.

Popov, Chris and Michael Radin. 1989. "An Analysis of Current Greek Government Policy on the Macedonian Issue." *Macedonian Review* 19 (2–3): 177–97.

Portes, Alejandro. 2000. "Globalization From Below: The Rise of Transnational Communities." Pp. 253–70 in Don Kalb, Marco van der Land, Richard Staring, Bart van Steenbergen, and Nico Wilterdink (eds.), *The Ends of Globalization: Bringing Society Back In*. Boulder, CO and New York: Rowman and Littlefield.

Poulton, Hugh. 1991. *The Balkans: Minorities and States in Conflict*. London: Minority Rights Group.

Poulton, Hugh. 1995. *Who are the Macedonians?* Bloomington, IN: Indiana University Press.

Poulton, Hugh, 1997. "Turkey as a Kin-State: Turkish Foreign Policy Towards Turkish and Muslim Communities in the Balkans." Pp. 194–213 in Hugh Poulton and Suha Taji-Farouki (eds.), *Muslim Identity and the Balkan State*. London: Hurst.

Poulton, Hugh. 2000. *Who are the Macedonians?* Bloomington, IN: Indiana University Press (2nd revised edition).

Poulton, Hugh and the Minnesota Lawyers International Human Rights Committee. 1989. *Minorities in the Balkans*. London: Minority Rights Group, Report No. 82.

Pribichevich, Stoyan. 1982. *Macedonia: Its People and History*. University Park, PA: Pennsylvania State University Press.

Pundeff, Marin V. 1969. "Bulgarian Nationalism." Pp. 93–165 in P. Sugar and Ivo J. Ledeter (eds.), *Nationalism in Eastern Europe*. Seattle: University of Washington Press.

Ramet, Pedro. 1989. "Religion and Nationalism in Yugoslavia." Pp. 299–327 in Pedro Ramet (ed.), *Religion and Nationalism in Soviet and East European Politics*. Durham, NC: Duke University Press.

Ramet, Pedro. 1992. *Nationalism and Federalism in Yugoslavia, 1962–1991*. Bloomington, IN: Indiana University Press.

Ramet, Sabrina Pedro. 1996. "The Macedonian Enigma." Pp. 211–36 in Sabrina Petra Ramet and Ljuibisa S. Adamovich (eds.), *Beyond Yugoslavia: Politics, Economics and Culture in a Shattered Community*. Boulder, CO: Westview Press.

Ramet, Sabrina Pedro. 1999. *Balkan Babel: The Disintegration of Yugoslavia from the Death of Tito to the War for Kosovo*. Boulder, CO: Westview Press.

Regional Headquarters Allied Forces Southern Europe Operation Essential Harvest— Achievements, 1 December 2001. http://www.afsouth.nato.int/operations/skopje/ACHIEVEMENTS.htm.

Rossos, Andrew. 1991. "The Macedonians of Aegean Macedonia: A British Officer's Report, 1944." *Slavonic and East European Review* 69 (2): 282–309.

Rossos, Andrew. 1995. "Macedonianism and Macedonian Nationalism On the Left." Pp. 219–54 in Ivo Banac and Katherine Verdery (eds.), *National Character and National Ideology in Interwar Eastern Europe*. New Haven: Yale Center for International and Area Studies.

Rossos, Andrew. 1997. "Incompatible Allies: Greek Communism and Macedonian Nationalism in the Civil War in Greece, 1943–1949." *Journal of Modern History* 69 (1): 42–76.

Rothschild, Joseph. 1981. *Ethnopolitics: A Conceptual Framework*. New York: Columbia University Press.

Roudometof, Victor. 1998a. "From Rum Millet to the Greek Nation: Enlightenment, Secularization, and National Identity in Ottoman Balkan Society, 1453–1821." *Journal of Modern Greek Studies* 16 (2): 11–48.

Roudometof, Victor. 1998b. "Invented Traditions, Symbolic Boundaries, and National Identity in Southeastern Europe: Greece and Serbia in Comparative-Historical Perspective 1830–1880." *East European Quarterly* 32 (4): 429–68.

Roudometof, Victor. 1999. "Nationalism, Globalization, Eastern Orthodoxy: 'Unthinking' the 'Clash of Civilizations' in Southeastern Europe." *European Journal of Social Theory* 2 (2): 233–47.

Roudometof, Victor (ed.). 2000a. *The Macedonian Question: Culture, Historiography, Politics*. Boulder, CO: East European Monographs, distributed by Columbia University Press.

Roudometof, Victor. 2000b. "Transnationalism and Globalization: The Greek-Orthodox Diaspora Between Orthodox Universalism and Transnational Nationalism." *Diaspora*: 9 (3): 361–97.

Roudometof, Victor. 2001. *Nationalism, Globalization and Orthodoxy: The Social Origins of Ethnic Conflict in the Balkans.* Westport, CT: Greenwood Press.

Roudometof, Victor. 2002a. "National Commemorations in the Balkans." In Michael Geisler (ed.), *Contested Ground: National Symbols and National Narratives.* Hanover, NH: University Press of New England, forthcoming.

Roudometof, Victor. 2002b. "Ethnic Heterogeneity, Cultural Homogenization, and State Policy in the Inter-war Balkans." In Steven B. Vardy and Hunt Tooley (eds.), *Ethnic Cleansing in Twentieth-Century Europe.* Boulder, CO: East European Monographs, forthcoming.

Rusinow, Dennison. 1968. *The Macedonian Question Never Dies.* New York: American Universities Field Staff.

Rusinow, Dennison. 1977. *The Yugoslav Experiment 1948–1974.* London: Hurst.

Rusinow, Dennison (ed.). 1988. *Yugoslavia: a Fractured Federalism.* Washington, DC: Wilson Press.

Safran, William. 1991. "Diasporas in Modern Societies: Myths of Homeland and Return." *Diaspora* 1 (1): 83–99.

Sassen, Saskia. 1996. *Losing Control? Sovereignty in an Age of Globalization.* New York: Columbia University Press.

Schiller, Nina, L. Basch and C. Blanc-Szanton. 1995. "From Immigrant to Transmigrant: Theorizing Transnational Migration." *Anthropological Quarterly* 68 (1): 48–63.

Schiller Nina, L. Basch and C. Blanc-Szanton (eds). 1992. *Towards a Transnational Perspective on Migration; Race, Class, Ethnicity, and Nationalism Reconsidered.* New York: The New York Academy of Sciences.

Schlesinger, Philip. 1987. "On National Identity: Some Conceptions and Misconceptions Criticized." *Social Science Information* 26 (2): 219–64.

Schmidt, Fabian. 1998. "Enemies Far and Near: Macedonia's Fragile Stability." *Problems of Post-Communism* (45) [July–Aug]: 22–31.

Schudson, Michael. 1997. "Lives, Laws, and Language: Commemorative versus Non-Commemorative Forms of Effective Public Memory." *The Communication Review* 2 (1): 3–17.

Schwartz, Barry. 1987. *George Washington: The Making of an American Symbol.* New York: Free Press.

Schwartz, Barry. 2000. *Abraham Lincoln and the Forge of National Memory.* Chicago: University of Chicago Press.

Schwartz, Barry, Y. Zerubavel, and B. Barnett. 1986. "The Recovery of Massada: A Study in Collective Memory." *Sociological Quarterly* 27 (2): 147–64.

Schwartz, Jonathan M. 1995. "The Petrified Forests of Symbols: Deconstructing and Envisioning Macedonia." *Anthropological Journal of European Cultures* 4 (1): 9–23.

Schwartz, Jonathan M. 1997. "Listening for Macedonian Identity: Reflections from Sveti Naum." Pp. 95–110 in Laszlo Kurti and Juliet Langman (eds.), *Beyond Borders: Remaking Cultural Identities in the New East and Central Europe.* Boulder, CO: Westview Press.

Schwartz, Jonathan M. 2000. "Blessing the Water the Macedonian Way: Improvisations of Identity in Diaspora and in the Homeland." Pp. 104–21 in Jane K. Cowan (ed.), *Macedonia: The Politics of Identity and Difference.* London: Pluto.

Seton-Watson, H. 1977. *Nations and States: An Inquiry into the Origins of Nations and the Politics of Nationalism*. London: Methuen.

Sfetas, Spyridon. 1995. "Autonomist Movements of the Slavophones in 1944: The Attitude of the Communist Party of Greece and the Protection of the Greek-Yugoslav Border." *Balkan Studies* 36 (2): 297–317.

Sfetas, Spyridon and Kyriakos Kentrotis. 1995. *The Albanians of Skopje: Questions of Ethnic Co-existence*. Thessaloniki: Institute for Balkan Studies [in Greek].

Shashko, Philip. 1974. "Bulgarian Literary and Learned Societies During the 1850s–1870s." *Southeastern Europe* 1 (1): 1–31.

Shashko, Philip. 1991. "The Emergence of the Macedonian Nation: Images and Interpretations in the American and British Reference Works, 1945–1991." Pp. 177–230 in B. Stolz (ed.), *Studies in Macedonian Language, Literature, and Culture*. Ann Arbor, MI: Michigan Slavic Publications.

Shaw, S. J. 1978. "The Ottoman Census System and Population 1831–1914," *International Journal of Middle Eastern Studies* 9: 325–38.

Shea, John. 1997. *Macedonia and Greece: The Struggle to Define a New Balkan Nation*. Jefferson, NC and London: McFarland and Co.

Shoup, Paul. 1968. *Communism and the Yugoslav National Question*. New York: Columbia University Press.

Simic, Predrag. 1998. "The Kosovo and Metohia Problem and Regional Security in the Balkans." Pp. 173–206 in Thanos Veremis and Evangelos Kofos (eds.), *Kosovo: Avoiding Another Balkan War*. Athens: ELIAMEP.

Simonov, Simon. 1990. "The Gypsies: A Reemerging Minority." *Report on Eastern Europe* [May 25]: 12–5.

Skopetea, Elli. 1988. *The Prototype Kingdom and the Great Idea in Greece 1830–1880*. Athens: Politipo [in Greek].

Skoulatou, V., N. Dimakopoulou, and S. Kondi. 1983. *Early Modern and Modern History [A-B]*. Athens: OEDB [in Greek].

Slijepcevic, Doko M. 1958. *The Macedonian Question: The Struggle for Southern Serbia*. Translated by James Larkin. Chicago: American Institute for Balkan Affairs.

Smith, Anthony D. 1979. *Nationalism in the Twentieth Century*. New York: New York University Press.

Smith, Anthony D. 1986. *The Ethnic Origins of Nations*. Oxford: Basil Blackwell.

Smith, Anthony D. 1991. *National Identity*. Reno, NV: University of Nevada Press.

Smith, Anthony D. 1995. *Nations and Nationalism in a Global Era*. London: Polity Press.

Smith, Anthony D. 1999. *Myths and Memories of the Nation*. Oxford: Oxford University Press.

Smith, M.P. and L.E. Guarnizo (eds.). 1998. *Transnationalism From Below*. New Brunswick: Transaction Publishers.

Sotiriou, Stephanos. 1991. *Minorities and Irredentism*. Athens: Evroekdotiki [in Greek].

Spillman, Lynette P. 1997. *Nation and Commemoration: Creating National Identities in the United States and Australia*. Cambridge and New York: Cambridge University Press.

Stavrianos, Lefteris S. 1944. *Balkan Federation. A History of the Movement toward Balkan Unity in Modern Times*. Northampton, MA: Department of History, Smith College.

Stavrianos, Lefteris S. 1958. *The Balkans since 1453*. New York: Harper & Row.

Stavros, Stephanos. 1995. "The Legal Status of Minorities in Greece Today: The Adequacy of Their Protection in the Light of Current Human Rights Perceptions." *Journal of Modern Greek Studies* 13 (1): 1–32.

Stokes, Gale. 1999. "Containing Nationalism: Solutions in the Balkans." *Problems of Post-Communism* 46 (4) [July–August]: 3–10.

Sumner, B. H. 1962. *Russia and the Balkans 1870–1880*. London: Archon.

Swire, J. 1939. *Bulgarian Conspiracy*. London: Robert Hale.

Tachiaos, A. 1974. *The National Awakening of the Bulgarians and the Appearance of Bulgarian National Movement in Macedonia*. Thessaloniki: Society for Macedonian Studies [in Greek].

Tamis, A. 1994. "The Image of Macedonia's Past in Australia." Pp. 83–118 in Faidon Malingudis (ed.), *Playing With History: Ideological Stereotypes & Subjectivism in the Historiography*. Thessaloniki: Vanias [in Greek].

Tashkovski, Dragan. 1976. *The Macedonian Nation*. Skopje: Nasha Kniga.

Taylor, Charles. 1992. *Multiculturalism and the "Politics of Recognition."* Princeton, NJ: Princeton University Press.

Thomas, William I. and Dorothy S. Thomas. 1928. *The Child in America: Behavior Problems and Programs*. New York: Knopf.

Tiryakian, Edward A. 2002. "Third Party Involvement in Ethnic Conflict: The Case of the Kosovo War." In George Kourvetaris, Victor Roudometof, Andrew Kourvetaris, and Kleomenis Koutsoukis (eds.), *The New Balkans: Disintegration and Reconstruction*. Boulder, CO: East European Monographs, distributed by Columbia University Press, forthcoming.

Todorov, Nikolai. 1969. "The Balkan Town in the Second Half of the Nineteenth Century." *Etudes Balkaniques* 21 (8): 31–50.

Todorov, Varban. 1991. "Nineteenth Century Federalism in Greece: An Attempt at Periodization." *Etudes Balkaniques* 4: 89–106.

Todorova, M. 1990. "Language as A Cultural Unifier in a Multilingual Setting: The Bulgarian Case During the Nineteenth Century." *East European Politics and Societies* 4 (3; Fall): 439–50.

Todorova, M. 1995. "The Course and Discourses of Bulgarian Nationalism." Pp. 55–102 in P. Sugar (ed.), *Eastern European Nationalism in the 20th Century*. Washington, DC: American University Press.

Todorova, M. 1997. *Imagining the Balkans*. Cambridge: Cambridge University Press.

Tounta-Fergadi, Areti. 1986. *Greek–Bulgarian Minorities: The Politi–Karloff Protocol 1924–1925: A study based on research in the archives of the Greek Foreign Ministry*. Thessaloniki: Institute for Balkan Studies [in Greek].

Trajkovska, Mirjana Lazarova. 1998. "Continuity and Efficiency in the Regulation of Citizenship in the Republic of Macedonia." *Croatian Critical Law Review* (3) (1–2): 187–90.

Triandafyllidou, Anna and Andonis Mikrakis. 1998. "A Ghost Wanders Through the Capital." Pp. 164–79 in Bernd Baumgartl and Adrian Favell (eds.), *New Xenophobia in Europe*. London: Kluwer.

Trix, Frances. 1995. "The Resurfacing of Islam in Albania." *East European Quarterly* 28 (4): 533–49.

Troebst, Stefan. 1994. "Yugoslav Macedonia, 1944–1953: Building the Party, the State and the Nation." *Berliner Jahrbuch fur Osteuropaische Geschichte* 2: 103–39.

Troebst, Stefan. 1997. "Yugoslav Macedonia 1943–1953: Building the Party, the State and the Nation." Pp. 243–66 in Melissa Bokovoy, Jill Irvine, and Carol Lilly (eds.), *State–Society Relations in Yugoslavia 1945–1992*. Scranton, PA: St. Martin's Press.

Troxel, Luan. 1992. "Bulgaria's Gypsies: Numerically Strong, Politically Weak," *RFE/RL Research Report* 6 [March]: 58–61.

Tsoukalas, Constantine. 1981. "The Ideological Impact of the Civil War." Pp. 319–42 in John O. Iatrides (ed.), *Greece in the 1940s: A Nation in Crisis*. Hanover, NH: University Press of New England.

Tzvetkov, P. S. 1993. *A History of the Balkans: A Regional Overview from a Bulgarian Perspective*, 2 vols. San Francisco: Edwin Mellen Press.

Ubicini, Jean Henri Abdolonyme and Abel Pavet de Courteille. 1876. *État Présent de l'empire Ottoman; Statistique, Gouvernement, Administration, Finances, Armée, Communautés Non Musulmanes, etc., etc. D'après le Salnâmeh (Annuaire Impérial) Pour l'année 1293 de l'hégire (1875–76) et les Documents Officiels les Plus Récents*. Paris: J. Dumaine.

United Nations. 1995. *Interim Accord Between the Hellenic Republic and FYROM*. Document 95–27866. New York, Sept. 13.

United States Department of State. 1991–95. *Country Report on Human Rights*. Washington: Government Printing Office.

Upward, Allen. 1908. *The East End of Europe: The Report of an Unofficial Mission to the European Provinces of Turkey on the Eve of the Revolution, With a Preface by the Late Major Sir Edward Fitzgerald Law*. London: J. Murr.

Vakalopulos, Apostolos. 1961. *History of Modern Hellenism*, vol. 1. Thessaloniki: n.p.

Vakalopoulos, Kostas. 1986. *Macedonia On the Eve of the Macedonian Struggle (1894–1904)*. Thessaloniki Barbunakis [in Greek].

Vakalopoulos, Kostas. 1987. *The Macedonian Struggle: The Armed Phase (1904–1908)*. Thessaloniki: Barbunakis.

Vakalopoulos, Kostas. 1988. *Young Turks and Macedonia*. Thessaloniki: Kiriakidi [in Greek].

Vakalopoulos, Kostas. 1994. "The Greek Minority of Skopje." *Tote* 46 [Jan.–Feb.]: 6–17 [in Greek].

Van Boeschoten, Ricky. 2000. "When Difference Matters: Sociopolitical Dimensions of Ethnicity in the District of Florina." Pp. 28–46 in Jane K. Cowan (ed.), *Macedonia: The Politics of Identity and Difference*. London: Pluto.

Vardy, Steven B. and Hunt Tooley (eds.) 2002. *Ethnic Cleansing in 20th Century Europe*. Boulder, CO: East European Monographs, forthcoming.

Vasiliev, Vasil. 1989. "The Bulgarian Communist Party and the Macedonian Question between the Two World Wars." *Bulgarian Historical Review* 1: 3–20.

Verdery, Katherine. 1993. "Nationalism and National Sentiment in Post-Socialist Romania." *Slavic Review* 52 (2): 179–203.

Verdery, Katherine. 1994. "Ethnicity, Nationalism, and State-Making." Pp. 33–58 in Hans Vermulen and Cora Govers (eds.), *The Anthropology of Ethnicity*. Amsterdam: Het Spinhuis.

Veremis, Th. 1995a. *Greece's Balkan Entanglement*. Athens: ELIAMEP.

Veremis, Th. 1995b. "The Foundation of the Albanian State and the Greek Claims," pp. 19–24 in Th. Veremis, Th. Couloumbis, and I. Nikolakopoulos (eds.), *The Hellenism of Albania*. Athens: Sideri [in Greek].

Vergopoulos, Kostas. 1994. *State and Economic Policy in the 19th Century: Greek Society 1880–1895.* Athens: Exantas [in Greek].

Vermeulen, H. 1984. "Greek Cultural Dominance among the Orthodox Population of Macedonia during the Last Period of Ottoman Rule." Pp. 225–55 in A. Blok and H. Driessen (eds.), *Cultural Dominance in the Mediterranean Area.* Nijmegen: Katholieke Universiteit.

Vickers, Miranda. 1998. *Between Serb and Albanian: A History of Kosovo.* New York: Columbia University Press.

Vickers, Miranda. 2001. "Tirana's Uneasy Role in the Kosovo Crisis, 1998–1999." Pp. 30–36 in Michael Waller, Kyril Drezov, and Bulent Gokay (eds.), *Kosovo: The Politics of Delusion.* London: Frank Cass.

Vihou, Marina, Dimosthenis Dodos, Panagiotis Kafetzis, and Ilias Nikolakopoulos. 1995. "The Minority's Political Presence." Pp. 59–102 in Th. Veremis, Th. Couloumbis and I. Nikolakopoulos (eds.), *The Hellenism of Albania.* Athens: Sideri [in Greek].

Vlassidis, Vlasis. 1997. "Macedonian Autonomy: From Theory to Praxis." Pp. 63–88 in Vassilis Vassilis, Giorgos Agelopoulos, and Iakovos Mihailidis (eds.), *Identities in Macedonia.* Athens: Papazisi [in Greek].

Voulgaris, G., D. Dodos, P. Kafetzis, Chr. Lyrintzis, K. Michalopoulou, I. Nikolakopoulos, M. Spourdalakis, and K. Tsoukalas. 1995. "The Perception and Treatment of the 'Other' in Today's Greece." *Elliniki Epitheorisi Politikis Epistimis* 5: 81–100 [in Greek].

Vouri, S. 1992. *Nationalism and Education in the Balkans. The Case of Northwestern Macedonia, 1870–1914.* Athens: Paraskinio [in Greek].

Vouri, S. 1993. "The Balkan Wars in the Slavic School Historiography." Pp. 299–326 in *Greece of the Balkan Wars 1910–1914.* Athens: ELIA [in Greek].

Vouri, S. 1996. "Greece and the Greeks in Recent Bulgarian History Textbooks." Pp. 67–78 in W. Hopken (ed.), *Oil on Fire? Textbooks, Stereotypes, and Violence in Southeastern Europe.* Hannover, Germany: Verlag Hahnsche Buchhandlung.

Vranousis, Leandros. 1957. *Rigas.* Athens: N. Zaharopoulos [in Greek].

Vryonis, Speros. 1978. "Recent Scholarship on Continuity and Discontinuity of Culture: Classical Greeks, Byzantines, Modern Greeks." Pp. 237–56 in Speros Vryonis, Jr. (ed.), *The Past in Medieval and Modern Greek Culture.* Malibu, CA: Undena.

Wace, Alan J. B. and Maurice S. Thompson. 1914. *The Nomads of the Balkans: An Account of Life and Custom Among the Vlachs of Northern Pindus.* London: E. P. Dutton.

Wallden, Sotiris. 1991. *Greece-Yugoslavia: Birth and Evolution of a Crisis and Balkan Realignments 1961–1962.* Athens: Themelio [in Greek].

Wallerstein, Immanuel. 1990. "Culture as the Ideological Battleground of the Modern World System." Pp. 31–56 in Mike Featherstone (ed.), *Global Culture: Nationalism, Globalization and Modernity.* London: Sage.

Walzer, Michael. 1994. *Thick and Thin.* Cambridge, MA: Harvard University Press.

Weber, Eugene. 1976. *Peasants into Frenchmen: The Modernization of Rural France, 1870–1914.* Stanford, CA: Stanford University Press.

Wilkinson, H. R. 1951. *Maps and Politics: A Review of the Ethnographic Cartography of Macedonia.* Liverpool: Liverpool University Press.

Winnifrith, Thomas J. 1987. *The Vlachs: The History of a Balkan People*. London: Duckworth.

Winter, Jay. 1995. *Sites of Memory, Sites of Mourning: The Great War in European Cultural History*. Cambridge: Cambridge University Press.

Wood, Paul. 2001. "The Rebels' Agenda," BBC News, Sunday March 1. http://news.bbc.co.uk/hi/english/world/europe/newsid_1213000/1213887.stm.

Woodward, Susan. 1995. *Balkan Tragedy: Chaos and Dissolution After the Cold War*. Washington, DC: Brookings Institution.

Xhudo, Gus. 1995. "Tension Among Neighbors: Greek-Albanian Relations and their Impact on Regional Security and Stability." *Studies in Conflict and Terrorism* 18 [April/June]: 111–43.

Yerushalmi, Yosef Hakim. 1996. *Zakhor: Jewish History and Jewish Memory*. Seattle: University of Washington Press.

Zahariadis, Nikolaos. 1993. "Politics, Culture and Social Science: A Commentary on Dr. Karakasidou's 'Politicizing Culture: Negating Ethnic Identity in Greek Macedonia.'" *Balkan Studies* 34 (2): 301–7.

Zahariadis, Nikolaos. 1994. "Nationalism and Small-State Foreign Policy: The Greek Response to the Macedonian Issue." *Political Science Quarterly* 109 (Fall): 647–67.

Zang, Theodore. 1991. "Destroying Ethnic Identity: Selective Persecution of Macedonians in Bulgaria." *Macedonian Review* 21 (1–2): 70–88.

Zelinski, Wilbur. 1988. *Nation into State: The Symbolic Foundations of American Nationalism*. Chapel Hill, NC: University of North Carolina Press.

Zelizer, Barbie. 1995. "Reading the Past against the Grain: The Shape of Memory Studies." *Critical Studies in Mass Communication* (12): 214–39.

Zografos, G. 1994. "The Real Situation of the Economy in Skopje." *Oikonomoikos Tachidromos,* 3 March, p. 94 [in Greek].

Zotiades, George. 1961. *The Macedonian Controversy*. Thessaloniki: Institute for Balkan Studies. (First published in 1954.)

Index

About the Author

VICTOR ROUDOMETOF is Visiting Assistant Professor in the Department of Sociology, Gerontology and Anthropology at Miami University, Oxford, Ohio. Among his earlier publications is *Nationalism, Globalization and Orthodoxy* (Greenwood, 2001).